THE LATE MEDIEVAL ENGLISH CHURCH

THE LATE MEDIEVAL ENGLISH CHURCH

VITALITY AND VULNERABILITY
BEFORE THE BREAK WITH ROME

G.W. BERNARD

YALE UNIVERSITY PRESS
NEW HAVEN AND LONDON

For information about this and other Yale University Press publications, please contact:
U.S. Office: sales.press@yale.edu   www.yalebooks.com
Europe Office: sales@yaleup.co.uk   www.yalebooks.co.uk

Set in Sabon MT by IDSUK (DataConnection) Ltd
Printed in Great Britain by TJ International Ltd, Padstow, Cornwall

Library of Congress Cataloging-in-Publication Data

Bernard, G.W.
   The late medieval English church: vitality and vulnerability
   before the break with Rome/G.W. Bernard.
      pages cm
   ISBN 978–0–300–17997–2 (hardback)
   1. English—Church history—1066–1485. 2 England—Social
conditions—1066–1485. I. Title.
   BR750.B47 2012
   274.2'05—dc23
                                                             2012000106

A catalogue record for this book is available from the British Library.

10 9 8 7 6 5 4 3 2 1

CONTENTS

ILLUSTRATIONS

PREFACE

INDIRECTLY absorbed an utterly conventional view of the inadequacies of the late medieval church from the low church anglican chapel at Reading School and from the history I was taught by an inspiring master, Frank Terry. Not that we ever directly confronted that late medieval church. It was more that within that chapel and within a history syllabus that began in 1485, and quickly moved towards a beneficent view of the reformation, the catholic church seemed obscurantist, superstitious and oppressive. It is hard now to imagine an intellectual world in which such attitudes seemed quite simply true. But in such a world it was not surprising that *The Economist*, wishing to condemn the Russian revolution on its fiftieth anniversary, should have described the soviet communist party as 'the most consecrated ideological barrier to progress since the medieval church'. In my Oxford entrance examination a few weeks later, I borrowed that formulation. I was not surprised that at my interview Charles Wenden and Peter Dickson pressed me on that: I was hoping for just such an opportunity. But I was—momentarily, but without being knocked off my stride—taken aback to be asked to justify *either* of those propositions. Deftly I turned the interview to what I thought I knew about, and an exhilarating discussion then ensued about communism, but my interrogators—neither of them medievalists (though, interestingly, many English medievalists would, I suspect, not have dissented)—never pressed me on what, for the first time, I realised was a proposition rather than a fact about the late medieval church. I suspect that the seeds of this book lie in that acute question.

At the time I did not have the slightest doubt. A list of books recommended to me by Peter Dickson when I asked him for advice on what to spend a school book prize included A.G. Dickens' classic *The English Reformation* (1964), which I had just begun to read when I went up to Oxford for my interview. That enshrined the conventional protestant views with which I had grown up. Personal experience of catholic intolerance when I had been in Munich two years earlier no doubt contributed something too. As an undergraduate studying the early modern wars of religion, I again absorbed a very protestant view of events. Hugh Trevor-Roper's Gibbonian mocking of the thousands of masses commissioned for his soul by Philip II—30,000, all at once, and as soon as possible after his death— and his equation of Spanish catholicism with 'obstinate bigotry' in an essay on the *Pax Hispanica*, the period of Spanish cultural dominance in the 1610s, offered vivid confirmations.[1] I can also remember being moved when Charles Wilson ended one of his Ford Lectures in 1969 by quoting John Motley's monumental *Rise of the Dutch Republic*. There Motley concluded his work with a eulogy of his protestant hero William the Silent, 'the guiding-star of a brave nation', and a translation of a contemporary report of his assassination in 1584: 'when he died, the little children cried in the streets'.[2] The catholic Philippe de Croy (1526–95), duke of Aerschot, was the villain of Wilson's account, a catholic nobleman who made a deal with the tyrant Philip II and so prevented the liberation of all the Netherlands.[3] Yet that did begin to give me pause. Why should Aerschot have taken such apparently wrong decisions? I do not recall that I developed such thoughts very far. But the periods I was spending in Germany and France did, I suspect, soften my attitudes to the catholic church, impressed as I was by the richness of the settings and the evident piety of worshippers, and the ordinary decency of catholic families with whom I stayed.

What did provoke a significant rethinking was when, as a graduate student working on the Tudor nobility, I first discovered architecture. I had by then already explored many of the churches of Paris, but it was only when I came across Pevsner's *Buildings of England* (which I quickly collected) that I began to look at buildings with an historian's eye. And as I marvelled at the rich heritage of late medieval English churches rebuilt in the Perpendicular style, I could not help asking how this could possibly fit within the conventional image of a late medieval church riddled with abuses, corrupt and oppressive, and over-ripe for a fall. Did not all these churches suggest rather that the church was maintaining, indeed increasing, its appeal to laymen and laywomen? Was there not rather something wrong with the orthodoxy which I had absorbed?

The early 1970s was a remarkable time in the study of history. Many scholars in many different fields were consciously thinking of themselves as 'revisionists' as they challenged long-established interpretations that had become solidified as 'facts'. For my part, I was questioning the tenacious belief in the decline of the nobility in Tudor England. Not a few scholars (most immediately for me, my college contemporary and friend Kevin Sharpe, and my sometime tutor Jennifer Loach) were revising the traditional history of early modern parliaments, denying that the natural condition of parliaments was to engage in conflict with the crown and denying that the English civil war of the 1640s was the inevitable culmination. Others, notably William Doyle and Colin Lucas, were repudiating the dominant social interpretation of the French revolution, denying that the revolution was intended as (or achieved) the triumph of the bourgeoisie over a feudal-absolutist monarchy and nobility. And in these years a group of scholars was revising the history of the late medieval church, calling into question just that protestant grand narrative of the speedy, inexorable and successful progress of the English reformation that I had absorbed at school, emphasising instead the continuing hold of what came to be called traditional religion. In my teaching I rode that revisionist tide and cheered as it gathered momentum. And in large measure I still hold with what was then being shown.

But as early as 1982, Cliff Davies, who had supervised my D.Phil., was asking whether historians of the late medieval church were not becoming too pietistic. And in many conversations over the following years we argued the toss over this. What, however, provoked my own rethinking was, paradoxically, an extraordinarily influential book which has consolidated the revisionist interpretation of the late medieval church, Eamon Duffy's *The Stripping of the Altars* (1992). Without wishing to dispute anything, details apart, of its overall view, I nonetheless was left with a sense that it did not tell the full story and that it left the subsequent reformation inexplicable.[4] That is not to read the history of the late medieval church as merely a prologue to the reformation. The historian cannot unknow that the reformation happened, and it is entirely legitimate to seek to explain it. For many years my principal scholarly concerns were to understand the causes, the course and the consequences of Henry VIII's break with Rome, and in that task I found it essential to form a view of the church as it was when he came to the throne. That pursuit increasingly led me to the conclusion that the very vitality of the late medieval church was marked by vulnerabilities which were being ignored or played down in much current writing. It is the counterpoint, or the tension, between vitality and vulnerability that I seek to explore here.

Jeremy Catto, reviewing a collection of essays on the late medieval church, originally given as papers at one of the annual conferences at Harlaxton, Lincolnshire, saw 'the independent paths of the contributors going in every direction' as an impressive monument to the historical tendency he labelled 'Harlaxton empiricism'. Not only could these papers not be 'corralled into a common focus on any specific theme', they were resolutely particularist in their approach. 'In many, perhaps most, cases they have started from a particular document or piece of material evidence and gone on from there.' But Catto noted limitations to this formula. 'The study of fourteenth- and fifteenth-century England needs the stiffening wind of controversial general ideas, developed at length.' It cries out, he urged, 'for a vigorous comparative and European approach'. All these contributors, he went on, 'would help to sweep the dust from these centuries by going to fewer conferences and writing longer, single-authored studies which challenge the tired assumptions of conventional late medieval English history'. They would then 'certainly fall to sharp and invigorating controversy'.[5] Whether this book can live up to Catto's demanding standards is not for me to say, but when I read his words I realised that they encapsulated what I was attempting to do. I present here an essay, a broad view offered by a single author, not a coldly efficient synthesis of a mass of particularities but rather an exploration of the church in the round. Above all, I seek to provoke questions, not least what the proper criteria for judging the late medieval church should be.

I owe great thanks to generations of students who have discussed these topics with me over the years. The late Tim Reuter read through some sprawling drafts and notes and offered characteristically acute observations. Barbara Harvey's encouragement at an early stage was far more helpful than I suspect she realises. I am most grateful to the British Academy for the invaluable and timely award of a Senior Research Fellowship. My study has been completed during tenure of a Leverhulme Major Research Fellowship, for which I very much thank the Trustees. I wish once again to express my gratitude for all the encouragement and assistance I have received from Robert Baldock, Tami Halliday and Rachael Lonsdale at Yale University Press. I acknowledge permission from Sutton Publishing to draw on material from an earlier paper on pilgrimage. Over the years I have enjoyed many stimulating conversations about the themes of this book with Cliff Davies, Peter Gwyn, Mark Stoyle, Alan Thacker, Alastair Duke, Colin Morris, Anne Curry, the late Brynmor Pugh and Greg Walker. Cliff Davies and Mark Stoyle in addition undertook the labour of reading and commenting on my text: I thank them warmly.

1

THE HUNNE AFFAIR

O N 4 December 1514, Richard Hunne, a prosperous London merchant, was found dead in his cell in Lollards' Tower at St Paul's Cathedral, where those such as Hunne, who were suspected of heresy, were detained while investigations were carried out. As was usual after any death in mysterious circumstances, an inquest was held. *The Enquirie and Verdite of the Quest panneld of the death of Richard Hune wich was founde hanged in Lolars tower,* a pamphlet printed around 1536, more than twenty years later, the reliability of which we shall consider later, offers a vivid account of what the coroner's jury saw. They went up Lollards' Tower and found the body of Hunne 'hanging upon a staple of iron, in a girdle [a belt worn around the waist] of silk, with fair countenance, his head fair kemped [combed], and his bonnet right sitting upon his head, with his eye and mouth fair closed, without any staring, gaping or frowning, also without any drivelling [flow of saliva or dribbling] or spurging [emitting of impure matter by fermentation] in any place of his body'. They spelled out details that convinced them that Hunne had not taken his own life. The girdle had no knot about the staple but was double cast; apart from four drops, there was no blood on Hunne's face, lips, chin, doublet, collar or shirt; the skin of both his neck and throat, beneath the girdle of silk, was 'fret [worn] and failed away'; Hunne's hands were 'wrung in the wrists'; there was nothing in the prison by which a man could have hanged himself, except for a stool which was extremely unstable; the girdle was not big enough (though exactly what that meant was not explained); the girdle, being made of silk, was too soft to have broken his neck or skin; there was a lot of blood in another corner; there was blood from the breast downward of Hunne's jacket; and there was blood within the flap of the left side of his jacket, a fold that Hunne could not have made after he was hanged.

From such precise observations the jury apparently determined that Hunne had been murdered: he had been smothered, his neck had been wrung, and then he had been hanged. And the jury named those responsible for the murder as William Horsey, the bishop of London's chancellor, Charles Joseph, the bishop's summoner, and John Spalding, the bellringer of St Paul's Cathedral.[1]

By any standard, that was a sensational matter: a prosperous London merchant found dead in an episcopal prison, officials and servants of the bishop of London accused of murder. That raises all sorts of questions about the late medieval church. First, though, we must reflect in more detail on exactly what happened to Hunne. This is by no means as straightforward a matter as might at first appear, not least since the Hunne affair has turned into something of a shuttlecock between those who defended the late medieval church and those who espoused the protestant reformation.

Who was Richard Hunne? He was a merchant tailor and a freeman of the city of London, easily worth 1,000 marks (£666) according to Thomas More,[2] and if so, just below the most successful overseas traders of aldermanic rank. For his protestant defenders he was 'of honest reputation, no man to the sight of people more virtuous'.[3] John Foxe, the martyrologist, described him as 'esteemed during his life, and worthily reputed, and taken . . . for a man of true dealing and good substance'.[4] Thomas More agreed that he was 'called a very honest person and of a good substance' and 'a fair dealer among his neighbours'.[5] But More drew attention to and emphasised his weakness, his 'spirit of pride': 'a man high minded and set on glory of a victory which he hoped to have in the praemunire [the legal action that he had undertaken against the church to which we shall return] wherof he much boasted as they said among his familiar friends that he trusted to be spoken of long after his days, and have his matter in the years and terms called Hunne's case',[6] an ambition which he has evidently realised. It is hard to deny that More's characterisation fits the facts, as does a modern historian's description of Hunne as 'a considerable pain in the collective ecclesiastical neck'.[7] For the details of his wrangles with the church do not show Hunne in a good light.

Hunne's son, Stephen, died on 29 March 1511 at the age of five weeks in the parish of St Mary Matsilon or Matfelon, Whitechapel, where he had been sent out to a wet-nurse, probably because Hunne's wife had died in childbirth or soon afterwards. Thomas Dryfield, the rector, demanded the bearing sheet (the cloth in which the baby was baptised) as a mortuary, a long-established routine gift claimed by the incumbent from the estate of a deceased parishioner as recompense for personal tithes unpaid at death (or for the privilege of burial). Hunne refused. He claimed that the baby had no title in the bearing sheet and that therefore the priest should not have it.[8] There is no record of anything more directly related to this dispute happening for over a year. But meanwhile, before the series of disputes which brought him posthumous fame developed, Hunne was involved in an obscure quarrel with the parson and churchwardens over a tenement burnt in a fire in the parish of St Michael Cornhill.[9] Then, on 26 April 1512, Dryfield, the rector who had asked Hunne for a mortuary, sent his chaplain Henry Marshall to the church courts to start a suit for the recovery of the bearing sheet. Unusually the case was heard not in the diocesan episcopal court but in the archbishop of Canterbury's court at Lambeth. Hunne was duly summoned on 28 April 1512; he appeared and denied the charge on 13 May 1512; but Cuthbert Tunstal, as chancellor, found for Dryfield.[10] Hunne's argument appears to have been a principled refusal on the grounds that his baby had not owned the sheet demanded by the church. Other instances of disputes over mortuaries arose when someone died away from home: no one, it would be claimed, owed tithes or mortuaries when simply a visitor. And if Hunne's baby died while put out to nurse outside his own parish, then it might have been understandable if Hunne had wanted to pay the mortuary there rather than to the priest of the parish where the baby died. But that does not appear to fit the terms of the bolder case that Hunne made against mortuaries in general. Hunne might have had something of a case had he objected to paying in the parish of St Mary Matfelon, but he was on much more controversial ground in seeming to deny his liability to pay a mortuary altogether.[11]

But the matter did not end there. On 25 January 1513 Hunne sued Henry Marshall, Dryfield's chaplain, in the court of King's Bench for defamation of character. Hunne alleged that, when he had gone to St Mary at Whitechapel on 27 December 1512, Marshall had said to him 'thou art accursed and thou standest accursed and therefore go thou out of the church; for as long as thou art in this church I will say no evensong nor service'. Hunne duly left but claimed that he had been defamed. In Hilary Term 1513 he brought an action under the law of praemunire against Dryfield and several church court officials.[12] That law had been designed to limit papal power in England but was more commonly being used to limit the powers of church courts. Laymen at odds with the church might seek to exploit its vagueness to gain an advantage in their particular quarrels.[13] That is what Hunne tried to do. The case was repeatedly adjourned in 1513 and 1514, on the last occasion to Hilary Term 1515. Unfortunately the legal record contains no indication of the likely decision.[14] Thomas More later claimed that by late 1514 it was clear that the case would go against Hunne, and that the judges would rule that disputes over mortuaries should be resolved in the church courts, not in King's Bench.[15] It was all fairly technical, and, as with most legal matters, a case could be at least argued both ways. But what Hunne was doing does make him appear somewhat litigious, somewhat provocative. Hunne was not the first layman to refuse a mortuary payment, but the fuss he made, and the apparently principled stand that he took, especially the recourse to the legal procedure known as the writ of praemunire, marked him out as unusually persistent.

Meanwhile—and we shall return shortly to the question of whether these matters were linked—the church authorities accused Hunne of heresy. In October 1514 Richard Fitzjames, bishop of London, ordered his arrest: he was held in Lollards' Tower in St Paul's Cathedral. On 2 December 1514 he was brought before the bishop of London at Fulham Palace and accused of a range of offences. According to what John Foxe presents as his transcription from the records of the bishop's court, Hunne had allegedly attacked tithes; he had said that bishops and priests were scribes and pharisees who crucified Jesus; he had defended one Joan Baker who had abjured heresy in 1510; and he had kept books in English that were prohibited by law, namely English translations of the Apocalypse, Gospels and Epistles, and the works of John Wyclif. Foxe cited Hunne's answer (though wondering whether it was a forgery): Hunne denied the charges, but admitted that he might unadvisedly have spoken words 'somewhat sounding to the same', and submitted himself to the bishop's charitable and favourable correction.[16] It is hard, on this evidence, to be confident that Hunne was indeed an heretic. If he had knowingly spoken up for Baker, an abjured heretic, that might be suggestive: though it was always possible that what Hunne objected to was the harshness with which an innocent woman had been treated by the ecclesiastical courts. Nor was Hunne's alleged possession of English translations of the Bible altogether compelling proof of his heresy: he may simply have been dabbling without quite realising the risks he was taking. The church authorities evidently felt that these charges were insufficiently damning. After Hunne's death he was subjected to a further trial, held between 11 and 16 December 1514, in which new articles were brought against him in a series of hearings attended by Archbishop Wolsey, Bishop Fitzjames, Bishop Smith of Lincoln, and the archdeacon of London. The involvement of leading clergy highlights the importance of the affair. The new charges were based on Hunne's possession of heretical books in which the holy canons were damned, the pope was called Satan and Antichrist, the pope's power to grant pardons denied, praying to and honouring saints dismissed, transubstantiation denied, the university of Oxford condemned.

Four witnesses testified that Hunne had possessed a banned English Bible. This offered stronger grounds for convicting Hunne than the charges made against him while he was alive. And Hunne was duly pronounced an heretic on 16 December and his body burnt on 20 December.[17]

But was Hunne an heretic? Were these charges falsely brought against him by the churchmen anxious to discredit his legal challenge to mortuaries? That was what Simon Fish claimed in his *Supplication of the Beggars* printed in 1528: anyone who accused churchmen of some misdeed was sooner or later accused of heresy. Charles Wriothesley's *Chronicle* would assert that Hunne 'was made an heretic for suing a Praemunire' against the bishop of London and his chancellor. When, Edward Hall recorded, the priests heard that Hunne was suing the priest in a praemunire, 'they did so much of malice that they accused him of heresy'. John Foxe would say the same, though attributing it to clerical fears that all laymen would follow Hunne's example.[18] Hunne had quarrelled with the church over money: the church responded by seeking his humiliation as an heretic. A problem with this line of argument is that Hunne sued his praemunire in early 1513: yet it was not till late 1514 that the church authorities accused him of heresy.[19]

Or was the sequence of events the other way about? Did Hunne bring the suit of praemunire against the church precisely because he was aware that his heretical activities had come to the attention of the church authorities and that he was on the point of being formally charged of heresy? That is what Thomas More claimed: Hunne 'was detected of heresy before the praemunire sued or thought upon'. If Hunne had not been accused of heresy, he would not have sued the praemunire.[20] For More, there was no doubt that Hunne was an heretic. According to More, drawing on the testimony of an Essex carpenter convicted and burnt for heresy six or seven years later who named Hunne as an heretic, Hunne had attended midnight lectures and readings of the scriptures in London. Hunne was thus, for More, part of a network of heretics. More also claimed that Hunne's English Bible was a book written after Wyclif: several passages dealing with the blessed sacrament were, in More's judgement, heretical.[21]

More's testimony is bold and definite. Yet doubts remain. Did Hunne see himself as an heretic? He was clearly angry, as his suit against Henry Marshall for defamation shows, to be denounced as 'accursed', that is excommunicated. A committed heretic might well have been less bothered. More interestingly still, John Foxe includes details in his account of the Hunne affair which suggest that Hunne was, if not orthodox, then by no means a committed heretic. Hunne was taken 'not only for a man of true dealing and good substance but also for a good catholic man'. 'To all true godly disposed men, Hun may well be known to be a virtuous and godly person, no heretic, but faithful and sound', Foxe wrote, only to muddy the waters by going on to add the qualification 'save that only he seemed rather half a papist; at least no full protestant, for that he resorted daily to mass, and also had his beads in prison with him, after the catholic manner'.[22] Foxe's confusions and near-contradictions are interesting here. He had clearly noted the evidence of one of Hunne's alleged murderers, John Spalding, the bellringer, who testified that, when he saw Hunne on the Saturday before his death, Hunne was saying of his beads.[23] Foxe also went on to pose the pertinent question, why did the church authorities not convict Hunne of heresy while he was alive if they were so certain of the case against him.[24] Foxe cited Hunne's supposed admisssion that while he had not spoken the charges laid against him 'unadvisedly I have spoken words somewhat sounding to the same, for the which I am sorry and ask God mercy'.[25] If Hunne did say that, and if that was not simply a ploy to avoid conviction, then it would lend support to the view that he was indeed as Foxe says 'no heretic'. And maybe 'unadvisedly' is also the aptest way to characterise Hunne's acquisition and possession of prohibited books. At first glance that appears to prove his heresy. But remarkably he does not seem to have hidden them, even when in trouble: did he realise that they were indeed heretical works? Is it possible that Simon Fish was correct when insinuating that if Hunne had not embarked on his praemunire action against a priest he would still have been alive 'and none heretic at all, but an honest man'?[26]

We are left then with the image of Richard Hunne as a deeply religious but not unorthodox man, yet one who was acutely critical of the financial exactions of the church, and stubbornly prepared to take his criticism almost to the limit. Faced by such irksome litigiousness, the church authorities supposed, wrongly but entirely sincerely, that it could be explained only by underlying heresy. And when the subsequent investigation found forbidden books and evidence of criticism of churchmen expressed in colourful language, such discoveries apparently vindicated the suspicion of heresy that Hunne's litigiousness had aroused. That misunderstanding on this scale was possible in itself highlights the vulnerability of the late medieval church.

So how did Hunne die? He was found dead on 4 December 1514. Had he been murdered? That is what has long been believed. But study of the Hunne affair has been tainted by reliance on a curious source, transcribed by Edward Hall and by John Foxe, and included in Hall's *Chronicle* and the 1563 edition of Foxe's *Acts and Monuments* respectively, and from them introduced into the historical mainstream. This is *The Enquirie and Verdite of the Quest panneld of the death of Richard Hune wich was founde hanged in Lolars tower,* a pamphlet compiled not earlier than 1536 (since it refers to the datable death of William Tyndale), printed (to judge from its typeface) in the Antwerp workshop of Peetersen van Middelburch and purporting to contain the report of the coroner's inquest held after the discovery of Hunne's body.[27] There is no doubt, as we shall see, that an inquest was duly held and that it did conclude that Hunne had been murdered, naming those responsible as William Horsey, the bishop of London's chancellor, Charles Joseph, the summoner, and John Spalding, the bellringer. But the details furnished by the pamphlet quoted at the beginning of this chapter are rather more problematic than at first glance they may appear.

If what had happened was a murder which the murderers had attempted to disguise as a suicide, then they had, on this account, made a terrible mess of it. It hardly seems credible that they would have left such clearly and immediately implausible evidence of suicide. And while the details given are manifestly intended to persuade the reader that Hunne could not have committed suicide, nonetheless they are often puzzling and contradictory, for example, the four drops of blood from Hunne's nose, a 'great cluster of blood' on the left side of his jacket under the folded flap of the jacket, and 'a great parcel of blood' in the corner of the room.[28] We shall return to the authenticity of such details: were they embellishments?

The pamphlet purporting to be the verdict of the inquest does not, however, stop there. There follows a series of observations and deductions designed to show that Charles Joseph, the bishop's summoner, murdered Hunne, having plotted it with William Horsey, the bishop of London's chancellor. According to the pamphlet, Joseph gave his keys to Horsey the day before Hunne's death and rode out of town the next morning but that was clearly intended to be understood as no more than a cover. Earlier, Horsey had been strict with Hunne, telling John Spalding, bellringer, now entrusted with the keys, to keep Hunne more strictly and allow him just one meal a day. He also made Hunne wear an unbearably heavy iron collar and chain on his neck. More puzzling still is the ensuing claim that Horsey went up to Hunne's prison, 'and kneeld down before Hun, holding up his hands to him, praying him of forgiveness of all that he hath done to him, and must do to him'. It is a very odd scenario. But it is intended to leave the reader with no doubt that Horsey, Joseph and Spalding must have been Hunne's murderers.[29]

The pamphlet continues with the confession that Charles Joseph apparently made in the Tower of London, admitting the murder. Joseph described how John Spalding, the key-holding bellringer, led the way, Joseph followed and Horsey came up last. When they found Hunne on his bed, Horsey said 'lay hands on the thief', and they murdered him. Joseph put the girdle round Hunne's neck; Joseph and Spalding 'did heave up Hunne'. Horsey pulled the girdle over the staple, and so, Joseph, concluded, Hunne was hanged.[30] This seems very strange. Why should Horsey have gone with Joseph? Why should he have cried 'lay hands on the thief'? Hunne was no thief.[31]

Some support for this confession comes, however, from the testimony of Joseph's servant, a woman (misleadingly for modern readers) called Julian Littell. She said that on returning home on Wednesday, Joseph had confessed to her that 'I have destroyed Richard Hunne'. When Littell pressed him, Joseph explained that 'I put a wire in his nose'. He had rather than a hundred pounds that it were not done—but what was done could not be undone. He had killed Hunne. Littell added that Joseph stayed at home in great fear on the Thursday and after going out briefly on Friday was again in great fear at home. Joseph had asked her to swear that she would not reveal what he told her; he refused to tell her the names of his accomplices.[32]

Littell's testimony is then followed in the pamphlet by the depositions of ten further witnesses. The text printed by Hall and followed by Foxe crucially omits a revealing phrase. It refers to 'the deposition of Julian Lyttell, late servant of Charles Joseph, by her free will, unconstrained, in the vi year of our Sovereign Lord King Henry the viii, within the chapel of our Lady of Bedlem [Bethlehem], showed to the inquest'. But the text of the pamphlet gives a precise date for Littell's testimony, namely 'the xiiii day of February'.[33] That detail, omitted by Hall and Foxe, makes it plain that the pamphlet cannot be a simple report of the coroner's inquest.[34] It is a compilation. It added to the verdict of the inquest material that was drawn from a later consideration of the case.[35] Here what Thomas More later wrote is pertinent. According to More, the matter was examined at Baynard's Castle, Henry VIII's residence in the city of London, before the king's council.[36] Almost certainly the depositions presented in the pamphlet are those made then. The bittiness of the depositions suggests that only a selection was included within the pamphlet—which must cast doubt on the representativeness of the sample. That said, the testimonies are somewhat miscellaneous. Various people had spoken of Hunne's imminent death. John Enderby, barber, testified how, on the Friday before Hunne's death, John Spalding the bellringer said that grievous penance was ordained for Hunne. It is unlikely that this amounts to evidence of any planned murder. After all, if Hunne were to be convicted of heresy, he would have to make penance, and he might even be burnt. More damaging, at first glance, were the testimonies of Thomas Chicheley, tailor, and Thomas Simonds, stationer, who had seen Joseph coming out of St Paul's on the fateful Monday morning. Moreover Robert Johnson, who lived at The Bell,

Shoreditch, said that Joseph kept a horse saddled all night and then rode out the back way at eight o'clock on the morning of Hunne's death.[37] Superficially these might hint at complicity and guilt.

But another witness, Peter Turner, Joseph's son-in-law, gave evidence that offers an alternative explanation. Here again there is a curious discrepancy between the text of the pamphlet printed by Hall and by Foxe in his 1563 edition of *Acts and Monuments* and the wording of the pamphlet itself. Turner deposed that Joseph rode out of town on Sunday, 3 December, at six in the morning. According to Hall and Foxe, Turner went on to say that 'the Sunday next before that' he was informed that Joseph would be arrested by 'divers sergeants' as soon as he could be taken: Turner accordingly warned Joseph, and Joseph escaped. But in the pamphlet it states that it was on 'the Saturday next before that' that this happened. The wording is a little obscure, but it must mean the Saturday before Hunne died, i.e. 2 December, as the context of Turner's evidence of what he and Spalding did the day before Hunne died further suggests. Joseph fled at six o'clock on Sunday morning, reacting to a warning passed to him on the Saturday by Turner. 'The same night' Horsey, the chancellor, gave John Spalding, the bellringer, the keys, and on 'the said Sunday' Spalding and Turner served Hunne his dinner at twelve o'clock. If Joseph was warned by his father-in-law on Saturday, 2 December, that he was in danger of imminent arrest, that is very significant. It shows that Joseph was evidently in trouble for something which had nothing to do with Hunne's death, since Hunne was then still alive. Could all that not explain his apparently suspicious comings and goings on Sunday and Monday?[38]

And whether Joseph did really confess that he had murdered Hunne, as the pamphlet suggests, is called into question by the inclusion, rather oddly at the end of Julian Littell's testimony, of Joseph's attempt to prove an alibi. He lay with a harlot in one Barington's house the night that Hunne was murdered: 'wherupon he brought before the king's council for his purgation the forsaid bawd, Barington's wife'. The compiler of the pamphlet at once dismissed this: 'which purgation we have proved all untrue', he asserted, citing the names of the other witnesses. What is intriguing for our purposes is that at the time of the investigation held before the king's council, Joseph evidently was denying that he had committed any murder: why would he have brought Barington's wife before the king's council to prove his alibi if he had already confessed his guilt?[39] And if Joseph sought refuge in a sanctuary in Essex on 22 December, that could readily be explained by fear. The bailiff of the sanctuary, Richard Horsnayle, testified that Joseph 'acknowlegeth him self guiltless of Hunne's death, for he delivered the keys to the Chancellor by Hunne's life [while Hunne was still alive]'.[40]

Thus the apparently compelling evidence for murder turns out to be problematic. The detail presented in the pamphlet lacks plausibility. There is, perhaps, Joseph's confession, though what we learn from the pamphlet is at best ambivalent. There is some circumstantial evidence about Joseph's behaviour and about talk at the time, none of which is conclusive and all of which is open to alternative explanations.

Most importantly, what is missing from any charge of murder is a compelling motive. It is difficult to see what the church, or what Horsey, Joseph or Spalding as individuals, had to gain from Hunne's death. If, as Foxe suggests, he had largely submitted to the correction of the church, it is hard to see what reason there was for murdering him.[41] A penitent and contrite living Hunne would have been far more valuable to the church than a murdered Hunne. He was scarcely so great a threat to the church for it to be worth murdering him. His praemunire actions were irritants, but hardly so fundamental and revolutionary a challenge that his elimination was the only way of stopping them. Foxe's confusions over the motives of the churchmen who allegedly had Hunne murdered, perceptively identified by Stefan Smart, are revealing here. Foxe attributes two contradictory motives to Hunne's alleged clerical murderers. On the one hand, Hunne was murdered so that once he was no longer able to defend himself he could be proved to be an heretic; on the other hand, Hunne was murdered to halt the praemunire case and then convicted of heresy to stop pursuit of the causes of his death.[42] Richard Wunderli has suggested that Joseph may have murdered Hunne in order to further his personal ambitions, seeking to re-establish himself in Horsey's eyes after his dismissal as summoner. Wunderli has noted that Joseph's name does not appear in the records of the Commissary Court books after 20 September. Did that mean that Joseph had been dismissed? According to the pamphlet, Joseph declared that he had been put out of his office because he would not deal with Hunne as cruelly as Horsey wanted.[43] Since Hunne was imprisoned in October, as Arnold's *Chronicle* states, the sequence of events is not a perfect fit: on that reasoning, Joseph should have been dismissed in late October or November, rather than losing his position as summoner in late September.[44] And claiming to have been dismissed because he would not treat an imprisoned man cruelly would have been an obviously self-serving defence against the charge that he had murdered him. A still more telling objection is that Joseph was evidently very much in favour with Horsey in the days immediately before Hunne's death: the details do not suggest that Joseph was there on sufferance. Above all, this line of argument is, in the end, only a subsidiary version of the claim that the church authorities wanted Hunne dead: it fails to deal with the principal objection that the church would have little to gain from Hunne's death.[45]

Yet it remains true that the coroner's jury did conclude that he was murdered. That, however, does not necessarily settle the matter. Any death in prison always looks suspicious. Given that a suicide was denied christian burial, given that any property owned by a man who committed suicide was, in principle, forfeited to the crown (in effect disinheriting his family) and given, at a deeper level, that suicide was seen as the greatest crime against God, the sin of despair which called into question God's justice and mercy, juries were often reluctant to return verdicts of suicide unless the evidence was utterly unequivocal. Juries would not have to be cynically calculating: jurors may simply have doubted that anyone would, in such circumstances, have committed suicide.

Many recent writers would put forward another version of events. Agreeing that murder was not in the church's interest, they suggest that Hunne was the unintended victim of accidental killing during torture or rough interrogation, carried out for the purpose of extracting more information about his alleged heresy and those who were involved with him. This is quite credible, and it would make sense of some of the details found by the coroner's inquest jury. Julian Littell's recollection of Charles Joseph saying he destroyed Hunne with a wire in his nose is relevant here, hinting as it does at torture that went too far.[46] Yet there is no explicit contemporary evidence. Those at the time who thought Horsey and the others responsible for Hunne's death saw their actions as deliberate murder, not as an accident.[47] To adopt such an interpretation is to question the coroner's inquest jury no less than to suppose that Hunne committed suicide.

Could the coroner's inquest have got it all wrong? On 6 December the jury accused Horsey, Joseph and Spalding of murder. As we have seen, what happened next was that the king's council held an inquiry at Baynard's Castle in the city of London in February 1515. This inquiry has not been adequately assessed. Until recent discoveries, all we knew was what Thomas More was to record in *A Dialogue concerning heresies*. Most historians have dismissed More's account, but, as we shall see, More was well-informed. 'The matter was examined at great length, before divers great lords spiritual and temporal of the king's council,' More says. More quoted a messenger who claimed that Horsey had in the end been indicted of murdering Hunne and then spent a great while in prison before securing a pardon through his friends. More then contradicted this messenger. First, More insisted that the king recognised Horsey's innocence. Secondly, More insisted that Horsey never sued for a pardon. What happened instead was that Horsey and the others were arraigned in King's Bench and pleaded not guilty: the king gave his attorney orders to confess their pleas of not guilty to be true. More's account has rarely been given much attention and, although in many ways supported by Edward Hall (though Hall thinks that Horsey bribed his way out of trouble), is not often believed.[48] It is perhaps not surprising that More has been dismissed because to accept his account would require a fundamental revision of our understanding of the Hunne affair.

That, however, More's account deserves credence is greatly strengthened by recent discoveries in the records of King's Bench which essentially confirm its thrust.[49] The document KB9/468 m. 14 gives the coroner's inquest jury's verdict. On 6 December [1514], we learn, the named jurors investigating the death of Hunne who 'per mandat Ric Epi London imprisonate et incaseratus fuit [on the orders of Richard, bishop of London, had been imprisoned and incarcerated]' declared that William Horsey, Charles Joseph and John Spalding maliciously and premeditatedly went to London, to St Paul's where Hunne was kept and 'ibm felonice ingulanerunt et suffocaverunt et collium eius fregerunt felonice interfecerunt [they feloniously strangled and suffocated him and broke his neck and feloniously murdered him]'. Hunne's body was then hung by a silk girdle upon a hook driven into a piece of timber in the wall of the prison. All this was fairly translated and included as the final section of the pamphlet of c.1536. But what immediately strikes the reader is that there is here none of the additional colourful detail in the pamphlet—the reasoning by which the jurors concluded that Hunne's death was murder—just their basic verdict.

When was this document written, and why? It is not the original verdict of the inquest, but a later declaration presented into the court of King's Bench. The brief endorsement states that it was delivered by Richard Broke, recorder, on Monday next after the octave of the purification in the seventh year of Henry VIII's reign, that is 11 February 1516.[50] What was going on is illuminated by two further documents. KB9/468 m. 13 is a writ of *certiori* dated 1 February 7 Henry VIII [1516]: ordering the recipient to deliver Horsey and others from Newgate into King's Bench following their indictment before the coroner in the city of London. Such a procedure was often used by those who had a pardon which they would then plead in the court of King's Bench, as a means of publicly confirming their innocence. That is more or less what happened here, though no pardon was involved.

On the controlment roll there is a corresponding entry recording what happened when the case duly came up in King's Bench, KB27/1019 rex. rot. 4. This began by repeating the inquest jury's verdict: the wording is identical to that in KB9/468 m. 14. Then it recorded how on the Saturday after the quinzaine of Easter in the seventh year of the reign of Henry VIII, i.e. April 1516, William Horsey appeared in person, and pleaded not guilty and submitted himself to trial by jury. The king's attorney-general John Earnley then—most unusually—declared that by virtue of a warrant directed to him by the king, the accused's plea was to be accepted:

> John Earnley our attorney greeting whereas William Horsey clerk stands and is indicted of and for the murdering of Richard Hunne late of London as by an inquisition taken before our coroner within our city of London and now remaining before us in our bench more plainly doth appear we for diverse considerations us specially moving will charge and command you our said attorney that all such plea or pleas as the said William Horsey will pleade or tend for his discharge of the premisses by what manner name or addition he be indicted that ye for us and in our name confess the same plea to be true so that he may be clearly against us for the said murder and every thing concerning the same clearly discharged And this bill signed with our hand shall be to you at all times against us sufficient warrant and discharge in that behalf given at our manor of Greenwich the xxvii day of November the viith year of our reign [i.e. 1515].

The sequence of legal events is thus quite plain. On 27 November 1515 Henry VIII discharged Horsey—that is to say, Henry, in effect, accepted his innocence, and instructed his attorney to accept any plea that Horsey might make. Horsey duly sued out a writ of *certiori* in February 1516 so that the case would be resolved. The coroner's jury's verdict was accordingly presented into court. In April the matter was duly heard in King's Bench and the king's attorney's acceptance of Horsey's plea of not guilty was formally recorded by the court. That meant that the case against him—in consequence of the coroner's jury's verdict of 6 December 1514—was finally dismissed.[51]

What this material highlights is the role of Henry VIII. The most significant conclusion to be drawn from the legal records is that they powerfully confirm what Thomas More later wrote. More, as we have seen, described how, when Horsey and the others were indicted in King's Bench, they pleaded not guilty, and, More tells us, the king gave commandment to his attorney to confess their plea to be true. 'After long examination of the matter' Horsey and the others were indicted, pleaded not guilty—'and thereupon the king's grace being well and sufficiently informed of the truth and of his blessed disposition not willing that there should in his name any false matter be maintained gave in commandment to his attorney to confess the pleas to be true without any further trouble. Which thing in so faithful a prince is a clear declaration that the matter laid to the chancellor was untrue.'[52] Hall confirms the detail, although, as we have seen, he explains it away by alleging bribery. That seems improbable in so important and public a matter. More had earlier scored a point against Simon Fish who claimed that Horsey had bought his pardon for £600: More noted that since his plea of not guilty had been accepted, he had not been convicted and therefore did not need a pardon.[53] Of even greater importance is what the fact of the king's intervention, stated by More, and now here emphatically confirmed by the judicial record, suggests about the circumstances of Hunne's death. It is, to say the least, unlikely that if Hunne's death was clearly the result of murder, Henry VIII and his council would have taken no action and that Henry would so unusually have instructed his attorney to accept Horsey's plea of not guilty. The king's action—for which we can no longer rely only on More's testimony—must cast severe doubt on the verdict of the coroner's jury that Hunne had been murdered by Horsey, Joseph and Spalding. Nor does evidence support the most fashionable recent interpretation that sees Hunne as accidentally killed in the course of torture or heavy interrogation. Rather, it points in support of More's vigorously argued claim that Hunne committed suicide. That indeed was what, according to the pamphlet, Bishop Fitzjames, bishop of London, asserted in the House of Lords.

More claimed to have known the matter 'from top to toe'—'I suppose there be not very many men that knoweth it much better'—and to have been present at various examinations and to have talked to almost all those involved. According to More, Hunne had come to see that he was going to lose his praemunire suit. He was also anxious about the charges of heresy. So 'he began to fall in fear of worldly shame'. 'It is to me much more likely,' concluded More, 'that for weariness of his life he rid him self out therof.' Elsewhere More stated that 'the man hanged himself for despair, despite and for lack of grace'. Perhaps, More speculated, he did it 'with a marvellous hope of that which after happed that the suspicion of his death might be laid to the charge and parell of the chancellor'.[54] In this context the testimony of Alan Cresswell, wax-chandler, as given in the pamphlet, is very interesting. He reported how one John Granger, a servant of the bishop of London, told him that he had been with John Spalding on the Sunday night before Hunne died. The keepers had set Hunne in the stocks; Hunne asked to borrow the keeper's knife; when asked why, Hunne had replied, 'I had leaver [rather] kill my self than to be thus intreated'.[55] That would appear to confirm More's impression of a man on the edge. Elsewhere More tells of Thomas Philip, who 'after that he was suspected of heresy and spoken to thereof, fearing the shame of the world, drowned him self in a well'.[56] More controversially, Thomas Chase of Amersham died in prison while under suspicion of heresy: Foxe said he was cruelly strangled—the authorities claimed he had hanged himself.[57] Even more interestingly, when the early reformer Robert Barnes feared that he would be burnt, and decided to flee to Antwerp, he was advised by a good friend to feign suicide by drowning. He should pretend to be desperate; he should write a letter to Wolsey and leave it on his table, together with a note saying where he had gone to drown himself, and another letter to the mayor of the town asking him to search for him in the river. It is interesting that such an action by an accused heretic should be thought of as providing a credible cover for an escape.[58] On 12 April 1540 a priest 'of the new sect', put in the bishop's house to be examined by the bishop of Winchester, hanged himself there.[59] That Hunne committed suicide is all too plausible.

What broader conclusions should be drawn from this affair? Does it show a deep and dangerous level of lay anti-clericalism? That would be to go too far. It is remarkable how little support there appears to have been for Hunne until he was found dead. There does not seem to have been any sign that he was becoming a popular hero. When he brought his defamation suit against Henry Marshall, he claimed that Marshall's exclusion of him from church had so damaged his credit and good name that merchants he had dealt with dared not trade with him any more.[60] That hardly suggests any great sympathy for his legal battles with the church (and, incidentally, calls into question any generalised lay anti-clericalism). And that is not surprising, since most Londoners would seem to have paid their tithes and mortuaries without the sorts of wrangles into which Hunne had fallen. Once Hunne was found dead, there was evidently uproar. Relatives and friends may well have made a fuss, not least to avoid the forfeiture of Hunne's property for heresy. There was evidently a good deal of sympathy towards Hunne's family. There was an unsuccessful attempt in parliament in 1515 to restore his property to his children. It is striking that the church was evidently so widely blamed for his death. That perception of the church as cruel in cases of heresy, as prepared to stoop to murder, casts an unhappy shadow, however unfairly, on the late medieval church, and hints at the anxieties about procedures in heresy trials that would surface in the supplication against the ordinaries in 1532 (and would be widely felt in the Low Countries). And murder by the church would become the standard protestant interpretation of Hunne's death. As Latimer put it when interrogated in 1533, he would prefer purgatory to the Lollards' Tower, for in the Lollards' Tower he might die 'bodily' for lack of meat and drink, or die 'ghostly' for fear of pain: 'my lord and his chaplains might manacle me by night', 'they might strangle me, and say that I hanged myself'—'as they did to Hunne', Foxe noted in the margin.[61] Bishop Fitzjames's lament that Londoners were so maliciously set in favour of secret heresies that they would condemn his clerk, were he as innocent as Abel, is revealing of the depth of unease.[62] But that may have also been an unfair, even mistaken, perception of the laity. Their unease may have reflected not any sympathy for heresy but rather distaste at the procedures used in such investigations and trials. That would be likely in this case if Hunne himself was not an heretic, but simply a cantankerous if idealistic critic of what he saw as the church's financial exactions.

The Hunne affair raises general themes that any assessment of the late medieval church must address. Manifestly it raises the question of lay anti-clericalism and, more generally, criticism of the church. Whether Hunne was or was not an heretic, the charges against him draw attention to the extent and nature of heresy. Hunne quarrelled with priests: the role of the clergy is central to our understanding of the late medieval church. Bishop Fitzjames is depicted unflatteringly in the pamphlet's presentation of the Hunne affair; but we must consider the position and actions of bishops more widely. And, maybe surprisingly, what a proper understanding of the Hunne affair highlights is the close involvement of Henry VIII. Accordingly, this study will begin with an examination of what will be presented as the 'monarchical church' in later medieval England.

2

THE MONARCHICAL CHURCH

IT is not to belittle the death of Richard Hunne to say that the most remarkable aspect of the Hunne affair is the decisiveness of royal intervention. Very quickly Henry VIII called together his council, held a special inquiry and then reached his own decision—which he then imposed. All that vividly illustrates how the late medieval English church was a monarchical church, that is to say that, in practice, kings exercised a great deal of control, a largely determining control, over the activities of the church. It was a relationship in which the crown held the upper hand. That is not to claim that kings always and effortlessly obtained what they wanted, nor to deny that the church had a sense of itself as an autonomous body, and that, much of the time and in most of their activities, churchmen acted according to their own sense of what was proper and what was just. Nor is it to say that the church was being assailed or marginalised by the crown, or that relations between crown and church were characterised by conflict: on the contrary, the Hunne case shows vividly how the church depended on and benefited from crown protection. It is rather to insist on the reality, in the final analysis, of crown power and clerical dependence.

It was ever thus. While the teachings of Jesus had been spread widely throughout the Roman Empire by missionaries and by writings, what that had produced was a remarkable scattering of christian communities: it was the decision of the Emperor Constantine to convert to christianity that had consolidated christianity in the Empire and offered a lasting model for the association of church and state. It was the Emperor Constantine who convoked the Council of Nicea, the first assembly of the whole church, in 325. Half a century later it would be the Emperor Theodosius who declared christianity to be the official state religion of the Empire. Following the fall of the Roman Empire, much was disrupted, and the extent of christian survival in England became problematic. The continuous story of English christianity traditionally begins with Augustine's mission in 597, begun 'with an almost clean sheet', and the conversion of Aethelberht of Kent.[1] From the seventh to eleventh centuries, all depended on the patronage of the royal and aristocratic families whose conversion had led to the imposition of christianity in England and across much of western Europe. From *c.*1000, rising population, increasing productivity, technological improvements, the growth of towns, significant migration and new sources of income (notably tithes), underpinned the flowering of a more ambitious and assertive insti-tutionalised high medieval church,[2] but even then that greater wealth and enhanced confidence were ultimately guaranteed and protected by royal power. We must be careful not to misrepresent the highest aspirations of churchmen for the superiority of the spirituality as evidence of the realities of power. Even at the zenith of the church's pretensions between the late eleventh and early thirteenth centuries, the age of 'the papal monarchy', from Pope Gregory VII (d. 1085) to Pope Innocent III (d. 1216), determined and strong secular rulers throughout Europe could in practice, whatever the theoretical pretensions of the church, impose their will against the papacy and their leading churchmen.[3] Even Thomas Becket has been seen as failing to 'win' his conflict with Henry II: 'It is doubtful that Henry II lost much if any power over the church by the martyrdom of Becket', making few if any concessions, and securing his aims by 'judicious interventions and subtle negotiations'.[4]

It has been even more common to argue that royal authority over the church grew later, especially from the fourteenth century. Certainly the schism and the rival popes of the years from 1378 to 1418 left the moral authority of the papacy lastingly damaged, perhaps the more so since the initial divisions largely reflected personal quarrels in the the papal court.[5] Efforts to resolve divisions by greater recourse to councils of the church, which included archbishops, bishops, abbots and representatives of univer-sities and also of secular rulers, and by the consequent development of 'conciliar' theories by which popes were subordinate to councils, again contributed to the weakening of papal power. It was Sigismund, king of the Romans and later Holy Roman Emperor, who was the prime mover in summoning the Council of Constance (1414–18) which ultimately resolved the schism. The papal court at Rome was re-established as the 'well of grace', the principal court of appeal throughout christendom, and peti-tioners sought justice in large numbers. But that reinforced the legalistic and administrative character of the papacy. The post-schism popes interfered less and less in the detailed workings of national churches; for example, as we shall see, in the nomination of bishops. And for kings across Europe, popes increasingly were seen much less as spiritual leaders than as allies or enemies in the complex and often bitter international power politics of the day.

It was monarchs who profited from the sacralisation of monarchy—the projection of monarchs as lieutenants of God, ruling not just with divine approval but at divine command. Monarchs emerged strengthened from the ceremonies of coronation which emphasised their semi-divine nature. The coronation, and especially the anointing with holy oil, or in the later middle ages with chrism, a mixture of balsam and olive oil, was held to make the king no longer only a lay man but also what the church called a clerk, though one without the power of saying mass or hearing confession. Coronation was above all a religious occasion. The procession from Westminster Hall to Westminster Abbey was a religious procession. The king was, throughout, attended by the abbot of Westminster and the ceremonies were led by the archbishop of Canterbury with senior bishops playing a prominent role. And the coronation liturgy was in many respects very close to the ceremonies by which a bishop was consecrated, with a similar pattern of examination, oath, litany, collect, anointing, delivery of crozier and mitre in the case of bishops, of sword, pallium, crown and ring in the case of kings, followed by mass. On the eve of the coronation the king was to give himself up to heavenly contemplation and prayer; the king was to meditate 'that he has been called to so high a position by God to be a defender of the catholic church, an extender of the christian faith, and to protect, as far as he can, this realm and country which God has given unto his charge'. All that emphasises the religious significance of the coronation. Kings were asked if they would follow the laws and customs of England, including the laws, customs and franchises of the church. 'Every good king in his kingdom ought to be protector and defender of the bishops and churches under his government,' the king was told; and the king promised to preserve and maintain the church as its protector and defender. All those requests and promises hint, perhaps, at the realisation that kings did not always behave as they should. Yet if the coronation ceremonies offered the church the opportunity to insist upon its claims, it was the king, now fully king, who emerged the stronger from the occasion. And it is worth noting, and emphasising, that in asking the king to protect it, the church implicitly acknowledged the king's superiority. Not least was that the case when churchmen asked the king to keep the laws, customs and franchises, followed by the crucial words, 'granted to the clergy by the glorious king St Edward your predecessor'. It was St Edward the Confessor who, the church recognised, had granted the church its liberties. The historical accuracy of that assertion does not matter here. What does matter hugely is that in the coronation liturgy, in a ceremony led by archbishop and bishops, when the church asked the king to uphold the liberties of the church which, it asserted, a past king had bestowed upon it, it implicitly recognised that these liberties were the king's to grant and to confirm.[6]

Anointed with holy oil, kings were then held to possess the power of magical healing. When they touched for the king's evil, or distributed cramp rings, it was as part of services led by churchmen. Rebellion against a king was denounced as rebellion against God, once more drawing attention to the semi-divine status of earthly kings. The church accepted all this, indeed collaborated in it. Kings, of course, may well have been deeply and sincerely pious, as we shall see, and a modern historian must guard against a naive cynicism in treating kings' religion as merely conventional or simply part of the projection of an image of power. But it would be equally misguided to deny the political significance of religious pomp, and the power over the church which it could reflect. With the support of the church, kings began to present themselves, if not quite as priests, nevertheless as men set apart from the rest.

A visible public aspect of this was the burial of kings in the greatest churches. Kings rebuilt them or added chapels in order to glorify distin-guished ancestors whose canonisation they sought and with whose piety or renown they thus identified themselves. The church offered kings invaluable associations which they vigorously exploited. Henry II secured the canoni-sation of Edward the Confessor in 1161. Henry III rebuilt Westminster Abbey in the mid-thirteenth century, at vast cost, to provide St Edward the Confessor with a truly fitting shrine. Edward I would turn the abbey church into a royal mausoleum, reburying Henry III there in 1290, and erecting an effigy above the embalmed body of his queen, Eleanor. His choice of Westminster Abbey reflected the contemporary development of Westminster as the centre of royal government, emphasising again the close and symbi-otic relationship between church and state. No doubt it was the unwilling-ness of those who held power immediately on Edward II's death to risk the development of a cult that explains his burial at Gloucester rather than Westminster. Edward III would be buried at Westminster. Richard II wanted to be buried at Westminster, though it was not until 1413 that Henry V moved his body. Westminster was not Henry IV's choice: he preferred Canterbury. Henry V, however, was buried at Westminster. What Henry VI's intentions were has been the subject of debate. He was buried first at Chertsey, then at St George's Chapel, Windsor. Twelve deponents testified in 1498 that he had, however, intended to be buried at Westminster and had chosen the spot next to the tomb of St Edward the Confessor, but such evidence is shaky and it may well be that Henry VI's true ambition was to be buried at Eton, the school he founded near Windsor. Edward IV funded the building of St George's Chapel, Windsor, and chose to be buried in a chapel there. Edward IV and his brother Richard, duke of Gloucester, then Richard III, reburied their father at Fotheringhay, Northamptonshire, and Richard may have considered being buried there himself before opting for a new chantry college at York. Henry VII, continuing the pattern of royal foundations, built the great chapel at Westminster that now bears his name with the aim of translating the body of Henry VI, whose canonisation he was seeking; in the event it was Henry VII who would be laid to rest there. Most, though not all, kings between 1290 and 1422 who were able to determine their place of burial chose Westminster; then, perhaps because the horseshoe chapel in which St Edward the Confessor lay was full, they tended to choose new foundations or greatly enhanced existing churches. It was individual kings, or in the case of deposed monarchs their successors, rather than churchmen, who made these decisions. The tombs of kings in the grandest of churches vividly displayed the monarchical church. It is necessary again to warn against too great a scepticism in treating the piety of monarchs—we should allow for the possibility that, at least near death, they were sincerely pious—yet the more cynical their motives, the more that would make the church a monarchical church, with its buildings and ceremonies ruthlessly manipulated by monarchs seeking to enhance their secular power.[7] Pertinent here too is the creation and development of quasi-religious chivalric associations, notably Edward III's mid-fourteenth century establishment of the Order of the Garter, a new order of chivalry dedicated to the Virgin and to St George, served in a lavishly refurbished chapel at Windsor Castle by a college of priests and poor knights. Here the church endorsed, indeed celebrated, the martial ardour and chivalric exploits of the king and his leading warriors.

A very direct and material illustration of the monarchical church was the extent to which successive English kings turned to the church for taxation. Obviously financial demands on the church go back a long way, but then the church had successfully claimed that only the pope could agree to financial demands on the church, and consequently the church as an institution had been exempt from taxes levied on the laity. Against that background it does appear that Edward I fundamentally changed the fiscal relationship between church and state. He claimed in 1279 that ' "the *communitas cleri* [the community of clergy]" live under our rule no less than the rest of the people' and should therefore contribute directly to the costs of defending the realm.[8] Taxes were duly levied on the clergy in 1279–80, 1283, 1286,

1290–1. The assessment of 1291 became a standard until the reforms of Cardinal Wolsey in the 1520s. The church was subjected to still heavier financial demands in the mid-1290s. Edward took advantage of the vacancy at Canterbury after 1292 and at Rome to impose very burdensome demands on the church in 1293 and 1294 (£80,000). Edward seized most of the alien priories, monasteries owing allegiance outside the realm. The clergy under Archbishop Robert Winchelsey resisted, not least instructed by Pope Boniface VIII, whose bull, *Clericis Laicos*, forbade clergy to grant money to a king without papal approval. The conflict reached its climax in 1297. Edward I threatened to withdraw his protection of the church: in the tussle Edward I emerged the stronger. Boniface VIII was, ultimately, prepared to co-operate with the king, and the church was not united against royal demands. It is telling that Edward was prepared to outlaw the clergy to get his way.[9] Thereafter it was accepted that, in an emergency, the king could tax the clergy. Again in 1340–1 there was a moment of great tension as the church under Archbishop Stratford resisted Edward III. The king declared that 'I believe that the archbishop wished me, by lack of money, to be betrayed and killed'. But once more it was the crown that won the day, with Archbishop Stratford humbling himself before the king, and Edward recovering his political position very quickly after seemingly yielding to his critics.[10]

Taxation of the church became a regular feature; when parliaments granted taxation from the laity, convocations made corresponding grants from the church. 'The formal de facto assumption of secular control over the taxation of the clergy represents one of the most remarkable and significant steps towards the decline of the church and the primacy of the state in the political life of later medieval Europe.'[11] What that meant was that, by the late fourteenth century, whenever clerical taxation was granted the king could expect to receive something approaching £13,500 from the southern province (as well as over £1,000 from the northern province); by the early sixteenth century the actual sums collected had fallen and each grant averaged £11,000 to £12,000.[12] The way in which clerical taxation was assessed became standardised (not to say fossilised), and in the fifteenth century what the church paid was not an up-to-date and accurate reflection of its wealth. In the years 1486 to 1534 the church paid an average of £9,000 a year in taxation. Some royal officials may have felt that the church was not paying enough. Henry VII's legal advisers, notably Sir James Hobart and Sir John Fyneux, have been seen as producing 'a campaign of fiscal intimidation so intense that a bill to preserve the liberties of the church was introduced into the first parliament of Henry VIII's reign'.[13] And in the 1520s Cardinal Wolsey significantly increased the weight of taxation on the church, just as he did that on the laity. Those financial demands were not directed disproportionately against the church, even if some clergy felt that they were. Nonetheless striking are the huge sums drawn from the church in these years. In 1522–3 the clergy were asked to lend the king a quarter of their annual income and of the value of their goods. The bishops produced £38,000, the general clergy £18,000, a total of £56,000, remarkable compared to the yield of the standard tax on the clergy, around £11,000 to £12,000. And, in 1523, just as the laity were asked to pay taxes based on fresh valuations of their wealth and income, so the clergy were asked to pay at the rate of 10 per cent for clergy with incomes over £8, and at 6.2 per cent for those with lower incomes. No details of sums received survive, but Wolsey calculated that each year should produce £24,000. Such taxation was obviously not welcome, but there was not much resistance. In 1514 or 1515, John Taylor made an impassioned speech in convocation against excessive and unnecessary taxation.[14] In 1523 convocation authorised the archbishop of Canterbury and the bishop of London to proceed against any clergy and monasteries who did not readily pay sums granted in taxation, hinting at expected resistance. In May 1524 there were difficulties at Boxley, where the abbot's attitude irritated Warham, the archbishop of Canterbury. And in 1525 clergy were prominent in refusals of the Amicable Grant, yet another financial levy, this time demanding one third from clergy with incomes over £10, one quarter from those with lower incomes. The clergy were prominent in preaching against the Amicable Grant, so the chronicler Edward Hall tells us, but that demand was generally refused before being abandoned by the king.[15] And, the Amicable Grant apart, there is not much earlier evidence of any significant clerical opposition to the increased financial burdens of the 1510s and 1520s. There is nothing to suggest that the church hierarchy was generally resisting royal demands. The crucial significance of the experience of clerical taxation here is that it vividly illustrates the reality of monarchical control over the late medieval church. Where the material interests of church and crown were not identical, it was the crown that largely got its way.

Moreover, as taxation was usually required in order to sustain war, grants of taxation unavoidably associated the church with the crown's diplomatic and military ventures. The association of church and war goes back a long way. Carolingian rulers secured masses, prayers and benedictions in support of their military campaigns against the Vikings, Saracens and Magyars. Holy banners were paraded before royal armies. There are early Anglo-Saxon traces of special services, of service books with masses in time of war.[16] Under Henry III the church offered prayers in 1242, 1256 and 1272. A letter of 1230 suggests that Henry III had asked for, and obtained, prayers for the success of an expedition. It was Edward I who turned this into a regular practice. From 1294, on virtually every occasion when he fought the French or the Scots, he ordered prayers to be said throughout the country. No doubt Edward I's motives were mixed. It would be unduly cynical to doubt his piety, however much that was combined with the maintenance and increase of his own authority.[17] Nonetheless, such prayers offered a splendid opportunity for propaganda, for explaining in detailed preambles the purposes of royal policy, and such prayers made it appear that the wars were holy wars approved by God.[18] Instructions issued in the province of Canterbury in Edward I's reign were precisely detailed, suggesting a novel procedure; later requests were terse and formal, suggesting a well-established routine. Special ceremonies took place on Wednesdays and Fridays, days on which it was permissible to substitute votive masses (masses for a special occasion) in place of the daily liturgy. By the fourteenth century the English church had thus come to accept even the secular pursuit of war as a religious virtue.[19] During the Hundred Years War the clergy of the realm prayed for the success of royal expeditions and for the peace that would follow a successful campaign; they preached sermons and organised processions.[20] By associating the cause of the king of England with that of God, by drawing on Old Testament parallels to present the English people as a chosen people, with a special relationship with God, churchmen further reinforced royal authority.[21] In 1412 Henry IV called for tears and fasting. Congregations were offered the customary reward of forty days' remission from purgatory for taking part in such special rites. In August 1415, on the day of the sea-battle off Harfleur, Henry V asked the monks of Sheen and the London Charterhouse, and the hermit of Westminster Abbey, to pray for an English victory.[22] Whether such propaganda was effective is a separate question; possibly not, as is suggested by the complaints of Bishops Chichele and Repingdon in 1418 that their instructions to clergy to organise patriotic liturgies were being disregarded. But what is at issue here is the close relationship between church and state that such actions reflected.[23] In his will Henry V asked for prayers from the whole kingdom, particularly at votive masses on Wednesdays and Fridays.[24] The association of church and war continued. In 1436 mandates were sent by the archbishop of Canterbury to dioceses ordering prayers and processions in support of the campaign of Humfrey, duke of Gloucester, aimed at relieving the siege of Calais.[25] In 1487 a *Te Deum* was sung in York Minster after news came of Henry VII's defeat of the rebel and pretender Lambert Simnel. Prayers were said before the French campaign in 1513. The diary kept by John Taylor, clerk of the parliament, during that campaign shows how important church services were. When Henry VIII arrived at Calais with his fleet, he was saluted by such firing of guns that, Taylor tells us, 'you would have thought the world was coming to an end', and conducted by a procession of clergy to St Nicholas's church. That Henry heard mass there two days later was more routine. But, significantly, it was at the high altar of St Mary's church that on 3 July the king ratified certain articles in the presence of the imperial ambassadors. When news came of the defeat of the Scots at Flodden Field, a mass was celebrated in a pavilion of gold and purple and a *Te Deum* sung. When Tournai fell, the king was conducted to the cathedral where a service was held.[26] A dozen years later, when news arrived of the defeat and capture of Francis I, king of France, at Pavia, Wolsey, after organising a series of bonfires in London, celebrated that great victory by officiating himself, assisted by four bishops and six abbots, at a *Te Deum* attended by great numbers of noblemen at St Paul's Cathedral. All that was aimed at drumming up support for the invasion of France that Henry VIII then planned and to encourage acquiescence in the Amicable Grant, the abortive huge financial demand that was intended to pay for the military campaign.[27]

If occasionally churchmen spoke out against war, as John Colet, dean of St Paul's, did in 1513, their voices were few. And some leading churchmen, by virtue of their status as landowners, were liable to provide military forces to serve the crown, and some of them served in wars themselves. That was especially true of the bishops of Durham and Carlisle. The prior of Durham regularly acted as treasurer during border wars. Border abbeys were used as headquarters. At Henry's request, Pope Leo X granted a plenary indulgence to the see of Durham.[28] At the king's and Wolsey's request, the pope granted an indulgence to assist the restoration of Norham Castle.[29] And, of course, Henry's invasion of France in 1513 was against Louis XII, a king declared schismatic by Pope Julius II, who issued a bull granting a plenary indulgence to all in Henry VIII's dominions who in the expedition against Louis XII of France served for at least six months, visited certain altars, made gifts or contributed to expenses.[30]

Taxation and warfare thus thoroughly associated the church with the crown. The church was 'comfortably integrated with the establishment', serving the crown faithfully, in return for the defence of its privileges.[31] In many ways such a close relationship was mutually beneficial; but it is not difficult to see that it was also, in various ways, compromising—especially when the wars that kings fought were not wars of national survival but rather more opportunistic attempts, at considerable cost in human life and suffering, to pursue dynastic quarrels and win chivalric glory.

Not only did the church pray for kings in time of war, it regularly declared to the people the right and authority of the king. In the general sentence or curse read four times a year to the people by the curate of every parish, until it was suspended by Archbishop Cranmer in 1534, enemies of the church were cursed, and, indeed, the preponderant thrust of the general sentence was the defence of the material interests of the church, especially against those who withheld tithes or fees or rents. But the general sentence also cursed all who were against the right of the king, all who sustained war against the king wrongfully; all who were robbers; all who maliciously despised the commandment of the king. It also cursed those who produced dissension—by bearing false witness or bringing false charges; all those who coined false money; all those who counterfeited the king's seal. We cannot know how seriously this was taken, whether those who heard it simply laughed or smiled inwardly; but anyone who was a committed christian could not but think that God wanted the king to be obeyed. It neatly illustrates once more the symbiotic relationship between crown and church.[32]

The English crown took a close, and increasingly restrictive, interest in the extent of the landholdings of the late medieval church. The lands which the church owned had, of course, originally been given by laymen and laywomen. The largest donations and bequests had been made centuries before the reign of Henry VIII. Pertinent to consideration of the nature of the relationship between crown and church were the restrictions that the crown came to place on such gifts. The statute of mortmain (1279) forbade laymen from alienating land to the church without royal licence. However much its provisions were in fact evaded, however much the statute was intended simply to raise revenue for the crown rather than to block grants to the church, with the royal licence to be seen as a kind of tax, however much some such control was inescapable if the church was not ultimately to become the greatest landowner in the country as each succeeding generation made bequests, nonetheless to enact such a statute was at the very least to assert a remarkable degree of royal control. The crown was in effect determining how much land the church would be allowed to hold.[33]

It is intriguing, too, in this context that the crown exploited the properties of the alien priories (monasteries directly under the control of mother houses abroad) and from 1294 dissolved them, taking over their lands. The suppression of the Knights Templar in 1324, with their lands forfeit to the crown, further illustrates the reality of crown control. As chantries—endowments supporting priests who were to say masses, usually for the soul of the founder (which we shall consider in detail in a later chapter)—became more fashionable in the later fourteenth and fifteenth centuries, so the crown took an increasing interest in the process by which laymen and laywomen alienated lands, and successfully controlled it in the early fifteenth century. Fines—in effect a fee charged on the granting of permission—increased from between one and three times the annual value of alienated property in the early fifteenth century to three to five times after c.1470 and then to between seven and a half to ten times in the early sixteenth century. 'Moreover the crown simultaneously became increasingly reluctant to grant licences in its attempt to halt the alienation of land into mortmain. In short it adopted a position profoundly hostile to the foundation of perpetual intercessory institutions.' Of course, in one sense the government failed, since would-be founders of chantries relied more and more on enfeoffments to uses, that is to say granting lands to named individuals who would then in turn grant revenues from them to the church, rather than on obtaining licences of mortmain permitting the outright grant of land. This reveals both the ambitions of successive governments to restrict the endowment of chantries and the considerable technical difficulties they faced in doing so.[34] Why the crown was so sceptical and hostile is not altogether clear. But the ambition and the conviction that the crown could legitimately determine such matters are clear.

The English church on the eve of the break with Rome was a monarchical church not least because English kings had long been responsible for the nomination of bishops, including archbishops. Since 1066, if not earlier, even in an era of papal provisions, kings had been the main successful petitioners to successive popes, but it was in the mid-fourteenth century that an enduring pattern emerged. Outwardly, appointments continued to be made by popes, but popes appointed men recommended to them by kings, who had themselves instructed cathedral chapters whom they should choose. In 1351 the statute of provisors forbade petitioning for, and acceptance of, papal appointments to benefices: Englishmen were not to lobby popes. Not all those appointed were obviously king's men, but there was no doubt that the crown was in command. 'Throughout the 1360s Edward III had little difficulty in securing the bishops he wanted.'[35] Under Henry IV, for example, all the king's candidates, save two, eventually found appropriate sees, although there were setbacks until 1407.[36] Martin V was the last pope to attempt direct interference; but, even so, few royal or governmental candidates were long disregarded by him.[37] Only once did the pope reject a suggested candidate between 1422 and 1461: Henry VI, having nominated Thomas Kemp for London, tried to substitute Bishop Lumley of Carlisle.[38] After the pontificates of Martin V and Eugenius IV, there was no further conflict over the pope's role in appointing bishops in England: by 1461 the question of provisors was a dead issue.[39] To a large extent this was because popes were more concerned with Italian power politics, and their consequent need for diplomatic support from rulers such as the kings of England encouraged them to give them whatever they wanted.[40] We shall look at what this meant in practice when we look more closely in the next chapter at the role of bishops. Clearly, since bishops were appointed for life, each new king inherited a bench of bishops in whose elevation he would have had little say, and it would consequently take time before the bench reflected his interests and preferences—but over time it would.[41]

Not only did English kings, in effect, control episcopal appointments: they were highly sensitive over papal appointments to the status of cardinal. Cardinals were originally the priests in charge of the parishes of Rome; from the late eleventh century popes appointed the principal office-holders in the *curia* as cardinals; and then some of the archbishops across Europe were appointed cardinal. The election of popes was entrusted to the cardinals. During the papal schism cardinals understandably grew in importance—but not for long. Royal sensitivities went back a long way: an early example was Henry I's concern over Hugh of Reading.[42] Henry IV blocked cardinalates for Thomas Langley (*c.*1360–1437), bishop of Durham, and Robert Hallum, bishop of Salisbury, in 1411; Henry V reacted vigorously when Henry Beaufort (*c.*1375–1447), bishop of Winchester, was made a cardinal in 1417.[43] Much has been made of Thomas Wolsey as cardinal. But it is plain that it was Henry VIII who wanted him promoted, seeing Wolsey's elevation as indispensable in the complex international power politics of the 1510s and as giving Wolsey powers to cut through vested interests when seeking to reform the church. As Wolsey declared, 'I cannot express how desirous the king is to have me advanced to the said honour to the intent that not only men might thereby perceive how much the pope favoureth the king, and such as he entirely loveth, but also that thereby I should be the more able to do his grace service and execute his commandments.'[44] Much the same was true of the additional and unusual powers that Wolsey was granted by the pope as papal legate. In 1520 Henry thanked Pope Leo X for renewing Wolsey's legatine authority for three years but added that he would have been better pleased if it had been prolonged for an indefinite period, as it would have enabled him to proceed with a greater vigour in the reformation of the clergy.[45] What needs emphasising here is what such remarks reveal about the location of authority within the church.

The church was also a monarchical church in a deeper and more subtle sense. The crown had long played a part in clerical appointments at lower levels in the church. From the thirteenth century the history of royal ecclesiastical patronage in general became very much a story of royal dominance. It was not a wholly one-sided relationship. Their early monopoly of literacy had made clerks the men to whom rulers turned when they sought counsellors and, above all, administrators and executors of their lands and policies; in the thirteenth and fourteenth centuries their numbers grew greatly. There were royal chaplains and almoners; clerks in chancery; scribes and accountants in the exchequer, chamber and wardrobe, the chief financial departments; justices in the king's courts; ministers responsible for royal manors and forests; sheriffs, constables, escheators. That in turn fostered a connection, a symbiotic relationship, between crown and church, as rulers rewarded those of their servants and officers who were clergy by granting them, or persuading others such as bishops or abbots to grant them, benefices within the church. Such clergy would in effect often make up a 'royalist' group within the church. They would not always, nor absolutely, support the king, as Thomas Becket would show Henry II to his cost, and, indeed, usually such clerks took up their new responsibilities and spiritual obligations with a degree of commitment. Yet mostly they did identify with the king's needs and wishes.

Tensions were understandable in such arrangements. There were practical hazards. If such beneficed royal clerks attended the king, they would not be resident in their benefices. Zealous bishops might seek to discipline them. There were also larger issues of principle about appointments. Quarrels might arise when, as in the twelfth and thirteenth centuries, the papacy aspired to make appointments to ecclesiastical benefices throughout christendom, and local bishops aspired to monitor candidates presented by laymen. That was never especially welcomed by English monarchs, who, particularly from the age of Becket, insisted that such patronage was to be supervised by royal courts in England, not papal courts in Rome, especially whenever there were any disputes. After all, it was claimed, benefices had originally been endowed by the laity.

Some benefices were always churches of the king's advowson, founded by kings, or in effect maintained by kings after someone else had founded them, and consequently giving the king the right to make nominations. When these benefices were in castle chapels, without parishes, problems were fewer. When such churches were collegiate, that is, staffed by several priests, but especially when they were single (that is, with a single priest), then there was increasing pressure in the twelfth and thirteenth centuries from bishops for them to be allowed to institute priests, not least since bishops were increasingly keen that priests should be resident, rather than that benefices were treated purely as a source of income. In such circumstances, bishops sometimes allowed the creation of vicarages, unequally dividing the revenues of a benefice between the absentee rector and the resident curate, though this was more commonly done for monasteries, and by bishops making appointments themselves, than for royal clerks.

Another set of opportunities for the crown occurred when a bishopric or abbey was vacant. Its patronage should, the crown claimed, be exercised by the crown during the vacancy, in the same way as during the minority of a tenant-in-chief the lands of the minor were administered by the crown. By King John's reign, if not earlier, this was a well-established practice. Moreover, skilful lawyers in the later years of Edward I's reign developed the notion that time could not run against the king, so that the crown could exercise powers of patronage even after an episcopal or abbatial vacancy had been filled. Such aggressive self-confidence on the part of the late thirteenth-century monarchy has been seen as reflecting 'an overriding belief in royal supremacy . . . the king's position in relation to the English church was marked by more and more clearly defined prerogative rights'.[46] Some churchmen saw all this as an intolerable abuse: Archbishop Winchelsey clearly deplored it. But by no means all churchmen would have disapproved of such trends. And it is worth noting that many initiatives, many requests for posts, most likely sprang from legalistic benefice-seeking clerks rather than from patronage-flaunting monarchs.[47] Not a few royal clerks would have benefited from these arrangements, and they depended on continuing royal power to protect their interests—not least if the benefice had already been filled by someone else. 'Royal clerks needed to advocate the king's prerogative in order (literally) to earn themselves a living.' When vacancies occurred, there would, for example, often be members of cathedral chapters willing and eager to support nominations made by the king, since they might see the interests of their church, not least the pursuit of legal claims, as best served by maintaining a close relationship with the court. And, in all this, the church was not so much losing its immemorial rights as failing to realise the greatest ambitions of the era of papal monarchy.

What was ultimately most remarkable was the extent of co-operation rather than conflict. Royal ministers often lent their support to the enforcement of decisions made by church courts, while the church supplied information for use in suits over advowsons heard in royal courts. Occasionally conflict did flare up, but usually 'not through preconceived rancour or aggressiveness so much as genuine local uncertainty upon the merits of a case'. Such a dispute could, of course, then raise questions of irreconcilable legal principle between church and crown; and the clash of personalities—Henry II and Becket, Henry III and Grosseteste—could make matters still worse. But such conflict remained rare. The crown's ultimate ability to confiscate a bishop's temporalities did rather give it the upper hand in practice, as Archbishop Winchelsey discovered. The later years of Edward I's reign have been seen as a turning point in relations: henceforth the church hierarchy would be more submissive, though never totally submissive, to the crown's demands.

Bishops were more and more drawn from the ranks of the king's clerks, symbolised by a churchman such as Simon Islip, archbishop of Canterbury 1349–66, previously keeper of the seal. And the imperatives of international power politics made later medieval popes unwilling systematically to support diocesan bishops against the king. Morever, the fact of royal patronage over the church doubtless influenced clerical attitudes at times of tension. A significant number of king's clerks—'graduates, lawyers, able and ambitious men who had looked to the king to provide them with benefices and bishoprics'—had divided the church by refusing to support Archbishop Winchelsey against Edward I over taxation in the 1290s. They were not cowards shirking a struggle; rather they saw their loyalty as owed to the king who had appointed them to their benefices and who was, in effect, already the supreme head of the church, rather than to the pope and to the church as an independent, ultramontane institution.[48]

There was also a remarkable increase in the extent of royal patronage: in the early thirteenth century eight to twelve clerks were presented by kings to benefices; there were twenty-seven appointments in 1290–1 and 1291–2, sixty per annum under Edward II, and over a hundred a year after 1337. 'The very existence of an enormous source of patronage at the king's court cannot but have affected the loyalties of the English secular clergy (i.e. those who were not members of religious orders) as a whole . . . The papacy, of course, remained the English church's unquestioned spiritual authority, but few could doubt that the king was its master.'[49]

Royal ecclesiastical patronage continued to be of great importance in the fifteenth and early sixteenth centuries. Co-operation was more common than conflict over appointments: a working compromise obtained. The church accepted that litigation over advowsons could take place in lay courts; but the crown allowed diocesan authorities to make inquiries in order to verify rights in dispute.[50] We have occasional glimpses of how royal influence worked. Bishop Oliver King of Wells revealed in a letter to Sir Reginald Bray in June 1502 that, on his consecration in 1495, he had promised to accept royal nominations to the chapter and that he had done so in appointments to the archdeaconries of Wells and Taunton, the latter that of Robert Sherburne, then Henry VII's secretary.[51] That was how a monarchical church functioned in practice. In effect a substantial part of the costs of government was met from the resources of the church.[52] In fairness to the crown, it might be countered that those resources had to a great extent first come from the crown: the church was in this sense a high-interest savings account.[53] And if successive kings exploited the church, in particular drawing on the resources of the church to support their own essentially secular purposes, especially by rewarding their officials and servants with benefices, that does not necessarily mean that kings could not be sincere in their own religious devotions or committed to reforming the church. But it does very clearly show how closely integrated were church and crown, crown and church.

Where did this leave the papacy? It would be wrong to disregard the continuing part that the papacy played in the working of English ecclesiastical life, especially when individuals or institutions who felt they had been wronged appealed in surprisingly high numbers to the courts in the papal *curia*, the apex of the system of ecclesiastical jurisdiction in christendom, for justice. Nonetheless, the part that the papacy played, for example in the appointment of bishops, was much more formal than real. Loyalty to the papacy was tempered by the crown's diplomatic and military needs. The hostility of the Avignon papacy (especially Benoit XII, Clement VI, Urban V) to English interference in France during the Hundred Years War must have encouraged English royal assertiveness against the interests and pretensions of successive popes. And from then on English monarchs increasingly tended to treat popes as secular powers, potentially useful allies in international diplomacy, but not possessing any special moral standing.

English kings had long insisted that appeals to Rome which threatened their interests should be restrained. That monarchical insistence went back to Henry II and indeed to William the Conqueror. A writ of 1306 noted that 'according to the custom obtaining in our realm, no one of our subjects may be drawn out of our realm in a cause [i.e. a legal case]'.[54] In 1353 a statute laid down that all who appealed to a court outside the realm on matters pertaining to the king's courts, or against judgments in them, were to answer for such contempt before the king's judges. This would especially be the case where men appealed to Rome to thwart the workings of the statute of provisors.[55] That statute, passed in 1351, had protected the rights of lay patrons to appoint to benefices and had in particular threatened those who attempted to implement papal appointments. Disputes over benefices were, it was declared, to be settled in England. In 1393 a revised statute of praemunire subjected those taking cases 'alibi' ('elsewhere') than the royal courts to its penalties. Implicitly this challenged the system—the hierarchical structure with the papal courts at the summit—of ecclesiastical courts as a whole: it made the theoretical supremacy of royal courts quite plain.[56] Of course, these fourteenth-century statutes were the product of particular disputes and problems, not stages in some calculated process; they were threats, rather than permanent restrictions, and their immediate practical results were nothing like as great as the principles which they proclaimed might have suggested. Nor were crown–church relations characterised by constant conflict over these issues. Such clashes as occurred were not the result of disputes over principle but often stemmed rather from confusions and uncertainty.[57] The fourteenth-century statutes are better seen as warnings than principled or revolutionary measures. It is tricky to bring them into precise focus. They did not aim at a fundamental repudiation of papal authority, nor did they, in practice, lead to any major shift in relations with the papacy.[58] Yet implicit in the making of such statutes was a firm belief in the superiority of royal sovereignty. All this could leave the church vulnerable in different circumstances.

In the fifteenth century, laymen, especially lawyers, began to make creative use of the statute of praemunire—technically, the writ of praemunire, a legal instrument that allowed cases to be brought—in disputes with the church. In 1434 convocation voiced fears that the law of praemunire was being deployed to secure the transfer of cases from the church courts into the court of King's Bench. Most likely, such manoeuvres reflected common lawyers' attempts to increase their business, rather than any principled anticlericalism. Nonetheless, the church was evidently rattled. In the difficult years of the mid-century, churchmen exploited the weakness of kings to press for concessions on these points. In 1462, at a moment of relative monarchical weakness, Edward IV, who had recently won the crown and who was seeking to stabilise his position, issued a declaration followed by a charter recognising that for many years prelates and ministers had not been permitted to enjoy their liberties, and forbidding all further process by praemunire facias against judges and parties in English church courts. Such statements lacked the force of parliamentary statute, and, despite renewed efforts by churchmen, notably a papal bull in 1476, and a confirmation of this charter by Richard III in 1484 (again in a period of monarchical weakness), they did not succeed in ending praemunire suits.[59]

Indeed, it seems that Henry VII and Henry VIII, and the common lawyers who advised them, did think that too many concessions had been made to the church during the years of civil strife. Henry VII and then Henry VIII consciously tried to turn the clock back. A series of legal actions from the mid-1490s, in which leading common lawyers were prominent, was intended to limit the autonomy and the immunities of the church. Richard Nix (c.1447–1535), bishop of Norwich, was vexed in 1504 that he and his servants had two years earlier been accused of offences under the statute of praemunire when he had excommunicated men who refused to attend church courts in disputes over tithes. Describing Sir James Hobart (d. 1517), the attorney-general, as 'the enemy of God and his churche', Nix declared that 'the laymen be more bolder against the church then ever they were'; 'if your fatherhood would favour me,' he appealed to Archbishop Warham, 'I would curse all such promoters and maintainers of the praemunire in such cases as heretics and not believers in Christ's church.'[60] All that reads intriguingly in the light of what we have seen in Hunne's case. It is interesting, too, that John Earnley, Hobart's successor as king's attorney, whom we have seen going to court and accepting Horsey's plea of not guilty, should in Henry VII's reign have sued eight several praemunire suits in 23 Henry VII (1507–8) acting 'for the king himself'. The 'frivolity of charges . . . the vagueness and inaccuracy of the indictments, suggest the group of actions was used perhaps as an intimidatory gesture towards more formidable clerical opponents', perhaps as inducement to enter into bonds and recognisances. Once more the church was being left under no illusions that it was a monarchical church.[61] And the church was always vulnerable to further encroachments and restrictions. The poet John Skelton was prophetic in his claim that 'the premenyre/ Is lyke to be set afyre/ In theyr jurysdictyons [the praemunire/ Is likely to be set on fire/ In their jurisdictions]'.[62]

The survival of special privileges (liberties) enjoyed by the church does not qualify the monarchical character of the church, since these liberties were held on sufferance and survived only in so far as the crown tolerated, and was prepared to recognise, them. A good deal has been made of the supposed iniquities of benefit of clergy and of sanctuaries but it should be emphasised that whenever there were any important difficulties, the crown saw matters resolved in its favour. Yet the church may well have damaged itself by being too prone to defend these privileges even when they were morally indefensible.

The practice of benefit of clergy was a source of tension. It was a concession made to the church by the crown after the Becket controversy. All clergy were to be exempt from punishment by the secular courts. After conviction, a clerk could plead benefit of clergy and then be delivered to ecclesiastical authority for appropriate punishment. The test of clerical status was the ability to read a passage of Latin, usually chosen from the psalter. Lay judges would determine the strength of such a claim, a procedure which gave them a say. But clearly such practices were open to confusion and to abuse. Varying restrictions were applied: some offences were considered too serious to allow exemption from trial in secular courts. From the fourteenth century, laymen who were literate successfully claimed the status of clergy in order to avoid punishment, or to face a lesser punishment, for their crimes. Individual cases could produce scandals. It is not surprising that there was controversy over benefit of clergy.

The church defended its principle of exemption. In 1399 convocation included violations of benefit of clergy in a list of grievances. In 1429 and 1439 convocation complained against false and malicious indictments against clerks. In 1446 and 1449 it petitioned again. Laymen protested against abuses: the House of Commons drew attention to them in 1449 and 1455. It is worth emphasising that it was much less principle than particular abuses that provoked disputes from time to time.[63]

Efforts were made in the half-century before the break with Rome to tighten the procedures: in 1489 an act limited the privilege by allowing laymen to claim it once only; in 1497 an act deprived those not in holy orders of any benefit in cases involving murder of a master; in 1512 an act withdrew the privilege in cases of murder and robbery in a church, on a highway or in a dwelling house.[64] It is not entirely clear on whose initiative these measures were taken. They were not in themselves new. Benefit of clergy had been denied in cases of arson and brigandage from the reign of Henry IV. Petty treason was disallowed under Henry VII. Treason cases brought by the crown were exempt.[65] One suspects that particular measures may have been prompted by some particular scandal.

In 1515 there was a huge row over benefit of clergy. Richard Kidderminster, abbot of Winchcombe, raised a storm when he asserted, in a sermon preached at Paul's Cross, that the statute of 1512, which would have to be renewed by the next parliament, was against the law of God. Minor orders of clergy, he declared, were as holy as major orders: those in minor orders could not therefore be punished by the secular courts. He went on to attack the practice of trying clerks in secular courts.

Henry VIII, strikingly, did not leave matters there. The king appointed several doctors of canon law to argue the point before his judges and 'temporal counsel' at Blackfriars. In that debate the canonist whose role it was to speak in support of the preacher failed lamentably to make his case: consequently some of the knights present asked the bishops to compel him to recant. And Henry received vigorous support from Henry Standish, provincial of the Franciscans, who as a friar was critical of the wealth and pretensions of the secular clergy. Standish was in turn cited before convocation in Michaelmas Term to answer what appear to have been trumped up charges of heresy, when his real offence was to have argued against Kidderminster.

Once again the matter was referred to royal judges: they declared that those who had attacked Standish were guilty of offences under praemunire. Henry then asked John Veysey, dean of the Chapel Royal, whether bringing clerks before temporal judges in criminal matters was against the law of God and the liberties of Holy Church: Veysey replied that it had always been the custom and that it stood well with the law of God and the liberties of Holy Church. A very formal debate was then staged before Henry VIII at Baynard's Castle. The archbishops of Canterbury and York knelt before the king. It is revealing that Warham and Wolsey should have done so: an explicit recognition of superior authority. They asked that the matter be referred to the pope: the statute under discussion was contrary to the law of God, they claimed, noting that several holy fathers had suffered martyrdom on this issue. Sir John Fyneux (d. 1525), chief justice of King's Bench, retorted that since the church had no authority to punish those who committed murders or felonies, there was little point in handing them over. The bishops had no answer. Then Henry VIII pronounced:

> By the ordinance and sufferance of God we are king of England, and the kings of England in time past have never had any superior but God alone. Wherefore know you well that we shall maintain the right of our crown and of our temporal jurisdiction as well in this point as in all others.

This was a very definite assertion of royal power.[66] The matter was not sent on to Rome for adjudication. And, revealingly, Standish and Veysey, who had so prominently defended the king's position, were appointed to the next available bishoprics.[67]

In 1531 and 1532 further acts were passed, referring to earlier attempts, and once again restricting the privilege of benefit of clergy. No person convicted of petty treason or of wilful murder or of robbing any church or robbing anyone in their house or robbing anyone on the highway or of arson should be admitted to the benefit of their clergy—except only those who were within holy orders, that is to say, of the orders of subdeacon or above.[68] In 1534 the privilege was withdrawn not just on conviction but on indictment for petty treason, wilful burning of houses, murder, robbery and burglary if the charge was not directly answered (for example, by staying mute, or escaping to another county);[69] in the next five years piracy[70] and buggery[71] and thefts of money or jewels by servants[72] were added to the list of offences for which benefit of clergy was not allowed. In 1536 a final paragraph, without any preamble, enacted that 'such as be within holy orders shall from henceforth stand and be under the same pains and dangers for the offences contained in any of the said statutes, and be used and ordered to all intents and purposes as other persons not being within holy orders'.[73] That did not abolish benefit of clergy as such, but it did make pleading benefit of clergy in court largely pointless since the penalties would now be the same. In 1540 several of these acts were renewed; it was also enacted that persons in holy orders admitted to benefit of clergy should be burnt in the hand in the same way as lay clerks were.[74]

It is possible to construct an account of benefit of clergy that sees it as a running sore, a continuous tussle over principle between crown and church. And undoubtedly there were at times crown lawyers and churchmen who did see it in terms of principle, possibly the more so in the mid-1510s. During the Pilgrimage of Grace in 1536 the northern clergy asserted that no clerk ought to be put to death without degradation by the church, and that a man ought to be saved by his book.[75] But, in practice, benefit of clergy was much less a matter of principle, more often a matter of awkward individuals or difficult cases. And generally the crown got its way.

Yet here, as in other areas, the church was in danger of losing out. On the one hand, the church could not and did not succeed in giving clergy unlimited immunity from prosecution and punishment for what were undeniably criminal offences. But, on the other hand, the church sometimes appeared to be asserting just such a principle and to be unjustifiably defending wrongdoers in practice. Moreover, the risks of abuse when literate non-clerics exploited these rules further tarnished the church when it tried to defend what many would have seen as a straightforward abuse. Perhaps some churchmen themselves recognised the risks: it is intriguing that in 1528 Wolsey gained new legatine powers summarily to degrade priests and others in holy orders and hand them over to the secular courts.[76] But it is not surprising that a modern legal historian should think the attitude of the churchmen defending the fictitious form of the privilege 'theologically vacuous, legally inept, politically bone-headed, and on any view irrational'. Arguably, the late medieval church would have done well to have taken the initiative much earlier and negotiated some such reform. It is hard to see that the church gained anything from the stand it took in the mid-1510s.[77]

The question of sanctuary was similarly a matter of intermittent concern, but once again what should be emphasised is that, when some scandal arose, the crown was keen to assert its authority. Sanctuaries were on the face of it significant gaps in the crown's control of the realm. Every church and churchyard was a common sanctuary; in addition there were large private ecclesiastical liberties. Those who had committed crimes for which the penalty was death might go to them for shelter from retribution. Temporary departures (to the toilet or because of fire or flood, or even to act as witness in a court) were permitted. According to common law, a criminal might stay for up to forty days in a sanctuary. He could then, under English custom, confess his crime (this went under the name of 'abjuration') and go into exile abroad. Or he could move to a special or private sanctuary which offered unlimited respite: for example, St Martin's-le-Grand, London, St John's Priory, Clerkenwell, St Peter's, Westminster, Beverley and Durham. Between 1478 and 1539, 469 self-confessed criminals sought the peace of St John in the sanctuary at Beverley.[78] Of the 243 crimes recorded in the register of St Cuthbert's, Durham, between 1464 and 1524, 195 were for homicide.[79] Sir John Huddlestone informed Thomas Cromwell

in June 1539 that the presumed murderer of one of his servants was in sanctuary at Westminster.[80] When Beaulieu Abbey surrendered to the king in
1538, the royal commissioners found thirty-two sanctuary men there,
accused of murder, felony or unpaid debts. They lived there with their wives
and children in houses with cultivatable ground attached; the debtors were
allowed to continue there for life.[81]

On the face of it, to the rational modern mind, sanctuaries appear an
obvious abuse, a serious interference with the administration of criminal
justice. Not much attempt was made to reform or to control them: 'they
seem . . . to have had the benefits of monastic life without the burdens of
its rule'. And there were contemporary critics, too. Polydore Vergil, papal
tax-collector turned historian of his adopted country, complained that
sanctuaries admitted 'all manner of criminals'; Thomas Starkey's Reginald
Pole called the practice 'a plain occasion of all mischief and misery'; and
Thomas More, in his History of King Richard III, has the second duke of
Buckingham attacking the protection given to thieves as indefensible: 'it is
pity the sanctuary should serve them'. 'What a rabble of thieves, murderers,
and malicious heinous traitors.'[82]

Yet sanctuary was not of any lasting avail in more serious matters, such
as treason. When Henry VII encroached on sanctuary in pursuit of those
who rebelled against him, notoriously when in 1486 the alleged traitor Sir
Humphrey Stafford was removed from the chapel of St Paul in the
Benedictine house at Culham, Oxfordshire, and then tried, convicted and
executed, it was claimed on the king's behalf that Culham's charter,
produced by the abbot, did not specifically mention traitors. The judges
then held that only the king could grant sanctuary for treason. Robin of
Redesdale, leader of popular uprisings in 1486, was apparently taken from
sanctuary in Durham and handed over to the king. In August 1487 the king,
after taking two further humble rebels from sanctuary at Hexham, assured
Thomas Rotherham (1423–1500), archbishop of York, that when seeking
the removal of convicted traitors he had not infringed the privileges of
Hexhamshire. Evidently Archbishop Rotherham and John Shirwood
(d. 1493), bishop of Durham, acquiesced in such infringements for what
they saw as the greater good. Henry VII had no need to invoke principles,
nor was he following any programme, any sustained policy: it was the
treason of those he pursued that mattered, not any anger against the
principle of sanctuary.[83] The pretender Perkin Warbeck surrendered, under
pressure, from sanctuary at Beaulieu Abbey, Hampshire, in 1497.

In Henry VII's reign two chief justices, Sir William Hussey (1481–95) and
Sir John Fyneux (1495–1525), mounted a judicial assault on sanctuaries. As
cases arose, they ruled restrictively. A spectacular cause célèbre in 1516, in

which a Gloucester justice of the peace, John Pauncefote, was murdered, and his assailants including Sir John Savage took sanctuary, led to a court case. How far did the sanctuary extend? Could sanctuary last for more than forty days? Did not sanctuary rest on royal permission? The matter eventually came before the king's council in November 1519. Henry VIII intervened personally. 'I do not suppose that St Edward, King Edgar, and the other kings and holy fathers who made the sanctuary of Westminster Abbey ever intended the sanctuary to serve for voluntary murder and larceny done outside the sanctuary in hope of returning, and such like, and I believe the sanctuary was not so used in the beginning. And so I will have that reformed which is encroached by abuse, and have the matter reduced to the true intent of the making thereof in the beginning.' Henry VIII was not seeking to abolish, but rather to control, the practice of sanctuary. Once again what is notable is the assertion of royal authority in general, with a pragmatic approach to particular disputes.[84]

In the next decade pleas of sanctuary were repeatedly contested by the crown and rejected by the king's courts. In the 1530s a series of acts criticised the abuses of sanctuaries and set out rules by which they should be regulated. For example, in 1531 an act was passed insisting that convicted murderers or robbers seeking sanctuary should remain there for life,[85] while in 1535 another was passed insisting that sanctuary men would have to wear a badge 'of the compass in length and breadth of ten inches' whenever they left the sanctuary, and that none of them was to carry any sword, knife or other weapon, other than their meat knives.[86] But in 1540 an act of parliament that appeared to regulate sanctuary in effect abolished it. If churches and churchyards were allowed to remain as privileged places of refuge, together with newly established sanctuaries in Wells, Westminster, Manchester, Northampton, Norwich, York, Derby and Launceston, sanctuary was nonetheless denied to those accused of murder, rape, burglary, robbery, arson or sacrilege. Other offenders were limited to forty days, unless they formalised their position and remained in sanctuary for life. In most cases sanctuary on such terms would not be worth having.[87]

Throughout, individual bishops and heads of monastic houses had repeatedly defended the privilege of sanctuary which particular churches or monasteries held. During the Pilgrimage of Grace, the northern clergy would assert that sanctuary ought to save a man for all causes in extreme need.[88] Once again it is hard to see that the church gained from such principled defence of sanctuaries. Moreover, its English practice appears at odds with how canon law was more generally interpreted in christendom: sanctuary was given to categories of criminals who would not have been protected elsewhere, including debtors.[89] If the late medieval church had

itself taken the initiative in reforming the obvious abuses of such a procedure, some compromise might readily have been found. By not doing so, it
left itself vulnerable to legislative criticism. And much opinion, not least
that of most nineteenth- and twentieth-century scholars, endorsed the
perception of sanctuary as an outrage.

More recently, anthropologically-minded modern historians[90] (though
not legal historians[91]) have tended to see sanctuaries as performing an
important and indeed indispensable local function: in the absence of a state
police force, they deterred victims of crime from taking matters into their
own hands, and they facilitated the resolution of disputes, not in the heat
of the moment but by reconciliation and arbitration, for example in cases
of accidental homicides that occurred when a quarrel got out of hand and
a fight turned into a murderous brawl. One Wolfe, servant of the earl of
Hertford, fought a master of the fence in St Martin's and killed him: he
sheltered in sanctuary in Westminster.[92] George Hogson, who took sanctuary in Durham in 1522, offered to pay £40 in restitution to the executors
of the man from whom he had stolen money: that may speak for how the
procedures were expected to work.[93] Some such defence of sanctuaries
might well have been elaborated by late medieval bishops, leading to a more
fruitful compromise with the crown. More difficult, but not impossible,
might have been a defence of sanctuaries as a bulwark against tyrannical
rulers, as 'a mechanism of local relief from an excess of government', neigh-
bourhood action as 'a potential independent force as a mitigator or critic of
the policies of government'.[94] Thomas More's *Richard III* includes a discussion of sanctuary. The queen knows that the life of her young son the prince
depends on sanctuary. The abuse of a thing does not destroy its use: ' "in
what place could I reckon him sure", demands the queen, "if he be not sure
in this the sanctuary whereof, was there never tyrant so devilish, that durst
presume to break" '.[95]

The monarchical character of the church was made quite plain in a
quarrel between churchmen in the early years of Henry VIII's reign. On the
thorny question of the probate of wills, there was a long-running dispute
between William Warham, archbishop of Canterbury, on the one hand, and
the bishops of Winchester, London, Lincoln, Exeter and Chester on the
other. When those bishops had appealed to the pope, Archbishop Warham
referred the matter to the king for arbitration; Henry VIII had passed it on,
in turn, to 'certain of our council'; and in February 1513 a set of proposals
was tabled. Some properties and rents were to be exempt altogether. The
demarcation between archbishop and bishop was set out: if testators died
leaving goods or debts worth more than £10 in a diocese other than that in
which they lived, then the archbishop's courts should deal with it, otherwise

diocesan courts should. Although this compromise gave him much of what he had sought (though he had wanted the threshold to be set at £5), Archbishop Warham refused to accept it, on grounds of principle. He thought that the king should allow what was clearly a spiritual matter to be determined by the papal courts in Rome, rather than that he should agree to a decision made under the auspices of the king in England that would, to an extent, impoverish his diocese.[96]

What is noteworthy is Henry's response. Henry at this point was engaged on an invasion of France: it is interesting that he found the time to deal with this at all. On 22 June he commanded Warham to observe the order—and immediately to send a letter confirming that he would comply.[97] When Warham not only refused to conform but summoned before his court an official of another bishop for usurping the archbishop's jurisdiction, Henry, in the midst of his military campaign, wrote from France to Catherine of Aragon about this incident. Catherine was to order Warham to cease vexing that official, obey the king's ordinances, and certify the king directly by letter that he would conform.[98] Yet Warham continued to defy the king until, ultimately, he was compelled to yield. What is interesting about this dispute is the king's concern, if merely for the very secular reasons of avoiding internal dissension while fighting a foreign war, to settle a dispute between archbishop and bishops. More arresting still is his easy assumption of authority over the procedures and privileges of the church, not least in his repeated and peremptory commands to Warham to certify his conformity in writing. That was not in itself novel, nor does it take us ineluctably along a road, say, to the prosecutions of bishops in 1530–1 for breaking the four-teenth-century law of praemunire, or to the submission of the clergy of 1532. But a king who could order his archbishop both to obey and to confirm that he was obeying—even if without getting his way immediately, though in the end he did—was a king who, if circumstances demanded it, would be prepared to exert all sorts of pressures on archbishop and bishops, as he notably did in the years 1529 and 1532. And in 1514–15 Warham was compelled to yield and to agree to almost exactly what had been proposed and he had refused a year earlier.

In the military campaign of 1513 Henry VIII conquered the city of Tournai. The young French bishop-elect (technically administrator, since he was under age) Louis Guillard, son of the second president of the Parlement de Paris, refused to do homage to Henry VIII, and by June 1514 Pope Leo X had declared the see vacant and appointed Thomas Wolsey as adminis-trator instead. A 'battle of the bishops' ensued. Officials of the contesting bishops competed to exercise authority and collect revenues, especially in those areas of the diocese in Flanders, under the rule of Margaret of

Austria. Both bishops appealed to the pope. Francis I's victory at Marignano in September 1515 greatly strengthened the French position, and in the Concordat of Bologna (agreed in December that year), Pope Leo appeared to have favoured the French over Tournai. In August 1516 Leo issued a secret judgment that, in effect, revoked Wolsey's appointment to administer the see, and ruled in favour of Guillard, including giving him permission to seek assistance from secular princes. Guillard's father was one of those whom Francis I entrusted with steering the ratification of the Concordat through the Parlement of Paris. Leo's judgment provoked a counterblast from Henry, which is the point of significance here. Henry wrote to his ambassador at Rome, Silvestro de Gigli. He asserted 'truth it is that we having the supreme power as lord and king in the regality of Tournai without recognition of any superior'. The pope 'attempts to take from us the superiority regal pre-eminence jurisdiction and authority that we have in the region and dominion of Tournai', in that he 'by his delegates called and adjourned us and our subjects out of the regality and territory to places unsure under the obedience of other princes in derogation of our honour and contrary to justice . . . If he in his person would thus rigorously without ground of justice proceed against us,' Henry added, 'we would not suffer it.' If the pope regarded his honour and surety he would revoke the bull, the king continued, 'but also be well wary how he grant the semblable bulls against the sovereignty of princes hereafter remembering the danger that may ensue unto him by the same'.

All this has been presented by T.F. Mayer as 'on the road to 1534', to the Act of Supremacy. Against that, C.S.L. Davies has rightly dismissed such claims as over-blown, and pointed out that what Henry said, embedded in a mass of (contradictory) observations in his letter to ambassadors, were entirely traditional and conventional sentiments expressed whenever rulers found themselves in conflict with the church. There was essentially nothing new here.[99] That said, however, the language *is* remarkable, and it confirms (not 'announces', as Mayer would claim, but 'confirms' because it is not new) that English kings saw the church in England and their other territories as a monarchical church, in the last resort under their control, and that they were conceptually equipped (to use a term Mayer would approve) to challenge papal authority. Of course the dispute in 1516 was a minor one. Of course those involved in disputes tended to use heightened language, making assertions in terms of principles which they were more than ready to compromise as soon as bargaining began over details (for example, denying a rival's jurisdiction completely but then negotiating over its application in particular cases). Of course grandiose statements of principle were called upon to justify disputes which they had not originated: political theories were invoked to justify pragmatic political decisions rather than stimulating action. Clearly in 1516 Henry had not the slightest intention of breaking with Rome and declaring himself supreme head of the church. There was no 'road to 1534'. But it would not be unreasonable to include Henry's words in 1516 in any discussion of his general attitude to the papacy. A ruler who could say this could also break with Rome. That is perhaps not saying much, since it could no doubt be said of most European monarchs, but it remains a point worth making, not least since the still influential Eltonian orthodoxy on the 1530s has been very much to see the break with Rome as revolutionary and unimaginable without the brilliance of Thomas Cromwell's insight. This letter helpfully illustrates royal attitudes in quarrels with the papacy. It does not in any way predict or make inevitable or likely a break with Rome; it is certainly not the origin or the first sign of, nor did it contribute to, the break with Rome of the 1530s. In making his threats, what Henry wanted (as was also true over his divorce a decade later), was to get his way in the matter in dispute, which he may, in part, have desired in order to raise the value in diplomatic bargaining of the return of Tournai to the French, not to secure the recognition by the papacy of some great and novel constitutional principle. And yet, and yet, the letter does reveal a frame of mind, a perfectly conventional frame of mind, but nonetheless one that could, in some unlikely circumstances, as a result of some quarrel between king and pope that could not readily be resolved, ultimately lead to a chain of events culminating in a renunciation of papal authority (itself also not an entirely unprecedented matter).

Late medieval kings did not directly claim to determine true religion, but the challenge posed by John Wyclif and by lollardy in the later fourteenth century led them to take a close interest in doctrine. In broader terms, that was not new. Kings had long dealt with heresy. Henry II had had heretics burnt in Oxford in 1163. But heresy had never been a significant feature of high medieval England: church and state were not troubled by cathars or waldensians. When confronted by the religious ferment stirred up by Wyclif, monarchs responded vigorously. The orthodoxy of Richard II, Henry IV and Henry V was crucial in the failure of Wyclif's 'premature reformation'. The involvement of successive monarchs in the struggle against heresy added a fresh dimension to the monarchical church. In 1408 Richard Ullerston's *Petitiones* presented the king as the protector of the church: only by royal exertion could heresy be defeated. No ecclesiastical reform was possible 'without the protection and strength of princes, considering the weakness of priests'. Measures against lollardy in 1414, 1416 and 1428 had governmental support. Henry V may well have sponsored the large-scale refutation of lollardy, Thomas Netter's *Doctrinale Antiquitatum fidei*.

Henry V's endowment of Sheen and Syon and planned foundation of Celestine—'in conception ... by far the most ambitious foundation attempted by an English king, and one designed to place the monarchy at the spiritual centre of English life'—more precisely defined what was to be seen as the truest piety of the day. The speed, self-confidence and assertiveness with which Henry V acted are striking. He set Syon's foundation stone himself on 22 February 1415. The authorities of the Grande Chartreuse accepted Sheen, under pressure from the king, in spring 1417, only after work on it had begun. Work on the Bridgettine and intended Celestine houses also began before negotiations with their authorities took place. It was only after the setting of Syon's foundation stone that Henry wrote to the Swedish mother-house. Under Henry V, Henry Chichele (c.1362–1443), archbishop of Canterbury, fostered the Sarum Use, and newer cults such as those of Corpus Christi and the Holy Name. That reflected a desire to control within the institutional church the best of those impulses that had fired the contemplative movements of the later fourteenth century.[100] And in 1421 Henry V assembled more than 350 monks and churchmen to voice his concern that the zeal of the past had become lukewarm and devotion had given way to negligence.[101]

After the Wycliffite and lollard emergency had passed, rulers continued their close interest in the church. Their interest was not directly in matters of doctrine. But Henry VI, notably—indeed notoriously—pious, took a close personal interest in his religious foundations, Eton and King's College, Cambridge, and these reflected a distinct strand of late medieval piety. Henry VII's mother, Lady Margaret Beaufort, was also deeply pious. Her interests again reflected and emphasised strands of piety fashionable in the later fifteenth century: a strict quasi-monastic regime of private devotions; an especial devotion to the Holy Name of Jesus (her chancellor Henry Hornby drafted the office for the feast of the Holy Name of Jesus which was approved for use throughout the province of Canterbury in 1488 and papally approved for the whole of England at Lady Margaret's request in 1494).[102] She purchased devotional works and translated some herself from French. While in many ways this was all perfectly conventional, the vigour with which she embraced conventional piety does suggest a depth of commitment. And in practising and endowing specific devotions, she was making choices: as queen mother her choices mattered.[103] Her son Henry VII also made explicit choices. His piety was above all expressed in charitable and educational works: the completion of King's College Chapel, Cambridge, the foundation of the Observant Franciscan house at Richmond, the establishment of the Savoy Hospital at Charing Cross as a nightly hostel for a hundred poor folks, Henry VII's almshouses, Westminster, as well as what we now call his chapel at Westminster Abbey. None of that was explicitly and directly a matter of doctrine. All of that patronage did, however, reflect emphases in contemporary piety and involved choices. The foundation of the Observant Franciscan house at Richmond, in particular, was significant and revealing. The Observant Franciscans aspired, as their name suggests, to a stricter observance than the existing, Conventual, Franciscans, and such aspirations were provocative and controversial. Henry's commitment to the Observants was total. When Pope Julius II attempted to combine the Observants with the Conventuals, Henry threatened to expel the Conventuals unless the pope agreed to the continuing independence of the Observants. Once more, royal preferences prevailed. Henry, meanwhile, used his influence to persuade the Conventuals to transfer at least three of their houses to the Observants: Canterbury, Newcastle and, possibly, Southampton. Intriguingly, two historians have commented, referring to this affair, that 'Henry's relations with the pope were not always smooth, and on occasion he exercised a guardian's role in the English church which in practical, though not theoretical, terms fell little short of his son's'.[104]

Henry VIII can be seen as continuing within the pattern set by previous monarchs. Official support of the church is shown in a note that the master of the rolls was accustomed to pay yearly at the rate of 1/2*d* a day for life all who within the realm converted to the christian and most catholic faith from any other erroneous faith and misbelief, an endorsement of conversion.[105] Much better known is Henry's stand against what he condemned outright as Martin Luther's heresies. He issued a royal proclamation in October 1521 requiring all mayors, sheriffs, bailiffs and constables to assist John Longland, bishop of Lincoln, in his efforts to seek out and punish those suspected of heresy.[106] He took a close interest in Luther's writings. In early 1521 he was sufficiently provoked to write a book against him.[107] In May he dedicated it to the pope, declaring that, as nothing was more the duty of a christian prince than the preservation of the christian religion, ever since he had heard of Luther's heresy in Germany he had made it his study how to extirpate it. By August the king had styled himself defender of the catholic faith and Christ's church: the pope would confer the title 'Defender of the Faith' in November.[108] Some have been sceptical about the depth of Henry's involvement. The pope said that he would not have thought that the king, necessarily occupied by other matters, could have done it, not least since men who studied all their lives were not capable of producing anything like it.[109] In 1539 George Constantine, a courtier's servant, would doubt that it was the king's work: it was rather that of Thomas More and Edward Lee, scholars then in the king's service. Although Henry was the most learned prince in christendom, he could not, Constantine went on, have had time to study, since as a king he would have been tempted by so many pleasurable pursuits.[110] Yet Erasmus wrote soon after the book was printed that, from what he heard, the king's work was his own.[111] And a few years later, while not claiming that the king had received no assistance in composing the book (for even the most learned sometimes seek help), he was sure that the king was both parent and author of those things which went under his name. No doubt recalling the time when the young Henry had been his pupil, Erasmus went on to say that the king had a vivid and active mind, with a capacity well above the average to bring off whatever he undertook: he never attempted anything in which he did not succeed.[112] Cardinal Campeggio, overcome with joy at reading the book, reported that all who had seen it said that nothing could be better expressed or argued. The king seemed to have been inspired by a spirit more angelic and more celestial than human.[113] Three years later Henry would write to Dukes John and George of Saxony, vigorously denouncing what he presented as Luther's poison. No faction was ever so universally pernicious as this Lutheran conspiracy, he declared, which profaned sacred things, and in preaching Christ trampled on his sacraments. It would lead to dissension, Henry warned, to the undermining of the power of laws: ultimately it would provoke the people to make war on the nobles.[114] But all this was not merely a negative attack on heresy—though it was certainly that—it was also a positive declaration of true belief. And once again it is remarkable how readily Henry involved himself in matters of doctrine.

Henry pressed Erasmus to make public what distinguished his teaching from that of Luther. In response Erasmus wrote a study *On Free Will*.[115] In November 1524 a copy of the book was presented to the king. Henry welcomed the passage in which Erasmus warned men against being immodestly curious about divine mysteries, a stand which much delighted him,[116] and a few days later Henry was reported as highly satisfied by Erasmus's warning men not to search too far into the secrets of divine omnipotence.[117] Here Henry seems to anticipate later rulers' attitudes to the reformation debates over predestination and free will. A few months earlier he had written to Dukes John and George of Saxony on the same subject. He complained that Luther's emphasis on God's grace in effect destroyed man's free will, licensed men to sin and made God the author of evil.[118] In 1525 Henry wrote to Luther arguing against his doctrine of salvation by faith alone and upholding free will.[119]

Henry was also interested in the general reform of the church, telling Erasmus in September 1527 that he had himself for some years felt the same desire as Erasmus to restore the faith and religion of Christ to its pristine dignity.[120] Significantly, in his denunciation of Luther to the dukes of

Saxony in 1524, he conceded that, at the beginning, some of what Luther had written had not been altogether bad—but now things had deteriorated so much that it seemed as if his early praiseworthy works had been intended rather to make his pollution saleable.[121] And, within England, Henry would encourage Wolsey's and other bishops' reforms of the church—especially the monasteries, as we shall see.

The church in England was thus a monarchical church, a church over which monarchs had, in practice, very considerable authority. In the final analysis, monarchs got their way. But their power was never complete, and the course of any dispute, if not its ultimate resolution, was never certain. Such a monarchical church was not incompatible with a significant clericalism, the claim by churchmen that the clergy, as servants of God, were superior to laymen, including the lay monarch, and that the forms and procedures of the church, its liberties and privileges, were not subject to royal control. Such views tended to be expressed either as somewhat bland and abstract general principles which had no very direct impact on events, or as principled justifications of the church's position when some particular dispute flared up—for example, Abbot Kidderminster's defence of benefit of clergy in 1515, or, more damagingly, some very small matter of disputed jurisdiction. This made the church vulnerable, since it gave it the worst of both worlds. In a sense, the church appeared to be claiming for itself vast privileges and authority overriding that of king and laity. In practice, it asserted such claims far more intermittently and pragmatically and made compromises with secular authorities frequently. But the church was left open to attack for its pretensions, and to criticism and jealousy of its actions. It may be that during the later fifteenth and early sixteenth centuries there was a heightened sense of self-confidence by the church in its claims. The charter of liberties extracted from Edward IV in 1462, a mysterious bill for the liberties of the English church (dropped from the House of Commons in 1510), John Colet's sermon in which he described the dignity of priesthood as 'greater than either the king's or emperor's: it is equal with the dignity of angels', Kidderminster's sermon and the assertiveness over benefit of clergy, and the vigorous pursuit of heresy can be seen as a notable reassertion of clerical privilege. In 1532 the first response of the church to the supplication against the ordinaries was in the same vein. 'We repute and take our authority of making laws to be grounded upon the scripture of God and the determination of Holy Church'; 'we, your humble subjects, may not submit the execution of our charges and duty, certainly prescribed by God, to your highness' dissent'.[122] Individual churchmen thought on these lines: in 1522–3 Edward Powell, a court preacher, prepared a treatise, *De immunitate ecclesiae*, proving, he said, that the church was derived from

God.[123] The memory of Becket and what he stood for remained vivid. Archbishops of Canterbury, including Warham, used seals which included an image of Becket.[124] Yet this did not amount to a coherent or, much less, a sustained campaign for the church. Such a campaign was unnecessary, since the church enjoyed considerable day-to-day freedoms. Tensions in particular areas, such as that of the jurisdiction of church courts, tended to arise from particular disputed cases, rather than from a settled set of principles. It was more, perhaps, a reflex defensive action—and, as such, likely to do more harm to the defendant than to anyone else. Whether it was all so new is doubtful: this may be an illusion created by the relative abundance of early Tudor evidence. And, in a sense, such intermittent, staccato assertiveness, provoked defensively by perceptions (or misperceptions) of royal intentions, offers the best evidence that this was a monarchical church, a church which enjoyed a close, indeed a symbiotic relationship with the crown, a church which benefited from the support and the protection of successive monarchs, a church which celebrated the liturgy and taught the truths of the christian religion, but a church which, in the final analysis, was always the king's to command and to control.

3

BISHOPS

WHATEVER we make of Bishop Fitzjames's exact role in the Hunne affair, his position vividly illustrates the complexities of the role of bishops. Indeed, it is not too much to say that the role of bishops was another area of vulnerability in the late medieval church. This is not to deny that there were many vigorous and effective bishops, especially Richard Sherburne (c.1454–1536), bishop of Chichester, William Atwater (c.1450–1521), bishop of Lincoln, John Fisher (d. 1535), bishop of Rochester, Nicholas West (d. 1533), bishop of Ely, and William Warham (c.1450–1532), archbishop of Canterbury, to name only those singled out by the best study of the early Tudor episcopate.[1] These men were worthy of comparison with the episcopal colleagues of Thomas Becket, as another modern historian has claimed.[2] Indeed, whenever any late medieval bishop has been studied in detail, 'his reputation has emerged much enhanced'.[3] Yet perhaps that should in itself sound a warning: perhaps here the method of inquiry determines the result. Such studies are based on administrative records which may well give an unduly favourable impression of episcopal activity: those who compiled them had every incentive to smooth over difficulties and present a picture of humdrum efficiency.

For there were many weaknesses. There was uncertainty about the precise function of bishops. In inherited tradition, they were the successors of the apostles. In his first epistle to Timothy, St Paul stated that[4]

A bishop then must be blameless, the husband of one wife, vigilant, sober, of good behaviour, given to hospitality, apt to teach; not given to wine, no striker, not greedy of filthy lucre; but patient, not a brawler, not covetous;

one that ruleth well his own house, having his children in subjection with all gravity . . .

What made that ideal an inadequate guide in our period was that it was concentrated above all on the personal and moral qualities of bishops, rather than on the bishop's work. Yet, by aspiring to such challenging personal standards, the church exposed itself to criticism whenever its leaders fell short. How many bishops could live up to such an exalted ideal? That was the more awkward given the post-Augustinian, and especially post-Gregorian, church's espousal of chastity as a clerical ideal. Such an emphasis on sexual morality did leave at least some late medieval bishops open to criticism. James Stanley (c.1465–1515), bishop of Ely, had three children—two sons and one daughter—by his housekeeper.[5] Thomas Wolsey had a son and a daughter by Mistress Larke, though well before his rise to fame. The young William Warham was archdeacon of Canterbury, and a modern historian has surmised that he was not the nephew of William Warham, archbishop of Canterbury, but rather his illegitimate son. There is no firm evidence.[6] In fairness, it should be noted that only this handful of bishops was open to such reproaches: and there is no evidence that late medieval bishops generally broke their vows of chastity while serving as bishops, rather than, as in these examples, at an earlier stage of their careers. This was not flagrant sexual promiscuity. In no sense could English bishops be described—as some French bishops were—as 'courtesans'. 'It is very hard to imagine Richard Sampson, Cuthbert Tunstal or Stephen Gardiner as lovers of the widow of the duke of Suffolk or of Lady Shrewsbury.'[7] Nor, for that matter, is there anything much to suggest that late medieval bishops were involved in violence or in crime.

How far did bishops set an example of piety, inspiring those whom they served as their shepherds? That was the ideal which underlay the poet John Skelton's humble ploughman Collyn Clout's complaint that bishops 'have full litle care/ How evil their sheep fare', and his wish that they should rather be 'lanterns of light'.[8] Of course there had indeed been some bishops whose lives were generally seen as so holy that after their deaths they were regarded as saints. Edmund Lacy (c.1370–1455), bishop of Exeter for over thirty years, lived a conspicuously holy life: by 1465 his tomb had become the focus of a developing cult, by 1478 many miracles were alleged to have occurred. Such evidence—including pilgrims, donations and wax votive offerings—has been taken to 'confirm the ability of the episcopal office in England to excite popular devotion, even after the office became so admin-istrative in function during the later middle ages'.[9] But such exemplary episcopal holiness was rare in the fifteenth and early sixteenth centuries.

Maybe the greatest weakness of the late medieval church was the sparsity of truly holy men whose evident sanctity would compensate for the human failings of the majority of churchmen. Yet that was already true much earlier.[10] Only five popes since 1000 have become saints, not all of them medieval, and none from the fourteenth and fifteenth centuries.[11] No late medieval English bishop resigned his office from motives of spiritual idealism, whether to join a monastery[12] or to devote himself to a parish. It is even difficult to find instances of conspicuous episcopal piety. John Fisher, bishop of Rochester, was seen as particularly devout, but that reputation is hard to disentangle from his later opposition to Henry's divorce, and to some extent it may have been his dedication to scholarship, rather than his piety as such, that won admiration from others such as Erasmus (who warned him not to spend so long in his chilly and draughty library).[13] Perhaps John Alcock (1430–1500), venerated at Ely as a saintly bishop and pastor, author of several devotional works, including *Mons perfeccionis* (*The Hill of Perfection*) (1496), comes closest of the late medieval prelates. Even John Bale, an early protestant writer who would excoriate the monks, recalled that Alcock 'having devoted himself from childhood to learning and piety, made such a proficiency in virtue that no one in England had a greater reputation for sanctity'.[14] Yet Alcock was untypical. And that leads an historian of the fourteenth century church to note that the *Ecclesia anglicana* of the later middle ages 'counted few men of deep religious conviction among those who were appointed to high office'.[15] To some extent, of course, such judgements partly reflect the surviving, largely administrative, evidence. Court records can give the impression of 'a hard, mechanical, institutional system',[16] with the emphasis on routine regulatory and judicial work.[17] Bishops were, of course, perfectly capable of giving appropriate spiritual advice, though it is unlikely to be found in such sources. In 1528 Archbishop Warham sympathised with the distraught Lady Greville, his niece, on the death of her husband Sir Giles Greville, a Worcestershire gentleman and comptroller of Princess Mary's household. He advised her to take it 'patiently and wisely', and not to make two sorrows out of one. That would displease God, hurt her and do no good for her husband's soul. If she used herself wisely and discreetly, and did not take 'such great heaviness', men would say that she was a sad (that is, serious-minded) and wise young woman, which would be better for her and for her friends. He was happy for his chaplain to stay with her as long as she thought necessary.[18] We cannot know how common such pastoral care (whatever its value) was, but there is no reason to suppose that it was rare.

If it was true that there were few men of the deepest spirituality in high ecclesiastical office, that also reflected the circumstances in which bishops

were appointed. Bishops were not chosen primarily for their moral qualities, despite the prevalence of such ideals. In what was, as we have seen, a
monarchical church, they were chosen by monarchs whose criteria were not
primarily spiritual. High office within the church was a means of rewarding
royal servants for their secular work in the central administration and in
diplomacy. Of course that does not mean that kings would necessarily
appoint unsuitable men.[19] Virtually all bishops were appointed after holding
a succession of benefices, though not necessarily after actually residing and
doing the work, including some key archdeaconries or deaneries, and often
after, in various capacities, serving the king or leading ministers.[20] But
bishops were not appointed because they had served outstandingly as parish
priests: if they held several parochial benefices, usually such men had not
been resident.[21] Moreover from the fourteenth century fewer and fewer
scholar bishops were appointed, especially to the more important and
wealthier sees.[22] Increasingly it was only for the bishoprics of Wales,
Hereford, Carlisle or Rochester that a man noted as a scholar or a preacher,
or a friar, might be chosen.[23] Richard Nix, bishop of Norwich from
1501, was unusual in that he had previously spent much time in diocesan
administration, rather than in royal service, before becoming a bishop.[24]
Occasional contemporary comments on an episcopal appointment offer
some illumination. When Archbishop Warham learned that Cuthbert
Tunstal (1474–1559) had been promoted to the see of London, he declared
himself pleased, and listed Tunstal's qualities: good learning, virtue,
sadness (we should say seriousness). Revealing just how far this was a
monarchical church, he added that Tunstal would be 'right meet and
convenient' to entertain foreign ambassadors in the absence of the king
and Wolsey.[25] Indeed, those of the king's servants who were employed in
diplomacy were often appointed to bishoprics in the belief that this
would enhance their status as ambassadors: Nicholas West (d. 1533),
John Clerk (1481/2–1541), bishop of Bath and Wells, Stephen Gardiner
(d. 1555), bishop of Winchester, Nicholas Heath (1501?–78), archbishop of
York, Edmund Bonner (d. 1569), bishop of London, and Thomas Thirlby
(c.1500–70), bishop of Ely, were all diplomats before they became bishops.[26]
Clerk served on diplomatic missions to Rome in 1519 and 1521. Appointed
bishop of Bath and Wells in 1523, he served at Rome until September 1525
and in France from July 1526 to August 1527 and April to September 1528.[27]
How far did such royal service inevitably prejudice the attainment of apostolic ideals of episcopacy—and even the lesser ideal of pastor and flock?[28]
Of course, engagement in royal administration and diplomacy did not
necessarily corrupt; but these were essentially worldly activities, and time
spent lying abroad for one's king was time that was not easily spent on

spiritual things. William Tyndale (d. 1536), the exiled early lutheran reformer and translator of the Bible, was unfair when he complained that contemporary bishops were 'more subtle and worldly wise' and 'less learned in God's word' than the earliest bishops since 'they come from stewardships in gentlemen's houses and from surveying of great men's lands, lords' secrets, kings' counsels, ambassadorship from war and ministering all worldly matters yea worldly mischief'[29]—unfair because his criticism implies the possibility of an alternative, unfair because it suggests that bishops were somehow wanton, self-interested, unaware that they were submerged in the ways of the world; unfair, then, in blaming them, but not inaccurate as a description. And this opened them up to attack, to Skeltonic satire, to idealising protestant invective. Tyndale's portrayal of bishops as 'worldly wise' raises the related question of how far bishops should be seen as careerists—interested above all in self-advancement. How typical was the cynicism that Francis Hull, Lady Lisle's correspondent, expressed when commenting on the resignations on principle of Bishops Hugh Latimer and Nicholas Shaxton in July 1539: 'they be not of the wisest sort, methinks, for few nowadays will leave and give over such promotions for keeping of opinion'.[30] How far did late medieval bishops have what we should recognise as a religious vocation? Of course the public roles bishops fulfilled did not necessarily or irretrievably compromise their inner dispositions[31]—but they undoubtedly made them more worldly, if only because their duties necessarily involved material concerns while leaving them little time for contemplation or prayer.

A fairer test of bishops' piety, and one that contemporaries would have recognised, was their willingness to use their resources for pious purposes. Bishops were expected to be charitable and to offer hospitality. Bishop West of Ely fed up to 200 poor daily at his gates with hot meals; Bishop Fox of Winchester provided the destitute of Winchester with food, clothing and money. Many bishops gave substantially from their revenues as bishop towards the cost of building or rebuilding at the cathedral church of their diocese. William Alnwick (d. 1449), bishop of Norwich 1426–36, built the porch at the west front of the cathedral and left money in his will for the great window at the west end of the nave, 'one of the most ambitious of its day'. Bishop Walter Lyhert (1446–72) renewed the choir screen and oversaw the huge project of vaulting the nave in a rich pattern of ribs and liernes. Bishop James Goldwell (1472–99) oversaw the remodelling of the arcades in the presbytery, and added the majestic vault, creating 'one of the finest and most interesting interiors of the English middle ages', and the spire. Bishop Richard Nix (1501–35) added vaults in the transepts. In each case heraldic devices and rebuses bear witness to the involvement of these bishops.[32]

A similar account could be offered of many other cathedrals. More telling still was episcopal endowment of a college or school. John Alcock, John Fisher, Hugh Oldham (c.1450–1519), bishop of Exeter, William Smith (d. 1514), bishop of Lincoln, Richard Fox (d. 1528), bishop of Winchester, and Wolsey were closely concerned with the foundation or refoundation of five colleges at Oxford and Cambridge between 1496 and 1529. Several of them supervised the drawing up of the statutes of their college.[33]

Such activity was undoubtedly significant. Perhaps it was almost a calculated policy, a response to the increasing sophistication of the laity. Its effect would, in the medium term, be to increase the number of educated parish priests. The weakness of all this was its patchiness. Schemes of improvement are no doubt laughable things but, nonetheless, without an overall plan the effects of such reforming ventures must have been limited and arbitrary: just some colleges, just some schools. For example, John Veysey (c.1464–1554), bishop of Exeter, a native of Sutton Coldfield, greatly lamenting the decay of his home town, secured 'a new privilege' from Henry VIII to restore its market. He began to repair old houses and to build new houses there. He obtained a licence to deforest the chase, on which he built several 'pretty' houses, leasing them to his poor kinsmen. He also endowed a grammar school, built 'a pretty pile of brick where he sometime lyethe', rebuilt the north and south parts of the church and the steeple, and erected a neat monument for himself in the wall of the north aisle.[34] Veysey's work can stand comparison with European ventures such as that of Cardinal Branda da Castiglione (1350–1443) who in his home village of Castiglione Olona, north-west of Milan, established churches, a convent and schools. It would be churlish to decry the value of such patronage and investment. But such activity was far short of the future Cardinal Reginald Pole's plan for every diocese to have a seminary in which the priests of the future would be properly trained. It is interesting that bishops chose to found new colleges in the universities of Oxford and Cambridge, rather than breaking their monopoly and founding new universities within their own dioceses: in other European countries many new universities were established in the fourteenth and fifteenth centuries, including Prague, Vienna and Heidelberg. Moreover, listing episcopal educational ventures also reveals those bishops who did nothing, or very little.

It would be unfair to suppose that self-glorification was the only motive for such actions. Yet this patronage may have been misunderstood and could have provoked resentment. That was Wolsey's experience. Henry VIII complained to him in 1528 about reports of the ways he had been raising money for his colleges.[35] And the inescapable fund-raising involved in such ventures was open to abuse. For example, in July 1528 John Longland, bishop of Lincoln, wrote to Wolsey asking for a favour for one of his kinsmen: if Wolsey would be his good lord and allow him to keep his prebend, then Longland would make a contribution of £200 towards the building of Wolsey's college in Oxford.[36] Perhaps no great harm was being done, but it could easily have looked bad. Wolsey has been singled out and much criticised for his excessive worldliness and unique ostentation. But this rests on taking literary sources' denunciation of Wolsey at face value and disregarding the very similar patronage of other churchmen which attracted little or no hostile comment.

What is striking is the general ostentation and display of late medieval prelates. Some bishops concentrated on the rebuilding or refurbishing of episcopal residences on a grand scale. John Morton, cardinal archbishop of Canterbury, the antiquary John Leland recorded, 'made a great piece of the palace at Lambeth. He builded at Alington Park. He made great building at Charing. He made almost the whole house at Forde. He builded also at the palace at Canterbury.'[37] The courtier-administrator Sir William Fitzwilliam would much admire the bishop of Chichester's residence near Arundel: apart from the king's and Wolsey's houses, not within a hundred miles, he claimed, was there 'a properer, a better cast house, more neatly kept, with fairer and pleasanter walls'.[38] Archbishop Warham built an immense palace at Otford, Kent, larger in plan than Cardinal College, Oxford. Bishop Alcock's tomb at Ely is no less ostentatious than Wolsey's (which was no more ostentatious than that of the cardinal of Amboise). The pride of Cardinal Morton, archbishop of Canterbury, who placed his rebus—a cardinal's hat and a tun—up and down the corner turrets of the great central crossing tower rebuilt at Canterbury Cathedral at his expense, is visible to this day. Wolsey was far less exceptional than has generally been suggested. And, to be fair, more generally such building celebrated the role and the office which these churchmen held as much as, or more than, their own persons. In an hierarchical society dominated by a landed monarchy and nobility, archbishops and bishops had to spend and to build and to live in a certain style in order to be accepted by those who wielded secular power. Yet, unavoidably, such worldliness was open to misunderstanding, misrepresentation and satire, another example of the vulnerability of the late medieval church. However much Wolsey, for example, may have claimed that he did not wish to accumulate the muck of this world, and insisted that he set no more store on its riches and promotions than on the rushes under his feet, but only for charity and in order to help his poor servants and kins-folk,[39] his enemies, so his servant Thomas Cromwell informed him, would hold his building and keeping too great a house against him.[40] Is a modern historian justified in criticising Miles Salley (d. 1517), simultaneously bishop of Llandaff and abbot of Eynsham, Oxfordshire, for showing 'rather less than the humility for which a follower of St Benedict should have striven' when requesting a flamboyant effigy tomb?[41] In the mystery plays it was not uncommon for Pharisees and Scribes to be dressed as bishops.[42] None of that in any way made a reformation inevitable. But it suggests a context in which it might be possible, a context in which bishops would not find it easy to defend themselves or the church in general against any determined attack supported or inspired by the king.

Moreover, bishops were not equal. It was not just that the archbishop of Canterbury held sway over the bishops of the southern province and the archbishop of York over those of the northern province. Bishoprics were equal neither in wealth nor in size. There had been no fundamental change to the seventeen English and four Welsh dioceses since soon after the Norman Conquest. It is curious that the challenge of lollardy did not lead to the subdivision of dioceses in the late fourteenth/early fifteenth centuries, since that was by then an established means of tackling heresy.[43] By contrast, there were some 250 bishoprics in fifteenth-century Italy, 131 in France, 56 in the German Reich, 33 in the Iberian peninsula, 27 in Scandinavian kingdoms, 12 in Scotland . . . and no fewer than 34 in Ireland, 'so poor currently that no honest and learned man of England will take them'.[44] English bishoprics were thus large by continental standards. Some were so large that they were unwieldy. The bishopric of Lincoln, which stretched from the North Sea coast to the Thames Valley, was particularly absurd (and owed its shape to the collapse of two bishoprics not restored after the Danish invasions).[45] William Barlow, bishop of St David's, argued that the location of St David's cathedral in the most ruinous and desolate part of his diocese ('so rare a frequented place [except of vagabond pilgrims]') was appalling, and urged in vain its transfer forty miles east to Carmarthen.[46] Another consequence of the large size of bishoprics was that twelve of the English dioceses were among the forty richest in Europe: Winchester the richest of them all.[47] One benefit of such relative wealth and size was that English and Welsh bishoprics were not, and had not been, dominated by local noble feelings or much associated with local or even regional sentiments. English sees were never mere appendages to aristocratic power, as was often the case on the Continent, especially in the Holy Roman Empire and in Italy (though rather less so in France and Spain). In the fourteenth and early fifteenth centuries some of the greatest sees were held by younger sons of noble families—Archbishop Arundel, whom we shall meet later, was one such— but by 1529 none of the English and Welsh bishops came from noble families (James Stanley, bishop of Ely, sixth son of Thomas Stanley, first earl of Derby, had died in 1515); a few had gentry origins (Booth of

Hereford, Blythe of Coventry and Lichfield, Standish of St Asaph, Oldham and Veysey of Exeter, and Tunstal of London and Durham—though as an illegitimate son of a Richmondshire gentry family); some were from yeomen (Warham, Skeffington of Bangor, Longland of Lincoln); some from merchants (Nix of Norwich, Fisher of Rochester) and some from artisans (West of Ely was a baker's son).[48] In many ways such a range of social origins was a source of strength, making bishops less remote from the population at large; but perhaps bishops from aristocratic backgrounds (and with lay noblemen as brothers and uncles and cousins) might have had greater confidence in standing up to Henry VIII.

How effectively did bishops carry out their diocesan duties? Over the past generation many substantial studies of diocesan administration have painted a generally favourable impression of episcopal rule. Bishops and their multifarious officers are seen as conscientiously and effectively running their administrations, notably by holding ecclesiastical courts and by carrying out visitations of their parish clergy. All that to some extent reflects the nature of our sources, in which court and visitation records are much more common than letters. Historians who defend late medieval bishops often praise a bishop who was resident for his energetic administration of his diocese while refusing to criticise those who were absent on the grounds that dioceses could run themselves perfectly well without their bishop. 'The church was a great bureaucracy, with well-developed administrative procedures': routine business therefore could be conducted whether the bishop was present or not.[49] 'Since their pastoral responsibility was mainly expressed through exercising their jurisdiction, administration and government rather than through close involvement with their subjects, it could virtually be as well attended to by efficient deputies as by the bishop himself'. 'In the day-to-day running of diocesan affairs, the vicars-general showed themselves to be competent and conscientious representatives of the type of chief executive increasingly employed in the early sixteenth century for routine business even by resident bishops'.[50] So were resident bishops necessary?

It is interesting that bishops quite often became resident after years of intermittent absence, usually reflecting their reduced role in central government. Geoffrey Blythe (c.1470–1530), bishop of Coventry and Lichfield, had been an active councillor in the early years of Henry VIII's reign, but, after (somewhat mysteriously) he was suspected of treason in 1523, he devoted himself to his diocese.[51] Fisher was also active in government in the early years of the reign, but then returned to Rochester full time.[52] Sherburne of Chichester was Henry VII's secretary, three times sent on diplomatic missions to Rome, but even before Henry's death he had settled in Chichester.[53] Tunstal was Lord Privy Seal between 1523 and 1530 while also bishop of London. But after his appointment as bishop of Durham in 1530, he was generally resident in the north though, to be fair, the responsibilities of the bishop of Durham had always included the defence of the Scottish borders, and, significantly, Wolsey had been a pluralist bishop of Durham for only a very short time.[54]

Contemporaries were aware of the issue. Richard Fox, bishop of Winchester, would, once retired from royal service, lament his earlier neglect of his dioceses. In 1522 he declared to Wolsey that for twenty-eight years he had been so negligent that, of his four cathedral churches, he had never seen Exeter or Wells, not to mention 'the innumerable souls whereof I never see the bodies'. He had now utterly renounced meddling with worldly matters, especially concerning war, 'whereof for the many intolerable enormities that I have seen ensue by the said war in time past, I have no little remorse in my conscience, thinking that if I did continual penance for it all the days of my life, though I should live twenty years longer than I may do, I could not yet make sufficient recompense therfore'. He would, he said, die in despair if he were now called into discussions of the fortifications that renewed warfare was calling for.[55] In 1522 Archbishop Warham informed Wolsey that he regretted that he had been absent from his cathedral in Lent four years running 'by reason of my calling to the king's grace's business and otherwise by your grace's commandment': he intended to stay at his cathedral next Lent and Easter to look after his diocese.[56] Wolsey himself would famously lament that 'if I had served God as diligently as I have done the king he would not have given me over in my grey hairs'.[57] In summer 1528 he told Jean du Bellay, the French ambassador, that if peace came and if the king had a son, then he would retire and serve God to the end of his days.[58] And Wolsey assiduously took up his pastoral responsibilities as archbishop of York after his fall in autumn 1529: he confirmed about 200 children in person.[59] Fisher regretted his absences:[60]

No man do I blame more than myself, for sundry times when I have settled and fully bent myself to the care of the flock committed unto me, to visit my diocese, to govern my church and to answer the enemies of Christ, straightways hath come a messenger for one cause or another sent from higher authority by whom I have been called to other business and so left off my former purpose. And thus by tossing and going this way and that, time hath passed and in the meanwhile nothing done but attending after triumphs, receiving of ambassadors, haunting of princes' courts ... whereas what have bishops to do with princes' courts? What this vanity in temporal things may work on you I know not but for myself I find it a great impediment to devotion.

All that hints at uneasy consciences and suggests that episcopal residence *did* matter.

How bishops came not to be resident is neatly illustrated by the arguments Wolsey deployed to try to persuade Giberti, bishop of Verona, not to devote himself to his church at Verona, as he had heard he was intending to do, but rather to continue to assist the pope by his presence and counsel. His absence from the papal court, Wolsey insisted, would be very prejudicial to the common weal. Henry VIII very much wanted him to continue there. Wolsey said that Giberti's wish to care for his church at Verona should not deprive christendom of his services: instead he should appoint a proper suffragan. If he withdrew from the papal court, rather than being praised for his zeal in serving God or loving virtue, he would be criticised for acting from despair and weakness, or for the ease of private life.[61] And some of the absentee-bishops were directly the responsibility of the king. The more affluent sees—Winchester, Bath and Wells, Exeter, Lincoln, Ely—were especially likely to be used by the crown for rewarding its servants, and consequently to have absentee bishops. The poorer sees— Rochester, Carlisle, Hereford—perversely were more likely to have resident and pastorally active bishops.[62] More generally, Henry VII and Henry VIII saw absentee bishops as the price that had to be paid for service at the papal court in Rome. The Englishman Christopher Bainbridge, archbishop of York, was resident in Rome between 1508 and 1514, fully engaged in the affairs of the *curia*, and consequently absent from his diocese. Italians who looked after English interests at Rome were appointed to English sees where they never resided. Giovanni Gigli was bishop of Worcester from 1497 to 1498, his nephew Silvestro Gigli from 1498 to 1521, Giulio de Medici, cousin of Leo X, from 1521 to 1522, and Geronimo (Jerome) Ghinucci, the papal nuncio in London at the time of his appointment, from 1522. Adriano Castellesi (c.1461–1521), bishop of Hereford from 1502 to 1504 and of Bath and Wells from 1504 to 1518, was similarly an absentee bishop (though he had spent four years in England in the early 1490s as papal tax collector). Lorenzo Campeggio (1471/2–1539), for many years Henry VIII's principal representative at Rome, was bishop of Salisbury between 1524 and 1534.

Other absentee bishops are less readily excused. Thomas Skeffington (d. 1533), bishop of Bangor, held that diocese jointly with the abbey of Beaulieu, Hampshire, and, not surprisingly, lived in the balmy south. In 1529 Thomas Cromwell was informed that he had not been in his diocese for fourteen years.[63] There were no visitations in his diocese in that period. Not that Skeffington lacked conventional piety: he requested 2,000 masses to be said for his soul, and he did spend considerably on the rebuilding of the nave and tower of Bangor cathedral.[64] Skeffington's successor,

John Capon or Salcot (d. 1557), lived at Hyde, in Hampshire, in the years from 1533 to 1539 when he was bishop of Bangor; he seems never to have visited his diocese.[65] After 1542 John Veysey ceased to live in his diocese of Exeter and returned to his home town, Sutton Coldfield.[66] It is worth noting that mere residence did not necessarily achieve much. If bishops were resident but unwell—like Edmund Audley (c.1439–1524), bishop of Salisbury, a very old man in his final decade as bishop—or resident but largely incompetent—like William Rugge (d. 1550), bishop of Norwich—the fact of residence counted for little. The absence of any general provisions allowing older bishops to retire created its own problems.[67]

Dioceses were run in the absence of their bishops by suffragan bishops and vicars-general. Suffragans in the diocese of Lincoln were becoming a more settled part of the church: their position generally was to be recognised in legislation in 1534.[68] There was a suffragan at Wells, Thomas Cornish, from 1486 to 1513, and at Hereford, Thomas Fowler, from 1505 to 1519. In Worcester there were the Franciscan Ralph Heylesdon, bishop of Ascalon (1503–23) and Andrew Whitmay, bishop of Chrysopolis, from 1525.[69] Thomas Cranmer had a suffragan, Thomas Doncaster (d. 1534), abbot of Newhouse, Lincolnshire, and another who went to Calais early in 1536.[70] Absentee bishops would appoint deputies and representatives of various kinds. For example, from the start of Bishop Silvestro Gigli's episcopate in Worcester, and most probably right up to his death in 1521, Bishop Fox of Winchester had oversight of the diocese as commissary, and was much involved in patronage. 'This suggests that Silvestro's presence in England did not matter and that the care of the diocese remained principally the responsibility of a leading government figure rather than of a foreigner who could hardly be expected to know the background of diocesan affairs and who perhaps could not be trusted in the matter of patronage.'[71] Vicars-general (often called chancellors) were appointed who were virtually bishops, exercising the bishop's jurisdiction, seemingly ordaining clergy, supervising monasteries, holding visitations every three years or so.[72] So the historian of the absentee bishops of Worcester would in effect reject the charge in the act of 1534 that 'the great hospitality, divine service, teaching, and preaching the laws, and examples of good living' had diminished.[73] Twenty-five sees of suffragan bishops were named: Thetford, Ipswich, Colchester, Dover, Guildford, Southampton, Taunton, Shaftesbury, Malton, Marlborough, Bedford, Leicester, Gloucester, Shrewsbury, Bristol, Penrith, Bridgwater, Nottingham, Grantham, Hull, Huntingdon, Cambridge, Berwick, St Germans in Cornwall, and the Isle of Wight. Every bishop desiring to have a suffragan was to name two honest and discreet spiritual persons, learned and of good conversation, to the king, who would choose one of them as bishop suffragan. Suffragans were allowed two benefices. Their powers were as had been accustomed.[74] Thanks to suffragans and vicars-general, the absence of a bishop was thus not an insuperable problem.

But what was missing when a bishop was not resident was a sense of urgency and dynamism applied to the more intractable of the problems facing him—whether among the parish clergy, or in the monasteries.[75] That was vividly expressed by Hugh Inge (d. 1528), archbishop of Dublin, and Lord Chief Justice Bermingham, writing to Wolsey from Dublin on 23 February 1527: 'Your Grace, we doubt not, heareth the sorrowful decay of this land, as well in good christianity, as other laudable manners; which hath grown for lack of good prelates and curates in the church. Wherfore your grace may do meritorously, to see such persons promoted to bishoprics, that ther manner of living may be example of goodness and virtue. The residence of such shall do more good then we can express.' The diocese of Meath was 'far in ruin, both spiritually and temporally, by the absence of the bishop there'.[76] And, at a different level, bishops who were not resident would fail to live up to the contemporary ideal of hospitality and might consequently slip in social respect.[77] Against such obvious negatives, the historian of the absentee Italian bishops of Worcester has concluded that 'the occupants of . . . offices under the Italians appear to have carried out their duties with conscientiousness and care, though without showing obvious signs of initiative, so that the letter of the law was enforced while its spirit may have been lacking: their principal concerns were administration and legal work'.[78] Yet, did subordinates play safe and slip into a dull routine?[79] Did visitations get overlooked, or were they held less frequently? Absentee bishops would be less likely to get involved in the detail of local needs: for example, the amalgamation of parishes promoted by Bishop Fox in Winchester.[80] The deputies of absentee bishops might run up against resistance from cathedral priories over precedence or from powerful monasteries over unsuitable elections. Dr Bell, vicar-general, unsuccessfully tried to depose the incompetent abbot of Pershore, William Compton, in 1524.[81] When Dr Thomas Hannibal, vicar-general in the diocese of Worcester, was concerned about the election of a new abbot of St Augustine's, Bristol, in 1515, he appealed to Bishop Fox of Winchester, who was acting as supervisor of the see of Worcester, for help. Fox responded by telling Wolsey that 'if I were within the diocese of Worcester, I could by calling the evil disposed persons before me soon remedy the matter. Mr Hannibal might do the same if he durst, but I perceive well that he is afeared.'[82] Episcopal authority was thought necessary to resolve disputes: vicar-generals such as Hannibal felt unable to intervene vigorously. And it is interesting that among Cardinal

Pole's reforms during Queen Mary's reign (1553–8) would be an emphasis on resident bishops.

Such criticisms raise the question of how far a bishop could, by close personal attention to the collations (appointments) and ordinations of priests, and supervision of priests in general, lead by moral example.[83] How far could a bishop stamp his personality on his diocese? It must be said that this was rare in early Tudor England—and possibly it would have been an unrealistic expectation.[84] A revealing test is offered by consideration of episcopal oversight of parish clergy within their dioceses. Bishops were responsible for the ordination of priests. A few, notably John Fisher, but also Alcock, Mayhew, Booth, Tunstal, Stokesley and Ridley, took this duty seriously, with Fisher (and, interestingly, given what we have seen of him earlier, Fitzjames) examining in person; by contrast Bishop Veysey of Exeter performed fewer than 400 out of 1,338 institutions himself.[85] Bishops were expected to hold regular visitations, a duty which they usually entrusted to deputies. There is little evidence of personal episcopal participation in parochial visitation and correction. Very few bishops were involved in the personal supervision of their parishes, just as very few modern university vice-chancellors are personally involved in the monitoring of their departments or in dealing with individual members of staff.[86] Warham unusually, indeed uniquely, visited all but one of his deaneries in 1511, but followed up only the heresy cases.[87] Of course, it is possible to be sceptical about the efficacy of such visitations. The lawyer Christopher St German remarked, 'as the common opinion goeth, commonly they reform nothing but as they find it, so they leave it'.[88] We shall return to this when we discuss the clergy.

A bishop could not be everywhere in his diocese; he would not get to hear of all that was amiss; and, as Edward Lee, archbishop of York, lamented, he could not put learning and the ability to preach in the heads of those who did not already have them.[89] Lee was writing defensively at a moment when he was being expected to enforce Henry VIII's royal supremacy. But the limits to episcopal power which he highlighted were real. In many dioceses, much was administratively outside the bishop's control. 'The actual authority a bishop could exercise was limited by all manner of local exemptions, customs, immunities and privileges.'[90] 'In a very real sense . . . there is actually no such thing as a diocese' since a diocese was 'a jig-saw puzzle of competing jurisdictions' in which the bishop was *primus inter pares*. Archdeaconries, especially in larger dioceses, could function as miniature bishoprics. The dean and chapter of a cathedral were usually determined to defend what they saw as their legitimate rights—and what others might see as unjustified privileges. The clash of personalities could deepen such institutional fissures.[91] In the diocese of Exeter, for example, several monasteries, including Tavistock Abbey and St Michael's Mount, claimed exemption from episcopal visitations, while fifty-two of the parishes were 'peculiars'.[92] Nor could bishops make appointments to every parish. Warham, it is true, could appoint to 190 ecclesiastical livings in a diocese of 239 parishes; but the bishop of Ely to just thirty-six out of 134, the bishop of Durham to thirty-five, the bishop of Rochester to thirty out of 122; the bishop of Norwich and the bishop of Worcester to just thirty each.[93] And these figures were, of course, theoretical. Bishops did not necessarily have the opportunity to exercise patronage. Without a vacancy there was no patronage, apart from anticipations: and vacancies might be infrequent, perhaps every ten years.[94] Veysey of Exeter lamented to Cromwell in 1539 how few promotions he had had the liberty to bestow on his chaplains who were learned and virtuous preachers.[95] Bishop Fitzjames of London made ninety-eight collations (of which forty-three were to his cathedral) between 1506 and 1522, or six and a half a year; Bishop Tunstal sixty-two collations (of which twenty-two were to his cathedral) between 1522 and 1530, or seven a year; Bishop Stokesley made ninety collations (of which thirty-three were to his cathedral), or eight a year; Bishop Fisher waited nearly two years before he could make his first appointment.[96] Moreover, bishops were subjected to external pressures when exercising patronage. Other bishops would press their suits, perhaps for a relative: for example, Bishop West told Wolsey that if his nephew received the benefice of East Dereham, he would send him abroad for five to six years so that 'he might have better learning, language and experience', and consequently be able to do Wolsey 'right acceptable service'. In exchange, as it were, West offered to give Mr Larke— brother of Wolsey's former mistress—the advowson of another benefice worth more than East Dereham.[97] Noblemen might nominate unsuitable candidates; for example, Lord Clifford's nominee, rejected by Wolsey's vicar-general at York since 'his cunning [learning] is marvellous slender . . . I have seen few priests so simply learned in my life'.[98] When making appointments, a bishop's priority would, moreover, be to reward his closest diocesan servants. A bishop's chaplains, household officials, and receiver-generals would have a high claim.[99] Often this went hand in hand with pluralism: the dozen collations Fisher made were shared between four men.[100] Bishops who moved diocese often took their closest servants with them, and would obviously seek to reward them as soon as possible.[101] It was accepted that a bishop would use part of his income and patronage to maintain his family.[102] In dioceses with monastic cathedrals, bishops were more dependent on rectories and vicarages to reward their officials and families: in secular cathedrals such men could be given prebends in the cathedral, that is, posts with no duties, literally sinecures in the sense that no cure of souls was involved.[103] It was a practical way of making things work, but it was open to misunderstanding and to abuse.

Several bishops used their powers of patronage, especially appointments to prebends, in order to promote learning and preaching. Bishops tended to give preference to graduates from the universities of Oxford and Cambridge. Bishops presented more graduates than other patrons.[104] Bishop Sherburne of Chichester founded new prebends to which he appointed men from Winchester College. But the outcome, measured by preaching and by residence, was disappointing. Prebends were, for some, more part of the road to greater prominence than posts to be held for their own sake. And it was not easy for a bishop to control those who held such posts, as Bishop Longland found in attempting to persuade the canons of Lincoln to reside.[105]

Some bishops showed what we should call leadership in other ways. Bishop Fox translated the rule of St Benedict into English for the benefit of the nuns of Wherwell, recognising that they understood their Latin Rule but imperfectly since they had no Latin.[106] But such episcopal pious literary activity was not very common. It is unlikely that bishops preached often. There was no early Tudor John Thoresby, who, as archbishop of York in the mid-fourteenth century, wrote a handbook for less educated priests and laymen, prepared a Latin and an English catechism, and got a monk of St Mary's York to make an expanded version of his own Latin catechism in English verse, including cycles of religious plays dramatising moral teachings.[107] That was not a canonical obligation. Only Fitzjames, Alcock, Fisher and Longland of the forty-four bishops between 1500 and 1534 left sermons. Skelton's Collyn Clout declared how 'The temporality say plain/ How bishops disdain/Sermons for to make/Or such labour to take', partly because of sloth, but mostly because they lacked the ability to preach.[108] When bishops were compelled to preach in defence of the royal supremacy in 1535, Rowland Lee (c.1487–1543), bishop of Coventry and Lichfield, declared that 'hither to I was never in pulpit', while John Stokesley of London was very reluctant.[109] Here, of course, the early protestants were applying a different set of values, or at least greatly emphasising the more humanist bishops' approach. In 1538 John Longland, bishop of Lincoln, would present Jesus as a model bishop—preaching to his people, teaching the most wholesome doctrine.[110] When William Tyndale, in *The Practice of Prelates*, declared that 'prelates appointed to preach Christ'—which expressed his ideal rather than the contemporary reality—'may not leave God's word and minister temporal offices', he was declaring a new standard. St Paul's Letter to Timothy laid down an obligation on bishops to teach,[111] but the force of the protestant emphasis on preaching was new. Protestants would expect their bishops to preach the word of God; pre-reformation bishops would not all have agreed.

Bishops did not always see themselves as a collective. They vigorously defended the privileges and rights of their dioceses, and that was often how they made their greatest impact. Did they spend disproportionate energy and time on complex jusrisdictional disputes with other bishops, abbeys, and secular authorities? Or is that the misleading impression left by the survival of documents relating to disputes? We have already seen the heated quarrel between Warham and the bishops in his province over probate. An earlier row over probate between Archbishop Morton and the bishop of London 'testifies mainly to the volume of rhetoric and emotion that churchmen could summon up at will'.[112] What a scholar has characterised as Morton's 'aggressive assertion of the rights of his own church' was striking.[113] Morton 'pursued a deliberate policy of invoking the papal courts in Rome to support the claims of his archdiocese'.[114] Bishop Fox of Winchester attacked Robert Sherburne's bulls on his consecration as bishop of St David's on 11 May 1505. Henry VII brokered a settlement in April 1506 and allowed Sherburne to go to Rome to clear his name, seemingly successfully; and Sherburne was promoted to Chichester in 1508. One historian has speculated that underlying this dispute was a quarrel between Fox and Archbishop Warham and that Fox saw Sherburne as Warham's tool.[115] Wolsey's 'compositions'—financial agreements—with bishops over their testamentary jurisdiction and his revival, on a small scale, of the practice of preventions reflected and continued such tensions between bishops.[116] Thomas Cranmer, archbishop of Canterbury (1533–56), and Stephen Gardiner, bishop of Winchester, apparently disputed over Cranmer's title as primate of all England and his wish to visit Gardiner's diocese. Cranmer remarked acidly, 'I doubt not but all the bishops of England would ever gladly have had the archbishop's both authority and title taken away'.[117] It is difficult fairly to evaluate all this. Maybe it should not be seen as central; maybe bishops were above all acting in self-defence, defending their inherited rights for fear that if they did not do so, if they did not litigate, then others would unscrupulously encroach on those rights.[118]

How far did bishops sense a need to deal with abuses, how far did they espouse a programme of reform? Inasmuch as they did, they show that the church was able at least to think of reforming itself, but they also implicitly offer some evidence for the existence of a malaise. For his modern biographer, Bishop John Fisher was 'no complacent defender of orthodoxy; rather he recognised that if doctrinal deviation was to be resisted the church itself must be regenerated'. The constant theme of his sermons was the need for penitence, contrition, for sins committed.[119] Alcock of Ely preached on the need for the clergy to set an example and urged the reformation of the clergy from within: what was needed were virtuous clergy who would observe their vows of chastity, obedience and poverty.[120] Cardinal Morton attempted a programme of reform through centralisation in alliance with the crown that anticipated the reforms of Wolsey.[121]

Wolsey's attempt at reform deserves more attention, and more sympathetic attention, than historians other than Peter Gwyn have usually been willing to give it. Wolsey went to a good deal of trouble to secure papal authority for the reformation of the clergy and visitation of the monasteries.[122] Before a council of bishops in May 1519, Wolsey declared his aims. No full version survives; but the headings make his concerns quite clear. Plain preaching of the articles of belief to the people in English; the administration of the sacraments; tithes and offerings; the duties of archdeacons and priests; jurisdiction and cognisance of matrimonial causes; holy days; appeals; the life and honesty ('honesty' being a synonym of 'chastity') of the clergy; non-residence; monasteries; repairs; immunities; simony.[123] That was quite an agenda. It has, however, struck an historian of the fourteenth-century church as empty. 'Devoid of spiritual fervour, the reformatory process constituted a hollow administrative and judicial exercise, expensive and burdensome for those who had to submit to it; of such a character was the process ostentatiously carried out by Cardinal Wolsey in the years immediately preceding the reformation.'[124] But that may be far too harsh. The matters highlighted by Wolsey all deserved attention and most, if not all, of them are dealt with somewhere in this book. Wolsey's injunctions, much more than those of other bishops, went beyond exhortations to follow well-established rules.[125] The difficulty was that such 'reform' might affect, indeed would very likely upset, established interests that might resist, for reasons good and bad, and it set standards that contemporaries did not live up to. In 1521 Wolsey wrote to Bishop Fox that he had fixed on a date in the near future to begin a reformation of the whole clergy. It is notable how ecstatically Fox greeted this news: he had desired to see this day as Simeon desired to see the Messiah, and he doubted not to see a more full reformation of the whole English hierarchy than he ever could hope for in this age. He had endeavoured to do within his own small jurisdiction what Wolsey had resolved upon in both the provinces of England.[126]

The problem with all this was that in so far as 'reform' meant that clergy should live more virtuously, it was asking a great deal of men who had not, perhaps, been led to expect that that was one of their obligations, and who had long been used to living by lower standards.[127] In his diocese Bishop Fox found the clergy, and especially the monks, so depraved, licentious and corrupt that he despaired of any being perfect.[128] But, nonetheless, he later wrote that he had never deprived anyone in any of his dioceses, and said that he had not been severe on secular clergy except for manifest fornication or adultery.[129] That neatly shows the difficulties facing any thoroughgoing reformer.

As well as trying to reform the clergy, Wolsey also attempted to create new bishoprics endowed with the wealth of dissolved monasteries. By the time of his fall he had secured papal bulls allowing him to proceed. This was a very significant attempt at restructuring and at redeploying resources. It was not very popular, it must be said.[130] Dividing a single diocese into smaller dioceses raised all sorts of hackles, affected vested interests, and raised difficult questions about the place of saints and relics. Creating new bishoprics or, more accurately, dividing one bishopric into two or three or more, meant making the original bishopric smaller, diminishing its standing, and, arguably, offending the saint to whom the bishopric was dedicated. Wolsey's fall from favour in 1529 meant that these plans were shelved; they would be revived, as we shall see, after the dissolution of the monasteries. Here we should simply note the vitality of the church as shown by Wolsey's reforming vision, but also the vulnerability of the church, both in the patent need for reform of various inadequacies and in the obstacles in the path of any would-be reformer.

And, in assessing the bishops overall, the best conclusion is that bishops made an awkward system work more or less: they muddled through. Their registers have been seen as 'a reflection of ever-increasing efficiency and professionalism', and there is little to suggest that episcopal administration was not adequately managed.[131] 'The determined and realistic efforts of Cardinals Morton and Wolsey to create order' and to embark on larger reforms have been praised.[132] But royal demands diverted their attention from spiritual and pastoral matters. Inevitably entangled in high politics, rebellion, diplomacy, and therefore worldly, Morton subordinated the church to the affairs of the king.[133] Wolsey's religious vocation has often been questioned and his efforts at reform seen as spiritually empty and as self-serving. It is then difficult to judge the work of bishops. Just as with modern university vice-chancellors, it is reasonable to say that the 'great majority' made a fair job of their responsibilities.[134] And yet it is also reasonable to conclude that that was not always enough.

4

CLERGY

W HENEVER bishops and critics spoke of reforming the church, they usually intended to begin with the reform of the priests.[1] For the condition of the clergy was widely seen as an area of vulnerability in the late medieval church. This is not to deny that there was much that was positive, but rather to claim that there was also much that was difficult to defend against the application of the highest standards.

The duties of clergy were first and foremost to administer the sacraments: to say mass, to baptise, to hear confession, to grant absolution, to marry, to anoint the sick and to administer the last rites to the dying. Clergy were also responsible for burials. They had to ensure that the necessary equipment for services was available, and they were responsible for the maintenance of the chancels of their churches. They were expected to offer instruction in the christian faith, and more general teaching, to the young. They were to give their parishioners pastoral care, including advice, hospitality, comfort in sickness, arbitration and peace-making, but they were also, when it was necessary, expected to discipline them. They were expected to set a moral example of good living, not least by being celibate. And, in order to support all their activities, they had to secure the correct payments of tithes and other fees and dues to which they were entitled.[2] All this amounted to a very complex range of responsibilities. Some involved the observance of basic duties, such as saying mass at the appointed hour. Some demanded administrative and technical skills. Others required financial and physical resources which might not easily be available. Much depended on the quality of the relationships which a parish priest might develop with his parishioners, relationships subject to all the vagaries of human character, as

Hunne's troubled dealings show. Chaucer vividly characterised the poor parson at his best: '. . . rich he was of holy thought and work/He was also a learned man, a clerk/That Christ's gospel gladly would preach/His parischens [parishioners] devoutly would he teach'.[3] But what was typical?

Episcopal visitations, in the course of which parishioners were invited to voice any complaints that they may have had against their parish priest, offer some evidence of how effectively clergy were seen to be fulfilling these duties. The most remarkable fact, which bears repetition, is that the numbers of complaints were low. In the diocese of Lincolnshire there were just thirty-four complaints against twenty-eight individual clergy from a total of some 700 clergy in 1499; there were just forty-one complaints in 1,006 parishes visited between 1514 and 1521 (no complaints were made against the clergy in 96 per cent of the parishes).[4] Where complaints were made, the most common subjects were the alleged sexual misdemeanours of priests, disputes over tithes, mismanagement of parochial property, and negligence in performing the liturgy.[5] The parson of St Mary Axe, London, had gone away without making any arrangements for divine service, preaching or teaching.[6] There was no priest at Sezincote in c.1511. Quarterly instruction was not taking place at Kirkby Malzeard in 1500.[7] The parishioners of All Saints, Lombard Street, London complained that their parson and curates kept no hospitality and were not resident.[8] The parishioners of Halifax complained that their vicar never attempted to resolve disputes between them.[9] Many more such examples of neglect could be cited, and their multiplication would make for a colourful, if somewhat repetitive, chapter, but the more important point is that overall the numbers of such complaints were low.

Priests had long been expected to be celibate. Was that an unrealistic expectation that was bound to cause problems for the church? As a modern historian has noted, 'the celibate priest embodied widely held ideals, perhaps even satisfied vicariously aspirations towards sanctity which most people were unable to achieve in their own lives'.[10] Yet, once more, only a few clergy were accused of falling short: five in 478 Suffolk parishes in 1499, nine in 260 Canterbury parishes in 1511, eleven in 230 Winchester parishes in 1527–8, eight in 200 Norwich parishes in 1537–8.[11] A handful of more or less racy stories can be told. The vicar of Budworth allegedly kept a woman in his house by whom he had had several children; the vicar of Runcorn had allegedly had between ten and a dozen children by one Agnes Habran.[12] The vicar of Mendlesham kept his 'woman' and children openly in his vicarage, declaring that he was married to her and that she was his lawful wife, and saying that the king knew that he was married. Consequently, his parishioners complained that 'men do refrain to do that their hearts would

serve them to do; and as to our ordinary [i.e. bishop], he dare do no thing'.
'His open crime . . . is abominable in the judgement of the lay people,' the
complainants insisted.[13] The parson of Burghfield had a concubine and
children.[14] The cathedral clergy of Wells evidently enjoyed the company of
townswomen.[15] All that provides entertaining—or depressing—reading. It
must, nonetheless, be reiterated that the overall numbers were small and
that the proportion of clergy so accused, tiny. That said, Simon Fish's
diatribe in his *Supplication of the Beggars* in 1529 would have been risible
unless it had at least some approximation, if not to realities, then at least to
popular prejudices.[16] And how much local connivance was there in priestly
concubinage, especially when priests were discreet and there was no public
scandal? It is interesting in this context that lay testators requesting masses
often specified that these be celebrated by virtuous and 'honest' priests:
again, what they meant was chaste priests.[17] Undoubtedly clergy were
expected to set a moral example. John Colet, dean of St Paul's, reasoned
that 'if priests that have the cure of souls be good, straight the people will
be good'.[18] But that placed an immense responsibility on the clergy. On the
same logic, it followed that if the clergy were not virtuous, their evil living
would harm the laity: consequently the clergy were open to the charge that
their iniquities were the cause of wider social ills. If Wyclif's proposition
that the clergy were owed credence only if their lives were moral was
followed, the church could be undermined.[19] Not surprisingly, would-be
reformers within the church, such as Colet, furiously denounced wicked
priests.[20]

But the church risked the worst of all worlds. In insisting upon sexual
abstinence, it set a tough ideal and left itself open to a justifiably deep sense
of betrayal if those standards were not met. Yet since, human nature being
what it is, some clergy were bound to fall short of that ideal, the church was
vulnerable to repeated and vivid criticism by those who wanted the ideal to
be achieved. There was 'an unavoidable tension between sacerdotal status
and the human fallibility of those ordained to the priesthood . . . expectations of priests were such as could never be fulfilled'.[21] Outspoken demands
for higher moral standards were a perennial feature of the medieval church,
from Bernard of Clairvaux to Colet. They fostered a view of 'the man who
celebrated the mass . . . as able to transcend the sexual and emotional needs
of other men' and thus as different, and superior.[22] And in that light,
'perhaps unconsciously, clerical unchastity was regarded in quasi-Judaic
terms as a ritual pollutant, an objective threat to the efficacy of priestly
functions as well as a dishonouring of Christ's body'.[23] Against that, the
Augustinian claim that the church was holy not because its members were
holy (though of course they should strive to be virtuous) but because it was

established by divine grace might seem hollow and involve the defence, or at least the acceptance, of evil living.[24] Henry VIII was able to quote to the papal legate Cardinal Campeggio in 1529 the lutherans' charge that churchmen, especially those of the court of Rome, lived very wickedly and strayed from divine law in many things; Campeggio recognised that churchmen did indeed sin, as they were but men, but his insistence that the Holy See had not deviated a jot from true faith was not an obviously stronger argument.[25]

It is hard to strike the correct balance, to determine criteria of evaluation. Should the fact that some arrangements made by those establishing chantries were very precise on the responsibilities of clergy, not least including provisions for dismissal, be regarded as implicit criticisms of parish clergy in general?[26] Did bishops tolerate all manner of abuses in practice because they had little choice, or because they came to have an understanding of the world as it is, rather than as it might be? However that might be, few clergy were disciplined and far fewer were removed once they had been appointed. Bishop Nix of Norwich deprived eleven between 1502 and 1532 (but nine of them in one year, 1532).[27] There were only isolated examples of deprivations elsewhere, most often for protracted non-residence or neglect of buildings.[28] Episcopal visitors did not often uncover 'dreadful examples of moral turpitude': concerns about the finances of the parish and the fabric of the church were more common.[29]

It is worth noting, in passing, that just as the work of bishops was not always assisted by the size and shape of dioceses, so the task of priests was often complicated by the geographical extent of their duties. Parishes had been created, or had emerged, in the tenth, eleventh and twelfth centuries. The logic underlying them is hard to fathom and doubtless reflects the inheritance of existing buildings, demographic pressures, the complexities of land tenure, a myriad individual and group initiatives which surviving sources hardly allow us to identify. A notable feature is the large number of parishes into which the largest cities were then divided: over a hundred in London. From then the overall pattern of parishes was little altered, even as population grew, or, after the Black Death, fell, or as new settlements were established. But there was a host of particular modifications as, for example, when a parish church was absorbed by a friary (in the thirteenth century) or as parishes were united. Were there too many churches in towns (forty-six parish churches in Norwich in 1496, for example[30]), too few in the country?[31] In some, mainly rural, regions with large parishes, parochial chapels dependent on the mother church were set up. In Cornwall there were more chapels—maybe twice as many—than parish churches: 188 in the ninety-five parishes of western Cornwall.[32] Everywhere there came to be

large variations between the populations and incomes of parishes, compli-
cating attempts by bishops to monitor, and priests to operate, the system.

And it must always be borne in mind that visitations inquired into what
was amiss. Surveys offering evidence of successes or of routine satisfactory
work are much harder to find. A rare surviving, remarkably full, survey of
equipment and books in the archdeaconry of Norfolk in the mid-fourteenth
century bears citing here (we shall return to it in greater detail in another
chapter). It shows that clergy were very conscientious in following requirements.[33] Can the impression left by that survey be extrapolated to the
period closer to the break with Rome? And is it fair to conclude that the vast
majority of the clergy were indeed performing their duties more or less
satisfactorily?

If services were regularly and fittingly conducted, how far, nonetheless,
was the ignorance of clergy another area of vulnerability? That turns on not
just how well educated late medieval priests were but on how well educated
we think they needed to be to perform their duties properly. Is it a fair judgement that 'it was a chronic weakness of the medieval church that it failed to
solve the problem of educating the parish clergy for their task'?[34] Were lay
expectations of the level of education appropriate to a priest rising, as is
often said? Clearly, priests were neither educated nor trained in the way that
has since become the norm. There were no seminaries in the late middle
ages. Cardinal Pole's vision, proposed in the Westminster synod of 1555-6,
of seminaries financed from the income of each diocese, and especially
from that of richer benefices, in every diocese, would be taken up and to a
large extent realised in the Council of Trent.[35] Implicitly, however, that
reform criticises the lack of relevant education and training provided for
priests earlier. Most late medieval clergy would have learned what they
knew from assisting and watching their parish priest when young—for
example, as holy-water clerks—supplemented by such private study of
handbooks as they had the chance to see.[36] Concerns that clergy were ignorant were widely expressed, though on the whole it is literary sources and
general remarks that offer support for them, rather than the detailed
evidence recorded in visitations. Richard Sampson, bishop of Chichester,
wished in August 1538 that all the ministers of the church were learned
enough to understand the offices, services and prayers which they said in
Latin.[37] Edward Lee, archbishop of York, lamented that the poverty of
livings in his diocese meant that he could not attract learned men. 'We are
fain to take those who are presented, if they are of honest conversation, can
completely understand what they read, minister the sacraments and sacra-
mentals, observing the due form and rite, though otherwise they are not
perfect'.[38] An increasing minority of clergy were university graduates,

exempt, it may reasonably be assumed, from such strictures. In Norwich only twelve out of 158 (8 per cent) were graduates between 1370 and 1449, but twenty-three out of seventy-one (32 per cent) between 1450 and 1499 and twenty-five out of sixty (42 per cent) between 1500 and 1532.[39] Contemporary reforming bishops (followed by many modern historians) tended to see graduates as those best qualified to be priests. Protestant churches and the counter-reformation catholic church would alike insist on the clergy becoming an ever more graduate profession. Yet it is increasingly being realised by historians that a university graduate may have been over-qualified for run-of-the-mill parochial duties.[40] If these essentially consisted of administering the sacraments and providing pastoral care, then university syllabuses in theology and canon law offered little that directly bene-fited pastoral practice.[41]

Clergy were expected to instruct their flock in the christian religion. But formal preaching was not a requirement and most clergy do not seem to have preached.[42] In the early centuries of christianity, preaching had been confined to the bishop.[43] Following the Lateran Council of 1215, by the constitution drawn up in 1281 by John Pecham (d. 1292), archbishop of Canterbury, all priests with the cure of souls were four times a year to declare to their parishioners in English the articles of faith, the Ten Commandments, the seven works of mercy, the seven deadly sins, and the sacraments. We know that similar instructions were issued by Bishop Fox in 1508 and Bishop West in 1528, suggesting that they were standard.[44] Such declarations of faith could be derived from manuals, and did not need to be delivered in the form of a polished sermon to be effective. And there is little sign that the laity were concerned by the lack or inadequacy of sermons: episcopal visitations do not reflect any such complaints.[45]

Preaching was often rather seen as a specialised matter, for an elite with the necessary ability and training. All secular cathdrals had 'some formal arrangement for the preaching of sermons'. Chancellors were expected to preach, or make arrangements for sermons. For example, John Taylor, when chancellor of Exeter, preached at least fifteen times between 1487 and 1491. Annual cycles of sermons—for example at Advent or during Lent—were common. Preaching was also often seen as the responsibility of friars rather than parish clergy: at Exeter the bulk of sermons in the late fifteenth century were given by Franciscan and Dominican friars.[46] Preaching was nonetheless seen as valuable. Perhaps through Bishop Fisher's influence, the University of Cambridge obtained a papal bull licensing the appointment of twelve preachers annually from the doctors, masters and graduates of the university to preach throughout the country to the clergy and people. The preachership endowed by Lady Margaret Beaufort at Cambridge carried with it the duty to preach six sermons a year at specified places in London, Westminster, Hertfordshire, Cambridgeshire and Lincolnshire. The statutes of St John's College, Cambridge, required a quarter of the fellows to give eight sermons a year to the people in return for exemptions from disputations and college office.[47]

If preaching was a specialist activity mostly carried out by a small number of highly educated clergy and by friars, there are nonetheless some hints that parish clergy did preach more than has been recognised. It is striking that many clergy were accused of preaching against the break with Rome and religious changes in the 1530s: are we to suppose that they found their voices only in adversity?[48] When those sympathetic to government policy in the mid-1530s lamented the lack of preachers, that may be evidence more of resistance to the break with Rome and associated changes or of fears that open preaching in defence of government policy could provoke risings than of any inability of late medieval clergy to preach. When Thomas Cromwell was informed that there were almost none in Yorkshire who sincerely, plainly, and diligently preached the Gospel, what his informant meant was that there were few enthusiastic advocates of the break with Rome and the dissolution of the monasteries.[49] When Archbishop Lee of York declared that he did not know a dozen secular priests there who could preach, and (as we have already noted) lamented that he could not put learning and cunning (ability) to preach into the heads of those who did not already have them, he too was explaining why the royal supremacy was not being preached, rather than making credible indictments of the ignorance of his clergy.[50]

Against such sweeping remarks, there are incidental references to preaching that make it appear quite a routine feature, attracting attention only when matters of controversy were raised. There is a tantalising hint in the terms of the episcopal licence granted to the Dominican friars of Exeter to preach that preaching by priests may have been more common. The Dominican friars were permitted to do so—provided that they did so at different times from the customary hours of rectors and vicars. Does this provision suggest that late medieval parish clergy in Exeter did preach regularly?[51] In 1534 Archbishop Cranmer issued an inhibition requiring any priests 'disposed to preach' to secure a new licence, including those priests previously licensed to preach. Cranmer's purpose was that all would-be preachers should be warned not to preach anything that might 'slander or bring into doubt . . . the catholic and received doctrine of Christ's church', but what is intriguing here is the hint that preaching was more common than is thought.[52] If the parishioners of Halifax complained that their vicar had preached at most twice in the past six years, that evidence cuts both ways, suggesting that this was dereliction of duty, not the norm.[53] The various statutes of the 1530s requiring priests to preach the royal supremacy or to exhort the people to be charitable to the poor appear to take it for granted that preaching was one of the routine responsibilities of priests.[54] In quite a few churches pews were being installed in this period—'a silent revolution' in furnishing[55]—evidence that sermons were regularly being preached.[56]

Sermons can of course range from the original and profound to the workmanlike and derivative—and worse. Still, by the late medieval period, and especially after the advent of printing, a good deal of material was available to parish priests who wished, as we might say, to enhance their performance as preachers: for example, *The Layfolk's Catechism*, commissioned by John Thoresby (d. 1373), archbishop of York;[57] or two works by the Augustinian prior John Mirk (*fl. c.*1382–1414), the *Instructions for Parish Priests*, 'an elementary handbook, presumably for a recently ordained priest' and the *Festial*, a collection of homilies for saints' days.[58] Some clergy left books in their wills: many of those books are likely to have been material of this sort. The inventory of John Baker (d. 1518), priest of All Saints, Ber Street, Norwich, gives the details of twenty-six books, including the basic textbooks on canon law, commentaries on canon law, including *Provinciale* by William Lyndwood (d. 1446), collections of sermons, including those by Bishop John Fisher and the Carmelite friar Richard Maidstone (d. 1396), and the *Legenda aurea* by Jacobus de Voragine (d. 1298), the influential collection of saints' lives.[59] Possibly it was mostly the better educated urban clergy who acquired such works.[60] But there was hardly a shortage of cribs; which again suggests that many clergy did preach in some way or another. William Melton (d. 1528), chancellor of York, urged that every ordinand should be capable of studying the scriptures on his own.[61] Bishop Veysey of Exeter ordered his clergy to learn part of the New Testament by heart every day.[62] Of course such aspirations might well remain no more than that. How much time would a conscientious priest have for study? Anthony Saunders, curate of Winchcombe, sounding like a hard-pressed modern academic struggling to get his research and writing done, lamented to Cromwell in 1535 that his parish was large, with a population of 2,000, and he was very busy with parish work: 'I have too little time to study and to preach and to read the lively word of God (which is my duty) as earnestly as I would be glad to do'.[63]

However demanding the tasks which priests faced, there was no general 'crisis of recruitment' in the late medieval church, although there were significant fluctuations in the numbers of clergy ordained. There does seem to have been a prolonged decline in recruitment in the late fourteenth and early fifteenth centuries,[64] perhaps reflecting the controversies provoked by John Wyclif's criticisms (to which we shall return).[65] But by the second half of the fifteenth century such problems had been resolved. In the diocese of

York there was a surprisingly large rise in the 1460s.[66] A study of Winchester ordination lists suggests that 'as far as recruitment was concerned the English church was in a healthy state in the half century preceding the Reformation',[67] and the evidence of strong recruitment in the early sixteenth century has been seen as 'a mark of confidence in the efficacy of conventional religion'.[68] Several studies nonetheless suggest that numbers of recruits did begin to fall.[69] In the diocese of Lincoln 172 men were ordained a year between 1515 and 1520, but only 141 a year between 1522 and 1527, and the even lower figure of eighty a year between 1527 and 1535, with just twenty-two a year between 1536 and 1546.[70] The decline began in the early 1520s. In the diocese of York it had begun in the mid-1510s, though it was not pronounced.[71] In Lichfield the numbers of ordinations fell from 1,059 between 1510 and 1514 to 931 between 1515 and 1519, 814 between 1520 and 1524, and 704 between 1525 and 1529. Ordinations of secular priests in that diocese peaked at 240 in 1518 and then broadly declined.[72] In London the turning-point had come a little earlier. The number of secular priests ordained in London rose from 404 between 1490 and 1499 to 645 between 1500 and 1509, but then fell to 484 in the 1510s and 306 in the 1520s (of which 158 were ordained in the first three years of the decade). A remarkable feature is that the church in London attracted few boys living in its parishes to become priests. Conversely, the dioceses of Lichfield and York recruited at least ten of their sons to the priesthood for every one native ordained in London, where 'the population was accustomed to viewing the priesthood as a calling more suited to immigrants from the country's deprived regions'. 'Only conjecture is possible about relations between London's parishioners and north country vicars and curates, whose backgrounds and dialects were so different.'[73] More broadly, the argument from numbers can cut both ways. The higher numbers of clergy ordained in earlier centuries have been seen as evidence that standards had been lax.[74] It is hard not to wonder about, say, the 1,005 clergy ordained by Bishop Walter Stapledon of Exeter on a single day, 21 December 1308.[75] And, conversely, it has been suggested (speculatively) that the declining numbers of clergy ordained in the 1520s reflected the higher standards being imposed by bishops, not least in the light of Wolsey's reforming zeal.[76]

Most clergy came from relatively humble backgrounds: they were the sons of yeomen, the better-off husbandmen, and the more prosperous urban craftsmen.[77] Considered from a different angle, about one in ten of the sons of some 1,500 Norfolk citizens whose wills from between 1370 and 1532 survive was described as a priest or monk.[78]

Many clergy, especially the more educated and the more ambitious, held more than one benefice. Of course, many of the posts that such pluralists held were sinecures, posts not involving the cure of souls. But a significant number of benefices that did involve the cure of souls were held in plurality. Of the clergy, 10 per cent held 25 per cent of the benefices.[79] The inevitable consequence was absence. Edward Lee, archbishop of York, complained that those who had the best benefices—meaning those with the largest incomes—were not resident.[80] That did not necessarily mean that pastoral responsibilities were neglected, since pluralists could afford to appoint deputies. And sometimes what, on the face of it, looks like pluralism was rather an arrangement by which a priest who retired received a proportion of the income of the benefice from his successor as a sort of pension.[81] The lack of formal provision for clerical retirement posed problems. In 1538 Cranmer pleaded on behalf of William Chevenay, parson of Kingston besides Canterbury, 'which being a very impotent man, above fourscore years of age, and also blind, is not able in his own person to discharge his cure, and would very gladly have licence to abide with his friends and kinsfolks, and would find an honest priest in the meantime to discharge his cure': the difficulty was that the revenues of his benefice were too small.[82] It was also seen as appropriate that a large share of the income of a benefice was used to support a priest who left his parish for a few years in order to study at university.[83] Perhaps 2,500 to 3,000 secular clergy were studying at Oxford and Cambridge by the end of the fifteenth century.[84] The personnel of the church courts were often supported and rewarded similarly. The kind of reorganisation that would have been called for if benefices had been made residential, and separate provision made for the administrators of church courts, was alien to the later middle ages.[85]

Moreover, benefices were treated as a form of property, associated with complex rights and duties. Incumbents owed their appointments to the working of patronage and consequently retained obligations to their patrons—whether bishops, abbots of monasteries, or laymen—that might interfere with the performance of their parochial duties.[86] A significant consequence was that ambitious churchmen might spend a good deal of energy on advancing their careers, lobbying potential patrons. Cranmer lamented 'what ambition and desire of promotion is in men of the church, and what indirect means they do use and have used to obtain their purpose'. Were these 'unreasonable desires and appetites', as Cranmer asserted, or were they unavoidable in any human institution?[87] And aspects of the ways in which clergy were appointed could appear as a financial racket, a murky world of bargains, collusion and pay-offs. Would-be ordinands had to demonstrate that they already had an income of five marks (£3 6s 8d); if they lacked private means, they needed to be able to say that they had been guaranteed a living—either a benefice or a position as a curate. Most such guarantees were offered by monasteries.

But monasteries offered far more such guarantees than they had vacant posts at their disposal. Presumably what was in it for monastic houses was that those ordained would make them some payments, though this remains puzzling as there is nothing in monastic accounts to confirm it (though the patchiness of survival of monastic accounts means that it is just as true to say that nothing refutes it). In any case, the sums could not have been large: yet some financial return seems the only reason why monasteries should have colluded in such arrangements. Whatever the truth of the matter, the damaging aspect of all this is that the ordination and appointment of priests had become a complex financial and legal business. Such practices made the church vulnerable to criticism: it was hard to defend them.[88]

And, when all is said and done, it must remain true that both a priest of a cultic church and a pastor of a church that emphasises preaching need to reside. According to one calculation, in the diocese of Lincoln no fewer than one parish in four was at some point between 1514 and 1521 held by a pluralist non-resident priest.[89] It is intriguing that the clerical beneficiaries of lay wills tended to be resident priests, including those not possessing a benefice.[90] A list of twenty-six Calais parishes showing that eleven incumbents were absent, one vacant, one dead and one unknown, does not offer a favourable impression, however much there might be mitigating circumstances, such as the small size of the parishes and the ready availability of alternative services and priestly ministration.[91] A statute of 1536 laying down constitutions for Calais included a section 'that spiritual persons shall be resident upon their benefices . . . for the more increase and maintenance of divine service'.[92] Legislation in 1529 had attempted to limit pluralism more generally.[93] But another act in 1536 noted that the exception made earlier allowing scholars to study at any university had been abused by those not apt nor intending to study but 'rather minding and intending their own ease singular lucre and pleasure', who went to Oxford and Cambridge 'where they under the said pretence and colour of study doth continue and abide living dissolutely, nothing profiting themselves by study at all in learning, but consume the time in idleness and in other pastimes and insolent pleasures, giving occasion and evil example thereby to other young men and students . . . little or nothing regarding their cure and charge of souls'. Spiritual persons under the age of forty would only be allowed to be absent from their benefices if they attended lectures and 'in their proper persons keep spohemes [sophisms] problems disputations and other exercises of learning'.[94] The statutes may have exaggerated, they may have drawn their vigour from some egregious events or arrangements now lost to us, but they

vividly illustrate contemporary perceptions. A dispute between the parishioners of Wembury and the prior of Plympton in 1535 turned on the consequences of the lack of a resident priest. Even though the benefice was worth
£50, the prior of Plympton would not supply the parish with a resident
priest as the priory was bound to do. As a result, many parishioners had
died without the benefit of the last rites, shrift or housel. Once, when a
priest was summoned to baptise a dangerously ill child, the father had been
waiting at the church for eight hours; but the priest arrived too late and
could do no more than bury the child. Only on Sunday was a priest sent
regularly to say mass, matins and (immediately afterwards) evensong, but
he then returned to the priory at Plympton for dinner. Mothers coming to
church on Easter Monday for the service of purification discovered that
there was no priest to officiate. The prior had threatened to evict any of his
tenants in the village who complained.[95]

The priests despatched to Wembury were most likely unbeneficed
clergy. At that end of the clerical spectrum there were a great many clergy,
though fewer than in the early fourteenth century (when the population
was greater).[96] There was no necessary connection between ordination—a
relatively straightforward matter—and the security of a benefice—a relatively difficult matter, since all turned on finding a suitable post. A priest
might wait for years before obtaining a benefice. Meanwhile he would seek
employment as an assistant, as a deputy, as a chantry priest or as a chaplain
in a domestic household (every household down to middling gentry would
have one),[97] for which there were many opportunities, especially in the
towns, given the proliferation of masses.[98] Many may well have remained in
their home towns: almost half those listed as unbeneficed in *Valor
Ecclesiasticus* recurred in the chantry returns of 1548, almost all at the same
chantries and chapels, which suggests local origins.[99]

Large numbers of unbeneficed clergy were not necessarily a cause for
concern. Many unbeneficed clergy were not much different in ability or
in the range of their duties from beneficed clergy.[100] The large numbers of
chantry priests allowed an increase in the numbers of masses (since canon
law permitted priests to celebrate no more than one public mass a day
except in exceptional circumstances). They also made more lavish
music, especially polyphonic music, a possibility. Some chantry priests may
well have been content to remain as such: they celebrated mass, sang,
assisted the parish priest, and often taught. Parish priests would welcome
them as assistants, whose costs were met by parishioners. In practice they
did play a considerable part in the religious life of a parish, despite lacking
any formal pastoral responsibilities.[101] Yet, against that perception, it
was the unbeneficed clergy who attracted most of the complaints against

the clergy.[102] Their relative poverty—chantry priests were paid roughly £6 in the later fifteenth century; stipendiary clergy somewhat less at £4 13s 4d—left them more open to worldly temptations. 'Unbeneficed clergy were', one scholar has gone so far as to say, 'the bane of the medieval church'.[103]

Unbeneficed clergy moved about a good deal and were consequently harder to monitor or to discipline. The career of Thomas Grey is instructive. The son of a smith, he went to school at Topcliff, where he was taught by a priest who was a steward of the earl of Northumberland. For three years he lived in Newburgh Priory, taught by a priest. Then he went to Oxford, spending four years as bible clerk and butler in St Bernard's College. He then travelled to Rome, via Troyes, Dijon, Savoy, Pavia and Florence, and was ordained a priest there. For the most part he begged his food and drink. At Calais he found employment for three months singing trentals for a noblewoman. In London he took up service with a parish priest, Edmund Bray, for twelve months. Then he was a soul priest for a year at Shere, Surrey, and a temporary parish priest for a year when Bray went to Morlez. Then he went to Bentle Green, Hampshire, serving as parish priest under the archdeacon of Surrey for three years. He then served in various places in Hampshire for different periods. We know about him because in 1538 he was interrogated under suspicion of treasonable communications: the assize judges found nothing against him but declared him to be a lunatic. We do not know what ensued, nor is his mental illness relevant to our theme. What is striking here, rather, is the complicated life he had been leading and how difficult bishops would have found it to handle such men.[104]

The clergy were not especially well off in the main. 'Parochial revenues almost universally declined after the Black Death, and continued to fall right through to 1535.'[105] Unbeneficed clergy were especially badly off, 'living . . . from death to death, literally singing for their suppers as one series of post-mortem masses followed another'.[106] It has been claimed that 'unbeneficed clergy were by no means as poor as reference to their stipends alone would suggest', on the grounds that the survey of movable goods carried out in 1522 shows that little more than one in five clergy was poor. Since movable goods cannot repeatedly be sold and spent, that claim is misleading.[107] True, almost all of the ninety-eight chantry priests of York who left wills between 1480 and 1530 left more than £5 in goods and money, and eight of them held lands; some had collections of vestments and service books. That has been taken as showing that chantry priests were far from an impoverished proletariat—but of course will-makers comprised a socially selective sample.[108]

Poverty, or relative poverty, left clergy, both with or without benefices, but especially those not totally committed to a life of renunciation, open to a variety of worldly temptations or involvements. These temptations might have deprived them of the time needed for the preparation of the administration of sacraments, let alone the leisure needed to write sermons. In some circumstances, poor priests might lose the respect of their parishioners. This might have made clergy more determined to pursue what they saw as their financial rights, with the damaging consequences that we saw in the Hunne affair.[109]

At least late medieval clergy were not like the stereotypical squire-parsons of the nineteenth century, independently wealthy, residing in grand rectories, scholarly and cultured, serving as JPs, charity administrators, school governors and poor law guardians, identifying themselves with county society and allegedly losing touch with the concerns of the rural poor. Such a view of the Victorian church may be unfair. But it is abundantly clear that late medieval resident parish clergy were an integral part of local society.[110]

Some clergy were, however, in danger of getting caught up in the worldly life of their patrons. The Perrots, a Welsh gentry family, used their advowsons to reward their household and retainers, in much the same way, in microcosm, that kings used bishoprics to reward their diplomats and closest advisers.[111] Laymen frequently used priests in their financial transactions.[112] The fourth earl of Shrewsbury sent his chaplain John Morton to court to collect the money due for a wood that the earl had sold to the king.[113] The lawyer Christopher St German described how laymen exploited priests by employing them as bailiffs and receivers: 'thay have by such occasion been much beaten and greatly exercised in such worldly business so that the inward devotion of the heart hath been in them as cold and as weak in manner, as in laymen'. Although less than ideal priests they were nonetheless appointed by their lay employers to benefices, in recognition of their work, or simply because they were good company. More devout clergy, especially those who would admonish laymen for their faults, risked missing out.[114] Domestic chaplains of noblemen and gentry (who might also hold a benefice or two) could even get caught up in the violent rivalries of landed families, perhaps taken along in case it proved necessary to administer the sacrament of extreme unction, more likely as articulate and literate witnesses who might testify in future court cases.[115] Once more, the clergy risked getting the worst of both worlds. The highest ideal of a christian priest involved the renunciation of worldly things: Colet's ideal of a priest was one who had died to the world.[116] Yet such idealistic clergy would equally find themselves criticised for not devoting themselves to the needs of those suffering in this world. And, surely most often, in practice clergy were inescapably involved in worldly matters. How far was that at the cost of their spirituality?

Such worldliness seems especially characteristic of cathedral clergy, who deserve special note. Ten English cathedrals were monastic, served by Benedictine monks at Canterbury, Coventry, Durham, Ely, Norwich, Rochester, Bath, Winchester and Worcester, and by regular canons at Carlisle. Nine English cathedrals were secular—that is served by secular canons. The distinction crystallised in the eleventh and early twelfth centuries. In some cathedrals, instead of property being communally owned, separate individual incomes were created—usually from estates or churches—known as prebends and allocated to individual canons. This was done at Lincoln, Salisbury and York in 1089–91. Salisbury then served as a model for Chichester, Wells and Lichfield. Similar forms of organisation emerged more gradually at St Paul's, London, Exeter and Hereford. Such canons were clergy who committed themselves to following a rule, comparable to the rule of a monastic order. In the case of the Augustinian canons it was the rule of St Augustine (d. 430), bishop of Hippo, North Africa, drawn from his teachings and originally intended for the clergy of his cathedral there. But, instead of following a rule within an enclosed monastery without much involvement in the world outside and with very specific obligations, they did so in a cathedral and with an explicit commitment to assist the laity. Such canons did a great deal to transform the church from a cultic church to a more pastoral church.[117] But with that transformation came worldly arrangements and temptations. The secular cathedrals 'developed into large corporations, between fifty and one hundred strong, with a complex hierarchy of office-holders'—dean, precentor, chancellor, treasurer—as well as canons. There were fifty-eight clerical office-holders at Lincoln, fifty-two at Salisbury, fifty-five at Wells, thirty at Chichester and St Pauls, thirty-two at Lichfield, thirty-six at York, twenty-eight at Hereford and twenty-four at Exeter. And there were also many minor clergy (whose position was becoming increasingly formalised)—vicars choral, chantry priests, altarists, choristers—backed up by a large number of servants. The deans of York and Lincoln enjoyed an income of over £300; the majority of dignitaries had incomes of over £50; in the poorest cathedral, the dean of Hereford enjoyed £38. Canonries varied widely in value from over £60 to 4s 4d at Hereford. Very little changed in the nature and structure of prebends. The principal function of cathedrals (and in this they were comparable to monasteries) was to offer the daily liturgy, often very elaborate, and involving very many masses, including those at many chantries, and obits.[118] But since, unlike monasteries—not least some of the largest monasteries—cathedrals were in the heart of towns, the laity were more readily involved in worship there. Cathedral clergy could not escape the world. Merely running so large a corporation meant much concern over rents and fees. The clergy of late medieval Wells were heavily involved in the property market with the burgesses of the city since the cathedral was a large landowner there.[119] Self-preservation demanded good and close relationships with local landowners. The bishop and chapter of Exeter sought the good lordship of the Courtenays; a significant number of fifteenth-century canons and minor clergy were in their service, four members of the family becoming canons, and one a bishop (Peter Courtenay between 1478 and 1487).[120] The Fitzalan earls of Arundel at Chichester, the Charltons lords of Powys at Hereford, and the Scropes at York did much the same. Perhaps that sort of relationship diminished in the early sixteenth century. Canons were often involved in diocesan administration, or in the service of kings, popes, bishops, and were perforce absent. Absence was condemned as a moral failing but accepted as a practical reality. Many cathedral canonries and prebends were held together with other posts, and their holders were often absent from the cathedral close.[121] Residence levels varied, but with no clear trends on the eve of reformation. 'At most cathedrals, except St Paul's and York, there was', it has been noted, 'a vigorous if sometimes small community of canons committed to residence.'[122] Archbishop Cranmer was very critical:

Having experience both in time past and also in our days, how the said sect of prebendaries have not only spent their time in much idleness, and their substance in superfluous belly cheer, I think it not to be a convenient state or degree to be maintained or established, considering first, that commonly a prebendary is neither a learner, nor a teacher, but a good viander. Then by the same name they look to be chief, and to bear all the whole rule and preeminence in the college where they be resident: by means whereof the younger, of their own nature given more to pleasure, good cheer and pastime, than to abstinence, study and learning, shall easily be brought from their books to follow the appetite and example of the said prebendaries, being their heads and rulers. And the state of prebendaries hath been so excessively abused, that when learned men hath been admitted unto such room, many times they have desisted from their good and godly studies, and all other christian exercises of preaching and teaching.

Cranmer wished it would stand with the king's pleasure that 'not only the name of a prebendary were exiled his grace's foundations, but also the superfluous condition of such persons'. 'I cannot deny,' he acknowledged, 'but that the beginning of prebendaries was no less purposed for the maintenance of good learning and good conversation of living than religious men were; but forasmuch as both be gone from their first estate and order, and the one is found like offender with the other, it maketh no great matter if they perish together.'[123] The modern historian of the brotherhood of canons reckons that Cranmer was 'unduly harsh'. 'Flagrant breaches of clerical discipline by residentiaries were rare.' He notes, '. . . their failure to live up to their religious vocations lay more in their readiness to accept a comfortable life in the close'. It was alleged that the canons of Exeter kept down their numbers so that they could enjoy a larger share of the revenues, though in fairness it should be noted that Exeter's basic prebends were lower than the norm, at £4. Cathedral closes did not attract the greatest scholars, who were more likely to be found in the universities or in episcopal households. Even John Colet, dean of St Paul's, lived in the Charterhouse at Sheen, not in the cathedral precincts. Cathedral clergy wrote remarkably few books. Barchester does not seem far away.[124]

If this impression of cathedral canons is unflattering, we should, nonetheless, note that a great many priests did reside in their parishes. Their local standing emerges most clearly in times of difficulty. Priests did act as leaders of their local communities in the rebellions in the north in 1536 and in the south-west in 1549. Governments would claim that, as Lancaster Herald, despatched by Henry to meet the rebel leaders, reported in December 1536, the clergy had been the greatest corrupters of the temporality and 'have given the secret occasion of all this mischief'.[125] But the government was keen to see the rebellions as the work of self-interested conspirators (the clergy) rather than as a reflection of far more widely shared grievances. It is hard to suppose that the laity would have allowed themselves to be persuaded by the clergy into highly risky demonstrations unless they felt just as strongly themselves. And, if large numbers of laymen were prepared to rise in defence of the church as they knew it, that does speak a good deal in favour of the parish priests of late medieval England.

Of course, it is desperately difficult to generalise about clergy who may at any one time have numbered some 40,000 men. Not all of them were suited to their calling. Under-paid, under-educated, under-inspired, with limited access to books, as one historian has noted,[126] how could they inspire the laity by their example, by their piety, by their learning? And how far were the more educated and the more affluent laity becoming more demanding in the later middle ages, both in the levels of education and in the standards of moral behaviour they were expecting from their priests? Was the church now failing to match rising lay expectations?[127] Or had the laity in fact always had realistic, but quite clear, and quite demanding, expectations of the moral behaviour and devotion to duty of clergy? If so, then the behaviour and the quality of the clergy were a perennial, rather than a new or an increasing problem. The danger for the church was that, in setting its priests such high standards, it was continually running the risk of falling short and thus disappointing the laity.[128]

How committed were the clergy of late medieval England? It is a hard test, but it is none the less true that few clergy would voluntarily abandon their livings for their faith in the sixteenth century. On the face of it, the reforms of Henry VIII's reign, and especially those of Edward VI's reign, were fundamental challenges to the church in which those priests had been ordained. Yet the conformity of Christopher Trychay, parson of Morebath, was far more typical than that of those few who refused.[129] Of course, clergy had little choice, and the pressures, political and material, making for conformity, were immense. Clergy did not often meet as a group: concerted action was never easy. Perhaps it was the sheer novelty of the changes that made speedy reaction difficult. But the general acquiescence of the clergy does raise wider questions about how zealous and how energetic priests had been. Did they see themselves as pursuing a vocation or simply as doing a job, demanding and important, but nonetheless when it came down to it, a job consisting of specific daily duties prescribed by authority? And how far did they just get on with them? How often did clergy bring something more, some charisma, some inspirational qualities, to their daily tasks? We cannot easily say. Reginald Pole complained to Bishop Tunstal in 1536 about the mechanical nature of services: 'I have seen twayne [two] say service in company together where as they have said divers psalms that none of them both remember whether they have said or no, and one ask the other whether they had done such a psalm or no',[130] though the context of his letter (a response to Tunstal's criticism of his attack on Henry VIII) complicates any assessment of the validity of his description. Most tellingly—though again this is a stiff test—there seem to have been few priests of exemplary devotion within the late medieval English church. In the fourteenth and early fifteenth centuries there were John Schorn (d. by 1315), vicar of North Marston, Buckinghamshire, who trapped the devil in his boot and developed unusually horny knees through long hours of prayer;[131] Philip of Beverley (d. 1323×5), vicar of Keyingham, Yorkshire, seen as unusually saintly; Richard Caister (d. 1420), vicar of St Stephen's, Norwich, praised by Margery Kempe as a holy man and effective preacher; and Richard Bovyle (d. 1359), of Whitstone, Cornwall. The graves of Schorn and Caister would become centres of pilgrimage. Yet we know very little in detail from strictly contemporary sources about how they carried out their duties as priests and what it was that created their reputations as holy men, even as saints-in-the-making. And it is hard to find later—fifteenth- and early sixteenth-century—examples of holy priests.[132]

Once again it is a challenge to the historian to strike the right balance. It is important to remember that, to all appearances, thousands of clergy did regularly celebrate mass and minister to their parishioners, and, to return to the rebellions of 1536 and 1549, those parishioners were prepared to rebel in defence of the church. Yet it seems fair to end this assessment of the clergy by noting a sense of weaknesses, of vulnerability, that in part at least reflected inescapable, and perennial, tensions between human aspirations and human behaviour.

5

LAY KNOWLEDGE

THE late medieval English church was very much a monarchical church. Bishops made the system work. Clergy administered the sacraments and undertook pastoral care in the parishes. But what of the people? How far were the people of England christian? What did they grasp of the teachings of Christ? One of the greatest areas of vulnerability of the church was ignorance and misunderstanding of christian theology. The richness and sophistication of that theology, not least as elaborated in the universities of high medieval Europe, could be grasped only by years of study and by the exercise of rare intellectual skills. It would have been too demanding to have required such depths of understanding from everyone. It has been perceptively noted that, while capable of 'infinite refinement and complexity', nonetheless 'Christianity's theology combined simple ideas which all could grasp'.[1] At its heart lies the very personal story of the life of Christ, not impossibly difficult to follow as such. And it is perhaps right to begin not by pointing to weaknesses, but by stressing the considerable extent of lay awareness of what faith was about. Indeed, one of the most common explanations of the sixteenth-century reformation stresses the increasingly higher levels of learning and literacy, and consequently heightened intellectual expectations, of the laity. But it is also necessary to indicate crucial areas of lay misapprehension that made late medieval piety especially vulnerable to humanist and protestant critiques. As well as functioning at very different levels of knowledge and understanding, christianity has been, and remains, remarkably open to rich and to poor, to the powerful and to the marginalised, as well as to different emphases, allowing, for example, both chivalric knights and aged widows to find a message that resonated with them (though one must beware of supposing that all knights or widows felt the same way). The many different forms the cult of the Virgin Mary would take over the centuries—from slow beginnings in specially dedicated churches in late antiquity to the elaboration of the doctrine of Mary's bodily assumption into heaven in the high middle ages to her appearances in nineteenth-century visions across Europe from Knock, Ireland, to Lourdes, France and to Marpingen in Germany—neatly illustrate the creative possibilities within christianity.[2] The risk was that approaches and emphases could diverge so much as to open the church to the charge of *nihil quia omnia*—of standing for nothing because it in practice allowed everything. The protean character of christianity—the simplicity of its central teachings, the complexity and fertility of its thought, the ease which which individuals, groups and localities could latch on to features which they might then highlight and exaggerate—was both a strength and a weakness.

How soon, and how far, was it expected that laymen and lay women should grasp the basic teachings of the church? It has long been supposed that in the early days of the christian church in western Europe, from the seventh to the eleventh centuries, accepted wisdom held that only a few could expect to attain heaven, and even then only after following an extremely rigorous system of penances, preferably in a monastery set apart from a wicked world. How far in such a context did abbots and monks, bishops and clergy, typically based in a *monasterium* (Latin) or *mynster* (Old English), 'minster' in modern English (and defined as 'a complex ecclesiastical settlement which is headed by an abbess, abbot, or man in priest's orders; which contains nuns, monks, priests, or laity in a variety of possible combinations, and is united to a greater or lesser extent by their liturgy and devotions'), regard it as their duty to instruct the laity at large?[3] A pioneering collection of essays provocatively entitled *Pastoral Care before the Parish* urged that they did, yet the 'pastoral care' offered seems to have consisted of baptism, the celebration of the liturgy in church services which the laity might attend (though the small size of many early churches raises questions about how many could do so), the maintenance of shrines of saints to which the laity came on pilgrimage and occasional proselytising by itinerant preaching clergy in rural areas.[4] Bede certainly believed passionately that it was the duty of the church to teach and to guide the souls of the faithful,[5] but just how far such efforts were made to realise such ideals in the eighth century, and with what success, remains controversial. Across the tenth, eleventh and the mid-twelfth centuries it is possible to discern a remarkably ambitious effort to extend the church's ministry to the whole population. In what must have been an astonishing enterprise—though it may well have been the fruit of myriad local decisions rather than the methodical implementation of any plan—by the mid-twelfth century, England was, or found itself, divided into parishes, each with a newly built church. Until well into the eleventh century these were mostly of timber (of which Greensted, Essex, 1063×1100 is the only survivor), then of stone: 'a white mantle of churches' as Rudolfus Glaber (d. *c.*1046), Benedictine monk, put it, in what has rightly been presented as a 'Great Rebuilding', a true revolution since such stone churches would last and could readily be adapted and enlarged. These parish churches, with a resident priest supported by a modest landed endowment, and often—but not exclusively—close to the lord's manor house, nonetheless functioned not as the lord's private chapel, but rather as genuine parish churches. Children were to be baptised in church and the dead to be buried in the churchyard by their parish priest, who was also to celebrate marriages. The profusion of surviving stone fonts in romanesque style from this time (dating is difficult and compelling pre-Conquest examples rare) suggests that baptism and christening in parish churches was widely practised, vividly demonstrating the importance of christian worship to all.[6] 'Exactly when, in the two centuries between 900 and 1100, the clerical group gave way to the one-church priest as the dominant agent of pastoral care remains very obscure.'[7] No doubt rising populations made some such attempt necessary, and no doubt increasing prosperity made it possible in practice. Theological developments—that is to say, reinterpretations and codifications of christian doctrine—played their part also. Something approaching the high medieval notion of purgatory is at least implicit in Gregory the Great's reference to 'cleansing fire after death' or in the account by Bede of Dryhthelm's or Fursa's visions of the afterlife.[8] And in the high middle ages a refined doctrine of purgatory, elaborating what had long been implicit in the masses and prayers offered for the souls of the departed as they awaited the resurrection that would come to the blessed at the Last Judgment (and spelling out in detail what had to be done), offered the prospect of heaven not just to a spiritual or a social elite but to ordinary men and women—that is to say, to ordinary people who were not saints and who had not led lives of unblemished virtue. After they died, their souls would go through purgatory, where their sins would be purged, and then heaven would await them.[9]

By our period everyone was to learn and to know the essentials of the christian faith. We have already noted Archbishop Pecham's instructions, drawn up in 1281, requiring all priests with cure of souls to instruct their flocks in the basic teachings of the church at least four times a year. What that meant was the Creed, the Ten Commandments, the Paternoster, the Ave Maria, the seven works of mercy, the seven deadly sins, the seven virtues and the seven sacraments. Lay people were expected to know these basic teachings of christianity by heart.[10] Such was the ideal. How far it was realised is extraordinarily hard to judge. Whether such exposition was done frequently and thoroughly enough for people to remember and to understand is obviously open to question. There were many late medieval manuals to assist priests in this task but no pre-sixteenth century catechism survives.[11] The style of the manuals was declaratory rather than post-reformation questions-and-answers.[12] There was no special emphasis on the religious instruction of children. There were no Sunday schools, no texts specifically designed for children; instead, children were taught informally by their parents, godparents, by local priests and friars.[13] Much (though far from all) medieval schooling was in the hands of clergy, so presumably such teachers took the opportunity to inculcate some religious knowledge, but this was not done as part of any systematic plan, and there was little general supervision, for example by bishops, of local schools.[14]

The single most important source of knowledge for the laity was the liturgy. Of course the liturgy was about devotional worship. But what must be asked here is how far witnessing and participating in the liturgy imposed an understanding of christian doctrine.[15] Eamon Duffy has powerfully argued that fashionable views of the late medieval church that see it as superstitious and obscurantist are seriously flawed because they do not take into account the power of the liturgy, the 'principal reservoir from which the religious paradigms and beliefs of the people were drawn'.[16] Everyone over the age of fourteen was expected to attend mass on Sundays and holy days. If they did, they must have learned a good deal.

Did they? Did people go regularly to church? 'It is exasperating,' a modern sceptic has noted, 'that we do not even know what proportion of a parish attended Sunday worship regularly.'[17] Another less sceptical scholar computed that 'the chances are that most people did attend fairly regularly, on Sundays especially'.[18] It is hard to know what to make of a handful of remarks on the subject in our sources. Bishop Veysey in 1523 thought that in Crediton the majority of the people were present scarcely four times a year at the principal Sunday mass.[19] John Barlow, dean of Westbury-on-Trym, found fourteen evil-disposed persons playing the unlawful game of tennis during the time of morning service at Yate, Gloucestershire; they were evidently protected by Lady Berkeley, the local landowner.[20] Defending his chaplain's failure to exhort people to pray for Henry VIII, Anne Boleyn and princess Elizabeth by name in April 1536, John Clerk, bishop of Bath and Wells, said that the congregation consisted of 'gross and rude people . . . disposed to gaming and pastime, and not to tarry long in the church'. They were at least there for a while, even if in an inappropriate frame of mind.[21] On the other side of the question, it is noteworthy how often rebellions and disturbances began with the gathering of crowds on religious festivals, implying that attendance was usually high: notably on Corpus Christi Day (the Thursday after Trinity Sunday) 13 June 1381.

Of course the liturgy was not simple. Not till 1543 was a single rite—the Sarum Use—enjoined throughout the province of Canterbury. Not till 1549 was a single order of service adopted throughout England: 'And whereas heretofore there hath been great diversity in saying and singing in churches within this realm; some following Salisbury use, some Hereford use, and some the use of Bangor; some of York, some of Lincoln; now from hence-forth all the realm shall have but one use'.[22] The most common rite was the Sarum Use, the forms developed at Salisbury, c.1197–1215,[23] when, no doubt building on earlier experiences of copying and writing devotional and liturgical works, the members of the cathedral chapter seem to have taken on the role of 'congregation of rites' to whom queries and doubts should be referred.[24] But there were several other rites, especially in the dioceses of Bangor, Hereford, Lincoln and York. It would thus be misleading to suppose that medieval men and women worshipped in the unified way they would later do once liturgical works such as the Book of Common Prayer were generally available. Careful scrutiny of the 110 surviving litur-gical books that can be linked with a specific church suggests that most books would have contained a good deal of material irrelevant to the church in which they were being used, for example because they presupposed several altars, or a more elaborate establishment than was likely in a parish church.[25] Yet it does seem that the Sarum Use was rapidly expanding in the fifteenth century: St Paul's, London, gave up its own rite in 1415; the fashionable new establishments of Eton, King's College, Cambridge, New College and All Souls College, Oxford, all adopted Sarum Use. Sarum Use was the rite in an overwhelming majority of surviving printed books to 1535 (thirty-two from Salisbury, five from York, one each from Abingdon, Hereford and St Albans).[26] While any detailed understanding of the liturgy needs to take these variations into account, the chief differences between the various uses lay in the elaboration of the details of ceremonies for particular feast days.[27] Far from there being a fragmentation of the church into a multiplicity of practices, there was an underlying common core.

Those, however many of them there were, who went dutifully to church, would witness an annual cycle: Advent, Christmas, Candlemas, Ash Wednesday, Lent, Holy Week, Easter, Whitsun, Corpus Christi.[28] 'On n'imagine plus à quel point le temps ordinaire a été organisé par la liturgie [it is hard for us now to grasp the extent to which daily life was marked out by the routines of liturgical observance].'[29] It would be hard not to grasp the essential significance of, say, the kindling of the fire at Easter, or the distribution of palms on Palm Sunday.[30] In counterpoint to the annual cycle of the church's year was the liturgy of every individual's own life-cycle: baptism, confirmation (though it is not clear how commonly this was practised), marriage (ideally to be celebrated by a priest in church but valid even without ecclesiastical approval), burial. All of these had their own ceremonies, especially burial, with the vespers, matins and lauds of the dead, the mass of the Trinity and Blessed Virgin Mary, the solemn high mass of requiem, and the burial service itself, followed by anniversary masses.[31]

At the centre of the liturgy was the mass, the heart of the liturgy.[32] The mass was held to have been introduced by Christ himself at the Last Supper. As St Paul wrote to the Corinthians:[33]

> For I have received of the Lord that which also I delivered unto you, that the Lord Jesus the same night in which he was betrayed took bread. And when he had given thanks, he brake it, and said, take, eat: this is my body, which is broken for you: this do in remembrance of me [in the Latin Vulgate Bible: *in meam commemorationem*]. After the same manner also he took the cup, when he had supped, saying, this cup is the new testament in my blood: this do ye, as oft as ye drink it, in remembrance of me [in the Latin Vulgate: *in meam commemorationem*]. For as often as ye eat this bread, and drink this cup, ye do shew the Lord's death till he come.

The medieval church taught, codifying its teaching in the Fourth Lateran Council of 1215, that the body and blood of Christ were contained in the sacrament of the altar under the appearances of bread and wine, transubstantiated by divine power, the bread into the body, the wine into the blood, of Christ. How far such a complex set of beliefs could be absorbed by un-tutored lay folk is difficult to judge. Yet the congregation would readily grasp that the priest was making a sacrifice, that the offering of bread and wine, transubstantiated into the body and blood of Christ, was something special, and that the elevation of the host, highly visible to the laity, was a transcendental moment—interestingly, the moment most frequently depicted in paintings of the mass. It was then that the congregation knelt as bells were rung, and the celebrating priest raised first the consecrated host and then the consecrated chalice high above his head.[34] As they saw the elevation of the host, parishioners looking from the nave would see the action of the priest framed within the rood, the image of Christ on the cross over the chancel arch.[35] The consecrated bread, or host, the body of Christ, was especially venerated: a previously consecrated host might be left exposed for public adoration.[36] The cult of Corpus Christi, the body of Christ, especially fashionable in the later middle ages, further reflected the impact of the mass. The congregation at mass was not simply passive. The laity participated in prayers. A pax—a wooden stick on which the crucifixion was carved—was passed round the congregation and kissed as a sign of peace.[37] At various times of the year congregations were involved in a range of liturgical ceremonies and processions. Music intensified the impact of religious services. Cathedrals, royal and noble chapels, and large urban parish churches, often had choirs performing elaborate liturgical music.

Most importantly of all, parishioners were expected to make an annual confession of their sins to a priest, perform prescribed penance, and then not simply attend mass, but also receive communion, usually at or around Easter. Episcopal statutes and penitential manuals laid down that practice. Did they just reflect the wishful thinking of the elite? There is a sufficient number of occasional references to confession throughout the middle ages to suggest that such scepticism would be excessively cautious. A rare early Tudor reference shows how demanding the obligation of confession and communion was—but also that it was just about met. In 1535 royal commissioners in Doncaster noted that there were over 2,000 people in the parish, 'whereof the said incumbent and other vij [7] priests, now resident in the said church, can scant hear the confessions of the said parochians [parishioners] from the beginning of Lent unto Palm Sunday, and then minister the blessed sacrament all the said week, with other requisite business to be done in the said church'.[38] The clergy of Doncaster were struggling—but their struggle was to do all that was required, not the indifference of their flock. And confession generally gave priests the opportunity to find out how much their parishioners knew, notably by asking them to say the Creed, and to offer them rudimentary instruction.

Some historians have seen a damaging transformation of the mass from an inclusive ceremony involving the laity in communion to an exclusively priestly liturgy in an incomprehensible and softly spoken language, the priest with his back turned to the congregation, and the laity as witnesses (and not even that if they could not see what was going on) rather than participants: 'le souvenir du repas en commun semble quelque peu s'effacer [the memory of communal meals seems somewhat to have faded]'. What was involved was less a communion, in the sense of a sharing of the gift of grace from God, than an epiphany, that is 'une serie de gestes magiques [a series of magical gestures]', culminating in a miraculous apparition in the midst of candles and incense, intended to provoke passive adoration.[39] All that does implicitly suppose some earlier period of perfection from which the later medieval church fell away: yet how frequent was communion in earlier centuries?

Duffy has riposted to this line of argument, that as well as principal or high masses celebrated at the high altar at the east end of the church, there were also plenty of low masses celebrated at minor altars in the side chapels off the aisles, including the aisles of the nave, so there was ample opportunity for parishioners to see from close quarters and so come to know what happened. Indeed, Duffy has teasingly suggested that distance from the altar and consequent mystification were more a feature of post-reformation high church English anglicanism than to be found in the medieval church itself.[40]

What we lack are sources to tell us how all that was felt by individuals, especially the less educated and the poor. We do, however, have some evidence for the great, which allows cautious extrapolation. It is illuminating to see how routine worship was for so richly documented a man as Henry VIII. On returning from hunting, he went to his privy closet to hear evensong, John Clerk informed Wolsey in May 1526, giving the impression that this was what he did every day.[41] In his will Charles Somerset (d. 1526), first earl of Worcester, referred to his chapel and private closet 'where I do kneel and hear mass every day'.[42] What we have in such casual references are glimpses of active piety; but, we cannot easily judge whether actions performed or donations made regularly were done routinely and unthinkingly, or from genuine devotion and commitment. How the mass was inwardly experienced we cannot know. What we do know is that those who could afford to do so maintained domestic chapels in their houses. Sometimes, we may note in passing, this has been seen as reflecting a damaging detachment from the parish community and selfish individualism, yet that would seem to be belied by gentry contributions to the rebuilding of parish churches, not least those in which they wished to be buried.[43] The increase in domestic chapels abundantly demonstrates a costly commitment to the practice of devotion, which is hard to square with ignorance or indifference.

Of course, one can only speculate on the effect produced by such regular worship. Did the routine of religious life lead to 'recitation, acceptance, acquiescence, and belief . . . rather than understanding'?[44] Did recitation like magpies allow any time for meditation?[45] Was all this a distraction, as the reformer William Tyndale claimed, from reading the scripture? Bishops, he alleged, had set out 'to occupy their preists with all that they should not study the scripture for barking against them set up long service wonderously intricate so that in a dozen years thou couldest scarce learn to turn aright unto it: long matinses, long evensongs, long masses, long diriges'.[46] But such a critique assumes not only that such matins and masses had limited value, but also that the liturgy had no biblical or theological content and that it left no deposit. That raises the question of how far attendance at church embedded knowledge of the Creed, the Lord's Prayer, and the Commandments. Printed service books reduced in size allowed larger numbers to purchase and then to follow services. Testators' prayers often reveal detailed knowledge of prayers from missal and breviary.[47]

Two rather more oblique approaches may shed light on the extent of lay knowledge of christian teachings. Some evidence survives of sceptics; and scepticism implies a degree of knowledge.[48] Among the accounts of miracles worked by Henry VI is the story of Edmund Crumpe, who condemned pilgrimage and the veneration of relics; he began to suffer burning pains over his body; his wife lectured him on the miracles of Henry VI; he sent her to get a silver penny, vowed it to the royal tomb, and recovered. Another tells how a man who mocked Henry VI's miracles was smitten by bodily pain, went mad for ten days, and then went on pilgrimage.[49] The point of these examples was to make the case for the sanctification of Henry VI. But the incidental details they reveal are intriguing. The men who mocked knew and understood what they mocked, even if their knowledge had led them to reject it. Moreover, it is clear that, in late medieval society, to be accused of being an heretic was very damaging. The supplication of the Commons against the ordinaries in 1532 made a good deal of the ease with which someone could be falsely accused and convicted of heresy. Significantly, it stressed how a man could be compelled by these procedures to make his purgation 'and bear a faggot to his extreme shame and utter undoing'. If being suspected of and punished for heresy was a source of shame and worldly undoing, then that suggests that orthodox religion—even if, as the supplication claimed, not always crystal clear—must have been generally understood, and indeed valued, for such social sanctions to apply.[50] And those accused of heresy often testified to the ubiquity of conventional pious practices which they, of course, had allegedly criticised.[51]

Another oblique approach to the question of lay knowledge is how those who could afford funerary monuments had themselves portrayed as devout. Henry VII had himself depicted kneeling in prayer with Elizabeth of York and their three sons and four daughters; Pietro Torrigiani's tombs show Henry VII and Elizabeth of York recumbent with hands clasped in prayer; earlier designs suggested kneeling.[52] Most probably this reflected genuine devotion; but even if this was hypocritical, the hypocrisy throws light on conventional beliefs and expectations.

Masses, especially high masses on feast days, could be elaborate ceremonies: they required a good deal of equipment. We lack full sources. But the remarkable surviving inventory of church goods in over 350 Norfolk churches in 1368 suggests that they were very adequately equipped for church services.[53] Practically all (352 out of 358) had missals or mass books, that is everything necessary for the priest when saying mass at the altar,[54] and almost all (346 out of 358) had graduals containing all the music sung by the choir during the celebration of mass.[55] Virtually all (355 out of 358) had chalices (340 of them silver).[56] Very many (328 out of 358) had locked chrismatories for holy oil,[57] and locked fonts for baptisms (326 out of 358).[58] Most (334 out of 358) had a manual, a portable volume containing the order of administering the sacraments, the offices of baptism, matrimony and extreme unction.[59] Virtually all (341 out of 358) had an ordinal (a guide to the rest of the service books, listing cues for each part of the service, together with the rubrics); almost all (340 out of 358) had at least one (the average was two or three) antiphonal, the music for anthems beginning and ending the psalms sung at canonical hours;[60] almost all (328 out of 358) had a lesson book or legendary, containing lessons read at matins, including readings from the Bible, homilies and sermons of doctors and fathers of the church, lives of saints.[61] Many (288 out of 358) had a martyrology, divided into sections corresponding to each day of the year, containing a short account of the lives and sufferings of saints and martyrs commemorated on each day.[62] Many (235 out of 358) had a breviary, not a compulsory work, but a very practically useful compilation of all the services said in the choir of the church, including antiphons and readings.[63] Almost all (333 out of 358) had a psalter (150 psalms arranged in the order in which they occurred during the course of the weekly office).[64] Many (262 out of 358) had a processional: music for Sunday and holy day processions.[65] Almost all (344 out of 358) had censers for incense at mass.[66] These are astonishing statistics. They are evidence of a remarkable commitment. They strongly suggest that the prescribed services were being observed in due form. Of course this is a single sample, from a period long before the break with Rome, but it is not obvious why mid-fourteenth-century Norfolk should have been unusually devout or why there should subsequently have been a marked decline in provision. It is much more reasonable to suppose that what can be counted in detail here was in fact typical. The remarks by a traveller from Venice c.1500 are pertinent: 'there is not a parish church in the kingdom so mean as not to possess crucifixes, candlesticks, censers, patens, and cups of silver'.[67] A study of pre-reformation book inventories concluded that churches were increasing their stock of liturgical books.[68] A sensitive analysis of the inventories of church goods compiled by a hostile regime in 1552 confirms the point. If the Norfolk returns were 'meagre and vestigial', that reflects the approach of the commissioners in that county: elsewhere, notably in the parishes of London, the returns offer 'an overwhelming sense of the lavish provision hitherto enjoyed'.[69]

The christian message was frequently encapsulated in art. At a fundamental visual level, churches and abbeys and cathedrals claimed attention. 'The church dedicated to Saint Thomas [Canterbury Cathedral] erects itself to heaven with such majesty that even from a distance it strikes religious awe into the beholders.'[70] But how far can christian art be seen not just as awesome but also as didactic in purpose and in effect? Wall paintings, stained glass windows and sculptures in churches offered representations of the Last Judgment, heaven and hell, a variety of scenes from the life of Christ, and the lives of the Virgin and the saints. These must have been an 'aide-memoire de la croyance'.[71] Fonts portrayed the seven sacraments. How far were such artistic artefacts deliberately intended to convey knowledge or to remind observers of aspects of the christian message, how far did they seek to evoke an emotional response, of pity, or of horror? Had Pope Gregory the Great's remark, that churches were painted so that those who did not know letters could at least read on the walls what they could not read in books, left a lasting impact? According to Bede, when Benedict Biscop founded Wearmouth in the late seventh century he brought from Rome pictures of the Virgin and the twelve apostles which were then erected on panels in the church 'so that all persons entering the church, even if unable to read, whichever way they went, should have before their eyes, at least in image, the ever blessed Christ and his saints'. [72]

Emile Mâle in a classic work argued that in the thirteenth century and beyond there was a quite deliberate effort by the church to disseminate a body of doctrine through sculpture and stained glass.[73] 'The symbolism of the cult familiarised the faithful with the symbolism of art.' Mâle accepted that not everything was symbolic and didactic: portrayals of animals and flora and fauna were not,[74] though perhaps earlier romanesque 'images of lust' were, being part of an iconography aimed at castigating the sins of the flesh.[75] But Mâle insisted that the main features of the medieval christian message were present in stone and glass. Scenes from the Old Testament were presented as prefigurations of Christ,[76] though such scenes, the Creation apart, were not very common in English wall-painting.[77] Christ's life was treated in three parts. The nativity, the annunciation to the shepherds, the massacre of the innocents, the flight into Egypt, the presentation in the temple and the adoration of the Magi made up the first part. Four scenes from Christ's adult life were commonly treated: his baptism, the marriage at Cana, the temptation and the transfiguration. Finally, there was Christ's Passion: the crucifixion, the entombment, the resurrection, his appearances after death, and the ascension. Only a few of the parables were portrayed, and then often symbolically, for example with the Good Samaritan seen as Christ himself saving mankind in person of the traveller.

Nor were the miracles at all common.[78] Quite a few apocryphal legends were artistically treated: the infancy of Christ, with the ox and the ass, or the midwives testifying to Mary's virginity.[79] The Virgin herself was also frequently depicted, with much use of the apocryphal gospels.[80] The apostles were a staple of sculptures:[81] 'thanks to works of art in particular, the faithful knew every event in the lives of the principal apostles,' Mâle claimed.[82] A further important category of artistic representation was provided by the lives of saints, seen as heroes and as intercessors, as protectors and as friends. Jacobus de Voragine's mid-thirteenth-century *Legenda aurea* drew on lives of saints in lectionaries and popularised them. Such works were in many ways very formalised, and simplified, but that did make them easy to understand once the code was understood. Each saint was identified by an emblem: some object relevant to their life or martyrdom.[83]

Finally there were direct attempts to warn. Most common were the representations of the Last Judgment which were to be seen in virtually every church over the chancel arch. In the centre Christ would be seated in judgment. Resurrected souls rising from their graves would be sent to heaven—or to hell, the pains of which were graphically depicted. Mary and the devil struggled to claim souls as their own when they were weighed on the scales, good deeds competed with bad deeds. Such paintings could also reflect changes in theological and liturgical fashions: for example, it has been suggested that depictions of the Last Judgment in English church wall-paintings gave Mary a highly prominent place in the fourteenth century but often omitted her altogether in the later middle ages, reflecting the increased emphasis on the suffering of Christ on the cross, depicted with his wounds and instruments of crucifixion, and some unease about the precise role of Mary.[84] Other morality paintings included depictions of the seven deadly sins and the seven works of mercy, the warning of the vanity of worldly power and riches in the contrast between the three living kings and the three dead kings, and warnings against swearing.[85] Paintings in naves of a full-length bleeding Christ, naked but for a loin cloth, and surrounded by the tools that parishioners used in their daily working lives, readily reminded parishioners, it has been suggested, that they should not work on Sundays and holy days but rather offer appropriate devotion to Christ whose suffering saved them.[86]

Was there a shift from symbolic icons of sanctity in the thirteenth century to a more theatrical illusionist depiction in the later middle ages? Did images of Christ increasingly stress his humanity, his suffering, his pain as 'a man of sorrows', more than his power as a worker of miracles?[87] Did that reflect a changing style of faith? 'Contempler l'image, ce n'est plus seulement alors se rememorer le sacrifice du Christ, c'est aussi participer émotionellement, personellement à ce mystère [to contemplate the image is no longer only to remind oneself of Christ's sacrifice, it is also to take part emotionally and personally in this mystery]'.[88] Did late medieval church-goers, then, know less, but feel more? Was there a larger difficulty here in the quality of their knowledge and understanding? Did the depiction of events from the life of Christ, of the Virgin, and of the saints, turn into a jumble of stories and images, without much grasp of the theological truths underlying and connecting them? How far did people grasp the body of doctrine such images were intended to convey? Was there a danger of simplification and exaggeration? Was not such a style of piety potentially vulnerable to the charge of encouraging an idolatrous, rather than simply reverential, attitude to these artistic objects?[89] Against the thrust of such claims, it could be urged that representations of the Last Judgment must have been pretty clear in broad outlines, even if open to subtle variation in details, such as whether purgatory was portrayed, or over the timing of events. So must much of the moralising thrust of such art. There can really have been little doubt about the emptiness of earthly rank and worldly riches, the ephemeral nature of secular pleasures, or conversely the value of study, vividly illustrated at Longthorpe Tower. Wall-paintings and stained glass were very common in churches,[90] and very likely they were also common in secular and domestic settings, such as rooms in castles, manor houses and merchants' houses. Longthorpe Tower, from the mid-fourteenth century, is the most remarkable such survival. But it was by no means unique. In his will in 1518, Robert Throckmorton left a bequest and detailed instructions for the glazing of his church with representations of central texts of the catholic faith.[91] In Leicester twenty-nine theologically sophisticated panels of religious glass were made c.1490–5 for a house rather than for a church.[92]

Colin Morris has suggested that there is very little evidence that paintings in church were understood by ordinary worshippers.[93] Jacques Toussaert declared that 'ces magnifiques distractions spectaculaires' were only of value to those already well versed in religious doctrine.[94] But it might be more helpful to see levels of understanding rather than either full under-standing or total incomprehension.[95] Again, the stylistic or artistic quality of such work was variable. Was there a general decline in wall-painting after 1400, was it coarser in design and execution, tending to caricature, and to stiffer poses?[96] But while that might have reduced the aesthetic appeal (or not, given how subjective such tastes must be), that would not necessarily have reduced the educational effect of such visual display. Protestant reformers such as John Bale thought painted images harmful, because they gave the wrong impression. For example, he was concerned how people interpreted the descent into hell. They should not believe it as they saw it presented in painted cloths or glass windows, or as he had presented it himself in a play: they must not suppose that Christ actually fought violently with the devils for the souls of the faithful. The crucial difficulty pinpointed here was that artistic representations of the scriptures tended to stress the physical, the corporeal, the material, perhaps at the expense of the spiritual, let alone the theological, meaning. But the very vehemence of the reformers' objections does at least suggest that such paintings and sculptures made an impact. Where, one might also ask, had the reformers' superior understanding come from? Where and how had they acquired their first knowledge of christianity and how had they moved on to criticise aspects of it? Does that not suggest that the church was getting its message across, even if some were provoked to disagree?

The Easter Sepulchre illustrates both the impact and problems of visual images. A re-creation in hundreds of churches of Christ's tomb in Jerusalem, it was an important part of Easter liturgies. By the fourteenth century it was usually to be found near an altar on the north wall of the chancel. It housed receptacles that would hold a cross or a host to be symbolically buried in it on Good Friday, the day of Christ's crucifixion. They varied from simple recesses to large arched recesses with a chest, table tomb and canopy, sometimes with an effigy of the donor nearby, sometimes further decorated by images of sleeping soldiers, holy women to witness the emptiness of the tomb, Christ rising, and the apostles witnessing the ascension. Sometimes images of Christ were placed within the sepulchre and then raised on Easter morning to dramatise the resurrection. How effective as a means of instruction was this? Reformers such as John Hooper denounced it: 'The ploughman be he never so unlearned, shall better be instructed of Christ's death and passion by the corn that he soweth in the field and likewise of Christ's resurrection, then be all the dead posts that hang in the church, or pulled out of the sepulchre with *"Christ resurgens"* '.[97] Still, this does hint at the power of these images.

In late medieval England, especially from the later thirteenth century, there was a profusion of devotional images in parish churches, especially those of Mary and of the patron saint of the church, as well as of saints seen as effective intercessors against illness and ill-fortune. Such images were mostly carved in wood, painted, and usually set above ancillary altars. They were didactic: they were certainly intended to teach. But they were not just didactic. They were intended to stimulate devotion and to serve as focuses of such affective piety; parishioners would place lights in front of them. It is hard to think that such images did not make an impact, not least in an age less saturated by visual images than the present. Most parishioners would have been very much aware of them. Through them they would have learned about the role of the Virgin Mary and about the intercessions of saints. Of course, such images may, through their corporeality and their very artistic qualities, have distracted viewers from what some might regard as more proper, that is to say purer, devotion. Such images may have become not so much objects of reverence as incitements to idolatry. Clearly the church might here be vulnerable to critics who saw such images as an idolatrous outrage. Yet the depth of protestant reformers' hostility to these kinds of images does suggest that they had been effective in transmitting their message, however much it was at odds with reformed christianity or, for that matter, the best practice of the late medieval church.[98]

How far did the religious plays of the later middle ages increase religious knowledge and understanding? Especially elaborate and lavish outdoor plays based on episodes from the Bible were regularly performed at York, Chester, Coventry, Ipswich, Kendal, Newcastle, Beverley, Norwich, Wakefield, Worcester and Lincoln; and probably at Canterbury, Lancaster, Louth and Preston, too.[99] There may well have been more on that scale, and there were undoubtedly many smaller, parish-based productions, perhaps linked to particular saints or cults.[100] The earliest recorded play in York is in 1376, in Chester in 1422, but in both cases that does not mean that that was the year of first performance: it is more probable that the plays were already well established by that time.[101] By the early sixteenth century, mystery plays had become traditional, but there is nothing to suggest that they were going out of fashion. Even after allowing for the distortion arising from greater survival of evidence, it is clear that there were significant developments at Coventry in 1519–20, at Chester in 1521, and in Norwich after c.1527.[102] Such plays had several purposes. Obviously they fostered the civic pride of a city and of its craft gilds[103] (though craft gilds may have been as much the product as the creators of these play cycles: few gilds are known to have existed before the first recorded play).[104] The burghers of Jerusalem welcoming the arrival of Christ were visibly the leading citizens of York[105]—though it is fair to point out that this may have been intended to make the presence of Christ immediate and real, rather than to elevate the local worthies. A Chester proclamation of 1531–2 saw the aims of the play as 'not only for the Augmentation and increase [of the holy and catholic] faith of o[ur s]aviour Jesu Christ & to ex[h]ort the minds of the common people [to good devotion & wholesome] doctrine th[ereof] but also for commonwealth & prosperity of this City'.[106] In a dense and by no means consistent argument, it has been claimed that religious plays were intended to foster 'social wholeness' in towns particularly prone to 'social differentiation'; plays offered urban societies 'a mythology and ritual; in terms of which the opposites of social wholeness and social differentiation could be affirmed, and also brought into a creative tension, one with the other'; 'the final intention of the cult was . . . to express the social bond and to contribute to social integration'.[107] A worrying technical objection to such an argument is that it assumes that surviving plays are complete, or at least a typical sample. More fundamentally, it says very little about the religious aspects of plays. However much weight is given to the secular and political purposes they may have served, it remains the case that the forms that these plays took were religious. That makes the claim that they reflected essentially secular concerns, lay and civic, not least against a powerful ecclesiastical establishment, somewhat implausible, or at best incomplete.[108] It is more plausible that these plays were in some ways connected with, or possibly inspired by, the new cult of Corpus Christi, a feast declared by Urban IV in 1264 consisting of a procession bearing the host—the body of Christ—through the streets of the town, escorted by clergy and the hierarchy of gilds. Perhaps it became the custom for gilds to display scenes from scripture, possibly those relating to their particular craft, and in time these scenes turned into *tableaux vivants* and then into plays.[109] But these plays are also associated with Christmas, Easter and other liturgical feasts, for example, an Assumption play at Leicester and a Pentecost play at Lincoln— and it would be wrong to think of them as only a genre of Corpus Christi plays, not least since we do not always, as in the case of the N-Town/ Towneley plays, have evidence of when they were performed.[110] Perhaps such plays are best seen more generally as a working-out of the dramatic potential of the church's liturgy—for example, the Rogationtide procession punctuated by halts at a series of 'stations' at which the gospels were read.[111] Here it has been suggested that aspects of the liturgy, especially processions and the ceremonies at Easter, became increasingly theatrical in the fourteenth century.[112] Moreover, it may be that, as with the extended doctrine of purgatory, the clue to the elaboration of the mystery plays is to be found in the increasing relative prosperity of townspeople, and their growing concern with their salvation, now seen as an entirely reasonable expectation for those involved in crafts and commerce.[113] Some plays were a substitute for pilgrimages, with the processions serving as a sort of surrogate pilgrimage.[114] At Chester, bishops issued indulgences offering forty days' remission from purgatory to everyone coming 'in peaceable manner with good devotion' to hear and see the plays there.[115]

The plays were always orthodox, respectful, clear-cut.[116] They were based on scripture. They were didactic in form. They concentrated on the central points of the christian faith, and stressed the need for repentance

in order to gain salvation. They reflect a moralising strain in late medieval
piety: they were seeking to offer examples of how men and women should
conduct themselves and so attain heaven. Wicked characters—Cain, Satan,
Herod, Pilate—might, as so often in literature and art, have the best parts,
but their wickedness was always made quite plain. All these plays dealt with
God's intervention in the world, especially the nativity and passion of
Christ. Often they were in the form of a chronological narrative taken
from the Bible, beginning with the Fall, and working through Cain,
Noah, Abraham and Moses, then the life (but with little on the ministry),
crucifixion and resurrection of Christ, followed by the work of the apostles,
and finally the Last Judgment.[117] They were evidently carefully and deliberately constructed: they were not some sort of folk art or street art.[118]
The plays included material in English.[119] We can rarely be sure of
their authors, though it seems likely that a monk from St Werburgh's
Abbey was involved in the Chester cycle,[120] and more generally the texts,
given the integrity of their message, would seem to have been composed
by learned theologians.[121] They might seek to promote a special intensity
of religious feeling, especially an emphasis on the passion of Christ, rather
like the mystical piety of some late medieval cults, while aiming to channel
such feelings along orthodox paths of repentance.[122] They might aim
to encourage people to identify their own everyday lives with that
of Christ.[123]

Of course, it is difficult to know just how much participants and
audiences grasped and understood. Perhaps the rich and powerful and
educated were more likely to attend than the poor and ignorant; but
perhaps the poor could hardly avoid seeing the spectacle in the streets of the
town in which they lived. Surviving texts may give a misleading impression
of what was actually performed in the streets.[124] But it seems reasonable to
suppose that religious plays were intended to, and did, inculcate and reinforce some elementary knowledge and some basic truths. The tableaux
were often supported by speeches of commentary, drawing out the implications of what was being performed, and warning against erroneous, especially idolatrous, interpretations.[125] Not every town had a mystery play,
though we cannot be sure that we know all the places which had one: the
silence about London is especially puzzling.[126] But it is likely that there were
plays of some kind in a great many towns and villages.[127] Much recent
research, especially that stimulated by the work of the Records of Early
English Drama, has shown how much more there must have been in
parishes: churchwardens' accounts list payments for materials, for costumes,
for playbooks, to players—along, sometimes, with tantalisingly brief
references to the subject of the play.[128]

Laymen and laywomen who were able to read and who could afford to commission manuscripts, and, once printing was established, purchase printed books, did acquire a good many. That suggests considerable commitment and knowledge. The production of books of hours in the fifteenth and early sixteenth centuries has been seen as a massive catechetical enterprise by the church in which a remarkably homogeneous overall message was transmitted, however varied individual volumes were.[129] These works contained prayers, detailed meditations on the life and passion of Christ, and stories of saints' lives; they might include contemporary or recent works such as the monk of Evesham's revelation of the afterlife, or the writings of Walter Hilton or Richard Rolle, accounts of the mystic Margery Kempe, or Caxton's translation of the Golden Legend, or the *Imitation of Christ*.[130] And they were illustrated by illuminations. The large numbers of such works produced have been seen as evidence of a huge demand for such religious reading-matter—catechisms, primers, hagiography, prayers—and thus of religious awareness, knowledge and commitment among those who, thanks to growing prosperity from 1250, had the means to acquire them and the leisure to read them. What would they have learned from them? Some indeed were not written directly to educate: hagiographies may have been intended more to foster the claims of one monastery over another, rather than primarily to stimulate lay devotion. How far aristocratic ladies had sufficient Latin to read the texts with understanding is moot.[131] And maybe one of the functions of such books, especially those most lavishly decorated with jewels, ivory, gold and silver, and illuminated images of the Blessed Virgin Mary, was to evoke the sacred, to stir passionate devotion, rather than to convey specific doctrinal truths in words.[132] But all the same, taken together, such works do suggest an intense lay piety that was more than just convention or the indulgence of the leisured.

It is hard to study the devotion of Lady Margaret Beaufort, Henry VII's mother, without noting her informed commitment. She commissioned the printing of the *Ladder of Perfection* by Walter Hilton and the Fifteen Oes (prayers attributed to St Brigitte of Sweden). She translated part of the *Imitation of Christ* (that dealing with the eucharist) from French. She attended masses daily (Bishop Fisher is our witness), took part in daily prayers, received communion twelve times a year. She listened to sermons by Fisher (which were printed in 1509). She had a special devotion to the feast of the Holy Name of Jesus. She owned relics, including a piece of the holy cross set in gold, a shield displaying the five wounds of Christ, and a tablet bearing an image of the handkerchief with which St Veronica was said to have wiped the face of Christ. She commissioned an image of the Lord painted on a cloth. She maintained a chaplain to sing before the image of

Our Lady of Pity at Westminster Abbey. She gave alms to the poor and needy. She maintained a scholar, Richard Mayne, at the London Charterhouse and visited Sheen Charterhouse in 1488. She gave Fisher a large sum, which he in turn gave to St John's College, Cambridge. In 1504 she took a vow of chastity. Her biographers interpret all this as showing 'personal sobriety' and 'a certain intellectual austerity'. It went far beyond the conventional. We can be less sure just how much theological knowledge and understanding this evidence of actions, commissions and possessions implies, and she may well have had little Latin, but it would be condescending to rule out the possibility that she was well aware of the significances of what she was doing. Her relationship with the scholarly Bishop Fisher is especially noteworthy here.[133]

A sophisticated liturgical and theological understanding has been seen beneath the most conventional piety. Successive generations of the Hungerford gentry family conformed to the most advanced practice of their time, with their various provisions and preferences being suppressed in turn by the next generation, implying some awareness of old and new, some individuality of decision-making, even if they were largely following fashion.[134]

At least, that was so among the more affluent: clearly, labourers could neither afford nor, for the most part, read, contemporary devotional works. In consequence, there are difficult problems in judging how many heard, read or saw such material, and just what they made of it. But we must equally beware a condescending dismissal of the ability of ordinary people to grasp quite sophisticated ideas, or to absorb them even if they could not read. Illiteracy does not necessarily mean ignorance, much less stupidity.

Protestant reformers would think all this devotional material quite insufficient, even when it was not, in their eyes, plainly erroneous. They called for the more thorough and coherent exposition of the word of God through substantial sermons. But preaching and sermons were not uncommon; they were not the invention of the reformation. Our evidence is again patchy, but nonetheless suggestive. It had long become quite widespread to include within the mass a vernacular section—a prone—to summarise the gospel; but this was fairly elementary.[135] The survival of over 200 pre-reformation pulpits hints at the importance of preaching.[136] More generally, an important distortion has arisen from the dissolution of the monasteries. That dissolution included the friaries. Mostly located in towns, friaries often disappeared more completely than rural monasteries, and it is necessary to consider, say, the Blackfriars at Norwich, a rare substantial survival, in order to get a sense of the importance and dominance of friaries in late medieval towns. Friars were above all preachers, and thus friary churches were characterised by large, open naves, designed with preaching in mind.

Incidental references to friars' preaching suggest that it was frequent. Of course, to attend a sermon was not necessarily to understand it. Erasmus had heard of women returning from church who enthusiastically applauded the preacher and graphically described his countenance—but could not repeat a word he had said, or explain the course of his argument.[137] But that may be exaggerated, or reflect a misogynist scholar's disdain for ignorant women. What is more important here is to take due account of preaching by priests and friars as an important means of instructing the laity in the faith. We have few details. But we learn from William Barlow, bishop of St David's, that three or four hundred attended a sermon in the cathedral on the feast of Holy Innocents in 1538: Barlow's tone suggests that this was by no means unusual.[138]

Protestant critics of the late medieval church (and their modern admirers) would make a great deal of the unavailability of the Bible to the laity. Indeed, no English-language version was allowed in England. That allegedly meant considerable lay ignorance which allowed the church to impose weekly, daily, hourly ceremonies, and doctrines such as purgatory and practices such as penance and auricular confession which, protestants alleged, were not to be found in the Bible properly regarded as 'the Word of God as originally written'. According to the modern biographer of Tyndale, 'The Church would never permit a complete printed New Testament in English from the Greek, because in that New Testament can be found neither the Seven Sacraments nor the doctrine of purgatory, two chief sources of the Church's power'. There was, he adds, a 'collective sigh of relief that accompanied the removal of a thousand-year-old wall built by the Church between the people and the Bible'.[139] Here the modern scholar is echoing the early reformers. Thomas Patmore, a draper accused of heresy in 1531, declared that the truth of scripture had been kept from them for a long time.[140] Yet there is little evidence that laymen and laywomen were clamouring to have the Bible in the vernacular. That the church's intentions were less conspiratorially selfish is surely shown by the willingness of churches in countries whose authorities were less troubled by recent heresy to allow the publication of vernacular translations of the Bible from the Vulgate—in German in 1466, 1470, and seven more by 1483, in French from c.1474; in Italian in 1471; in Catalan in 1478; in Czech in 1488; and in Dutch in 1477.[141] Beyond that, to say that 'an elementary working knowledge of the Bible, the ultimate root of the Christian faith, could only have been developed within Protestantism'[142] is to adopt a particular interpretation of what the christian message was. If belief in justification-by-faith-alone and its elevation to the central doctrine of christianity is the test against which understanding of christian teachings and of knowledge of the Bible are being judged, then, indeed, the middle ages were unchristian and ignorant. Yet such a deduction is not as significant in any evaluation of what the laity knew and understood as might at first be supposed. After all, if they did not know what the church did not attempt to teach, then the ignorance of which reformers complained was a feature not of the laity but of the church as a whole—bishops and theologians included. In fact, access to the Bible was far greater in medieval christendom than the reformers' criticisms would seem to imply. Any serious scholar would learn Latin and be readily able to read the Vulgate Bible. It is worth noting in passing that the absence of the Bible in English was not total. A few texts were to be found in monastic libraries.[143] And the essentials of the christian message, as the church saw them, were necessarily distilled for the edification of the less learned. Such distillations included stories from the scriptures and extracts in such devotional and liturgical works as books of hours and primers, lives of Christ, meditations, in which quotation, paraphrase and free comment were combined. Our Father, Hail Mary, the Creed and the Ten Commandments were readily available in English. Apologists for the late medieval church see such works as going 'a long way towards satisfying lay eagerness for knowledge of the Gospels'; its critics dismiss works such as Nicholas Love's *Mirror of the Blessed Life of Jesus Christ* as 'the Gospels-as-pap'.[144] What such criticisms of the medieval church do helpfully point to, however, is its potential vulnerability to the scripturally based critique to which it was subjected in the early sixteenth century. It was open to the charge that it concealed—and burnt—the Word of God. And the Bible in its richness and ambiguities did offer scope for the development of different emphases of the christian message, although there was nothing inevitable about such a process. That fear underlay Pope Paul V's rhetorical question in 1607, with nearly a century of the division of christendom behind him: 'do you not know that so much reading of scripture destroys the catholic religion?'[145] But it is a protestant shibboleth that lay reading of the vernacular Bible is indispensable to christian understanding. Art, images and the stories drawn from devotional works could take unlettered laymen and laywomen a long way.

Has all the discussion of what people knew been fatally flawed, however, because popular religion essentially consisted of an underlying pagan-cum-magical religious understanding upon which christianity had more or less been superimposed, but without making much impact? Was christianisation incomplete and shallow? Was the christianity we have been considering in this chapter no more than the views of a minuscule bookish clerical elite? And was that elite brutally oppressing a superficially christianised mass of people living in a world of oral culture and magic—in short, steeped in rural superstition?[146] Were most people absorbed in such a magical and superstitious world consequently indifferent to, or opposed to, the established church?[147] Was there a body of religious practices specific to the lower laity, a good part of which was reprehended by the church—at least by the higher clergy—as a survival of pagan ritual?[148] What should we make of cunning men, astrologers, witches and wizards, wise-women? Was there a host of recreational, sexual, healing, marital and folkloric customs, showing plebeian autonomy, custom and initiative, amalgamated with more official religious practices, but often attacked by the church?[149] How far did bishops use the term 'superstition' to eliminate unauthorised cults? How did such cults survive in popular memory into the nineteenth century?[150] However interesting such speculation might be, in the end 'there is not much evidence that pagan survivals, [or] magical beliefs . . . formed a genuinely alternative belief-system or ideology to which peasants in general gave more adherence than they did to the church'.[151] What could be found were various 'utterly disjointed' beliefs, notably about spirits and demons whose malevolence and supranatural powers might do people harm,[152] disjointed beliefs which were not in themselves part of a systematic and coherent alternative faith, and by no means incompatible with entirely conventional attendance at church services. Even in the immediate post-conversion period there is very little evidence indeed of surviving or residual pagan worship: 'the spiritual culture of the eighth- and ninth-century English countryside was christian'.[153] Indeed, it may well be that it was intellectual clerics who were fascinated by magic—by formulae, and by bizarre charms.[154] Pressure for prosecutions of witches may have come from ordinary people, but the theory of witchcraft was elaborated and systematised by an educated elite. And protestant reformers may have exaggerated what they saw as idolatrous aspects of the medieval church.

More plausible than to postulate some independent semi-underground pagan survival is to reflect on how far laymen and laywomen might have distorted official and learned christianity by developing what were arguably semi-magical practices within it. Was the laity's understanding of christianity essentially a distortion of it as a semi-magical faith? And did the church continue to make too many concessions to such attitudes, just as the earliest Anglo-Saxon church had, while condemning idolatry and sacrifices, nonetheless won over pagans by absorbing a good deal of their charms and cures, by building a christian church or erecting a cross on the site of springs or trees or rocks or woods popularly regarded as possessing magical powers?[155] The host could be seen as possessing magical qualities, especially of healing. Much the same was true of attitudes to relics, for example, the girdle of Our Lady that Henry VII's queen hired when pregnant.[156] Thomas

More gives an account of a Franciscan friar, preaching in Coventry, who asserted that whoever repeated daily the psalter of the Virgin would escape damnation: a parish priest who warned his parishioners from the pulpit against this was abused as an enemy to the Virgin.[157] Masses could be seen in magical terms, trivialising the intellectual content of faith.[158] If one mass was good, then surely several masses were better. In the later middle ages it became increasingly fashionable to pile up masses. Long before, monks had said hundreds or thousands of masses, for example at Fulda and Saint-Riquier for the family of Holy Roman Emperors, or at Cluny. Eleventh- and twelfth-century lay patrons made offerings in hundreds. Yet those figures were more symbolic of profusion, of a multitude, or they were symbolic in using numbers such as five for the five wounds of Christ; they did not involve careful counting and accounting. Monasteries, it is true, were devoted to *perpetual* prayer. But, especially in fourteenth-century France, wills began to suggest an arithmetical, accumulative approach. Testators sought the maximum possible prayers and masses in the first hours, days and months after death. 'Desormais, le passage dans l'au-delà parait avoir une durée variable que chaque testateur semble evaluer, mesurer, en prevoyant avec soin les celebrations [from now on, entry into the afterlife seemed to be of variable duration, which each testator appeared to measure and to calculate, carefully preparing the celebration of masses]'.[159] There was a multiplication, a 'parcellisation' [a division] of bequests, to as many as fifteen to twenty beneficiaries.[160] Indulgences—rewards granted by the pope or by bishops in return for some worthy action, from going on crusade to making a charitable donation to the church, but, crucially, rewards which specified precisely how many days or years of remission from the pains of purgatory the recipient would enjoy—were collected and accumulated. Perhaps the precision reflected legal provisions of an earlier age when penalties for offences were set according to a complex tariff.[161] A strange book-keeping developed.[162] 'Avec l'essor de la piété flamboyante, la quête de Dieu, qui avait été le fondement de toute la religiosité médiéval, dégenère en une comptabilité de l'au-delà [with the flourishing of such ostentatious piety, the search for God, which had been the foundation of all medieval religious sentiment, degenerated into a book-keeping of the afterlife]'.[163] Some churchmen—such as Thomas Arundel (1353–1414), archbishop of Canterbury—did object to crudely material worship of relics.[164] The development of the Corpus Christi feast has been seen as, in part, an attempt to wean the citizens of York away from superstitious temptations and to promote sorrowful compassion instead.[165] All this raises the question of ecclesiastical control. How far were liturgies and devotions, in practice, compromises which accommodated the desires of the faithful? Was popular religion contributing to the creation of orthodoxy, not just being policed by it? How far was popular religion a blending of popular practices with initiatives from above?[166]

It is important to note that, if the laity were indeed developing extra-liturgical and semi-magical practices, then that contradicts the supposition that they knew little of the christian faith. Such extensions or distortions of the truths of christianity imply some sort of comprehension, even if these went off into superstitious directions. Moreover, if people were inarticulate, stupid, ignorant, spasmodically taking the practice of a faith they half understood into more magical directions, then they would hardly seem to be good material for a protestant conversion. It was rather the extent to which the official church made concessions, in effect, to popular attitudes that rendered it vulnerable to Erasmian and protestant critiques.[167] Late medieval clergy did not speak with one voice: some, especially the less educated, may well have shared the more magical views of the laity.[168] The veneration of saints has been seen as precariously balanced between magic and religion.[169] The distinction between magic and miracles was difficult. Prayers were intended to be intercessions rather than attempts to harness supernatural power. Yet the eucharist was a daily miracle. And even the most sensitive defender of medieval miracles sees a vulgarisation in the fourteenth and fifteenth centuries, a decline from the high middle ages.[170] Had 'the element of superstition become disproportionately great in the late medieval church', with much that bordered on idolatry and magic?[171] Had biblical stories become 'entangled in a web of fantasy'?[172] We shall return to this when looking at pilgrimages and the cult of saints in a subsequent chapter.

Against such critics, Eamon Duffy has attempted a vigorous defence of late medieval religion, questioning the distinction between an educated, cerebral, rational understanding of christianity, and a lay, popular, magical approach. It is worth noting that such a claim fails to take account of the wealth of writing by late medieval theologians precisely criticising what they saw as superstitious practices, trying to distinguish what was accept-able from what was not.[173] Moreover, the weakness in Duffy's approach is that such a playing down of differences will lead to the conclusion that late medieval religion generally could be seen as 'magical'.[174] Duffy concedes that a good deal of *all* late medieval religion, clerical and lay, elite and popular, went beyond the text of scripture,[175] that it was interwoven with non-christian divisions and uses of time, that the piety expressed in the belief in the power of the mass to heal was somewhat credulous,[176] that straightforward catechetical instructions were often mixed with charms,[177] that certain passages of the Bible, or books such as primers, were seen as holy in their own right,[178] that prayers were, at one level, close to spells and charms,[179] that apocryphal legends proliferated,[180] that the *Horae* were full of charm-invocations,[181] that belief in the physical presence of the devil was widespread.[182]

That such semi-magical understandings should have been socially and geographically ubiquitous is not surprising. Jacques Toussaert, assessing the religious sensibility of the inhabitants of late medieval Flanders, claimed that 'christianisés, ils cherchent toujours aide et protection dans leurs diffi-cultés de la vie, très particulièrement lors des malheurs multiples du moyen-âge, ils s'agenouillent aux pieds de ceux qui, de près ou de loin, peuvent les aider [once christianised, they were always seeking help and protection in the face of life's hardships, most especially as the manifold misfortunes of middle age beset them, kneeling at the feet of those who, near or far, could help them]'.[183] In *Religion and the Decline of Magic*, Keith Thomas elaborated such an analysis and articulated an 'enlightened', 'liberal' view of religion—especially of its superstitious and semi-magical forms—as the result of inadequate scientific knowledge and lack of technological control. He claimed that 'Men were locked into a system of belief in the supranat-ural by the brute facts of life—a hazardous, unpredictable world could only be understood in terms of the operation of possibly arbitrary spiritual forces'. Life was nasty, brutish and short. Infant mortality was high. A half to a third of the population lived close to subsistence. Fires were common in towns. Most people were frequently in pain. Dietary deficiencies led to a variety of diseases. Epidemics were common. Primitive medicine was expen-sive, ineffective and dangerous. Agricultural production was at the mercy of the weather. Livestock were prone to diseases. Shipwreck disrupted coastal and overseas trade. It is arguably not surprising that men and women sought assistance from supernatural power. As George Gifford (1547/8–1609), a clergyman of puritanical inclinations, put it, 'for this is man's nature, that where he is persuaded that there is the power to bring pros-perity and adversity, there will he worship'.[184] Those sentiments were vividly expressed by the Victorian poet Arthur Hugh Clough who observed that 'almost everyone when age/ Disease, or sorrows strike him/ Inclines to think there is a God/ Or something very like him'. Is this a sufficient explanation of medieval religion? The evidence of cults and pilgrimages is telling. How far did the terror of plague stimulate religious devotion and bequests? Is it significant that there was a dramatic increase in offerings to cathedral shrines in the second half of the fourteenth century?[185] As we shall see, seven out of ten of the miracles attributed to Henry VI involved cures of illnesses or injuries or physical afflictions.[186] Henry VIII's devotions increased in intensity during the sweating sickness of 1528.[187] It was not just

the king: the French ambassador—not without a note of cynicism—
reported that 100,000 wills were said to have been made and the notaries
were having a fine time of it.[188] All this devotion stimulated by suffering
does suggest at least some sort of understanding and commitment. And
maybe it explains the semi-magical character of late medieval piety?

Yet such an interpretation is open to fundamental objections. The most
telling difficulty is that of explaining how and why these sorts of beliefs in
a magical universe, and especially the fear of magic, disappeared from the
attitudes of educated members of the English elite in the seventeenth
century. That shift to a markedly increased degree of scepticism and ration-
alism, and a new confidence in the potential of human action in this world,
did not correspond with any obvious change in man's control over the environment, not least over disease: plague, disease, fire and flood continued to
wreak their devastating effects; and yet in the minds of the elite these were
less and less seen in magical ways. And that development has implications
for our understanding of late medieval religion, suggesting that 'lack of
control over the environment had not been a sufficient condition for the
holding of magical beliefs'.[189] The link between distress and religious
conviction proves to be more tenuous than it first seemed.

Even so, perhaps it is unwise to suppose conscious thought on such
questions. People did not choose their religion in the way that it is often—
perhaps wrongly—supposed that people choose their religion (or their
politics) today. They rather grew up in a world in which they absorbed the
religion and took part in the religious practices of their parents and relatives, and their locality. Watching and taking part preceded learning,
knowing and understanding. Did this trivialise central aspects of the faith,
draining them of their intellectual content?[190] Was religious observance
merely mechanical, coarsened, lax, cheapened and trivialised?[191] Were the
majority of people singularly inarticulate and confused about their faith?[192]
Was this a religion in which doing was more important than learning and
understanding?[193] Did church music foster a sense of devotion far more than
understanding? Was it more important that the laity should assume a
proper and necessary role in the drama of the mass rather than develop and
show an intellectual grasp of eucharistic doctrine? They were observers
rather than participants at masses: 'the people of the time were witnesses of
a ritual rather than the holders of a faith'.[194] How far did, and could, people
understand the complex theological doctrine of transubstantiation? It has
been powerfully argued that for the laity the mass was 'less a ceremonial
representation of eucharistic doctrine or Christ's original sacrifice than a
sacred rite uniting them with God, the Church and each other'. The laity
were like courtiers at court: their presence was necessary, and gave a sort of

'gestural consent'. Lay participants would have made connections between the mass and secular ceremonies: standing, doffing of hats, saluting, kneeling were part of the ceremonies of secular lordship; the offertory was comparable to almsgiving.[195] But in that sense the mass 'se réduit le plus souvent pour eux à une série de gestes magiques [was most often reduced in their eyes to a succession of magical gestures]'.[196] It might, of course, have chanced that 'the same people who in their daily life mechanically follow the routine of a rather degraded sort of worship will be capable of rising suddenly, at the ardent word of a preaching monk, to unparalleled heights of religious emotion'.[197] Yet that, by and large, did not happen in late medieval England. Margery Kempe's uncontrollable weepings are the most stunning English manifestation: any account of her life readily shows that while she was never wholly without clerical admirers, she was effectively marginalised.[198] Bouts of extreme asceticism, practices such as flagellation, characteristic of Italy, northern Germany and the Low Countries, are not so readily found in England. And few charismatic preachers lit up the fire of faith in late medieval England.[199]

If much of late medieval religion was thus largely conventional, if what men and women had absorbed was some sense of the humanity of Christ, including the great moments of his life, especially the passion, an emotional attachment to the intercession of the Virgin and of the saints, some grasp of the lives of saints and the miracles attributed to them, but little grasp of theology—that is to say, the underlying ideas that connected and explained what would otherwise be disparate actions or events—then, however consoling, such a faith was not well placed to defend itself against more searching intellectual critiques. Would it not leave even those who were most visibly devout vulnerable and empty-handed when that faith was challenged? How could such lay folk defend themselves against those who claimed that doctrinally informed understanding and participation were essential?[200]

A somewhat different tack is taken by those historians of the continental reformation who have gone so far as to explain it as a reaction against the excessive burdens of late medieval piety, especially the confession, which included, if confessors' manuals are to be believed, increasingly intimate questions about sexual misconduct. If the practice of confession was indeed oppressive, that would at least suggest that the laity were being made very directly aware of what knowledge and behaviour were expected of them. But it is much more likely that confession was not so terrifying, that it was less a special moment of searching one's conscience, more a rite of seasonal purification, 'une toilette [a cleansing]' more than a burden.[201]

How fearful were people? How far is it true that 'late medieval men and women lived in fear of damnation in the after-life, and the whole gamut of their worship and beliefs was designed to provide reassurance at the moment of death'?[202] Did the disasters of plague and associated infectious diseases reinforce this? The multiplication of indulgences and masses for the dead has been seen as prompted by just such unease.[203] The increasing theatricality of worship, and its more obsessive character, has been seen as reflecting a heightened fear of death, anxiety about the world beyond, and even terror that God and the saints will irremediably desert men and leave them to an awful destiny: 'le sentiment d'être toujours trop loin d'un Dieu qui échappe desormais à toute saisie intellectuelle [the feeling of always being too far away from a God who from now on evaded any intellectual grasp]'.[204] This reflected not some decadence but rather 'une malaise dans la civilisation'. The exaltation of the consecrated host has been seen as a compensation for the rarity of communion. Yet while the adoration of the host offered a personal link with God, it was nevertheless unsatisfyingly distant; it did not reflect the assimilation offered by communion, through the memory of the Last Supper. That led to a sense of isolation, an aware- ness of the immeasurable distance between God and man. The need to see the host again and again, everywhere, has been interpreted as evidence that for the majority of the faithful, the sight of the sacrament within the mass was not sufficient. 'La ferveur ne fait aucun doute, mais l'éclatement des dévotions, l'obsession de la présence réelle, l'accumulation des suffrages trahissent cependant une crise de tous les rapports avec l'au-delà [Their zeal was not in doubt, but the splintering of their devotions, the obsession with the real presence, the piling up of prayers betrayed, however, a crisis in all relationships with the afterlife]'. Nominalist philosophy led to doubts that it was possible to reach God by reason. People were, above all, afraid of a solitary death, without rites. Moreover, they were, it has been claimed, conscious of a new solitude, deracinated, cut off from their ancestors, orphans, in an age of plague, high mortality and migration. Masses were a desperate, yet ultimately unsuccessful, attempt to recreate such links. Mysticism—efforts to reach God personally through prayers and devotions, undertaken with great emotional intensity—was another response to this perceived void. Late medieval men and women were ever conscious of, and frightened by, the presence of devils.[205] It was a powerful, if somewhat vague, evocation of fear of damnation and fear of spiritual solitude.

Such an argument does, it might be noted, again suggest a good deal of knowledge and understanding of christian teachings, even if not always understood in the ways that we ourselves would, together with significant levels of dissatisfaction. But is it well founded? Can one speak in such

generalised terms of 'une grande melancolie [a great sorrow]'? Were not
these experiences those of an exceptional devout minority, of fearful individuals? True, if *some*, especially among those who took their faith most
seriously, were fearful, and ever conscious of the distance that separated
them from God, then that would point to another area of vulnerability for
the late medieval church. Luther's struggle with salvation irresistibly comes
to mind here.[206] Yet it does not seem probable that the majority of men and
women spent most of their lives in a state of religious unease, that they were
more pious, less worldly, than their successors.[207] Reading sources based on
state papers, such as the volumes of *Letters and Papers of Henry VIII*, does
not offer much evidence of desperation about the world to come, rather a
mixture of a relish for life with a concern for practical day-to-day details.
Even the monasteries—perhaps especially the monasteries—appear dominated by secular and practical concerns, as we shall see in a later chapter.

Whatever one thinks of the overall picture derived from visitations, there
can be little doubt that *some* clergy and monks and nuns were so little
worried about retribution in the world to come that they were prepared to
risk their souls by breaking their vows. And as for the laity, William Langland,
writing in the 1380s, remarked that 'The mooste partie of this peple that
passeth on this erthe/ Have thei worship in this world, thei wilne no bettre;/
Of oother hevene than here holde thei no tale [the majority of those who live
out their lives on this earth, if they enjoy worldly success and a high reputation, desire nothing better; they can't be bothered about any other heaven
than that here]'.[208] 'The thing that we desire most in this world is to live long
and the thing that we most fear is to die soon,' said the shepherd in the early
sixteenth-century *Shepherd's Kalendar*. It is revealing that the subsequent
reproof, 'a man ought to perform his life in this world corporally that they
may live spiritually without end', nevertheless adds 'and also by this point
and none otherwise shall be accomplished the desire of long living in this
world'.[209] How much scepticism was there? Margaret Roper's sister laughed
when seeing Thomas More's hairshirt:[210] does that hint at a broader scepticism, unlikely to be recorded in our sources unless it was seen as evidence of
unacceptable heresy, about piety and ascetic practices? Bishop Longland
informed Cardinal Wolsey in 1525 that the king approved his proposals
to bind merchants and stationers under recognisances never to import
forbidden books: the king approved this, especially the recognisances, which
many would fear more than excommunication.[211] This is a revealing perception: the risk of financial penalty in this world was seen as more fear-
inspiring than the threat of eternal damnation. An act against forestalling
and regrating of fish spoke of many of the king's subjects as 'nothing
regarding the displeasure of Almighty God and of the King's Highness'.[212]

Moreover, the argument that reformers were releasing people from fear seems misconceived. As has been pointed out, protestants and catholics alike saw the fear of judgment and punishment as inescapable and offering useful 'moral regulation in this world'. Reformers had a 'vision of a right-eous God who decreed eternal punishments for the wicked and . . . expected fear to animate but not to overwhelm his servants'. 'That any writer should simply seek to banish fear on the grounds that it contributed to the misery of the human condition was quite inconceivable.' Protestants invoked hell rather than purgatory, arguably more frightening. What the reformers were liberating men and women from was not fear of hell but rather what they saw as the confidence trick of purgatory, and from all the financial costs of providing masses and chantries and so forth.[213] Reformers would offer the certainty of salvation through faith rather than the uncertainty of always having to do more—though whether, given human frailty, that was altogether a more comfortable position than always being able to hope to do better, is a matter of judgement.

Here it is worth noting that it obscures rather than enlightens to see organ-ised religion as no more than a means of social control, as the ideological expression of a moralising concern for order and discipline. Undoubtedly, christian teachings had immense, even implacable, implications for how men and women should live, how they should behave towards each other, empha-sising chastity, sobriety, duty, charity. Such ideals permeate all manifestations of christianity over the centuries. But they readily spring from the hope of salvation—or the fear of damnation—in the world to come: there is no need to invoke social control in order to make sense of them.[214] Nor should christian teachings be seen as the ideology of a controlling political elite: if Jesus did not espouse any kind of active political engagement, if he believed in rendering to Caesar that which was Caesar's. Nonetheless, the thrust of Christ's appeal to all men and women, to each and every one of them as individual human beings, to renounce all worldly things and join him, was potentially deeply subversive of human social hierarchy.

But it may well be the case that more people in the later middle ages were trying to live model christian lives, stimulated by the example of the saints and by the writers they read. How far did people respond to the dynamic seen as shaping religious culture from the eleventh century onwards—namely to go beyond the normal obligations and to try to share in the life of priests and monks, through household 'devotions, books of hours, asceticism, penitential actions, charitable giving'?[215] Vitality indeed; but vulnerability also, since the efforts of those who strove to live better danger-ously showed up the inadequacies of those who did not.

6

LAY ACTIVITY

L AYMEN were much involved in the running of parish churches. They might hold the advowson—the right to choose the parish priest. They could employ chaplains. At a lower social level, they served as church-wardens, typically a two-year tour of duty involving the financing and administration of the parish church, an office which seems to have developed in the early to mid-fourteenth century. Surviving churchwardens' accounts (nine from the fourteenth century, thirty-three from 1400–49, seventy-five from 1450–99 and 196 from 1500–49[1]) show in remarkable detail the close supervision that churchwardens exerted over all aspects of parochial religion, including the provision of charity, tax collection and even military organisation.[2] They also, intriguingly, show that twenty-five women served as churchwardens between 1425 and 1547.[3] It is unnecessary to postulate grand theories of 'communalism' or 'communalisation' or to see churchwardens as controlling parish clergy; rather, the work of church-wardens illustrates the extent and range of lay involvement in the church. From the thirteenth century, and very likely in places well before, parish churches became less proprietorial (that is, controlled by a single large land-owner) in character and more reflections of the local communities in which they stood. Laymen had come to be involved as office-holders and collectors and treasurers of revenues. Parish churches and churchyards were never exclusively devotional: sheep were grazed in churchyards, markets and fairs were held, not least since naves of churches were the only large indoor communal space available to them, prompting a range of attempts to enforce more seemly order on holy places. Church houses were built in the fifteenth century so that such profane activities, including church ales intended to raise money for the church, did not have to take place in the church itself.[4] Laymen, and to some extent laywomen, were active in gilds and confraternities, in the rebuilding of churches. They took part in processions. They were involved in the running of hospitals and schools. If they lived in towns, they had a considerable choice of churches to which they could go for religious services. If wealthy, they made complex provisions for their funerals—choosing whether to be buried in a monastery (in the high middle ages), in a friary church (especially popular in the late thirteenth century), or in their parish churches (increasingly the preferred location by the fifteenth century)—and for their souls, perhaps taking over the initiative from the clergy.[5] Of course, all this may well have concerned only a minority of the laity, but it was nonetheless a significant and socially and politically influential minority. No doubt some may have taken part out of a sense of duty or social obligation. But when all these qualifications have been made, it remains hard to doubt that such activity must have demanded, and stimulated, a fair level of knowledge and understanding of the christian message.

The fifteenth and early sixteenth centuries were a great age of church rebuilding—the subject of my current research—and however much some of the most famous examples were the gift of individual wealthy benefactors, nevertheless there are many examples of contributions from a large cross-section of benefactors. It is hard to stand, say, at the west end of the nave of Cullompton, Devon, and remain entirely sceptical about the vitality of the late medieval church. This chapter will consider remarkable illustrations of that vitality in which the activity of the laity was central: confraternities and chantries; and pilgrimage.

(i) Confraternities and Chantries

Confraternities and chantries were extraordinarily flourishing features of the late medieval church. But in their very strengths there also lay certain weaknesses. They were not part of the essential core of the official church. No canonical legislation, no general council, dealt with them before Trent. Bishops rarely took any interest in confraternities, not including them in their visitations. Their rise and development were in a sense unplanned. They were not imposed from above. They went back to the high middle ages and presumably reflected a depth of lay piety that went beyond what a parish church and conventional worship could offer. They may well have been influenced by the apostolic ideals of the eleventh and twelfth centuries as reflected in models of piety of prayer for fellow monks and veneration of saints by means of the maintenance of a wax candle at a relic, as practised notably by Benedictine monasteries (the earliest references to confraternities are to St Peter, Abbotsbury Abbey, 1016), adjusted for a more secular setting. Colleges of secular priests, without parochial responsibilities, especially in towns, and urban craft gilds, many of which included a devotional dimension, offered further models. Nevertheless, confraternities were, in many ways, part and parcel of the life of parish churches, which they might enhance, and it would be wrong to see them as an institution necessarily apart from the mainstream.[6]

The very existence of confraternities testifies to levels of devotion. Where membership of the parish was automatic, joining a confraternity was, allowing for all sorts of social pressures, an exercise of free choice.[7] Men and women would not have been prepared to give time and money for such purposes without some degree of conviction that this might be worthwhile. Whether parish fraternities were the 'truest expression of medieval men and women's priorities and preoccupations' is impossible to say. But clearly they were important. In late medieval London some 150 to 200 different voluntary associations of laymen and laywomen have been traced, half of them first recorded in the later fourteenth century, but new foundations continued to be established into the sixteenth century.[8] Some confraternities became wealthy. The Gild of the Blessed Virgin Mary at Boston had, in the 1520s, after sending a hugely expensive delegation (including Thomas Cromwell) to the papal *curia* in Rome, acquired a perpetual Jubilee indulgence, that is to say that anyone who visited the church on the Marian feasts, and went from altar to altar three times, would secure remission from the pains of purgatory (a matter to which we shall return). The *Scala Celi* (ladder of heaven) indulgence (granted at a celebrated chapel in Rome) was tied to the altar of the gild chapel. Collectors were sent around much of southern England (their expenses absorbing a quarter of the receipts). The gild's indulgence receipts peaked at £1,550 in 1521–2. If individuals typically gave 2s 6d then that implies some 10,000 subscribers.[9] The gild of Holy Cross at Stratford-upon-Avon and that of Holy Trinity at Coventry were among the greatest, with a large membership, drawn from all over the country. There were three significant fraternities in Salisbury, two Jesus gilds in St Thomas and St Edmund's, and the Holy Ghost fraternity in St Martin's.[10] There were five pious confraternities in Norwich.[11] The Corpus Christi gild at York included many noblemen and gentry among its members.[12] In some towns such confraternities proliferated: there were seventy in King's Lynn, forty in Bodmin.[13] But in other cities, such as Bristol, there were few.[14] It is not clear why such variations occurred. It may have been a response to particular circumstances, but it may simply reflect the chance incidence of individual pious commitment.

What did those lay folk who founded confraternities seek? Why did their own parish church not satisfy their needs? There are virtually no theoretical treatises which can enlighten us. Nor do the administrative records of confraternities explicitly touch on theological issues. These must rather be inferred from requests and actions.[15] Some confraternities were clearly founded to meet some specific, practical problem: the repair of a church, the provision of water, remedies for a natural disaster.[16] Some people were noticeably very concerned with the salvation of their soul and those of their families. Here the belief in purgatory was crucial: and so obvious and widespread that it did not need to be spelled out. If the sufferings of souls in purgatory could be assuaged by prayers and masses said on their behalf, then the benefits of establishing institutions to offer such assistance are clear. Every confraternity would employ a chaplain, which ensured that such prayers and masses were said.[17] Moreover, confraternities would often be dedicated to particular intercessors—whether saints, the Virgin, or Christ himself, in the growing cult of the Corpus Christi—allowing members to call upon that special aid. The confraternity ensured that its members received as much help as it could give after they died. It arranged the burial and associated masses. That met a real concern. It arranged prayers and masses for the souls of departed members: the fear of a solitary death, bereft of holy rites, terrified contemporaries more than anything else.[18] Above all, it held an annual mass followed by a feast which all members were supposed to attend in order to reinforce the prayers for those who had gone before. That marked out a confraternity from a simple chantry.[19] In 1410, 108 out of 245 members attended the feast of Holy Cross, Stratford-upon-Avon; 200 often gathered at the feast of Corpus Christi, Coventry.[20] Such days might be marked by processions and a series of church services. Interestingly, these masses do not appear to have involved lay communion.[21] Much care was given to the arrangement of the annual feast.[22] A member of a confraternity could enjoy the expectation that his soul would be given appropriate and substantial assistance after he died.

Confraternities pre-date the Black Death, but perhaps it is not surprising that the half-century following it saw the greatest flowering of confraternities, at a time when mortality was high and sudden, and could leave people without relatives and friends to pray for them. In some broad sense, then, confraternities were substitute families, perhaps attractive to migrants, but analysis of early fifteenth-century French confraternities suggests that over half the members joined as married couples, showing that they were not then primarily institutions for the widowed, orphaned or abandoned.[23] The pioneers may have joined from religious commitment; once such institutions were long-established, motives may have been more mixed. Some may have followed the example of older family members; others may have been stimulated by seeing the chapels maintained by the confraternities in the parish church.[24] It was not necessary to pass any test or undergo any ceremonies of initiation, at least in so far as the statutes are a full guide to members' obligations.[25] Some who joined were no doubt pious. Others may simply have been joining what, at one level, were dining clubs, occasions of conviviality, or associations of the important men in a town, with whom business might be done, including lending or borrowing money, or local disputes resolved, though even such members may have welcomed the element of insurance against suffering in the afterlife. On occasion, the annual feast degenerated into a display of gluttony, which became a target for satirists and, later, protestant reformers.[26] Possibly the erection and use of their own buildings, sometimes distant from the parish church, reinforced such secularising trends.[27]

The experience of confraternities was very varied. Some grew rich and were able to employ several clergy, to contribute to the maintenance and rebuilding of the churches in which they were housed, not through their members' physical labour, but by supplying funds, and to offer charity to the poor, however symbolic or didactic, rather than practical, this was.[28] Such confraternities might in time take on responsibility for local good works, such as the maintenance of roads, bridges and wells, and in a broader sense look after the interests of the town or village.[29] But it would be straining the evidence to see these as a 'bourgeois' movement against 'feudal-aristocratic' control of towns, much less a 'democratic' movement, though those most involved are likely to have been the leading merchants in towns and the *coqs de villages*, if only because they were best placed to make contributions to running costs.[30] Others led a less settled existence and appear only intermittently in the records, though dissolutions (as opposed to unions) of confraternities were unusual.[31] Joining a confraternity meant paying an annual subscription, which obviously confined membership to the relatively better off; but, if the poorest were in effect excluded, some humbler craftsmen were to be found as members, for example in the Gild of the Assumption of Our Blessed Lady at Westminster.[32]

It would be impossible to guess what proportion of the population were members. It has been estimated that in Devon and Cornwall in the years 1535–41 there was an average of five gilds in towns and six in villages; as many as 57 per cent of testators making wills in those counties in 1520–9 left bequests to religious gilds. In other regions the percentage was lower: 24 per cent in Somerset, 14–15 per cent in Durham, York and Lincoln archdeaconry, 10 per cent in Huntingdon archdeaconry, 5 per cent in Suffolk and 2 per cent in the archdeaconry of Buckingham in 1520–30.[33] Confraternities, like all collective organisations, required a certain number of people in order to function; that meant that they were more likely to develop and to prosper in centres of population than in sparsely inhabited rural areas. Apart from that, there was nothing necessarily urban about confraternities, and some can be found in the country. Active members of the larger urban gilds were, however, likely to be leading merchants and craftsmen; noblemen and gentry members of confraternities did not play a very active part.[34]

It would be wrong to see confraternities as in some sense apart from, or hostile to, the parish churches. Indeed, by employing additional clergy, as chaplains, they might serve to increase the divine service available, notably providing additional weekday masses. They may well have played a spectacular part in making possible the development of polyphonic music in the later middle ages, financing the essential professional choirs. At Boston, St Mary's gild maintained choirmen and an organist within its own chapel in the parish church. John Leland admired St Botolph's, Boston: 'for a paroche [parish] church the best and fairest of all Lincolnshire, and served so with singing, and that of cunning men, as no paroche [parish] is in all England. The society and brotherhood belonging to this church hath caused this, and now much land belongeth to this society.'[35] Confraternities may have encouraged devotion to a local cult. They often organised the collection of funds for the rebuilding of naves and aisles. There is not much recorded tension between confraternities and parish priests. On the contrary, at Salisbury there is evidence that the gild supplemented the stipends of the parish clergy, including that of the parish priest of St Thomas, in 1531.[36] Moreover, there is nothing to suggest that the church authorities ever saw confraternities as anything but orthodox in late medieval England (unlike in thirteenth-century Languedoc).[37]

Chantries served similar functions to confraternities but at the level of an individual and family. Someone of wealth, anxious about the fate of his or her soul, could, while alive or by a last will, arrange the foundation of a chantry, securing the services of one or more chantry priests to pray and say masses for the soul of the founder. Chapels could be built within, or tacked onto, parish churches for this purpose. Lands or revenues could be set aside to finance such chantries. Once again the development of the doctrine of purgatory was crucial to such events. Again the incidence of chantry foundation, in so far as the sources offer trustworthy information, suggests that it began well before the Black Death but such obviously heightened concern with mortality intensified the movement. Chantries should not be seen as selfish or elitist: in an hierarchical society it was accepted that those who enjoyed greater wealth should spend it proportionately. Perhaps, too, those with the greatest responsibilities and with the greatest opportunities to sin needed to make correspondingly greater efforts at expiation. It has been estimated that eighty-five aristocratic families established chantries in the fourteenth and fifteenth centuries;[38] how many did not? Motives may have been more altruistic, for example, to safeguard the future of a long-serving chaplain and confessor.[39] And chantries, just like confraternities, could benefit the whole parish, not just their founders, by leading to the increase of divine service: chantry priests were available to serve as acolytes, in choirs, or as local schoolmasters.[40] Some chantries had almshouses, hospitals or schools attached to them.[41] That familiar clause requiring chantry priests to pray for all christian souls, for 'all the faithful departed', should not be seen as mere form.[42] Henry V declared that he was founding Syon 'both for ourselves, and our progenitors, and all our successors, our whole kingdom, and every one of our subjects, healthfully to consult the salvation of our souls'.[43]

The profusion of chantries within parish churches (highly visible) reminded parishioners of the importance of prayer and intercession.[44] 'To walk into a parish church around 1500 was', Colin Richmond has written, 'to enter . . . an ante-chamber of purgatory. Almost everything was labelled with the names of local souls who required assistance.'[45] That clergy, notably bishops, founded chantries, especially in cathedrals (for example, the magnificent chapel built by Bishop Stillington at Wells 1477–87[46]) should show that there was nothing intrinsically hostile to the established institutional church in the chantry movement, even if most chantries were founded by laymen and laywomen. That John Colet sought and obtained a licence to found a chantry near his school in St Paul's Churchyard in January 1514 testifies to the continuing attraction and importance of chantries to reforming and humanist churchmen.[47] It is difficult to discern clear trends. Some historians have detected a decline in testatory bequests for masses and prayers for the dead in the 1520s[48] but chantries were still being founded in the 1530s. As late as 1538, George Talbot, fourth earl of Shrewsbury, then in the last year of his life, secured a licence to found a chantry on the site of the recently dissolved monastery of Flanesford, Herefordshire.[49] One scholar concludes that 'although overall support for intercessions had in general remained substantial until about 1530, it thereafter entered an unmistakable and sometimes drastic decline'. New chantry foundations between 1500 and 1530 were strong in Lincolnshire, Wiltshire and Yorkshire, much less so in Essex, Kent and Warwickshire; and diminished rapidly in the 1530s to negligible numbers in the 1540s.[50] But those changes were the consequence of the break with Rome and the dissolution of the monasteries, not a reflection of how chantries had been regarded till then.

The profusion of chantries was untidy. There was no central direction or control. Fraternities, and more especially chantries, came and went. It was easy for William Tyndale to mock the increasing impracticality of prayers for the dead: 'if they should do all that they have promised from the first founder unto this day v hundred monks were not enough in many cloisters'.[51] A brief exercise in arithmetic will quickly show that he was not wrong. Testators often expressed a measure of uncertainty as to whether their pious intentions would be put into practice.[52] They were right to be wary. Some prospective chantries were never set up, for example the planned chantry of William Paston (1378–1444) in Norwich Cathedral, unfounded by his son and grandsons.[53] Other chantries were merged or allowed to fall into disuse, abandoned by later generations. James Gunwyn, canon of Southwark, noted in January 1536 how they were bound by the will of William Wykeham, bishop of Winchester, to have five masses said daily in their church: they had not been said for over forty years.[54] A study of the Hungerfords shows that they generally neglected the chantries of their predecessors. Walter (d. 1449), first Lord Hungerford, and Margaret (d. 1478) suppressed chantries at Heytesbury, Upton Scudamore and Calne, diverting the endowments to other purposes, despite local opposition and appeals to bishops. If they acted within their legal rights and according to contemporary standards, they were not observing the spirit of the original founders' wishes, but rather, according to contemporary understanding, imperilling their souls. That such suppressions and diversions were carried out hints at the potential financial and administrative burdens placed by these endowments on succeeding generations.[55] Larger economic trends— such as rising real wages, falling returns from lands rented out—might add to the costs.[56] All that offers a context for the relative absence of opposition to their dissolution. Some, especially the more recently founded, chantries would have continued to evoke the loyalty of the families who had endowed them. But many would have seemed too remote. Laymen's chantries in England were especially located in founders' parish churches. On the whole, and unlike the people of the southern Netherlands, the English laity were not much involved in the greater collegiate and cathedral churches,[57] though there were significant gilds in the cathedrals at York, Lichfield, St Paul's, London, and fraternities at Lincoln and Salisbury.[58]

Moreover, the theology of purgatory was ambiguous and full of contradictions. What happened after death? Did the souls in purgatory remain in the same state as they entered or could they increase in grace and charity? The reformer John Frith made much of the contradictions between Bishop Fisher (who espoused the former view) and Thomas More (who espoused the latter).[59] More's position implied that there were two judgments, one

final at the end of time, the other provisional, immediately after death,
Fisher's emphasised the Last Judgment. On this difference turned the best
course of action. If inert souls awaited the Last Judgment, then perpetual
masses offered them greatest assistance. If some kind of provisional judgment was made straight away, and a brisk start made on purging sins, then
it made sense to arrange as many masses as possible at the funeral and in
the immediately succeeding days and months, since that would reduce the
time spent purging sins in purgatory, and hasten progress to a better state.
But such an attitude led to what, as we have seen, has been called 'la comptabilité de l'au-delà'—the book-keeping of the hereafter.[60] It was open to
crude simplifications such as the claims of one Stanley, in Grantham church
in 1535, that, on giving a penny to a priest, souls were released from purgatory and went straight to heaven.[61] In a late fifteenth-century Carthusian
miscellany there is a charming illustration of souls in the flames of purgatory with, above them, a large basket full of souls suspended at the end of
a rope pulled by a priest saying mass and a man giving alms to the poor: the
caption reads 'these saules are drawne vp oute of purgatory by prayer and
almos dede [these souls are drawn up out of purgatory by prayer and alms
deed]'. An accompanying rhyme reinforces the message: 'The saules that to
purgatory wendes/ May be relyfed thorowe helpe of frendes [The souls that
to purgatory wends/ May be relieved through help of friends]'. It explained:
'for so large is holy kyrk tresir/ That it is ynoughe to paye therefore/ And
for al the paynes that det be/ Of al the men of cristiante/ The pardon in
purgatory avayles' [for so large is holy kirk treasure/ That it is enough
to pay therefor/ And for all the paynes that death be/ Of all the men of
christianity/ The pardon in purgatory avails]'.[62] The notion of a treasury of
merit on which all could draw was a vital system of belief with its own
logic, yet desperately vulnerable to Erasmian or protestant critiques. Writing
of late medieval lay devotion, Jack Scarisbrick asked: 'was its preoccupation
with purgatory and the enormous multiplication of intercessory prayers for
the dead, especially masses, entirely healthy?'[63]

(ii) Pilgrimage

Pilgrimage—a devotional journey to a sacred object or place—was still a
vital part of English religious life in the early sixteenth century, as the
vigour with which it was attacked by protestant reformers shows. It is
revealing that the leaders of the largest movement of protest against religious change in the reign of Henry VIII called it a Pilgrimage of Grace. A
great many shrines attracted pilgrims. A few Englishmen even went on the
hugely expensive and often dangerous pilgrimage to Jerusalem—notably

Sir Richard Guildford, who died there in 1506, Richard Torkington, a protégé of Sir Thomas Boleyn, who went in 1516–17, and Roger Wood, a Norfolk gentleman, who went in 1520. Anne Boleyn's fool had been to Jerusalem, presumably on pilgrimage. Obviously such examples are few and rare, but they testify to a continuing strand of devotion.[64] Some Englishmen went on pilgrimage to Rome. The hospital of the English college at Rome welcomed eighty-two visitors between November 1504 and May 1505, 202 between May 1505 and May 1506, and 205 between May 1506 and May 1507: presumably these were mostly pilgrims.[65] Santiago de Compostela in Spain attracted the steward of Tattershall College in 1479, John Bewde of Woolpit, Suffolk, in 1501, Robert Langton, treasurer of York Minster, in 1510, and Sir Thomas Boleyn in 1523. Anne Boleyn's father had vowed to go on pilgrimage to Santiago de Compostela during a violent storm while crossing to Spain in 1522: he had just begun his journey there when Henry VIII recalled him for diplomatic duties.[66] Robert Langton (1470–1524), ecclesiastical pluralist, wrote a book entitled *The pylgrymage of M. Robert Langton clerke to Seynt James in Compostell and in other holy places of Crystendome* (1522) about his travels; in the prologue he declared that he had been to Jerusalem as well.[67]

Within England, Walsingham was among the most popular of pilgrimage centres. Richard Pynson printed a ballad history in 1496. Henry VII visited it in 1487, 1489, 1498 and 1506.[68] Wolsey went there in September 1517 (though he came away with a fever).[69] Sir Robert Wingfield vowed to go there in 1517;[70] Sir Richard Wingfield was keen to accompany Wolsey there in 1520.[71] The duke of Buckingham made an offering in March 1519;[72] the marquess of Exeter in June 1525.[73] The bishop of Ely was riding there before Michaelmas 1523.[74] Queen Catherine of Aragon asked in her will for someone to go there on pilgrimage for her.[75] Lord Lisle, in 'marvellous danger' with 'hope gone' on board a ship which had struck a rock, called upon Our Lady of Walsingham for help and comfort, and vowed that, if it pleased God and her to deliver him from that peril, he would eat neither flesh nor fish till he had seen her.[76] Elizabeth Newhouse, by her own account 'a poor widow', who had just been to Walsingham, sent her son in London a Walsingham brooch as a token.[77] Four men from Lincolnshire went there just before Christmas 1536,[78] as did some Cornish soldiers.[79] According to the *Valor Ecclesiasticus* £260 12s 4d was donated to the chapel, the highest recorded amount by far for any shrine in the country; and 133s 4d was given over nine days a little later.[80]

Canterbury, too, remained an important shrine. Foreign visitors marvelled at its gold and jewels.[81] Cardinal Campeggio went in procession to the high altar in 1518. The Holy Roman Emperor Charles V visited it in 1520. In

1520, the jubilee, celebrated every fifty years on the canonisation of Becket, was expected to be attended by a large confluence of people; though it seems that it did not in fact take place because Pope Leo X refused to grant a plenary indulgence unless half went towards St Peter's rebuilding costs.[82] 'It might well be surmised,' Barrie Dobson suggests, 'although it cannot be proved, that there were few late medieval Englishmen (and even Englishwomen) who did not harbour at some time or other of their lives the desire to go on pilgrimage to Canterbury.'[83] The power of Becket's shrine is vividly demonstrated by the large number of souvenirs—ampullae (vessels containing water or oil from pilgrimage shrines) and badges—which archaeologists and metal detectors have discovered.[84] The vehemence of the attacks on Becket in the late 1530s reflected the continuing potency of his cult.[85] Comments made after the dismantling of the shrine in 1538 testify to the continuing influx of pilgrims right to the end. John Hales asked Cromwell to show favour towards the city and mayor and secure them the grant of the watermill and lands belonging to St Augustine's: a great part of their yearly costs used to be paid, he said, by the victuallers and innholders of the city 'having then great gain by pilgrims and others which heretofore came to the said city of Canterbury and now not so continuing'.[86]

The town of Thetford would later claim that it had 'ever been greatly maintained relieved and preserved by the resort and trade of pilgrims there passing through . . . but now the pilgrims are abhored exesepulsyd [expulsed] and set apart for ever, wherby a great nomber of people be idled and like to be brought into extreme beggary'. Pilgrims had come to the parish church, where St Audrey's smock was kept 'as a great jewel and precious relic'.[87] Ellis Price, commissary-general of the diocese of St Asaph, described how people came daily in pilgrimage with kine, oxen, horses or money to the image of Darvell Gadarn, at Llanderfel, near Bala, in whom they had 'so great confidence, hope and trust'. It was of wood, like a man of arms in harness, holding a little spear in his hand and with a casket of iron hanging about his neck with a ribbon. Some 500 to 600 pilgrims, he said, had offered there on 5 April 1538, believing, he claimed, that the image had the power to fetch persons that be damned out of hell. A little later the parson and parishioners would offer £40 that the image should not be conveyed to London.[88] Hugh Latimer highlighted people flocking from the west country to the blood of Christ at Hailes,[89] and described the image of Our Lady at Worcester as 'our great Sibyl' who had been 'the devil's instrument to bring many, I fear, to eternal fire'.[90] The image at Cardigan of a taper burning in the hand of the Virgin was 'used for a great pilgrimage to this present day', the prior testified in 1538, 'so worshipped and kissed' by pilgrims that it yielded twenty nobles annually as a pension to the abbot of Chertsey.[91] The prior of the Cambridge Blackfriars said that there had been much pilgrimage to an image of Our Lady in that house, especially at Stowbridge fair.[92] John London recorded that there was 'a great pilgrimage' to Caversham, Oxfordshire.[93] Even when he was there pulling down the image and defacing the chapel, 'not so few as a dozen with images of wax' came in.[94]

John Foxe, the martyrologist, frequently testifies to the popularity of pilgrimage. At Dovercourt, ten miles from Dedham, there was a rood, 'whereunto was much and great resort of people', 'an idoll' of such power that no man was strong enough to shut the door of the church.[95] The antiquary John Leland's *Itinerary* is peppered with references to shrines and pilgrimage, and often to 'great' or 'much' pilgrimage.[96] The Rood of Grace at Boxley was much sought after by people from 'all parts of this realm', Archbishop Warham noted in 1524, adding that it was 'so holy a place where so many miracles be showed'.[97] When it was dismantled in 1538 it was recorded that 'the inhabitants of Kent had in time past a great devotion to the same and to use continual pilgrimage thither'.[98] A London chronicler, recording Bishop Hilsey's sermon, described the Rood of Grace 'that had been many years in the Abbey of Boxley in Kent, and was greatly sought with pilgrims'.[99] Many wills, of course, record bequests for candles to be lit at particular shrines. When pilgrimages were attacked, there was often trouble. When Latimer spoke against pilgrimages in Bristol in the early 1530s, the people were not a little offended.[100] It is interesting that the commissioner William Herbert was ordered to take down the image of Our Lady at Penrhys 'with quietness and secret manner'.[101] When three commissioners came to make an end of the shrine of St Swithun at Winchester, they did so at about three in the morning.[102] Henry, lord Stafford, ordered to remove the 'idol' that 'ignorant persons' called St Erasmus, sent for it, as instructed, the next morning, early.[103] What this catalogue cannot well convey, for lack of appropriate evidence, is the felt experience of many thousands of ordinary pilgrims, not least of women—if Margery Kempe can be seen as in any way representative—and the place of pilgrimage in their often hard lives.

What is abundantly plain is that pilgrimage was prevalent and popular in the late fifteenth and early sixteenth centuries. I must dissent from Keith Thomas's remark that 'in the fifteenth century pilgrimages and hagiography were on the decline',[104] and from Colin Richmond's questioning of Geoffrey Dickens's assertion of a 'crazed enthusiasm for pilgrimages around 1500'.[105] Of course, most of the cults mentioned so far were long established. But two new cults, in many ways very different, vividly illustrate the continuing vitality of pilgrimage, and call into question the claim that 'the impetus behind the worship of the saints seems to have slackened considerably during the fifteenth century'.[106] My first example, familiar but open to more forceful emphasis, is the development of the cult of Henry VI in the later fifteenth century. In many ways it does seem a popular cult. Offerings to an image of the king in York Minster were recorded by 1475.[107] In 1480 the London Mercers' Company advised its members that pilgrimages to Henry VI had been forbidden, compelling evidence that they had been taking place.[108] A year later, in August 1481, the inhabitants of Westwell, Kent, looked to Henry to release and bring back to life the body of a small boy who was trapped below the water wheel of the mill.[109] The social setting of the 174 miracles attributed to Henry VI in the collection compiled in Henry VII's reign as part of the campaign for his canonisation presents the cult as very much a popular phenomenon, with its emphasis on healing, especially of children.[110] Pilgrim badges confirm that impression. Pilgrims commonly brought back badges from the shrines they visited, attached by pins to clothing and to hats, usually decorated on one side. Erasmus's character Ogygius arrives covered with scallop shells, stuck all over with leaden and tin figures.[111] Such badges are interesting evidence of the popularity of pilgrimages. By 1978 some ninety pilgrim badges from the shrine of Henry VI had been found, including in Ludlow, Oxford, Salisbury and Bristol, compared with some 300 that survive from Canterbury, but produced over a much longer period of three and a half centuries.[112] From 1982 the Museum of London worked together with metal detectors, especially with members of the Society of Thames Mudlarks, and, by 1998 some 800 additional pilgrim souvenirs and badges had been discovered on the Thames foreshore. The number of Henry VI badges unearthed grew fourfold: 'the sheer size of the assemblage of badges is impressive testimony to Windsor's enormous, if relatively short-lived, appeal to pilgrims'.[113]

As late as the mid-1530s Robert Testwood saw pilgrims, especially from Devon and Cornwall, coming to Windsor with candles and images of wax in their hands, to offer to Henry VI.[114] One of the miracles attributed to Henry VI is especially interesting in showing the fluctuating attitudes to different saints. A nine-month-old boy swallowed a silver badge of Becket and choked upon it: significantly, it was when his parents invoked Henry VI that the boy drew breath and spat out the badge.[115] Clearly the cult of Henry VI had political dimensions too. Was it the safest way in the 1470s and early 1480s to express Lancastrian sympathies and implicitly to question the legitimacy of Edward IV's crown?[116] It was certainly important enough for kings to challenge or to foster. The translation of the shrine of John Schorn, the holy priest, parish priest of North Marston, Buckinghamshire, in the early thirteenth century, to Windsor in 1478 has been seen as an effort to create a counter-weight to the attraction of Henry VI.[117] What were Richard III's motives in having the body of Henry VI moved from Chertsey to Windsor in 1484: genuine piety, guilt as the king's murderer, hypocrisy, political cunning, a desire for political reconciliation? Was this, as has been suggested, 'a generous move' by Richard? [118] 'He may', another scholar has written, 'have wanted to be associated with a king with a posthumous reputation for sanctity.'[119] Or was this perhaps an attempt 'to effect the recreation of concord in a disordered body politic by the reintegration of the defeated and marginalised', the power of a saint being 'not the least' of later medieval England's 'resources of compromise and conciliation'? 'In reaching this conclusion there is always a danger of mistaking rhetoric for reality': 'the proclamation of harmony could become the assertion of a still-disputed hegemony, which only served to remove the conflict from one arena to another'. But the ideal of reconciliation and harmony nonetheless remained, and the cult could contain the political struggle.[120] That sort of interpretation seems to treat with excessive intellectual sophistication what was more likely to have been an instinctive political reaction. Was not the body of Henry VI transferred to keep closer watch over the cult, and to neutralise its political implications by locating it close to the body of Edward IV?[121] And just how much of Henry VI's holy innocence, and reputation as a peacemaker, would have rubbed off on to the reputation of Richard III, had time allowed, must remain problematic. Possibly, in the long run, a royal saint such as Henry VI might contribute to an 'enhancement of the spiritual status and claims of the English monarchy', reinforcing 'the growing conviction that kings stood in an especially close relationship to God'; but, apart from the somewhat questionable assumption about the earlier spiritual status of kings, this would seem more a long-term consequence than, in any specific sense, a plausible cause of protection and encouragement of the cult.[122]

Whatever Richard III's motives, under Henry VII the cult of Henry VI developed still further. Henry VII began to reconstruct the Lady Chapel at Windsor, intending to make it into a shrine for the remains of his uncle, and to be buried there himself. He asked for a papal commission to inquire into Henry VI's miracles, a request granted in 1494. Then in 1498 the king's council debated where Henry VI should lie: should he be reburied in Westminster Abbey, as the abbot and convent claimed, or Chertsey (as claimed by the abbot), or remain at Windsor (as claimed by the dean and chapter). Witnesses asserted that Henry VI had often visited Westminster Abbey and had chosen the exact spot where he wished to lie, immediately north of St Edward's shrine. Henry VII appears to have been convinced, and announced his intention of reburying Henry VI in a new Lady Chapel at

Westminster Abbey, where he himself would also be buried. Chamber accounts show that £14,856 was paid between 1502 and 1509; an indenture dated 13 April 1509, eight days before the king's death, entrusted the abbot and convent with a further £5,000; Henry's will instructed his executors to see the chapel perfectly finished. Thus far the story is one of vitality and development; but, with Henry VII's death in 1509, the momentum disappears, and Henry VI remained at Windsor, the chapel intended for him at Westminster being turned into one for Henry VII.[123] We shall briefly return to this; meanwhile, we should note the continuing vitality of the tradition of 'political saints' in the later middle ages.

It is entirely correct to claim that if 'political canonisation was an aspect of gaining and maintaining political legitimacy', nevertheless 'without real power it was ultimately useless'. But that was no novelty of the fifteenth century: it was no more true of the later middle ages than it had been earlier. Perhaps 'the heyday' of political saints in England is indeed, as has been argued, to be found in the thirteenth and fourteenth centuries, yet it seems that the cult of Henry VI admirably fits into the world of 'political canonisation and political symbolism' that has been seen as most characteristic of earlier periods.[124] The cult of Henry VI shows the continuing potency of political saints.

My second example of a new cult comes from the 1520s and is in some ways more remarkable. A display of mass piety surrounded Elizabeth Barton, the nun of Kent. We only know about this from the later sermon denouncing her political predictions against Henry VIII's marriage to Anne Boleyn and from the summary of a non-extant book by Edward Thwaites in William Lambard's *Perambulation of Kent*.[125] But the scenes described by John Salcot, then bishop-elect of Bangor, in November 1533, and by Lambard had occurred well before Henry sought an annulment of his marriage to Catherine of Aragon.[126] Barton was a servant of one of the archbishop of Canterbury's tenants at Aldington, Kent. She fell ill. She correctly predicted the death of her master's desperately sick child, 'the first matter that moued her hearers to admiration'. She was able to tell them of things that happened in places where she was not present. She told them what meat the hermit of the chapel of Our Lady at Court of Street had for his supper and many other things about him. She spoke of heaven, hell and purgatory, and of the joys and sorrows that sundry departed souls had or suffered there. She preached against the corruption of manners. She urged attendance at church, hearing of mass, confession to priests, prayer to Our Lady and the saints, and was prone to make declamations about the seven deadly sins and the Ten Commandments. She said she had seen the joys of heaven, where St Michael weighed souls and where St Peter carried the keys.

She herself had been with Our Lady at Court of Street, and implored her to cure her sickness. Our Lady had responded by ordering her to make an offering to the taper in her honour there, and to declare boldly to all christian people that it was Our Lady at Court of Street that had revived her from the point of death, and that the bell should be rung to tell of a miracle. Moreover, the voice that spoke in her announced that if anyone were to die suddenly, without the opportunity to make a final confession of his sins and so to remain in mortal deadly sin, if he had made a vow to Our Lady heartily then he would receive the last rites, and then depart from this world with God's blessing. The parish priest reported to Archbishop Warham how she spoke 'of high and notable matters in her sickness, to the great marvel of the hearers'. Warham declared that such words were the words of God and that they should be recorded. Barton's trances continued. In one such speech she announced that she would on a certain day go to the chapel of Our Lady at Court of Street and be restored to health by a miracle. According to Lambard, she went there but was not immediately cured. Nonetheless, her reputation had grown so great that those appointed by the archbishop to investigate her claims joined her on her next visit to Our Lady at Court of Street. Many priests and monks were present, as were many ladies and gentlemen of the highest degree, together with some 2,000 to 3,000 people, who went on procession, singing the litany and saying divers psalms and orations on the way. At the chapel, mass began. Barton was by now in a trance. According to Cranmer, she was brought there and laid before the image of Our Lady. 'Her face was wonderfully disfigured', Cranmer went on, 'her tongue hanging out, and her eyes being in a manner plucked out and laid upon her cheeks, and so greatly disordered. Then was heard a voice speaking within her belly, as it had been in a tun; her lips not greatly moving; she all that while continuing by the space of three hours and more in a trance; the which voice, when it told anything of the joys of heaven, it spake so sweetly and so heavenly that every man was ravished with the hearing thereof; and contrary, when it told any thing of hell, it spake so horribly and terribly, that it put the hearers in a great fear. It spake also many things for the confirmation of pilgrimages and trentals, hearing of masses, and confession, and many such other things'.[127] After the mass was over, Elizabeth knelt before the image of Our Lady at Court of Street and declared that she was perfectly whole. The miracle was reported to the archbishop by Dr Edward Bocking, doctor of divinity and cellarer of Christ Church, Canterbury. In a vision Elizabeth was then commanded to become a nun at St Sepulchre, Canterbury. As was customary, she was assigned a spiritual adviser. Edward Bocking was chosen since, in one of her trances, a voice had stated that that would be God's pleasure.

She continued to have visions and revelations weekly or fortnightly. As a result, and also because of the 'great perfectness' that was thought to be in her, many came to see her, both great men of the realm and lowly men, many learned men and especially many religious men, hoping that through her they might know the will of God.[128] One Ellyn, a maid living at Tottenham, who had been troubled by trances and revelations, had been to see her: Barton told her that the revelations were but illusions of the devil and that she should cast them out of her mind. Ever since, she later declared, she had been less troubled by them.[129] Barton continued to go often to Court of Street, performing miracles such as lighting candles without fire, moistening women's breasts that were dry, curing the sick, and even, we are told, 'reducing the dead to life again'.[130] A book was written of the whole story and put into print, according to Cranmer, 'which ever since that time hath been commonly sold and gone abroad amongst all people'. Moreover, by reason of the miracle of her cure, 'there is established a great pilgrimage, and ever since many devout people hath sought to that devout . . . lady of Court of Street'. The hermit of Our Lady at Court of Street was enriched by the daily offerings made there,[131] further evidence of the popularity of the pilgrimage. Of course, all this might easily be condemned as imposture, as it was in John Salcot's sermon, in which he claimed that she had completely recovered before the day of her miraculous healing.[132] It is quite plausible to read these events as stimulated by the clergy—Richard Master, the parson of Aldington, in the first instance, and the Canterbury Charterhouse monk Edward Bocking later (though he does not seem to have been involved until attending the miracle of healing). Master was alleged to have spread reports of Barton's trances and speeches 'by cause he would have increased the devotion of the people in coming on pilgrimage to a chapel set in Court at Street . . . within his said parish . . . for his own lucre and advantage' (yet it was not in fact within his parish). In her trance on the day that she proclaimed her miraculous recovery, Barton urged that the chapel of Our Lady should be better maintained and staffed by a priest who would sing mass daily.[133] Master and Bocking between them allegedly devised the miraculous healing.[134] It was Dr Bocking who first prepared a great book of the wonderful work done at Our Lady at Court of Street, a study evidently taken further by Thomas Master, Edward Thwaites and Thomas Lawrence of Canterbury (the archdeacon of Canterbury's registrar). Dr Bocking had 500 copies of the book, and the printer 200.[135] John Dering, another Canterbury monk, would compile a tract in defence of the nun's revelations.[136] Edward Thwaites's book—'a little pamplet, containing four and twenty leaves'—called *A marueilous worke of late done at Court of Streete in Kent*, was printed by Robert Redman, but survives only in

Lambard's *Perambulation*. Bocking then allegedly got Barton to have revelations about the king's marriage. Still, and especially if Barton's revelations were invented by a priest and a monk, it is powerful testimony to popular beliefs that critics of the king's divorce should have thought that revelations given to, and prophecies uttered by, a nun would have the greatest effect in spreading their opposition. Yet the display of lay piety revealed by the mass procession, the large numbers of men and women who hoped for, and believed in, miracles, is perhaps more significant than the truth of, or the persons behind, Barton's political revelations, and it vividly shows the continuing strength, on the eve of the break with Rome, of popular belief in the healing power of an image visited in pilgrimage. This is a story that, if one did not know when it occurred, one might think dated from the high middle ages, the twelfth and thirteenth centuries of Jonathan Sumption's *Pilgrimage* or Ronald Finucane's *Miracles*, or the early middle ages of Patricia Morison's French tenth- and eleventh-century hagiographies.[137] Here in Kent in the 1520s something very similar is—still—happening: we are—still—in the middle ages. As related here, the orderly story reveals no mass hysteria; but something more emotional does not seem far away. This is not a comfortable, measured, moderate, lukewarm Barchester-style religion free from extremism and enthusiasm.[138] And it is worth emphasising that but for the nun's involvement in the king's divorce, we should know next to nothing about her.[139] How many more local, popular cults were there, unrecorded for posterity?

Many parish churches contained relics or, much more commonly, images to which pilgrimage was made. Often our knowledge rests on a single, passing, reference, in Foxe's *Acts and Monuments*, or a brief mention at the dissolution. For example, in Buckinghamshire, apart from the well-known shrines of John Schorn at Marston and of the holy blood at Ashridge, there were relics of St Rumwold in the parish church at Buckingham, a rood at Wendover, images of Our Lady at Missenden, an image of Our Lady at Bradwell to which offerings were made, and a chapel and image of the Virgin at High Wycombe.[140] Robert Whiting, who has studied Devon and Cornwall intensively, found several local cults in parish churches and local chapels, including an image at Looe to which a hundred pilgrims came one feast-day just on the eve of the 1530s.[141] Just outside Coventry offerings were made at two chapels to an image of Our Lady and to a rood.[142] Chapels in churchyards have been described as 'an area of growth in late medieval religion': some became important pilgrimage centres, such as Buxton in Derbyshire, and Muswell in Middlesex.[143] Local cults could develop rapidly. For example, the newly appointed parish priest of Morebath gave the parish a statue of St Sidwell: soon the altar was surrounded by candles and received bequests.[144] A study of the late medieval church in Rouergue, south-west France, found that in 1524–5 one in ten parishes included a pilgrimage site.[145] Were there as many in England? According to Bishop Barlow of St David's, in his diocese 'idolatrous abused images' did 'horribly . . . abounde'.[146] There must have been many images such as that at Ashford, a rood in a chapel in the north aisle, before which stood a box to receive offerings: people made daily reverence to it, it was claimed.[147] At Leintwardine, Herefordshire, the abbot of Wigmore used to preach on the Nativity of the Virgin, where the people had been wont to offer to an image.[148] On Midsummer Day pilgrims came to a chapel of St John at Broughton, Oxfordshire, where (instead of at the parish church) the curate said mass.[149] Pilgrimages were made to hermits' chapels, such as St Augustine, Brampton Ash, Northamptonshire, or at Colnbrook, near Windsor.[150]

It would be tempting to put forward a social explanation of the development of pilgrimage along the same lines as Sir Richard Southern's influential exposition of the development of the doctrine of purgatory in the eleventh and twelfth centuries. Just as purgatory offered a system of religious discipline and hope for the afterlife to a much larger number of the laity than had been effectively catered for by the more cultic church of the dark ages, so the practice of pilgrimage, the veneration of saints and their relics, offered to the whole population a religious challenge and balm. In the same way as purgatory, pilgrimage was the fruit of a society enjoying a greater degree of economic prosperity, internal peace and an elaborate system of church discipline.[151]

Pilgrimages attracted the poor and the uneducated but also the rich, the powerful and the learned. Rulers sought the assistance of the saints in the destruction of their enemies. In 1487 Henry VII prayed devoutly before the image of the Virgin at Walsingham that he should be delivered from the wiles of his foes. After his victory at the battle of Stoke, he sent Christopher Urswick to Walsingham with the military standard used in battle to offer thanks.[152] Erasmus vowed to make a pilgrimage to Walsingham in 1512 for the success of the church against the schismatic Louis XII of France.[153] Catherine of Aragon was intending to go on pilgrimage to Walsingham on hearing of the victory against the Scots at Flodden, to see Our Lady 'that I promised so long ago to see'.[154] This was connected to a continuing belief in the power of saints to bring victory. Saints served as protectors in war. Thomas Ruthal, later bishop of Durham, testified to the power of St Cuthbert in his account of the battle of Flodden in 1513. Thomas, Lord Howard, had led the vanguard, followed by St Cuthbert's banner. The banner men won great honour and gained the king of Scots' banner which now stood beside St Cuthbert's shrine. In his own hand, Ruthal added that

all believe that the victory had been wrought by the intercession of
St Cuthbert, who never suffered injury to be done to his church unre-
quited.[155] When in 1522 Thomas Lord Dacre informed the bishop of
Durham about the condition of Norham Castle, he reported that the inner
well was finished and of that strength 'that with the help of God and the
prayer of St Cuthbert it is impregnable'.[156] In autumn 1523 Henry VIII
ordered the earl of Surrey 'in nowise' to go further than St Cuthbert's
banner could go with him.[157] It would be wrong to be dismissive of all this,
to see it as insincere and manipulative.

Why did the third duke of Buckingham go on pilgrimage so often?
His accounts show that in 1508 he visited shrines at St Augustine's Bristol,
Glastonbury, St Anne in the Wood, Keynsham, Our Lady of Pew at
Westminster, Our Lady of Barking and the Holy Rood at Greenwich, all
between April and July. In the months before his arrest for treason in 1521 he
visited Our Lady of Kingswood, St Aldelm, Malmesbury, Our Lady of
Bellhouse, Bristol, the relics at Hailes, the Child of Grace at Reading and Our
Lady of Eton at Windsor.[158] In the autumn of 1520, Buckingham had vowed
not to shave until such time as he had gone on pilgrimage to Jerusalem.[159]
One senses an emotionally troubled man seeking spiritual solace.

But what principally underpinned the practice of pilgrimage was the
hope of relief from sickness and disability. About 170 miracles were
described in the compilation claiming Henry VI as a saint: of these, fifty
involved a sick or afflicted adult, thirty an adult injured in an accident,
twenty-seven an injured child and fifteen a sick child.[160] A man crippled for
ten years after falling from a horse made the pilgrimage and was cured.[161]
A four-year-old boy drowned in a mill stream—at the invocation of Henry
VI he was rescued and revived.[162] A girl suffering from swelling of the tibia,
could not move or bear to be touched for fifteen weeks; as many as twenty
skilled doctors, physicians and surgeons were called by her parents in a
single week; but it was her parents' invocation of Henry VI that cured her,
and, once restored to health, she made a pilgrimage with her parents to
Henry's tomb, leaving her crutches there.[163] Healing was a central feature in
Elizabeth Barton's activities, as we have seen. That the belief in saints as
healers was universal is suggested by Hugh Latimer's admission that 'I have
thought in times past that divers images of saints could have holpen me, and
done me much good, and delivered me of my diseases'.[164] The ballad
printed by Richard Pynson stressed the miracles of healing that had
occurred at Walsingham: the sick cured, the dead revived, the lame straight,
the blind able to see.[165] It was during a period of widespread sickness
that Wolsey went to Walsingham in 1517.[166] Saints were (or possibly had, in
the later middle ages, become) specialists in healing, each with different

expertise.[167] The shrine of St Guthlac and his bell at Repton was thought to alleviate headaches.[168] The old chapel at the east end of Sonning church, Berkshire, attracted many pilgrims 'for the disease of madness'.[169] St Audrey's smock at Thetford was specially useful 'in putting away the tooth ache and swelling of the throat'.[170] The hat of Thomas earl of Lancaster, venerated at Pontefract, was thought to be good for headaches.[171] So was an image called Maiden Cutbroghe, at Thelsford, under whose feet was a trough of wood descending beneath the altar. Those in search of a cure put a peck of oats into the trough.[172] The image of John Schorn at Marston, Buckinghamshire, standing blessing a boot into which he had conveyed the devil, was much sought after for the ague.[173]

Pilgrimage saints were also much invoked to mitigate the pains of childbirth. The images of St Anne of Buxton, and St Modwyn of Burton on Trent with a red bow and staff, attracted 'women labouring of child in these parts' who were 'very desirous to have with them to lean upon and walk with it'.[174] Commissioners in the 1530s found the girdle of St Mary, Haltemprice; the girdle and part of the tunic of St Francis, Grace Dieu; part of the shirt of St Thomas, at St Mary's, Derby; the girdle of St Bernard, at Melsa, Holderness; the girdle of St Saviour, at Newburgh; the girdle of St Ailred, Rievaulx; the finger of St Stephen, at Keldholm; the necklace called agnus dei at Holme Cultram; the girdle of St Mary, at Calder; the girdle of St Mary, at Conishead; the girdle of St Werburgh, at Chester; the belt of Thomas earl of Lancaster, at Pontefract; the belt of blessed Mary, at Kirkham; the girdle of St Bernard, at Kirkstall; and the girdle and book of St Robert, at Newminster. Were these girdles and tunics borrowed temporarily, implying that someone went to or from the shrine to collect them?[175] In August 1535 Richard Layton sent up the chains of St Peter from Monkton Farleigh 'which women of this country used always to send for in time of childbirth to put about them to have thereby short deliverance and without peril'. Layton himself was not impressed and sneered 'I suppose the thing to be very mockery'. He sent up Our Lady's girdle of Bruton, made of red silk, 'which', he noted, 'is a solemn relic sent to women travailling, which shall not miscarry in partu', and Mary Magdalene's girdle, also sent with great reverence to women travailing.[176] Here, clearly, there was a gendered dimension to late medieval religion: these features of piety were especially suited to the social, psychological and, above all, physiological needs of women. Vows of pilgrimage were often made by those who were ill. It was when he was sick that the fourth earl of Shrewsbury evidently resolved to go on pilgrimage to Doncaster;[177] it was when he was sick that Thomas Alen, the fourth earl of Shrewsbury's chaplain, vowed to ride to Canterbury on pilgrimage.[178] It was during the sweating sickness of 1528 that Bishop Longland of Lincoln promised a pilgrimage to Walsingham 'as soon as my strength will serve me'.[179] In a series of events similar to those involving Elizabeth Barton, Sir Roger Wentworth took his twelve-year-old daughter, who suffered from violent fits, on a famous pilgrimage to the shrine of Our Lady of Grace, Ipswich, after a vision of the Virgin looking as she did in the picture and statue of Our Lady of Ipswich effected a cure. A thousand people escorted her; the abbot of Bury travelled thirty miles on foot 'of pilgrimage'. But a relapse occurred after a promised repeat pilgrimage was delayed. Four thousand then attended a renewed pilgrimage, at which others were also cured. The girl then became a nun. Wolsey and Catherine of Aragon visited the shrine in 1517 and Wolsey's statutes for his college at Ipswich drew upon Gracechurch, which obtained a fresh papal judgment in 1526.[180]

So vibrant a faith might seem firm against criticism. Yet there were potential weaknesses within the system of belief and practice represented by pilgrimages. In general terms, the distinction between what was true religion and what was superstition or magic was not always easy to maintain.[181] The official line of the church was to stress that pilgrimages and prayers to saints were intercessions and aids to piety, inculcating obedience, humility, reverence, forbearance, charity; that contemplation of saints' lives and relics inspired men and women to emulate their conduct.[182] But the church could not deny the occurrence of miracles—from the Creation itself to the daily miracle of the mass. And miracles had been essential instruments of conversion in late antiquity and the dark ages, implanting the first seeds of faith among the pagans.[183] The seventh and eighth centuries were the English 'age of saints': it is indeed possible, though unprovable, that 'virtually every religious community had its own saint'.[184] The church of the high middle ages, beginning at the Benedictine reform in the 960s, was more sceptical of miracles, making miracle an explanation of last resort, and the canonisation of saints an increasingly lengthy and difficult process. But, in practice, people might have had rather stronger hopes than the church would have preferred to allow that their specific requests in prayer would be granted; and there were obvious temptations for those clergy or monks involved in a pilgrimage site to make claims on behalf of their saint and relics, treating miracles as a 'primary advertisement for the shrine or saint', not least when seeking funds to build or rebuild a church. The whole procedure could take on a mechanical quality, not very different from magic, as significant numbers of miracles were reported as having taken place at saints' shrines, as saints were seen as having almost divine powers of intervention in this world.[185]

Elizabeth Barton claimed to have seen souls in purgatory, and in particular to have watched the disputation of the devils for the soul of Cardinal

Wolsey after his death: by her penance he was brought to heaven.[186] Such mechanical and magical approaches to salvation were readily attacked by reformers. William Barlow denounced those who saw saints such as St David as having the power not just on earth but also in heaven 'to give it whom he would, to discharge hell, to empty purgatory, to pardon sin, to release pain, yea to save his beneficial friends, to curse and kill his unfavorable adversaries': such power, Barlow insisted, was rather God's alone.[187] It is always tricky to generalise on trends in such matters, but had there perhaps been a drift towards a more magical conception of sainthood in the fifteenth and early sixteenth centuries? Was the late medieval church more tolerant of such things, less prepared to prohibit and to excommunicate, less forward in explaining the distinction between magic and faithful intercessory prayer, less prepared to prune the luxuriant growth of abuses?[188] Were there fewer bishops willing as Bishop Grandison of Exeter (1292–1369) had been to prohibit the offering of public veneration to those who had not been canonised, to expose a supposed miraculous recovery of sight as a financial fraud or to complain at a developing but unauthorised pilgrimage to a chapel with an image at Frithelstock, Torrington?[189]

However that may be, late medieval pilgrimages increasingly involved images made by men—statues, paintings, crucifixes and crosses—rather than the relics of saints: such man-made images were perhaps more vulnerable to be turned into a form of worship approaching idolatry.[190] Can we believe Robert Testwood of Windsor's description, recorded by Foxe, of pilgrims at St George's Chapel 'licking and kissing a white lady made of alabaster' in a wall behind the high altar, wiping their hands on it and then stroking their eyes and faces?[191] It would be easy to claim that the worship of saints had taken the place of that devotion due to Christ, to assert, as Erasmus's Menedemus did, that he had never read a commandment that he should entrust the care of his daughters, maids and wife to the saints.[192] But that is not wholly fair, since one of the most fashionable late medieval devotions was that to the stricken Christ on the cross. Many roods were claimed to have worked miracles, for example, those at Chester, Brecon and Tremeirchion.[193] Perhaps, however, 'the power of the individual rood itself, rather than the merits of the great sacrifice of which it was the symbol [was] . . . assuming the largest place in the worship of its devotees'.[194] Certainly the popularity in the later middle ages of the iconography of the instruments of Christ's passion, and of the five wounds of Christ, is remarkable.

More directly vulnerable to criticism was the heightened devotion to the Virgin Mary in the late middle ages, another very fashionable practice. The rosary, especially, lent itself to mechanical observance.[195] The specialisation of late medieval saints (each with areas of responsibility) reinforced that

approach—and was easy to ridicule.[196] For example, a list of relics compiled
by the commissioners in 1535 (no place is mentioned) includes the wimple
of St Etheldreda, 'through which they draw knotted strings on silken
threads, which women think good for sore throats', the wimple of St Audrey
for sore breasts, the comb of St Audrey for headaches, the rod of Aaron for
children troubled by worms, and the ring of St Ethelred for lying-in women
to put on to their fingers.[197] Monasteries that accumulated a miscellaneous
collection of relics—such as Bury St Edmund's shirt of St Edmund, blood
of Christ, some parts of the Holy Cross, the stone with which
St Stephen was stoned, the coals with which St Lawrence was roasted, the
parings of the nails and hair of St Edmund in a pyx, some skulls, including
that of St Petronilla, which the feverish put on their heads, the boots of
St Thomas of Canterbury, the sword of St Edmund, the bones of St Botolph
carried in procession during droughts—invited satire and incredulity.[198] As
we have seen, Richard Layton in August 1535 judged the chains of St Peter
at Monkton Farleigh, which women in childbirth used to send for, 'to be a
very mockery'. They also had Mary Magdalene's comb, St Dorothy's comb,
St Margaret's comb: 'they cannot tell how they came by them, neither have
anything to show in writing that they be relics'.[199] At St Augustine's Abbey,
Bristol, Richard Layton found relics which he sent up: 'first two flowers
wrapped in white and black sarcenet that one Christmas even, *hora ipsa qua
Christus natus fuerat* [at the same hour that Christ was born], will spring
and burgeon and bear blossoms', according to the prior of Maiden Bradley.
He also sent a bag of relics, 'strange thinges' such as 'God's coat, our Lady's
smock, part of God's supper *in cena domini*'. The '*pars petre super qua
natus erat Jesus in Bethelem* [part of the rock on which Jesus was born in
Bethlehem]' prompted the sarcastic comment 'belike there is in Bethlehem
plenty of stones and some quarry, and maketh their mangers of stone'.[200]
At Reading Abbey, John London made an inventory of the relics: two pieces
of the holy cross, St James's hand, St Philip's stole, the bones of Mary
Magdalene, St David, St Edward the martyr, St Jerome, St Stephen, St Blase,
St Osmond, St Margaret, St Anne, and of many more obscure saints.[201] At
the priory of Coventry Cathedral, Dr London listed part of the holy cross,
a relic of St Thomas of Canterbury, a piece of Our Lady's tomb, St Cecilia's
foot, a cross with a relic of St James, an image of St George with a bone in
his shield, a relic of St Andrew, a rib of St Lawrence, an image of one of the
children of Israel, a small shrine of the apostles, a relic of St Katherine, Our
Lady's milk in silver and gilt and a piece of the most holy jaw bone of the
ass that killed Abel.[202] The churchwardens of Wisborough Green, Kent,
surrendered a crucifix with a crystal containing a little quantity of Our
Lady's milk, relics of tombs and vestments of St Thomas of Canterbury, a

hairshirt and bones of St James, a cloak in which St Thomas the martyr was killed and his blood, St Peter's beard and hair, stones with which Stephen was stoned, and St James's comb. Sage men of the parish claimed that these 'have been used and offered unto time out of mind'.[203] At Caversham, Oxfordshire, as well as an image of Our Lady, there was the holy dagger which killed Henry VI, the holy knife that killed St Edward, and an angel with one wing that brought to Caversham the head of the spear that pierced Jesus's side upon the cross.[204] At Bangor, Richard, bishop of Dover found the servant's ear that Peter struck off.[205] More of the holy cross had been found than three carts could carry.[206]

As presented by the commissioners, all this is intended to provoke incredulity when it does not simply shock. But it would be wrong to suppose that these relics were the neglected leftovers from a distant past. On the contrary, the possession of relics continued to matter and demand the attention of rulers of church and state within this period. The dispute over the location of the body of Henry VI, determined by Henry VII's council, shows that well. Another quarrel illustrates it clearly. The early sixteenth-century dispute between the abbey of Glastonbury and Archbishop Warham over the relics of St Dunstan might have come from a saint's life from the twelfth century. Archbishop Warham had directed a search at Canterbury in 1508, which found the coffin and bones of St Dunstan. Glastonbury, however, maintained that the saint's relics had been brought there from Canterbury, and that tradition held that the larger bones were now at Glastonbury, the smaller remaining at Canterbury. Moreover, Glastonbury suggested that the relics at Canterbury should be concealed till the truth was established. In response, Warham questioned the authenticity of the relics at Glastonbury and claimed that it would be impertinent for him to conceal the relics at Canterbury which he had himself seen. He ordered instead that Glastonbury's relics should be brought before him.[207] This shows how much such practices were still part of a living tradition: no doubt, it might have continued indefinitely. But it does seem to me to be desperately vulnerable to any kind of searching scepticism. As even Jack Scarisbrick was provoked to ask (when reviewing Eamon Duffy's book), 'had veneration of relics come close to mere magic?'[208]

The more-or-less automatic sale and distribution of indulgences at pilgrimage sites reinforced such mechanistic attitudes. Since the twelfth century, popes, cardinals and bishops had offered indulgences—often specifying the number of days remitted from penance in purgatory, forty as the fourteenth-century maximum, a hundred by popes in the fifteenth century—to those who went on pilgrimage to named shrines and contributed money towards their maintenance. By the late fifteenth century, it was accepted (and ratified by Pope Sixtus IV in 1476) that indulgences could be used to assist those who were already dead. Abuses could readily arise if monasteries and churches competed to attract pilgrims by offering ever more generous indulgences; leading, as we have seen with chantries, to an accounting mentality in which the faithful sought to accumulate ever more indulgences, exacerbated when pardoners selling indulgences behaved with all the unscrupulousness of salesmen in marketing their wares.[209] There is no doubting the popularity and ubiquity of indulgences: people actively and vigorously sought them out. 'There is sometimes a sense of a papacy besieged by petitioners, and possibly losing control of the process.' Did people collect indulgences in the spirit that we collect tokens or Air Miles? How far were theological and devotional impulses present? Did some buy indulgences not because they believed in the theology or wanted to reduce their or their family's time in purgatory, but because they valued the more immediate or even the secular uses to which their donations would be put, such as the rebuilding of their parish church or cathedral or of a bridge or the maintenance of a hospital? Whatever the case may be, undoubtedly indulgences offered an easy target to satirists and reformers.[210]

The habit of promising to make a pilgrimage if a saint worked the miracle—by curing an illness, or by calming a storm—tended to reinforce the mechanical quality of pilgrimage. A remarkably high proportion of the miracles attributed to Henry VI followed the bending of a coin in his honour and the making of a vow to take it as an offering to his tomb.[211] Pilgrimage by deputy again tended to make the relationship between saint and intercessor more commercial than devotional. Erasmus's Ogygius went on pilgrimage to Santiago de Compostela because his wife's mother had vowed that he should do so if her daughter had a son born alive.[212] In September 1526 a servant of Sir Henry Willoughby was paid 12d 'by my master's commandment when he went of pilgrimage', probably to the Holy Cross at Garendon.[213] Miles Salley (d. 1517), bishop of Llandaff and abbot of Eynsham, offered £10 in his will to an honest and trustworthy man prepared to go on pilgrimage in his name to Santiago de Compostela and a shrine of our Lady in Castile.[214] If you cannot yourself perform a good work, the next best thing is to encourage someone else to do it; but the risks of abuse are obvious.

A great deal would depend on the spirit in which pilgrims went on pilgrimage. If they went selfishly, as Erasmus mocked, maids praying for handsome and rich husbands, philosophers for a solution to their problems, countrymen for showers, priests for the best benefices, then the whole venture became dangerously mechanical.[215] Of course, pilgrimage had always included an element of tourism and entertainment, and that too offered a target for satire.[216] William Worsley, priest and hermit, was accused in 1530 of having said that no man riding on pilgrimage, having under him a soft saddle and an easy horse, should have any merit thereby.[217] According to John Hewes, draper, the vicar of Croydon had said that much immorality arose from pilgrimages to Willesden and Muswell.[218] Mistress Cottismore of Brightwell allegedly said that 'when women go to offer to images or saints, they did it to show their new gay gear . . . folks go on pilgrimage more for the green way than for any devotion'.[219] Should those pilgrim badges, most of them a cheap alloy of tin and lead, be seen as sacred objects, almost 'secondary relics', for those who acquired them, or more like the souvenirs that day trippers buy today?[220] It is a question of striking a balance: medieval pilgrimage has been compared to modern museums, full of half-comprehending tourists, of young people having a day out, yet with serious and scholarly purposes at their core.[221] Are the experiences of those who go church-crawling, or visit the blockbuster exhibitions in art galleries, or go to concerts at all comparable? Does the ritual of pilgrimage meet a perennial human need?[222] It has been suggested as a general rule 'that all flourishing centres of pilgrimage must by definition attract an inseparable, if uneasy, agglomeration of the genuinely needy, the genuinely devout, and those for whom curiosity is a stronger motive than either need or devotion'.[223] Historians should take care not to be too pietistic. 'Uppermost in the minds of believers who journeyed to Walsingham or Ipswich were the images of the Virgin to be found at those places,' wrote one scholar.[224] Uppermost, no doubt, in the minds of *believers*, but how many of those who went on pilgrimage were believers? How many pilgrims took part in pilgrimages in much the same part-materialistic, part-sentimental way that many nowadays treat Christmas? A no doubt unenforceable royal proclamation of 1473 claimed that, on pretext of pilgrimage, far too many people were wandering about in vagabondage: in future no one should go on pilgrimage without a letter of authority under the king's great seal, stating the reasons for the pilgrimage, the pilgrim's place of origin and his destination.[225]

The difficulty for the church was that pilgrimage was so large-scale and so varied an activity, much of it inherited from an obscure past, involving monasteries that were often exempt from episcopal supervision, or informal shrines in remote places, and relics whose authority was based on miracle[226] that controlling, or even monitoring, it was almost impossible. How much did that matter? 'To have a favourite relic or statue, and to honour and cherish it, and indeed to have a favourite saint—perhaps identified with one's trade or guild—is, short of obsession, as harmless and indeed congenial as having a favourite sentimental possession, football team or pop group, providing comfort, identity, vicarious excitement and inspiration—albeit misplaced, no doubt, in many cases.'[227] But when in the late 1530s pilgrimage shrines were subjected to unprecedentedly close scrutiny, as part of the dissolution of the monasteries, what was discovered (sometimes, it seems, almost accidentally) was by no means easy to defend. Thomas More had argued that people did not confuse images and reality: 'I trust there be no man so mad nor woman neither but they know quicke [living] men from dead stones and tree from flesh and bone . . . there is no dog so mad but he knoweth a very coney [rabbit] from a coney carved and painted'.[228] All the same, one does wonder about images such as that of Darvell Gadarn, Derfel the Mighty, at Llanderfel, a wooden image of a warrior in arms, on horseback, carrying a little spear in his hand and a casket of iron about his neck, who was believed to have the power to fetch the damned out of hell.[229] Commissioners in 1538 investigated the alleged blood of Christ at Hailes. Bishop Latimer claimed that pilgrims 'believe verily that it is the very blood that was in Christ's body, shed upon the mount of Calvary for our salvation, and that the sight of it with their bodily eye, doth certify them and put them out of doubt, that they be in clean life, and in state of salvation without spot of sin'.[230] It seems that the initiative for the investigation came from Stephen, the abbot of Hailes, who wrote to Thomas Cromwell expressing his thanks to God 'that ever I was born to live to this time of light and knowledge of his true honour'. Having embraced the truth from the bottom of his heart, he now wished to set apart everything that appeared as superstition or idolatry. Referring to the blood at Hailes which had long been held to be a miracle, he said that 'I have a conscience putting me in dread lest idolatry be committed therein'. He hesitated to put it away on his own authority but asked Cromwell to send down commissioners to investigate and to take such order that the blood was no more an occasion of idolatry.[231] (Similarly the prior of Cardigan, examined about the pretended taper of Our Lady there, confessed that he had been deceived by it, saying that he had seen only its nether end.) A little later the abbot of Hailes asked Cromwell to license him to pull it down 'every stick and stone' since he was afraid 'lest it should minister occasion to any weak person looking thereupon to abuse his conscience therewith'.[232] In October the king accordingly issued a commission to Bishop Latimer, the prior of Worcester, the abbot of Hailes and Richard Tracy.[233] They opened the cask in the presence of a great multitude and took it out of the round silver-bound barrel in which it was enclosed. Bishop Latimer examined it carefully and found it to be 'an unctuous gum'. It had 'a certain unctuous moistness'. When in the glass, it looked a glistening red, rather like blood; yet when even a little was taken out it looked yellow like amber or 'base gold'. It cleaved like gum or birdlime. What it was not was blood.[234] The commissioners decided that it was simply honey mixed with saffron (not duck's blood, as some had claimed). In November Bishop Hilsey of Rochester preached at Paul's Cross, displaying the blood, and declared that it was 'honey clarified and coloured with saffron, lying like a gum, as it evidently had been proved and tested before the king and his council'.[235]

The commissioners also exposed the mechanical contrivances which worked 'miracles'. The Rood of Grace, at Boxley Abbey, near Maidstone, Kent, was an image of Christ crucified. Its singularity was that Christ nodded his head, winked his eyes, turned his beard, moved his eyes and lips and bent his body. According to Foxe, if the gift offered was a small piece of silver, the rood would hang a frowning lip; if it were a piece of gold, then his jaws would go merrily.[236] No doubt these contrivances grew in the telling, yet there is no doubt that the head and eyes of the image did move.[237] It was revealed in 1538 that these miracles were worked by wires through little pipes—'certain engines and old wire with old rotten sticks in the back of the same, that did cause the eyes of the same to move and stir in the head thereof, like unto a lively thing, and also the nether lip in likewise to move as though it should speak'.[238] Was this just 'good propaganda' for protestants, justifying the reformation?[239] But surely it provided them with effective arguments precisely because such practices were not readily defensible. It is hard to defend them, and harder still to enter into the mental world of those who operated them. Were these images, whose origins lay deep in the mists of time, now the inherited responsibility of a small handful of guardian-monks, with most of their fellow monks happily uninvolved in the details of their operation? Jeffray Chamber, who found out how the Rood of Grace at Boxley worked—as he presented it, by chance—when the monastery was being defaced, and its images plucked down, thought it 'not a little strange'. He accordingly questioned the abbot and the older monks, but they declared themselves ignorant of it.[240] Perhaps 'those responsible for the shrines might be as much the dupes of their own contrivances as the pilgrims themselves'.[241] Interestingly, Stephen, abbot of Hailes, said that there was one monk, over eighty years old, who had 'kept' the blood for almost forty years: the abbot himself feared he could be accused of 'changing and renewing it with drake's blood'.[242] The clergy and monks described by Erasmus appear somewhat defensive, evasive and embarrassed when taxed with some of the oddities of the cults and relics over which they had charge. 'What need to ask such questions,' responded a canon showing Ogygius the holy milk of the Virgin when Ogygius asked for proof.[243] The attendant priest at Canterbury could make no answer when John Colet asked whether some of Becket's riches could be taken to relieve the poor.[244]

Or perhaps it was all more like the Easter Sepulchres we have already touched upon. In the later middle ages an image of the living Christ with a host on his breast or in his hands would be secretly inserted into the Easter Sepulchre in order to be dramatically raised from it on Easter morning: 'the "miraculous" appearance of an image of the resurrected Christ displaying a consecrated host in his breast would have increased the impact of the *elevatio*'. It would have looked rather like a tableau from a Corpus Christi procession.[245] It was not exactly deceitful. But it was a set of practices desperately vulnerable to Erasmian, protestant or simply commonsense rationalist critiques.

And it could easily be presented as just a financial racket, as monks cynically exploiting the innocent devotion of the faithful people for their own material gain. In fact, the financial benefits of shrines are somewhat elusive. The by-no-means unbiased Richard, bishop of Dover, claimed that two images at Bangor, including 'the holiest relic in all North Wales' were worth twenty marks a year to the friars—which is not a vast sum.[246] The canon of Notley Abbey, Buckinghamshire, who served the image of Our Lady at Caversham, Oxfordshire, had the offerings for his living, which suggests that they were a few pounds a year.[247] If the monasteries did receive a large income from the voluntary gifts of parishioners and pilgrims, it did not appear in the pages of the commissioners' returns in the mid-1530s. Oblations and the income from the church services made up only a very small part of the monastic spiritual budget recorded there. Oblations were very considerable in one case only, that of St Mary's Walsingham which had received £260 12s 4d. Becket's shrine at Canterbury had only received £36 2s 7d, the rood of Hailes £10. Were these figures 'suspiciously low?'[248] It is possible that monks and clergy at pilgrimage centres (except Walsingham) concealed their revenues or received non-monetary gifts or used different accounting practices—and the figures for Canterbury, with a remarkable collapse in revenues after 1420, are baffling (from £370 p.a. between 1390 and 1439 to £27 p.a. between 1440 and 1489 and just £14 p.a. between 1490 and 1535).[249] Two opposite deductions from such evidence are both risky: on the one hand that the market in pilgrimages was saturated and in decline; on the other hand that pilgrimage centres were grand financial rackets.[250] But whatever the truth of the matter, the perception that the monks had profited, however little, from deceit was obviously damaging. It quickly provoked the charge that the money might better have been spent on the poor.[251] Was there resentment that people had been duped? According to Jeffray Chamber, when he showed the deceit of the Rood of Grace at Boxley openly to the people on market-day at Maidstone, 'to see the false crafty and subttle handling thereof to the dishonour of God and illusion of the said people', they had the matter 'in wonderous detestation and hatred'.[252] William Barlow, not a disinterested witness, reported after the removal of images in summer 1538 that 'the people now sensibly seeing the long obscured verity manifestly to display her brightness, whereby their inveterate accustomed superstition apparently detected, all popish delusions shall soon be defaced, so that erudition, the parent of virtue and unfallible foundation of all ordinate policy . . . might . . . be planted here'.[253] But not everyone felt like that: a local woman claimed that the image of Our Lady at Walsingham had wrought a miracle even after it had been dismantled and sent up to London (though apparently she was set up in the stocks at Walsingham on market-day, and then sent round the town in a cart, with the boys and young people throwing snowballs at her).[254]

What makes pilgrimage so tricky to assess is that, as these examples show, the practice ultimately rested on an act of faith, which many, if not all, both educated and ignorant, powerful and powerless, held, and which it may be something of an impertinence, perhaps, for a modern historian to call into question. What, for example, should we make of Elizabeth Barton's visions of the Virgin Mary? We may prefer explanations such as those of Hugh Trevor-Roper, who suffered from hallucinations—seeing bicycle races, horse races, landscapes, trains—as his sight deteriorated. 'If you lose the capacity to see,' Trevor-Roper later said, 'the brain gets cross and invents an artificial reality for the reality that's lost. It creates it out of the dregs of the unconscious memory—hence the bicycle races . . . Now I know all about ghosts. It's perfectly obvious to me that they're created out of the rubbish of the brain, in the same way as are the hallucinations of Charles Bonnet Syndrome', the condition from which he had been suffering.[255] Visions are thus very real to those who experience them. Since, however, there is no way that they can prove to others that they have indeed experienced a vision, anyone who believed Elizabeth Barton was, in the last resort, making an act of faith. And as such, the belief in visions, pilgrimages and miracles was always open to rationalist critiques, whether from intellectual theologians or from the homespun down-to-earth first-principled approach of the unlettered. There had always been a few sceptics, like Guibert of Nogent in the twelfth century, critical of the credulity of the people and all too aware of the inadequacy of written proof of the authenticity of relics,[256] or Wyclif in the late fourteenth, deeply suspicious of postbiblical saints (if 'remarkably silent about image worship and pilgrimages'[257]), or those accused of heresy in the fifteenth and early sixteenth centuries, whose alleged wrong beliefs consistently included criticism of pilgrimages as unscriptural, incredible, mercenary and noisy (and whose penances when they abjured often included going on pilgrimage). Satirists such as Langland,

Chaucer and Skelton mocked the worldly features of pilgrimage. But one must be cautious in drawing on their satires. Langland hits out at fraudulence but pilgrimage is still the symbol of conscience's quest at the end of the poem.[258] Skelton's biting satire of the church would later be printed by protestants but was prompted by what was a wholly orthodox, moralising and idealistic view of what the church could be. None of that criticism was likely in itself to have brought about the collapse of pilgrimage: pilgrimage had so far rather triumphed over such dissenters, moralists and sceptics as there were.

Nonetheless, pilgrimage was in two senses vulnerable. First, the more doubtful practices associated with pilgrimage left the church perennially exposed to criticism, and open to the threat of a more fundamental and systematic attack on the whole system of salvation through the intercession of saints. It is notable that Thomas Bilney, one of the first Englishmen to have been influenced by Luther's doctrine of justification by faith alone, should, as early as 1527–8, have preached sermons at the shrines at Ipswich and Willesden, denouncing pilgrimages and urging that men should address their prayers instead directly to God.[259] Secondly, pilgrimage, like the church as a whole, was dependent on the continuing support of the government. Any institution that depends on physical sites and popular participation will find it hard to survive against official disapproval if the government is more or less united and determined. The continued support of the authorities—above all of the king, leading ministers and churchmen—was vital to the survival of practices such as pilgrimage. The close relationship between church and state had in many ways been an indispensable source of strength to the medieval church, but it left it highly exposed to any change in royal attitudes. Once government policy took the wholly unpredictable turn that it did in the 1530s, it would have been very hard for the church to have resisted it.

Henry VIII is, in a sense, the *deus ex machina*, or the *diabolus ex machina*, of this story. Although Henry's accounts record payments to shrines, and although he was reported to be intending to go on pilgrimage to Master John Schorn at Windsor in gratitude for recovery from fever ('to procede forth on his pilgrimage to master John Schorn in giving lauds and thanks to God [though it must be noted that Henry's thanks would be to God, not to John Schorn] of his speedy and soon convalescence and amendment') in 1521,[260] he does not strike me as a committed pilgrim. He cannot be compared, say, to Catherine of Aragon, that 'indefatigable pilgrim' as David Loades and Christopher Haigh called her, who went to several shrines in the late 1510s and early 1520s, unaccompanied by her husband.[261] It is perhaps suggestive that it was after his accession to the throne in 1509 that the momentum for the canonisation and transfer of the body of

Henry VI seems to have petered out; in his will, Henry VIII wished the tombs of both Henry VI and Edward IV to be made more princely in the same place where they then were, reflecting perhaps a sense of a neglected commitment but also a revealing unwillingness to mark Henry VI out as different from, or as more worthy than, Edward IV.

When, in the 1530s, official formulations of faith expressed doubts about the value of pilgrimage, and when, in the late 1530s, pilgrimage shrines were dismantled, that hostility to pilgrimage, not least from the king, was not directly the result of an endemic undercurrent of scepticism (why should that lead to a change of policy?), nor the result of the adoption of lutheranism. It reflected more the development of the king's active anti-papalism (itself the somewhat accidental consequence of the divorce) into a rejection of practices seen as associated with Rome, such as indulgences, the idolatrous worship of images, and anything that might be seen as potentially a threat to his rule, such as monasteries (putative fifth columns of papal power) and the shrines which they housed. But since that hostility to pilgrimage came from the top, from the king and his leading ministers, and because it was imposed by force and by pressures, it was irresistible. Abbots and bishops and monks and priests could do very little here. Five bishops— John Clerk of Bath and Wells, John Stokesley of London, John Longland of Lincoln, Cuthbert Tunstal of Durham, William Rugge of Norwich—tried their best, probably in 1537, when the statement of faith known as the Bishops' Book was being debated. They boldly defended pilgrimage. 'The bodies of saints, and, namely, the relics of holy martyrs, are to be honoured most sincerely, as the members of Christ. The churches builded in their names, deputed to the service of God, to be gone unto with faithful and good devotion; and not to be contemned: and pilgrimage to places where Almighty God sheweth miracles, may be done by them that have thereunto devotion.'[262] It was a clear expression of conviction—but it was not really an argument, and the critics of pilgrimage, not least the king, proved the stronger. Official hostility to pilgrimage shrines could, moreover, readily be justified by the abuses now revealed. Physical destruction vividly publicised these abuses, and empty shrines then mocked the impotence of the images to protect themselves.[263] There was, of course, a large-scale popular protest—the Pilgrimage of Grace in 1536—against religious changes, before the most important shrines were attacked; but it failed, and its failure on the one hand associated pilgrimage, its declared purpose, with treason in the eyes of the government and, on the other hand, helped to deter further rebellion in 1538 and 1539 when the larger monasteries surrendered and the pilgrimage shrines they housed were dismantled. Conformity does not mean more than acquiescence. In countless ways devotion to the saints survived in popular memory, and even perhaps in attenuated practice, as in the visiting of holy wells in Cornwall and in Wales in search of cures.[264] The disappearance of pilgrimage must have been a shock to many. Some, probably a minority, accepted the criticisms now made of pilgrimage: the spell was broken; others, though even fewer still, may have seen the dismantling of the shrines as justifying the plain scepticism they had always felt.

How then should pilgrimage be characterised? A flourishing and fervent devotion, or merely a social pastime, or a superstitious road to idolatry? It was, or it could be seen as, all of these. And in its combination of vitality—in its profusion and popularity—and of vulnerability—vulnerability to criticism and scepticism, and vulnerability to attack and dismantling by a determined royal government—it epitomises the strengths and the weaknesses of the late medieval church as a whole.

1 Above. The interior of St Andrew, Cullompton, Devon. A sumptuous late-medieval rebuilding; long, light and broad, with a fine roof.

2 The tower and spire of St James, Louth, Lincolnshire. The tower is *c.*1440–5, the spire was built between 1501 and 1515 and cost £305 7s 5d, a magnificent reflection of piety and urban pride.

Orate' pro anima Jacobi Hobart, Militis, qui Ecclesiam hanc Parochialem de Laddon, A primo Fundamento condidit, suis Proprijs Bonis: etiamq' Dominã Hobart uxore ouq' Pontem Sancti Olaui unã cum uia strata ad õum Ducente Proprijs guis Impensis Boni Publici ergõ Ædificauit

5 Sir James Hobart (d.1517) and his wife Margaret at prayer, Holy Trinity, Loddon, Norfolk (panel painting, south aisle). The inscription urges the onlooker to 'pray for the soul of James Hobart knight who established the parish church of Loddon from its foundations from his own wealth, as well as for Lady Hobart his wife, who built St Olave's Bridge together with the [cause] way leading to it, at her own expense for the common weal'. The text over their heads declares 'Lord Jesus, the means [mediator?] through the cross and passion, you give to us pardon and remission for our sins'. If the rustic quality of the faces points to an early seventeenth-century date, the invocation to the viewer to pray for the soul of Sir James but for Lady Hobart suggests that the inscription was composed after his death but while she was alive, pointing to an early sixteenth century date for the original image, which may have been the foot of a stained glass window that does not survive. Perhaps this panel painting and copies now at Blicking (dated 1614) and Lincoln's Inn were commissioned by Sir James's great grandson, James, who is buried in Loddon church.

Detail of top left corner.

6 *A description of the Lolards tower, where M. Rich. Hunne was first murthered*, in John Foxe's *Acts and Monuments*. Illustrating and reinforcing the account of the Hunne affair given by the martyrologist John Foxe in the 1563 edition of the *Acts and Monuments*, and in particular depicting the details of his alleged murder as recorded in the pamphlet 'The Enquirie and Verdite of the Quest panneld of the death of Richard Hune wich was founde hanged in Lolars tower' printed *c*.1536 and reprinted by Foxe. Hunne was allegedly strangled but then left hanging to make it look as if he had committed suicide.

7 Bishop Alcock's Chantry, Ely Cathedral, begun in 1488. Lavishly decorated chantry of John Alcock (1430–1500), bishop of Ely, perhaps the most saintly of late medieval bishops.

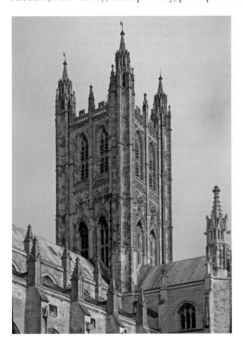

8 Bell Harry, and detail of Cardinal Morton's rebus, Canterbury Cathedral. John Morton (d. 1500), cardinal archbishop of Canterbury, financed the building of the great central tower of Canterbury Cathedral; his rebus – a tun under a cardinal's hat – is repeated up the corner turrets of the tower: see the initials M, O and R going clockwise, with the tun in the centre.

9 Unknown artist, Thomas Wolsey, sixteenth century. Thomas Wolsey (d. 1530), cardinal archbishop of York, papal legate, Lord Chancellor, was Henry VIII's leading minister from 1514 to 1529, and in many ways a committed reformer of the church.

10 Exterior of Henry VII's chapel (Lady Chapel), Westminster Abbey, London. Financed by Henry VII with the intention, not realised, of reburying Henry VI there, increasingly venerated as a saint. Instead it has become known as Henry VII's own mausoleum. Begun in 1503 and completed c.1512, it was almost certainly designed by William Vertue. An extraordinary profusion of turrets and panelling.

11 *The South Prospect of Black-friers Church in Norwich* by Wenceslaus Hollar.

12 Bird's-eye view of Blackfriars, Norwich. Friaries dominated late medieval towns and cities but their buildings have largely vanished. The rare survival of the Blackfriars in Norwich offers a vivid impression of their importance. Blackfriars' church is set in a complex much changed by modern development but the plan of the partially surviving cloister is nevertheless recognisable. The octagonal tower shown in Hollar's engraving collapsed in 1712.

7

CRITICISM

RICHARD Hunne was assuredly critical of the church. He made principled attacks on its financial demands and legal procedures. He was
eventually arrested and, as we have seen, he was found dead in his cell. His
opposition to the church has long been seen as emblematic of lay anti-
clericalism; and his death has been read as showing that his hostility to the
church was amply justified. Undoubtedly, the Hunne affair reveals several
areas of tension, to say no more, between the laity and the church. But
whether lay anti-clericalism deserves the prominence it has until recently
been given, not least in explanations of the reformation, is much less sure.
A.G. Dickens wrote of 'the vast body of evidence for anti-clerical forces
within English public opinion', and linked the growth of towns, the expansion of education, the increasing sophistication of the laity and the greater
self-confidence of the common lawyers in a great anti-clerical tradition.[1]
Some contemporary observers commented on it. The poet Skelton's Collyn
Clout regretted 'such temporal war and bate/ As now is made of late/
Against holy church estate . . . the temporalty/ Accuseth the spiritualty;/
The spiritualty again/ Doth grudge and complain/ Upon the temporal men';
Skelton's Parrot noted 'so hot hatred against the Church, and charity so
cold'.[2] In 1529 the newly arrived imperial ambassador Eustace Chapuys
opined that 'nearly all the people hate the priests'.[3] Writing about 1532, the
common lawyer Christopher St German declared, as an undoubted fact,
that 'division hath risen between the spiritualty and temporalty'.[4]

Despite such colourful contemporary remarks, more recently the extent
and significance of anti-clericalism have been vigorously played down by
many historians, notably Christopher Haigh. It is certainly very difficult to

see a crescendo of hostility towards the church in the early sixteenth century. What there was then, as there had always been, was plenty of criticism of the church and of clerics: 'dissatisfaction with the state of the church for one reason or another is as old as christianity itself'.[5] And, of course, a constant cannot explain a change, as Haigh has pointed out; if such criticism was a normal feature of medieval life, it cannot therefore of itself account for the reformation. Yet that does not mean that such criticism was unimportant. As Haigh has written of the English civil war, 'there is always a danger that in rightly denying that religious division led directly to civil war, we deny that there was religious division'.[6] Similarly, it might be said that 'there is always a danger that in rightly denying that anticlericalism/ criticism of the church led directly to the reformation, we deny that there was anticlericalism/criticism of the church'. And if anti-clericalism in no way made the reformation inevitable, nonetheless it was important. What we must do is assess the nature of that criticism.

Much of it was in response to the financial demands the church made on the laity and to the legal claims that underlay such demands. As Euan Cameron has observed, the constant process of haggling and negotiation over rights and dues inevitably left somebody dissatisfied and so swelled a reservoir of deeply felt, if not necessarily justified, grievances.[7] The church was once more in danger of getting the worst of all worlds: inadequate revenues and lay opprobrium. And lively and vigorous argument over money always risked turning into something more fundamentally challenging, calling into question not just the immediate financial demand but also whatever principle underpinned that claim.

The very existence of such criticism of the church offered opportunities to those who might wish to exploit it for their own ends, notably lay monarchs who found themselves in a quarrel with the papacy. An intriguing illustration of this comes from the third duke of Norfolk's letter to William Benet, one of Henry VIII's agents in Rome, in 1532 (or possibly 1531). 'On my behalf,' Norfolk began, 'ye may surely affirm to his holiness, that notwithstanding the church hath in this realm many wringers at their high authorities, yet no thing hurtful shall be done, unless the fault be in him in proceeding wrongfully and ungratefully against the king.' If the pope granted Henry his annulment, all would be well; the king would protect the church from the 'infinite clamours' of laymen in parliament 'against the misusing of the spiritual jurisdiction'. If the pope offered Henry 'ill and unkind handling' then Henry might not protect the church. Meanwhile, Norfolk assured Benet, 'this realme did never grudge the 10th part against the abuses of the church at no parliament in my days as they do now'.[8] None of that should be taken at face value and quoted as uncomplicated evidence of general lay attitudes to the church. But nor need it be completely dismissed. Endemic quarrels over money and over jurisdiction were one of the vulnerable features of the church, a sore that a monarch quarrelling with the pope might deliberately seek to inflame.

In 1529 several anti-clerical statutes were passed by parliament. They restricted and regulated probate and mortuary fees and clerical pluralism. It is just possible even more was briefly contemplated, including disendowment of the church. For that we have a copy of a petition from 1410 and a longer undated petition, most likely from 1529, vituperative in its onslaught against the church.[9] It is not clear that anything like that was put to parliament. But Bishop Fisher did vehemently protest against various measures.[10] The most plausible explanation is that Henry VIII was exploiting lay discontents on a range of issues in order to put churchmen on the defensive as he pursued his campaign for a divorce. That means that this anti-clerical legislation cannot be taken at face value in its presentation of the weaknesses of the church. As we shall see, studies of particular aspects have tended to show that the criticisms were disproportionate. Yet if the criticisms had been wholly absurd there would have been nothing for the king to exploit. And Bishop Fisher's reaction itself shows that he feared that lay anti-clerical sentiment was strong.

The Hunne affair showed that financial relations between the church and the laity were a rich source of disputes. That quarrel had begun over a dispute over mortuary fees, with a dramatic and tragic conclusion. According to Christopher St German, who was writing after parliamentary legislation in 1529, priests continued to tell their parishioners that unless they paid mortuaries at the old rates rather than what was laid down in the new statute, they would not be saved. 'There were few thinges within this realm that caused more variance among the people,' St German noted; 'the curates loved their mortuaries better than their lives'.[11] In a colourful tale told by the antiquary John Leland, the vicar of Brackley, Northamptonshire, was buried alive by a lord of the town displeased with him over a horse taken, as some said, for a mortuary. The lord then, it was said, went to Rome for absolution and took great repentance.[12] True or not, and it sounds fantastic, the telling of such a tale shows that it was not instantly dismissed as implausible. And there were certainly a few instances—one study found five between c.1509 and 1526—of the insensitivity of priests when exacting payments after the death of a child, always a dreadful experience.[13] Parliament passed a bill regulating mortuaries in 1529 but this bill should not be taken at face value. It has rightly been seen as 'probably part of a carefully orchestrated campaign to pressurise the church into conformity with the royal will rather than [reflecting] spontaneous popular opposition':

in 1529 Henry VIII was wanting to put pressure on the church over his divorce.[14] Yet that does not dispose of the issue. If there had been no grievance over mortuaries, then the king would not have been able to make use of it to harass senior churchmen. That there was, as a study of the archdeaconry of Chester has found, an increase in the number of mortuary suits, from eight between 1500 and 1529 to thirteen in 1530, the year after a new law had been passed, hints that mortuaries were not a matter wholly indifferent.[15] And further legislation in 1534 was directed at exactions within the archdeaconry of Richmond, Yorkshire, whose inhabitants were 'sore and grievously exacted and impoverished by the parsons vicars and other such as have benefices and spiritual promotions within the same', who took from everyone who died what they called 'a pension', ranging from one-ninth to one-third of the deceased's goods and chattels. The sums involved were not small: Robert Holdsworth, vicar of Halifax, would complain in 1535 that the legislation cost him over 80 marks (£53 13s 4d).[16] Mortuaries, then, were a source of resentment and disputes. Some churchmen may have acted uncharitably, or even illegally, and that would have given the impression of the church as a forbiddingly powerful and grasping institution. But it would be as misleading to suggest that priests always and only behaved like that. And, above all, it must be emphasised that disputes over mortuaries were, as far as recorded evidence shows, few and far between.

Tithes were an even more immediate cause of disputes between laity and church. Long ago the Carolingian church had struggled to free itself from excessive dependence on lay lords. That led to the development of tithes—dues payable by a wide cross-section of the population in return for the services of a parish priest—first recorded in England in the 920s. In the Gregorian era efforts were made to extend the principle of tithes to non-agrarian sources of income. By and large tithes were effectively collected in late medieval England. But there was much fertile ground for dispute, especially the vexed questions of how to value animals and how to assess fluctuating urban wages. If the principle of tithes was widely accepted, there was conflict over the scope of the tax and over the rates demanded. Henry Tankerd, vicar of Barfreston, Kent, ignored the local tithing customs in 1511 and demanded higher rates; those who refused were denied holy bread and holy water. The parish was united in opposition: and Archbishop Warham removed him. In Hayes, Middlesex, there was a lively argument over tithing customs, which the local alehouse-keeper refused to pay at Easter 1530, threatening the vicar and his curate. The matter went before the court of Star Chamber. Arrangements for assessing and collecting tithes were particularly bothersome in London, partly because parish boundaries were unusually uncertain, partly because attempts to resolve the issues, as

in 1453 and in 1528, failed to work definitively. Henry Gold, parson of
Aldermary, London, was in dispute with his parishioners over how much
was due from the owner of an odd (that is to say not easily divisible)
number of lambs.[17] All that said, the number of tithe cases, however
dramatic their details, was never great. In the diocese of Canterbury,
250 parishes yielded fourteen suits in 1482 and four in 1531; 1,148 parishes
in the diocese of Norwich yielded ten suits a year in the early 1520s;
339 parishes in the diocese of Winchester yielded two suits in 1527 and two
in 1529; 650 parishes in the diocese of Lichfield yielded ten suits in 1525,
four in 1530. Any particular conflict might prove spectacular and make for
a good story; but conflict was not typical. It is interesting that some 70 per
cent of London testators included in their wills bequests for tithes unpaid,
revealing a recognition and acceptance of the necessity of tithes. No doubt
the events of the 1530s led to a greater unwillingness to pay
tithes. Tithe suits became more frequent in the 1540s.[18] A statute of 1535
denounced 'divers numbers of evil disposed persons' who 'having no respect
of their duties to almighty God, but against right and good conscience have
attempted to subtract and withhold in some places the whole and in some
places great parts of their tithes and oblations' due God and Holy Church;
and disobeyed the ecclesiastical courts 'in more temerous and large manner
than before this time hath been seen'. The king as supreme head willed that
the spiritual rights and duties of the church should be preserved and therefore enacted 'by authority of this present parliament that all his subjects
should, according to the lawful usages of their parishes, pay the tithes of
holy church'. The operation of the act was suspended until the committee
of thirty-two persons, named by the king to review the ecclesiastical laws of
England, had completed their work; and it was provided that any party to
a suit could argue in court as if the act had never been made.[19] The act
recognised that there was a problem, indeed an increasing problem; but the
reluctance of the king to make an immediate order to his subjects to pay
testifies to hesitations and uncertainty about the place of tithes. If the basic
principle of tithe as a tax paid to the church was straightforward and unex-
ceptionable, that was often not so in particular cases. If, for example, a
monastery had in the distant past undertaken to supply a priest for the
parish in return for receiving a proportion of the tithe, that could readily
arouse misunderstandings and resentments as resources were taken away
from the parish. If long ago a layman had made some such arrangements,
payments to their lay descendants could seem even more inappropriate. On
the whole, it must be emphasised, tithes were duly paid. 'Many people
surely appreciated that the parochial system, which they generally supported,
depended upon the payment of tithes.'[20] Yet the complexities of the system

meant that tithes were always a potential source of disputes—in short, another area of vulnerability in the church.

The probate of wills was an ecclesiastical responsibility with financial implications. Here a common accusation was that clergy exacted fees beyond the limits laid down by statute. A study of Lincolnshire shows that 118 out of 412 executors in 1505–6 paid more than the supposed 5s maximum.[21]

At a more general level there was irritation at or jealousy of the wealth of the church. Some think, said Christopher St German, that the church should have no possessions, that it has too much.[22] There was lay resentment in Suffolk in early April 1525 when it was (wrongly) believed that the clergy were not being asked to make an Amicable Grant; the commissioners responded by insisting that the clergy would pay double,[23] and it is indeed the case that in the 1520s the clergy paid at higher rates than the laity. Reporting the gossip that the churchmen would be deprived of their temporal wealth, John Husee, Lord Lisle's London agent, added that many were glad and few bemoaned them.[24] Such jealousies and tensions are tricky to assess. In Germany the so-called peasants' war in 1525 revealed a startling degree of hatred of the church. But that was a society in which bishops, cathedral chapters and monasteries exercised significant legal rights over the laity and made financial exactions that were condemned as rapacity. In England during the same year clergy and laity were, in contrast, seen as making common cause against unprecedented royal financial demands.[25] Nonetheless, the financial demands of the church could not but leave the church vulnerable to criticism. Christ had lived for the day and urged his followers to renounce material things. Many heard, and still tried to follow, that message. But it was hardly realistic for the church as an institution—as opposed to christians as individuals—to espouse poverty: institutions presuppose staff and buildings, in short, income and expenditure. And those buildings and that establishment, as well as the regular taxation that maintained them, could quickly make the church appear grasping and extravagant, far removed from the ideals of apostolic poverty. 'How better to express—consciously or unconsciously—bitterness over the misuse of manpower by the ecclesiastical establishment than to represent Annas and Caiaphas in the mystery plays of York, Chester and other cities as contemporary bishops.'[26]

Financial disputes stirred the sharpest tensions between the laity and the church. It has often been held that ecclesiastical courts—which were run by senior clergy—also triggered much lay protest. Such a claim is much less tenable in the light of the studies of episcopal administration by the past generation of scholars which have revealed church courts operating sensibly and fairly.[27] Much of their business came not from churchmen seeking to prosecute lay miscreants but from laymen who saw church courts as appropriate places for the pursuit of their claims. They were speedy and convenient in matters involving debt, marriage, the sort of sexual misconduct that was seen as a public nuisance (above all prostitution) and slander.[28] It is hard, then, to decry church courts as inefficient or as a racket or as oppressive. So why was there so much heated criticism of them in contemporary writings, offering colourful quotations much drawn upon by historians until recently? The explanation is that much of the criticism of church courts was self-interested. In specific cases it might be no more than the discontent of a losing plaintiff.[29] More broadly it reflected a continuing struggle between common lawyers and church court lawyers for business, not least in areas of overlapping jurisdiction, rather than any generalised lay hostility to the church. Such tensions were unusually acute in the early sixteenth century because, it has been suggested, of falling levels of litigation in King's Bench and Common Pleas: common lawyers desperately needed to seek new business.[30] A legal historian has suggested that the 'insecure peace' between the two jurisdictions was 'nearing a crisis' in the early sixteenth century. Readers in the inns of court—teachers who outlined the state of the law in significant cases—took an increasingly restrictive view of ecclesiastical liberties: for example, John Hales in 1514. There was a 'substantial current' of private suits in King's Bench in the later fifteenth and early sixteenth centuries which turned on the legitimacy of the church courts in certain areas. Writs of prohibition or writs of praemunire could be obtained from the royal courts to halt proceedings in the church courts. In 1496 judges in King's Bench held that a suit in an ecclesiastical court was a case of praemunire. The king's lawyers used the writ of praemunire after 1500 in campaigns to restrict the jurisdiction of church courts, and to bring matters such as debt and slander within the scope of the royal courts in which they practised. Some fifty such cases between 1500 and 1532 have been uncovered. Maybe the novelty of all this has been exaggerated: there may have been similar actions earlier. But what is undoubtedly true is that the secular courts were restraining the operation of church courts in the years from 1495.[31] Sir James Hobart (d. 1517), attorney-general, shared 'the common lawyer's suspicion of the church and its courts'. He used writs of praemunire to attach the jurisdiction of the courts of the bishop of Norwich. Bishop Nix was angry and anxious, as we have seen. In 1504 he lamented to Archbishop Warham that 'the laymen be more bolder against the church than ever they were' and said that if the archbishop would support him 'I would curse all such promoters and maintainers of the praemunire in such cases as heretics and not believers in Christ's Church'.[32]

Of Sir John Fyneux, chief justice of the King's Bench, one historian has written that 'his judgments worked consistently to undermine the position of the church courts', especially, as we have seen, over sanctuary.[33]

Yet all this cannot be taken as evidence of general lay hostility to the church courts, or more widely to the church as a whole. Revenues and jurisdictions were obvious points of tension. It is not surprising that there should have been quarrels, at times, over particular financial demands or over legal rights. But here, above all, it is essential to strike a balance. There is a good deal to support the claim that the church was vulnerable in these areas: all these disputes and arguments left their deposit of irritation and mistrust. But there is nothing to suggest that such disputes reflected general or overwhelming hostility to the church. It is intriguing that the two judges whom we have just been considering were far from wholly anti-clerical. Hobart rebuilt Loddon church in Norfolk, and completed Bishop Goldwell's choir in Norwich Cathedral where he was buried in a chapel erected at his expense in the north arcade of the nave, and Fyneux wanted to be buried in Canterbury Cathedral near Becket's altar. They may have wished to shift the demarcation line between church courts and royal courts, but their actions reveal a conventional piety. Should we emphasise their aggressive encroachment on the procedures and resources of the church—or their evident conventional devotion? How far were they themselves aware of such tensions?[34]

Relations between townsmen and the church, especially cathedral or abbey, could be strained. In Canterbury the city and cathedral priory were at odds. The city complained that the convent's servants had cut the river bank, so stopping the mill which had been granted to the town by the king, and that the prior and convent fished in the river, the right to which belonged to the mayor and commonalty.[35] There was a long-running dispute between cathedral and city at Norwich, with flashpoints in 1272 (when a crowd set some of the priory buildings ablaze and killed some thirteen people, though seemingly no monks) and 1443 (when the commoners cried 'Let us burn the priory and kill the prior and monks', though they did not, on that occasion, come to blows); it seems to have eased somewhat in the later fifteenth century, and in 1524–5 two royal charters went the citizens' way.[36] It has been claimed that tensions between towns and monasteries were high and violence never far away between 1272 and 1399, but that such tensions much diminished in the course of the fifteenth century.[37] That overlooks a serious quarrel between the monks and townsmen of Sherborne in 1437, sufficiently vividly remembered for John Leland to describe it in his *Itinerary* a century later—an unusual inclusion. The townsmen were increasingly having their children baptised not in the nave of St Mary's Abbey, which served as their chief parish church, but in a chapel, All Hallows, which abutted the west end of the nave of the abbey. One Walter Gallor, a stout butcher, 'defaced clean the font'—the location of which was crucial to this dispute—and the 'variance' grew into 'a plain sedition'. The earl of Huntingdon (probably John Holland [d. 1447], later first duke of Exeter) took the townsmens' part, the bishop of Salisbury that of the monks. Then a priest from All Hallows shot 'a shaft with fire'—presumably a burning arrow—into the top of the partition dividing the monks' part from the townsmen's part, and since the partition was thatched, the roof caught fire and the whole church was gutted, the lead and bells melted. The abbot prosecuted, and the townsmen were compelled to contribute to the rebuilding of the abbey, first the east end, and then the nave—which remained roofless till it was rebuilt between 1475 and 1504, more than forty years after the fire. If for a time All Hallows was used as the parish church, once the rebuilding was complete parishioners were required to proceed from their church into St Mary's for Easter baptisms. Only after the dissolution of the monasteries, when the parishioners acquired the abbey church for their own worship and the church of All Hallows, now surplus to requirements, was demolished, was the dispute finally laid to rest.[38] That incident was the most spectacular dispute between monks and parishioners who shared the same church building. It is worth noting, in passing, that the conflagration was actually started by a priest of All Hallows who clearly took the townsmen's side against the abbey: this was not a completely clear-cut clash between church and laity. From quarrels elsewhere, it is clear that whenever they could parishioners were keen to increase and enlarge the spaces available to them, and to assert their independence, but the telling evidence of wills suggests that hostility between monks and parishioners was far from the norm: of 261 parishioners from nine monastic-parochial churches, over 50 per cent left bequests to the monastery with which their church was shared—a high proportion.[39] In Salisbury there was an awkward relationship between city and cathedral. Conflict was spasmodic. Issues included the raising of tallage, oaths sworn to the bishop's servants, legality of gifts of land in mortmain to the corporation.[40] Yet in Bury St Edmunds members of the social elite continued to request burial in the abbey and were involved in the reconstruction of the tower damaged by fire in 1465, so qualifying the supposedly strained relationship between abbey and town.[41] Conflict was not continuous; there was plainly much contact and some support; as ever, the challenge is to strike the right balance.

The attitude of medieval townsmen to their local cathedral was, it has been suggested, rather like that of their successors to modern universities: 'an ambiguous mixture of slight suspicion and considerable incomprehension was alleviated by a natural pleasure that this corporate giant might contribute to their own prestige and economic welfare'. Some might feel pride at the display of continuity of family and religion. Cathedral clergy were often local men, local townsmen and, therefore, links were strengthened between church and town in a way that is unlikely between modern universities and towns where only the mature students are local, and most of the younger students, and virtually all of the staff, have come from elsewhere.[42] And, furthermore, this analogy may underestimate the very real resentment of local inhabitants in many university towns against students, especially towards their excesses.

If lay anti-clericalism had been as widespread, as deep-seated and as passionately felt as many historians of an earlier generation declared, it might have been expected to lead to violence directed against priests and assaults on church property. Yet there was very little by way of physical attacks on the church. The spectacular violence in 1381—Archbishop Sudbury of Canterbury was murdered—reflected less any generalised hostility to the church than resentment at the way in which Sudbury, in his role as Lord Chancellor, was formally responsible for the hated and oppressive poll tax. Again, the murders of churchmen in 1450 were provoked by the politics of that year, not by some groundswell of anti-clericalism. The enclosure of cathedral closes with walls and gates (Lincoln in 1256, York in 1258, Exeter and Wells in 1286, Lichfield in 1299, Salisbury in 1327, Hereford in 1389) has been seen as 'a response to the dangers in the close, especially when the clergy were vulnerable to attack as they went to matins'. It was the brutal murder of Walter Lechlade, precentor of Exeter in 1283 that led to Exeter's enclosure.[43] Of course, what clergy may have feared was straightforward theft. Some 'evil disposed' persons stole surplices and other ornaments, perhaps worth less than the thieves imagined, from Mortlake church one Friday night.[44] In 1520 Newnham Abbey, Devon, was assailed by a crowd which took more than £600.[45] A silver chalice was stolen from the church of Morebath, Devon, in 1534: interestingly, 'the young men and maidens drew themselves together and with their gifts and provision they bought in another chalice with out any charges of the parish'.[46] In 1535 Bishop Rowland Lee interrogated the 'greatest nest of thieves robbers of churches that was heard of many years': based in Gloucestershire, they confessed to robbing eighteen churches.[47] Later that year there were thefts from the churches of Pembridge, Herefordshire (a chalice) and Brentmarsh, Somerset (including four or five chalices, a pyx and a silver and gilt cross sold to a Gloucester goldsmith for over £20), and a break in at Camden from which nothing was taken because there was nothing to be had.[48] Two parish churches in Canterbury were robbed in 1538.[49] Robberies were a perennial problem, as the watching or guard chambers over the altar or shrines in great churches such as St Albans and the *custodes* above the entrance porches at Christchurch, Hampshire, and Hereford and Exeter Cathedrals show.[50] The medieval world was no nirvana; but robberies should not be elevated into an ideological objection to the church.

In Henry VIII's reign some twenty-six cases of assaults against clergy were heard in Star Chamber, mostly over tithes or financial dues.[51] A canon of Brinkburn was murdered in 1521 in a complex dispute over tithes. Since the relationship between parish priest and parishioners was affected by all the vagaries of human character, it is not surprising that in some disputes men and women occasionally resorted to force. But there simply does not seem to have been any widespread, recurring and systemic violence against the church.

Criticism of the church from the laity was neither as general nor as disinterested as it was once fashionable to claim. And it is also revealing and significant that much of the most forceful 'anti-clericalism', many of the most quotable and most quoted phrases, came from *within* the church, from men such as John Colet, dean of St Paul's, or from the priest-poet John Skelton, already drawn upon. Undoubtedly 'the late medieval church was its own sternest critic'. After all, most of the early protestants, in England as in Germany, came from within the church, often attacking with especial venom the very institutions from which they had sprung.[52] That certainly reflects the difficulty of reforming the practices of a well-established institution, but, in a back-handed way, it is also testimony to the dynamism of the church and its capacity for self-renewal, if sometimes to the point of schism. From another perspective, the work of reforming bishops, discussed in chapter 3, can also be seen as a form of criticism of the church from within.

That, moreover, suggests that what at first appears to us as full-blooded criticism of the church, whether from churchmen or from the laity, was rather an aspiration to achieve higher standards of moral conduct. Rather than reflecting hostility to the church, it was an assertion, or reassertion, of the most demanding clerical and monastic ideals. It was a criticism not of the church but of those who betrayed those ideals. Jack Scarisbrick has helpfully termed this 'loyal' anti-clericalism.[53] It should not be taken as evidence of rising lay anti-clericalism in the sense of outright hostility to priests. But nor should it be dismissed as irrelevant to an assessment of the late medieval church. It suggests that for some influential insiders, standards were inexcusably low. Such clerical anti-clericalism was matched by those lay critics of the clergy for not living up to the highest standards, especially in matters of sexual morality, and for failing to reside and administer the sacraments. 'Some covet their bodily ease and worldly wealth, in meat and drink . . . more than commonly any temporal man doth.' That was the thrust of the complaints that the lawyer Christopher St German reported, impugning non-resident clergy, priests who did not fast at Advent or who ate meat in Lent, priests who swore, priests who went to taverns, monks who left their monasteries on the business of this world.[54] The priest-poet John Skelton's Collyn Clout offers biting criticisms of churchmen from just such a wholly orthodox but moralising perspective: bishops who failed to preach, neglected their pastoral responsibilities, paying little attention to their flocks, failing to set an example as 'lanterns of light';[55] clergy who were ignorant ('some cannot scarcely read'), preoc-cupied with their legal and financial rights,[56] and failing to observe their vows of celibacy—indeed flaunting their breach by hanging tapestries in their halls of 'naked boys striding/ With wanton wenches winking'.[57] It is important to emphasise that such concerns were not new. For example, the House of Commons petitioned against clerical non-residence in the parlia-ments of 1401, 1402, 1406 and 1425–6.[58] The problem was that its professed high ideals of sexual purity and religious observance left the church vulner-able to satire. It ran the risk, once more, of getting the worst of all worlds: lofty aspirations clashed with very mixed practice.

The church took the line that human failings did not invalidate the authority of the office: the sacraments were valid whatever the personal failings of the priest who celebrated them. However sound in logic, that was to take up an exposed position, with the church in practice appearing complacently to accept as inevitable, or openly to defend or too readily to forgive or to cover up, lapses and worse. There was always the danger that a scandal, or a perceived scandal, could suddenly undermine confidence in the church in general. 'Of all the contradictions which religious life of the period presents,' Johan Huizinga observed, 'perhaps the most insoluble is that of an avowed contempt of the clergy, a contempt seen as an undercur-rent throughout the middle ages, side by side with the very great respect shown for the sanctity of the sacerdotal office.'[59] Yet maybe Huizinga was wrong to see this as a contradiction. It was possible to criticise the behav-iour of individual priests while—indeed, because—greatly respecting the office of priest (much as Bruce Truscot, in Red Brick University, satirised the shortcomings of Professor Deadwood while offering a very idealistic impression of universities in general).[60] Thomas, Lord Darcy, who drafted a petition to the king in 1529 declaring that 'there is no manner of state within this your realm that hath more need of reformation, nay to be put under good government, than the spiritual men',[61] was, in 1536, to stand with the northern monasteries in the Pilgrimage of Grace. It is a mistake to read all criticism as intended to humiliate or to destroy its object: what critics of the late medieval church wanted was a church that was more what it ought to be. And satire could powerfully work to reform and to cleanse the church. Satire implies shared values, or perhaps values that ought to be shared, or, at the very least, lip-service to shared values. That purifying aim of critics and satirists was as true of earlier critics, whether St Bernard in the early twelfth century, or Chaucer and Langland in the fourteenth. But if critics and satirists were voicing their concerns from an idealistic and high-minded belief in the church, that does not explain away what they said. Late medieval versions of the Robin Hood ballads have been seen in this light, combining deep attachment to the mass and the Virgin Mary with monks being presented as uncharitable and grasping landlords.[62] Above all, the very fact that so much about the church seemed to be deserving of criticism, especially from those who were in many ways conventionally devout, further reveals the vulnerability of the church.[63] Much satire may have drawn on a stock of tropes and stereotypes,[64] yet most stereotypes exaggerate rather than invent, and some stereotypes may have become stereotypes for the very good reason that they were at least partially and perennially true. That admitted, if (for the sake of argument) Richard Hunne is taken as the archetype of an embittered lay critic of the church, he cannot be seen as a non-believing, thoroughly secular man. On the contrary, he wanted to attend evensong, and in protesting that he had been wrongly excommunicated, he showed that he accepted that it was the role of the church to attend to the salvation of souls, and of priests to celebrate the sacraments. But perhaps Hunne falls into a special category of critics of the church, namely that of heretics. And we shall consider heresy in the next chapter but one.

8

THE CONDITION OF THE MONASTERIES

WE must now turn to a feature of the English church to which the Hunne affair did not draw attention, namely the condition of the monasteries. In itself that prompts the question: had they become irrelevant to the religious life of the capital? However that may be, English monasteries in the years before the break with Rome and leading up to the dissolution illustrate again the combination of vitality and vulnerability that characterises the English church as a whole. It is important to emphasise vitality, since it tends to be underplayed—a reflection not least of the unfashionability, until very recently, of the study of late medieval monasticism. But it will also be essential to discuss difficulties and weaknesses.[1]

Monasteries were communities of monks or nuns who had made a lifelong commitment to the service of God through prayer and devotions, who lived their lives according to the *regula*—the rule—laid down by the religious order they had joined. The sixth-century Rule of St Benedict, very likely a codification of what was then current practice, had long been the most influential. Monasteries maintained an elaborate round of liturgical observance, day by day, hour by hour. The details varied from order to order: there might be matins at midnight, lauds at two a.m., prime at six a.m., terce, sext and none in the morning, vespers and compline in the afternoon and evening. Meals and bedtimes were arranged around these observances.[2] Worship was central to the life of the monastery, so central indeed that there are relatively few references in the sources. It was taken for granted. When (perhaps tactically) the larger monasteries were officially praised in 1536, the words chosen were that 'religion is right well kept and observed', highlighting that that was the core of monasticism.[3] In the nature of things, regular observance is less likely to be recorded than some breach of the rule. There are thus only chance references that show due devotion. For example, when the parson of Holford was sent by Lord Audley to see the abbot of Athelney, he found him in the church coming from mass at ten a.m.[4] It is only when what is normal comes under attack that its very normality emerges in our sources. The reports of royal commissioners reporting on the monasteries in the mid-1530s are revealing in this respect. When John Whalley told Cromwell in 1535 that the monks were 'exceeding superstitious, ceremonious and pharisaical, and wonderfully addicted to their old mumpsimus', he was testifying to his own religious convictions, but, unwittingly, also to how conscientiously they were observing their self-imposed devotions.[5] When Richard Layton told Cromwell that the monks were 'more superstitious than virtuous', long accustomed to 'frantic fantasies and ceremonies right far alienate from true religion', which they held in greater regard than either God or their prince, he was in a backhanded-way admitting the strength of their pious observances.[6] Similarly, when John ap Rice described the abbot of Bury St Edmunds 'to be addict to the maintaining such superstitious ceremonies as hath been used heretofore', he too was revealing the vitality of religion there.[7] Beyond those daily devotions, fundamental to the religious life, was a principled renunciation of the vanities of this world, characterised most notably by total abstinence from any sexual relationships and, ideally, the renunciation of any personal property.

Overall, in the early sixteenth century there were nearly 900 religious houses in England, around 260 for monks, around 300 for regular canons, and 142 for nuns; there were also 183 friaries. In the early sixteenth century there were almost 12,000 inmates in all: almost 4,000 of them monks, almost 3,000 regular canons, almost 3,000 friars, and some 2,000 nuns. If the total adult male population was around 500,000, that meant that one in fifty adult men was in religious orders. There were many different orders of monks and nuns, each with their own rules or practices: it is a weakness of modern scholarship to treat monasticism *en bloc*. For example, half of the 136 English nunneries were Benedictine, nearly a fifth Cistercian, nearly a sixth Augustinian, and a tenth Gilbertine.[8]

Monasteries pass the most basic test of vitality, that of recruitment. 'One of the most impressive features of the late medieval English monastic orders was their ability to maintain stable recruitment until (almost) the very end', as Barrie Dobson put it, citing the numbers of monks at Carlisle: thirteen in 1366, twelve in 1379, sixteen plus the prior in 1396, twenty in 1438, twenty-three in 1540.[9] Manifestly the Black Death, which killed between a third and two-fifths of the population, must be borne in mind whenever we consider long-term trends. In the reign of Henry VII 'monastic numbers stood at between two-thirds and three-quarters of the 1320 level'.[10] Romsey Abbey had ninety-one nuns in 1333, eighteen in 1478, forty in 1521.[11] At Winchester numbers fell a little from more than sixty in 1261 and 1325 to only forty-six in the late fourteenth century, forty to forty-five in the fifteenth century, and thirty-five in 1495–6, but then recovered to forty-five in 1532–3.[12] If there had been a significant fall following the Black Death, that is unsurprising and in no sense evidence of any unpopularity of the monasteries. As a proportion of the population, the numbers of monks, nuns and friars may well have remained more or less constant before rising by c.1500.[13] Nor was there much sign of poor recruitment in the years immediately before the dissolution. At Glastonbury, for example, numbers rose from forty-six in 1525 to fifty-two in 1533–4 and to fifty-five in 1538: allowing for deaths, there were at least twenty-two new monks, eight of them admitted after 1534. At Durham there were fifty-nine monks in 1483 and seventy-four in 1532; eight new monks were recruited in 1535.[14]

Recruitment was very localised. Westminster Abbey continued to recruit monks from the local urban society, despite the increasing commitment of parishioners to their parish church, St Margaret's, Westminster. Anyone living in Westminster would have been familiar with the life and work of monks, and such recruitment suggests at least 'the largely passive respect of their secular neighbours'.[15] The great majority of Durham monks recruited between 1383 and 1446 came from within thirty-five miles of the city.[16] 'Drawn from the rural and urban elites in the hinterland of their monasteries, the Yorkshire religious formed an integral part of local society.'[17] Similarly, the recruitment of monks at Canterbury Cathedral and Norwich Cathedral was overwhelmingly local.[18] Monastic tenants' sons were typical recruits.[19] 'Most of the community [at Winchester] were closely connected to the Hampshire and Wiltshire areas in or near which many of the priory estates were located': fifteen from Winchester, fifteen from Basing, six from Marwell, six from Salisbury, five from Enford.[20] The monks of Canterbury Cathedral were drawn from the middling ranks of East Kent, including the city itself.

There were very few from great families. 'The social inferiority of the English monk, and even of the English abbot, to the English gentleman is', as Barrie Dobson has remarked, 'a factor of fundamental importance to the history of the late medieval monastic orders.'[21] Nor, contrary to tenacious belief, were nunneries full of the daughters of nobility and gentry, an impression perhaps created by the relative ease of identifying nuns from noble and gentry families in the post-dissolution pension lists. A study of over 1,700 references to 542 nuns in eleven female monasteries in the diocese of Norwich between 1350 and 1540 concluded that far more nuns came from middling (and lower) ranks of society than from aristocratic and upper gentry families. Only seven came from titled families; eighty-one (15 per cent) from upper gentry; 345 (64 per cent) from parish gentry, eighty-six (16 per cent) from townsfolk and twenty-three (4 per cent) from yeomen. 'A majority of nuns', that study concluded, 'came from parish gentry families.'[22] A study of 2,390 daughters from elite families between 1450 and 1540 found that just fifty-three (2.47 per cent) became nuns (2,006 or 94 per cent married). Of 958 nuns identifiable from the list drawn up in 1538–9 and the pension lists of 1538–40, only 3.75 per cent were daughters of noblemen or knights. Of 393 noblemen and knights leaving dowries to daughters before 1535 only nine left money either for a marriage portion or to enter a convent. Of fifty-three who had four or more daughters, twenty-seven found marriages for all of them. 'Very few aristocratic women entered convents, and, in general, convents played a rather peripheral role in their spiritual and philanthropic lives.'[23] The remarks of Robert Aske, that the daughters of gentlemen were 'brought up in virtue' in nunneries, cannot be used in support of the presumption that monasteries were repositories for superfluous aristocratic daughters: he meant that they were educated there, not that they became nuns.[24] That too was what Rowland Lee, bishop of Lichfield, meant in 1536 when he wrote in support of the nuns of Aconbury, saying that the gentlemen of Abergavenny, Talgarth, Ewyas Lacy, Brecon and Herefordshire 'have had commonly their women children brought up there in virtue and learning'.[25] Nor did noble and upper gentry families use religious houses with which they had some association as 'dumping grounds' for unmarried daughters to whom they could not afford to give a dowry, or for widows.[26]

What is true is that those relatively few nuns who came from great families did tend to go to the wealthiest nunneries in their locality. Most of the nuns from upper gentry backgrounds in Norfolk went to the wealthiest house in the diocese, Campsey Ash Priory, or to comparable convents just outside, including Chatteris and Denny in Cambridgeshire and, further afield, Barking in Essex.[27] Amesbury, in Wiltshire, was especially socially exclusive.[28] It is tempting to suppose that, for women, nunneries offered a socially acceptable way of life that did not involve marriage, an escape from patriarchal oppression, and the opportunity, usually denied them, to hold office, but it is very hard indeed to find support for what on the face of it sounds the reasonable proposition that convents 'provided medieval women with the means to break the boundaries within which society held them'.[29] Another scholar has noted that 'there is no evidence that elite women considered convents viable or desirable alternatives to marriage, or that they valued them as female communities',[30] and we must be alert to the dangers of viewing medieval nunneries through modern feminist lenses. It is salutary here to note that if the statistics given above are correct, then just one adult woman in 250 was a nun: there simply would not have been sufficient places in nunneries for any substantial number of women wishing to avail themselves of the supposed unconventional freedoms of monastic life. And it is important to recognise that nunneries were, for the most part, branches of male monastic orders rather than independent female institutions, and they required male priests for the performance of their liturgical duties.[31]

Child oblates had been banned by the Lateran Council in 1215 and recruits were expected to come forward voluntarily.[32] Most monks and nuns joined in their late teens or as young adults. At Westminster Abbey monks were usually between seventeen and twenty-one when entering, but perhaps as young as fifteen in the half-century before the dissolution.[33] The pioneering historian of medieval nunneries, Eileen Power, found just three examples of nuns younger than thirteen. There are scattered references to under-age monks: for example, two fourteen year olds and one fifteen year old at Ramsey.[34] On what did John London, one of the commissioners persuading monasteries to surrender in 1538, base his remark that many nuns had been professed aged ten or twelve?[35] Hugh Cooper, dissident monk at Winchcombe, claimed that he had been 'enticed by fair promises' when not yet fourteen and when he lacked the knowledge of their manner of living that he had acquired since.[36] How typical was the story of William Bell, Augustinian canon of Leicester, who claimed in his defence in 1529 that he had first received the habit when he was just seven, that he had frequently run away but been captured and finally compelled to make his profession when he was thirteen, escaping and then marrying when he was twenty-two? His landlord corroborated his account, but we have no way of knowing whether this was all fantasy.[37] If, despite such a colourful tale, we suppose that by and large the canonical instructions were being observed, that does not entirely dispose of the issue. Entry to monasteries even at the canonical age of sixteen must strike a modern reader as problematic. How many had reached the intellectual and emotional maturity to make so far-reaching a decision over the course of their lives? How far had impressionable children been put upon?[38] It is far from unreasonable to question the vocation of recruits to monasteries and nunneries in late medieval England. Recruitment to monasteries has been characterised as comparable to a comprehensive school's mixed intake with all its associated problems.[39] Certainly, finding employment for men and women of a diverse range of abilities and temperaments was a perennial challenge.[40] Of course, there is no knowing the mixture of motivations that led young men and women to follow religion. A modern temptation is to see single-sex institutions attracting those with homo-social or homo-erotic leanings. As we shall see, such evidence as there is of monastic sexual misconduct would not offer a great deal of support: the most common—but not very common—breaches of the vow of chastity (masturbation apart) were relationships between monks and women, between nuns and men. It is not altogether obvious that religious houses in which monks and nuns were required to live according to a demanding rule were sites for the realisation of personal freedoms as we should define them. And such speculations presume that young men and women were aware of, conceptualised and responded to their sexuality in ways that we assume early twenty-first-century teenagers do, and that late medieval society expected, tolerated and encouraged consequent behaviour. All that risks crashing anachronism.[41] Much more plausible in grasping monastic callings are the remarks of Hugh Latimer, the later preaching bishop, who declared that 'I have been minded many times to have been a friar, namely when I was sore sick and diseased'.[42] One can only wonder whether some such experiences influenced the vocation of others.

In the greater monasteries novices underwent some sort of training. Barbara Harvey has described how at Westminster Abbey novices took part in divine service, absorbed the custom of the monastery, and studied on the lowest slopes of grammar and theology. By 1500 there were signs at Westminster of a two-stage noviciate, with senior monks given responsibility for oversight of particular novices. Young men seeking to become monks would need to show that they were literate and could sing. They would serve several months on probation before making their profession.[43] There are also signs, in the collections of manuscript books, of some attention to the needs of novices and practice in other houses. The Franciscans did use the noviciate as a sort of spiritual probation and formation, as post-Tridentine orders would very much do. Elsewhere in the late medieval period there are only hints. The career structure in which a novice might serve for four years and then be ordained first as sub-deacon, then as deacon and finally as priest, does imply some sort of training and assessment. The noviciate of women was shorter, since nuns would not exercise sacerdotal functions.[44] A manuscript addressed to two sisters of Amesbury priory, probably dating from the early sixteenth century, was a response to a request by the sisters for spiritual counsel at the time of their profession. The author expressed his purpose 'to show after my simple ability, both by authorities and examples of scripture, somewhat of the manner of living that Christ calleth every religious person to'. He insisted on poverty, rejecting the retention of individual goods, emphasised obedience to the will of the prioress, distinguished (rather oddly) between chastity of the body and chastity of the soul or mind, and called for daily devout prayers to God. His text assumed no deep knowledge of Latin but did take it for granted that his readers would know the evangelists and church fathers and could follow quite complex arguments. It is striking that 'the novices were considered by the author to have been seeking a spiritual dimension or depth to their lives', that 'such an emphasis on the spiritual was not out of character with the practice of religious life in early sixteenth-century England' and that 'the author expected this form of life to be attainable at Amesbury'. That two novices should have sought such advice reveals 'both a serious interest in their religious vocation and a genuine desire to live the religious life well'.[45] How typical such attitudes were of monks and nuns in the bulk of small and poorly endowed houses is another matter.

Few monks and nuns appear to have left their houses. It had, since the late fourteenth century, been accepted that, for good and serious reasons, monks and nuns might be given dispensations from their vows, and monks be granted 'capacities' that allowed them to serve as secular priests freed from the obligation of obedience to their abbots. Not until the mid-1530s, however, did significant numbers request such permission. Donald Logan has argued that apostasy was quite common in the twelfth century (one in eight, even one in four), but that family pressures to enter monasteries lessened in the demographic context of the fifteenth century, with the consequence that there were fewer monks and nuns who should never have taken the vow. Even if by 1535–6 circumstances were changing, such late evidence does not tell us very much about earlier attitudes. Some scholars would rather emphasise 'the number of religious prepared *of their own accord* to abandon their way of life in 1536 . . . already testimony enough to the degree of demoralisation in their communities'.[46] Certainly the royal visitors did find monks who wished to leave, including half a dozen at Denny with tears in their eyes.[47] A faculty office had been set up in Lambeth in 1534 to process requests from those who wished to leave their houses, and from late 1535 any religious wishing to be dispensed could leave. Yet not all that many expressed any such wish and fewer actually left, even at a moment at which it was clear that there would, at best, be a shake-up of monastic institutions. In the diocese of Norwich there were monks wishing to leave in just three out of thirty-three houses. In the north only in twenty-five out of 111 houses did anyone wish to leave: sixty-seven religious out of a total of 1,441, seventeen of whom did not, in the event, leave. 'When the chance to leave was given, when the monastic gates were thrown wide open, when anyone could leave without reproach, only about fifty religious from the north of England, less than four per cent, actually left', as Logan has calculated.[48]

More remarkable than these hints of disaffection is the evidence garnered from disparate sources of monks and nuns who continued to live together after the dissolution. The nuns and priest-monks of Syon divided themselves into seven households and attempted to carry on. Elizabeth Shelley, the last abbess of St Mary's, Winchester, was living with five of her community at her death in 1547, making a will in 1547 granting a chalice to Winchester College on condition that the 'nunnery of St Mary's in Winchester should have it again in case it be restored and come up again in her own time'. Morphita Kingsmill, the last abbess of Wherwell, Hampshire, was living with six of her community at her death in 1570.[49] Some former monks from Monk Bretton may well have continued some kind of communal life. William Browne, the last prior, acquired a house in Worsborough, Yorkshire, where he lived with Thomas Frobiser, sub-prior, and two other former monks; he reassembled 150 books from the monastic library. In his will in 1557 he made provision in case the monastery was restored and left bequests to seven of his former colleagues.[50] Several of the monks of the Cistercian abbeys of Roche, Yorkshire, and Rufford, Nottinghamshire, 'were ready and waiting to revive their former abbeys' in Mary's reign.[51] At least two, possibly more, of the nuns of Shaftesbury continued to live together in a house near the site of their former nunnery: the evidence is a survey of precincts of 1562–7.[52] Two nuns of Campsey Ash stayed together and taught a school in Dunwich. Elizabeth Dawrey, formerly prioress of Blackborough, and Ela Buttery, formerly prioress of Campsey Ash, both left all their possessions to fellow ex-nuns.[53] Three will-makers in the 1540s left bequests to three ex-nuns of Campsey Ash who were sharing quarters in the parish of St Peter Hungate, Norwich. Ex-nuns of Shouldham lived at St Stephen's, Norwich. Elizabeth Throckmorton, formerly abbess of Denny, Cambridgeshire, lived with two ex-nuns in the family manor of Coughton.[54] Ten wills known to have been made by former Yorkshire nuns contain references to no fewer than twenty-four other sisters: 'for many years after the dissolution, in some cases until their deaths, some nuns strove to keep alive ties of friendship and may even have tried to continue a form of the religious life'.[55] A small number of the monks of St Albans lived on there, even though unbeneficed. Thomas Kingsbury (d. 1545), prior at the time of the surrender, requested burial at the parochial chapel of St Andrew, the only surviving place of worship from the former abbey buildings, next to John Albon (d. 1540); the witnesses were former monks. Had they established some kind of common life?[56]

One scholar has presented all this as post-traumatic stress disorder, with many religious unable to accept the fact of dissolution, clinging to the hope that monasteries would be re-established, secretly saving books or vestments.[57] More prosaically, groups of monks or nuns who had, in effect, become friends may have continued for reasons of sociability and practical convenience to live together. Or should we see such behaviour as defiance, reflecting not an inability to cope with exclaustral life but rather a determination to continue the religious life, come what may?

This suggests that monks and nuns were committed to their vocation. What that meant was commitment to the often demanding daily liturgy; they also had to administer their monasteries. But those duties, burdensome though they were, ought to have left time to spare, not least for study. How far were monasteries centres of learning? Dark age monasteries were crucial to scholarship: virtually all learning took place in monasteries. With the emergence of universities in the twelfth and thirteenth centuries—part outgrowth from monasteries, part reaction against the burdens of liturgical observance—the relative place of monasteries in learning diminished. Many of the newly founded monasteries of the high middle ages, especially the smaller foundations, never developed any substantial commitment to learning. And, until recently, the consensus has been that late medieval monasteries were at best scholarly backwaters. That may not be an altogether fair judgement, even if true. In a sense, the rise of universities reflected a beneficial specialisation and division of labour. Many late medieval monasteries made arrangements to send their most intellectually promising young monks to university. 'The progressive exposure of increasing numbers of monks and regular canons to academic study' was the 'single most important new departure in late medieval religious life'. One in four Durham monks, one in seven Norwich monks, one in eight Christ Church Canterbury monks, one in nine Worcester monks, one in fourteen Ely monks, and one in fifteen Winchester monks received some form of university education.[58] Of the average complement of 48 monks at Westminster Abbey, at any one time two or three would be away at university in the thirteenth and fourteenth centuries, and five or six in the later middle ages.[59] Of the thirty-five to forty-five monks at Winchester, two or three would be at Oxford.[60] Bury St Edmunds sent two monks to Louvain.[61] For some monasteries, notably Canterbury and Gloucester, the relationship between monastery and university was very close, with Oxford colleges linked to the monastery. Of course, while such study must have stimulated learning in general terms, it is likely that the characteristic scholastic curriculum in theology at university may not have made such students better or more committed monks. If long periods of absence from the monastery were necessary for intellectual development, then that in itself cast a less flattering light on monasteries. Does it suggest that there was not much of a self-sustaining monastic educational culture, that monasteries were in a sense parasitic on universities?[62] To claim that 'monastic thought now became more closely aligned to contemporary secular trends' highlights the vulnerability as well as the vitality of monasteries with graduate monks.[63] It is intriguing that, at Winchcombe, Abbot Kidderminster (1488–1525) recalled how there was scarcely a day in the week that did not have one graduate monk expounding the Old Testament or another the New and how he himself had twice a week expounded the *Sentences* of Peter Lombard, the staple university text in theology. The cloister of Winchcombe 'conducted itself no differently than if it had been another new university (though a small one)'. Abbot Kidderminster cited 'the incredible learning' of the Venerable Bede—who flourished centuries before the emergence of universities—against contemporary monks 'who think there is no place of learning apart from the universities'. Was his ultimate aspiration, sadly never realised, to devise a programme of training and instruction to be undertaken within the monastery that would make it unnecessary for monks to be absent at university?[64]

In many monasteries intellectual interests did flourish. Joan Greatrex has written of the 'enduring presence of a scholarly tradition in the cloister'.[65] Late medieval monks continued to be occupied in writing and copying manuscripts, binding and repairing books.[66] Several monasteries had size-able libraries, for example those of Bury St Edmunds (where Henry of Kirkstead [d. *c*.1378], monk and librarian, catalogued more than 1,500 books) and of Winchester (where at least sixty works have been identified). The large old-established Benedictine houses continued to develop and expand their collections in the later fifteenth and early sixteenth centuries. And they took full advantage of the invention of the printed book. Benedictine houses quickly had more printed books than they ever had manuscripts. Indeed, several monks were involved in the production and publication of texts, as patrons to local printers or even establishing presses within their own precincts. Surviving books of proven monastic provenance are our evidence of wide-ranging activity: one of the most intellectually exciting areas of recent scholarly enquiry has been the painstaking working out of such details and the compiling of catalogues.[67] At Abingdon in *c*.1528 John Scolar produced a printed edition of the monastery's own *Breviary*. The first monastic press was at Tavistock, though the monk who ran it did so more as a printer responding to secular patrons' requests than as a scholar. At St Albans in the 1530s John Herford, the printer, produced several works, often with high quality decoration: a breviary, a grammar book, a work of arithmetic, a justification of the monastery's stand in a dispute with a Danish monastery over the location of relics, and a confuta-tion of the early protestant John Frith.[68] Many monasteries were ready to invest in printed books, including multiple copies for use in divine service, in the training of novices and in teaching. Some monks amassed large personal libraries. Abbot Kidderminster of Winchcombe was buying books in 1532; Philip Hordern of Evesham had eighty books. Such libraries reflected broad intellectual interests, including Erasmus, the Italian humanists, classical texts, and even early reformation theology.

The greater monasteries were energetic in keeping up with, and even inaugurating, developments in the practice of liturgy, especially in worship of the Blessed Virgin, and the creation, maintenance and development of small groups of trained singers—specialist choirs established to give special distinction to services at which the Virgin was worshipped. Lady chapels, intended for the daily celebration of a mass dedicated to Our Lady, were a development of the thirteenth century. They were often staffed by a quali-fied musician who taught and rehearsed the boys who sang daily at those services. There were some fifty Lady chapel choirs at the better known Benedictine and Augustinian houses. From the 1480s the greater monas-teries played a prominent part in the enhancement of divine worship by the development of polyphonic music to be sung by choirs rather than a handful of soloists.[69]

Moreover, some monks not only collected and read manuscripts and books—they also wrote them. We do not know the authors of most of the late medieval mystery plays, but we do know that the author of the Chester cycle was a monk of St Werburgh's Abbey, and a case has been made that those at Bury St Edmunds were written by the monks of the abbey.[70] Earlier monasteries had been in the forefront of the writing of mystical and contemplative piety so characteristic of the later fourteenth and fifteenth centuries: Richard Rolle (1305×10–1349), adviser to the nuns of Hampole, Yorkshire, whose prolific writings included an influential gloss on the first two-and-a-half verses of the Song of Songs; Walter Hilton (c.1343–96), Augustinian canon of Thurgarton, Nottinghamshire, author of *The Scale of Perfection*; Nicholas Love (d. 1423/4), prior of Mount Grace, Yorkshire, who translated and adapted the *Mirror of the Blessed Life of Jesus Christ*, surviving in hundreds of manuscripts.[71] Such piety was not to protestant taste, nor to that of modern liberal historians, but its influence in broad terms is hard to doubt. In the early sixteenth century priest-brothers from the Brigittine nunnery at Syon wrote devotional works, including Thomas Betson's *Right Profytable Treatyse* (1500) and Richard Whitford's *The Werke for Householders* (1530), intended for devout lay people.[72]

Yet the importance and extent of all that have been questioned. Vincent Gillespie's study of Syon suggests that most of the accessions at Syon are attributable to just two men, Richard Reynolds (d. 1535), and John Fewterer (d. 1536?), confessor-general, who donated seventy-seven volumes (including nine volumes of Erasmus's edition of Jerome), so calling into doubt the level of intellectual engagement of the rest of the house. There is no sign of significant literary activity or awareness of contemporary intellectual trends among the other brethren. Nothing was acquired after 1524—no late sermons by John Fisher, no works by Thomas More. Most of the material was printed sermons (the single largest category) and canon law. It was an eclectic, chronologically layered collection. And Gillespie is sceptical that monks did very much with their books.[73] That may, perhaps, be too severe a judgement on Syon. It seems to underestimate the writings of John Whitford. But it is a salutary corrective to the temptation to attach excessive importance to detailed studies of individual texts. More telling is the point that even if all the evidence of scholarship and book-collecting is taken at face value, the numbers of monks and nuns involved, and the numbers of monasteries at which significant interest in learning can be identified, amount to no more than a small proportion of monks, nuns and monasteries as a whole. Many, perhaps most, monasteries were not places of learning. It is remarkable how many of the details and examples just cited come from the great Benedictine monastic cathedrals: it would be much harder to find university graduates among the Cistercians or the Augustinian canons. And, of course, nuns were excluded from university study.

At least thirty of the older and larger monasteries are known to have offered teaching by establishing or maintaining schools, usually associated with the almonry. There were, for example, thirteen boys receiving free instruction in the *scola grammaticalis*—the almonry school—of Norwich Cathedral Priory in 1535.[74] We have already noted the use that gentry and parish gentry families made of nunneries to educate their daughters. 'The education of the laity was one of the last features of monastic life to founder at the end of the 1530s.'[75]

Many monasteries, and especially the larger monasteries, were centres of pilgrimage, as we have seen. Many of the more important shrines—St Thomas Becket at Canterbury, St Cuthbert at Durham, the image of the Blessed Virgin Mary at Walsingham, the Holy Blood at Hailes—were to be found in monasteries. The monks of Lynn Priory may have been actively involved in promoting a new pilgrimage cult when they financed the restructuring of a chapel to house the image of Our Lady of the Mount, Lynn, in 1505–6.[76] In these terms, then, monasteries played a vital part in late medieval life as custodians of relics and as stimulants to devotion. And disputes over relics, such as that between Glastonbury and Canterbury over St Dunstan, show that they were still part of a living tradition. It is significant that when Elizabeth Barton claimed to have been miraculously cured, it was to a nunnery and to the pastoral care of the monks of Canterbury Cathedral that she was assigned.

Monasteries remained significant sources of charity. During the Pilgrimage of Grace, Robert Aske emphasised the alms that monasteries distributed.[77] In 1529 one of the complaints against Cardinal Wolsey was that the taxation that he had imposed on the monasteries had diminished their charitable capacities.[78] And there is a good deal of evidence that monasteries did take their charitable obligations seriously. Accounts show considerable spending. Westminster Abbey, in many respects worldly in its practices, nonetheless spent c.£400 per annum (10 per cent of its gross income) on alms. Its monks often tried to be discriminating in their charity, favouring the local deserving poor, but they were often constrained by the detailed requirements of lay benefactors' wills, which insisted on distributions on special occasions, such as their own anniversaries, feast days, or deaths of monks, when it would be more difficult, if not impossible, to distribute alms to those who needed them most.[79] After the dissolution of the smaller monasteries in 1536, Thomas Gibson remarked that when the legislation had gone through it had been thought that it would not damage the king's poor subjects. Yet what had happened 'showeth plainly unto us that a great hurt and decay is thereby become and hereafter shall come to this your realm and great impoverishing of many your poor obedient subjects for lack of hospitality and good householding that was wont in them to be kept to the great relief of the poor people of the countries adjoining to the said monasteries beside the maintenance of many servants, husbandmen and labourers that daily were kept on the said religious houses'.[80] There were many comments on the charitable role of monasteries. The priory of Catesby gave much relief to poor people.[81] So did St James Abbey, Northampton, giving alms daily to three to four score.[82] Wolstrop offered good hospitality and relief to the poor.[83] At Carmarthen hospitality was kept daily for the poor and rich: weekly alms were given to eighty people.[84] Cleeve Abbey, Somerset, kept great hospitality.[85] Christchurch, Dorset, fed the poor daily 'with bread and ale purposely baked and brewed for them weekly'.[86] In Colchester there were many poor people who received relief daily from St John's.[87] Of course, those comments were made when these houses were under sentence of dissolution, and there may be an element of special pleading. Henry VIII certainly thought so. 'As to the relief of poor people,' Henry wrote, responding to the Lincolnshire rebels in 1536, 'we wonder you are not ashamed to affirm that they [the dissolved smaller monasteries] have been a great relief, when many or most have not more than four or five religious persons in them and divers but one; who spent the goods of their house in nourishing vice.'[88] That does not come over as an unbiased assessment. And not only did monasteries assist the poor but they also offered hospitality more widely. Michael Sherbrook, Elizabethan priest of Wickersley, near Rotherham, declared how 'no wayfaring person could depart without a night's lodging, meat, drink and money; without being demanded from whence he or she came, and whither he would go'.[89] That might be tinged by romantic nostalgia (Sherbrook was born in 1535 and, therefore, dependent on what he had heard from his elders); and it may be that hospitality had become increasingly institutionalised and less personal, and that charity was distributed with an eye to the interest of the monastery. Yet the volume of protest when monasteries were dissolved, especially smaller monasteries more rooted in their localities, suggests that monasteries were indeed thought to be fulfilling vital charitable functions and serving their communities. The most thorough modern investigation has concluded that the monasteries, cathedrals and colleges recorded in the *Valor Ecclesiasticus* were giving some 7 per cent of their revenues to the poor; for those dependent on monastic charity, the dissolution must have meant great hardship.[90]

In that respect the friars were a distinctive sub-set of those in religious orders. Friars had been, in one sense, a reaction against the unworldly, even extra-worldly, character of the most austere monasteries established in the twelfth century, the Cluniacs and the Cistercians. Friars were intended to work very much in the contemporary world, especially in the burgeoning towns, and they saw it as their mission to preach, notably against heretics. But, if they were thoroughly engaged in the world, they renounced, at least in their ideals, the riches of that world; friars were to beg for their living. Such a mixture of worldly involvement and idealistic renunciation of material reward struck a chord. The Franciscans (the Greyfriars), followers of St Francis of Assisi (d. 1226), and the Dominicans (the Blackfriars), the order of Preachers, followers of St Dominic (d. 1221), were the largest orders of friars. There were also Augustinian Friars (shortened in English to Austin Friars), following an adaptation of the Rule of St Augustine of Hippo, and the Carmelites (the Whitefriars), looking to the hermits on Mount Carmel in the Holy Land for inspiration. These orders of friars quickly spread throughout England in the thirteenth century. On the eve of the break with Rome, friars were a ubiquitous feature of the urban scene: there were some 180 houses and 3,000 friars in England. But, by then, many bequests from laymen and laywomen had left some friaries comfortably endowed, and inevitably they became embroiled in worldly business, for example, appearing as plaintiffs in litigation over debt. Not all friars lived as they were supposed to: some friars were accused of theft, as well as indiscipline. Friary churches, nonetheless, became fashionable places for wealthy townsfolk to seek burial. Friars acted as confessors and scribes. Judging from wills, friars retained their popularity right to the end, though some of the fluctuations and variations are hard to understand. In London between 13 per cent and 20 per cent of wills between 1373 and 1417 contained bequests to friars; thereafter the percentages were lower, ranging from 9 per cent to 13 per cent between 1417 and 1483.[91] In the 1520s the percentage of wills with bequests to friars was 28 per cent in the dioceses of Durham and York, 22 to 23 per cent in the diocese of Exeter and the archdeanconry of Lincoln, and 16 per cent in the archdeaconry of Huntingdon.[92] In the diocese of Salisbury, excluding the city, 14 per cent of wills included bequests to friars.[93] If in Bury St Edmunds the number of bequests to friars was low, there was nonetheless, a steady increase in requests for trentals (a set of thirty masses to be said for the soul of the deceased) celebrated by friars (perhaps because friars were freer to celebrate frequent masses than secular clergy?).[94] Recruitment at York peaked in the 1500s, with sixty-seven Greyfriars ordained, the second highest number over the past century, falling to thirty-four in the 1510s and fourteen in the 1520s (but high mortality in the city may have been a factor).[95]

Friaries have sometimes been seen as an alternative to, or even as opposed to, monasteries of the traditional type; but it makes more sense to see the orders rather as another illustration of the refashioning of the underlying monastic ideal. That makes especial sense in understanding the divisions within the orders of friars. The Franciscans would, over time, split between those who sought stricter observance of the ideal of poverty espoused by St Francis—the Spiritual Franciscans—and those who saw the institutionalisation of the order as unavoidable—the Conventual Franciscans. In the mid- and late fourteenth century many houses of Franciscan friars joined a new grouping of Observant Franciscans, notable for their strict observance and austerity, but efforts to reunite the disparate Franciscans proved unavailing. Surprisingly little is known in detail about the activities of late medieval English friars: 'one can only conclude', one historian has written about the majority of them, 'that they remained in their convents and quietly pursued their pastoral vocations'. Since it was only if they were involved in property transactions or accused of some offence that their names would be found in surviving records, 'their anonymity therefore might be taken as a sign of the success of their pastoral work'.[96] Of course, there were significant tensions in the role of friars almost from the start. When they lived up to their ideals of poverty and preaching, they implicitly showed up the failings of the more institutional church. There could be more practical and particular quarrels with parish clergy, for example, over burial dues or the hearing of confessions. Friars were not easily monitored or disciplined by bishops, especially if they preached too freely. And two friars, Girolamo Savonarola in Florence and Martin Luther in Wittenberg, would disrupt or divide the church. There was, then, something untidy in the relationship between friars and the larger church.[97] Yet in England, if not on the continent, that untidiness does not seem to have led to any dramatic quarrels.

How, then, should the general condition of the monasteries on the eve of the break with Rome be described? For all their professed ideals, late medieval monasteries were very much part of the world. Many monasteries were wealthy institutions, thanks to the extensive lands with which they had been endowed many centuries earlier. Glastonbury, Canterbury Cathedral, Westminster Abbey, St Albans, St John Clerkenwell all enjoyed annual revenues of over £2,000 a year, another nineteen were worth between £1,000 and £2,000. The overwhelming majority of religious houses, however, received less than £200 a year. Moreover, there was great variation in the value of ornaments, jewels, plate and fittings between different houses. The gross annual value of the monasteries as a whole was £152,517 18s 10¼d, the clear annual value (that is, after deducting various charges) £131,607 6s 4¼d, more if the *Valor Ecclesiasticus* is an under-estimate, as comparisons with receipts for alms and individual records of spending on alms tend to show.[98]

That wealth was reflected in the considerable volume of building and rebuilding at many of the larger late medieval monasteries (but much less often at smaller houses). At Chester, the south transept, tower, and south aisle of the monastic church were completed under Abbot Ripley between 1485 and 1493, and the nave clerestory, the roof of the north transept and the west front under Abbot Birkenshaw between 1493 and 1524.[99] Notable building work included Bath Abbey; the central tower at Canterbury; the Tower and Lady Chapel at Gloucester; Winchcombe; the choir at Evesham; the fan-vaulting at Sherborne; the cloisters at Hailes and Lacock; and the gatehouses at Montacute and Cerne. And there was much remodelling, re-roofing, tiling, reglazing. Whether, though, 'the restoration of the outward fabric of the monasteries' shows, as has been asserted, that 'there was a corresponding revival of the monastic rule and a general transformation of religious life' is moot.[100]

At a different level, such building campaigns were also distractions—as Thomas, Lord Dacre, pointed out to the prior of Lanercost in 1524. The prior 'being so often occupied as well in outward works and businesses as building, oversight of workmen, quarryers, masons, wrights, wallers, as others needful to be seen to for the common weal of you all, your monastery, servant and store cannot have times convenient and space to see to the inward part of your church as to take heed and see the service of God continually maintained, the order of Religion with the ceremonies of the same within the Church, Cloister, dorter and frater observed and kept so well as needful it were'. Dacre went on to recommend a named sub-prior, hinting at a more self-interested reason for his comments, but, nonetheless, they may stand as evidence of lay awareness of the costs of supervision of building and of lay attachment to monastic ideals.[101] In some respects, late medieval monastic rebuilding created a different atmosphere, that of a comfortable country mansion, rather than a renunciation of the world, something especially true of abbots' lodgings, of which Much Wenlock offers a tellingly grand example.[102] Of course, as with bishops, abbots needed to keep rank with secular lords, especially those (mostly Benedictine) abbots who sat as spiritual peers in the House of Lords, the more so since few abbots were themselves from aristocratic backgrounds, and much of what they did might be seen as matching expectations and standards set by the laity.[103] Yet the worldliness remained (especially when abbots socialised and hunted with lay noblemen) as did the corrosion of the highest ideals of poverty professed by monks. It opened the monasteries to the sort of criticism expressed by Sir George Lawson, writing from York to Thomas Cromwell in February 1533, just before moving northwards to defend the borders. He thought the abbeys should bear more of the charges in those parts—in other words, pay more in taxes. God's service could be as well maintained, Lawson claimed, and yet the king's highness might have a good part of what the abbots and priors wastefully and prodigally spent.[104] It is not, however, for a modern historian to criticise too moralisingly; simply to note aspects of monastic life that left monasteries open to criticism.

Monasticism was supposed to involve the renunciation of the world; but late medieval monasteries were landowners living off rents drawn from the profits of farming, and even friaries often amassed properties and incomes. There was an inescapable tension between ideal and reality. If it is hard to see how any human institution can subsist without a degree of worldliness, nonetheless the worldliness of the monasteries made them vulnerable to satire, criticism and contempt. The imperatives of running landed estates— dealing with tenants, collecting rents, sorting out leases—were at odds with the ideal of withdrawal from the world. The sheer multiplicity and complexity of sources of income meant that all this could not be handled simply and quickly. Rents came from urban lands and tenements; from corn mills at which tenants were compelled to have their corn ground, from fulling mills for cloth; from coal mines (for example, Lacock in Wiltshire); from stone quarries; from rents for stalls in market places; from fisheries; from sales of timber. Rents paid by tenants on agricultural holdings were the principal source of income. Some rents were payable in kind—wool, lambs, pigs, eggs, corn, barley, hay. Some direct farming survived: for example, Winchcombe Abbey's sheep.[105] All in all monasteries were businesses.

Much effort has been devoted to drawing on surviving monastic accounts to delineate broad agrarian and economic trends, but the experiences of individual houses were too diverse to make generalisation reliable. The huge fall in population during and after the Black Death led monasteries to shift from direct management of their estates to leasing out farms for rent. It may well be that their revenues fell, though so did the numbers of monks and nuns, and much depended on the particular circumstances of each house. Monastic orders, notably the Cistercians, which had employed lay brothers to cultivate their lands, now found they no longer needed them. But the scale of building in the larger monastic houses in the late fifteenth and early sixteenth centuries suggests at least a degree of prosperity. Monasteries that were in any way involved in the production of wool should not have done too badly. And here it is vital to note that the evidence of debt and the assertions of poverty in the immediate years of the dissolution reflect the pressures of that time, and not necessarily anything long-term. The complaints of the friars of Worcester that they were not able to live 'for very poverty' and that no charity had come to them 'as before was wont to do' tells us about the situation of 1538, and the comparison with former times confirms the recent onset of their difficulties.[106] Surrendering in September 1538, the Greyfriars of Reading noted that the people had withdrawn their former support: the poor people there stole all the things that could be had from them, including clappers from the bells.[107] The Whitefriars and Blackfriars of Norwich presented a bill to the duke of Norfolk asking him to take the surrender of both their houses, saying that 'the alms of the country is so little that they are not able to live any longer unless they sell all the goods of the houses': 'the cold and small charity' of those days was insufficient to live on.[108] The friars at Boston—Dominican, White and Austin—piteously lamented their poverty. The devotion of people was 'clean gone'.[109] But those movingly gloomy comments simply highlight the contrast with the evidently plentiful support of previous times.

Whatever the long-term trends, many smaller religious houses were very poor and consequently struggled to maintain their buildings from an inadequate budget. In Yorkshire the modesty of the monastic buildings described by the commissioners in the mid-1530s has been seen as evidence of monastic poverty. Chimneys were rare, glass scarce. Exploitation of demesne lands was crucial to their survival.[110] Nunneries were especially likely to be poor: as many as a third enjoyed annual incomes of less than £50: Nunburnholme, in North Yorkshire, for example, supported six nuns on an income of £8 15s 3d.[111]

Many parishes had been appropriated by monasteries in the twelfth century. Laymen who had founded a church, or their descendants, felt increasingly uncomfortable as, in a sense, its 'owners', and they in effect granted to a local or neighbouring monastic house a share, usually two-thirds, of the tithes due: sometimes, but not always, retaining the right to appoint the priest. It is not easy to say how monasteries fulfilled these assumed obligations, and in particular whether they despatched one of their monks to serve the cure of souls regularly or not. What all this meant was that, by the mid-thirteenth century, monasteries were often patrons of a church, acting as its rector, or corporate rectors, presenting its vicar, and keeping a greater share of the tithes. Such arrangements were often highly complex, legally and financially. The assessment and collection of tithes were often tricky, offering innumerable opportunities for dispute: and the task was often entrusted to lay officials who were either paid a lump sum and left to take what profit they could or allowed to keep for their pains a set fraction of the sums they raised: 'the unfortunate consequence was that the monasteries had little contact with their appropriated parishes and were seen by the parishioners only as the recipients of portions of their crops and livestock'.[112] The vicars who had to get by on low incomes would have their own resentments, and they would have less to give in charity. Some monastic houses became unhealthily dependent on tithes from parish churches. The abbot of Welbeck warned Thomas Cromwell in 1533 that if that order's monks who were serving as vicars (with appropriate papal bulls and royal grants) were called home, and their benefices given to secular priests, it would undo a third of their houses.[113]

No doubt monasteries were no worse than the crown, noblemen or bishops in the ways in which they raised revenues. But the contrast between professed other-worldly ideals and mundane financial realities was more flagrant; and there was always something dubious about the system of appropriation. It was always tempting for a monastery to treat such patronage as merely a source of revenue, and it is possible that the quality of pastoral care suffered to some extent.[114] It has often been supposed that there was a connection between monastic impropriations and the neglect of chancels.[115] Outright neglect of cures was rare but when it occurred it was usually because monastic rectors failed to supply vicars. In 1520 Bishop West of Ely cited five religious houses to answer charges of neglect of their churches; the livings were sequestered when no representatives came. Bishop Veysey of Exeter acted similarly in the 1520s.[116]

Even when a monastery's financial affairs were honestly and efficiently managed, it all inescapably took time to administer, especially when there were disputes and difficulties. It was impossible in such circumstances for monks to live a desert-style life of self-sufficiency and enclosure. No wonder that so many abbots protested in 1535 and 1536 when Thomas

Cromwell, as vice-gerent, attempted to impose strict rules of enclosure. And those monasteries which housed shrines that attracted pilgrims became absorbed in a different kind of worldliness.

Visitation evidence suggests that the norm was 'sound observance'. It is dangerous to dramatise instances of scandal in the late medieval period and contrast them with the supposedly unblemished life of eleventh- and twelfth-century monasteries, for which we lack visitation records.[117] The earliest visitation records from the thirteenth century already show misdemeanours that were supposedly characteristic of the later middle ages.[118]

What monks and nuns have most notoriously been condemned for is sexual misconduct. Monasticism involved the total renunciation of what the world saw as the pleasures of the flesh. Celibacy was an immensely challenging ideal and, human nature being what it is, not surprisingly (at least to a twenty-first-century historian), it was not always met. The evidence of the visitations in 1535–6 suggests, however, that the ideal of celibacy was honoured more in the observance than in the breach, and even then masturbation was a far more common breach than were sexual relations with women and, still less, sexual relations between men.[119] Once again the church was hoist by its own petard. A demanding—an impossibly demanding—ideal; messy realities, leading to local scandals; a wider tarnishing. It might well be that 'a good monastery is not one where no faults are committed but one where faults do not go uncorrected',[120] but to expect faults is to illustrate the point. Yet, for all that, sexual scandal was uncommon. The greatest difficulty in judging the condition of monasticism is in deciding appropriate criteria. This is particularly so for historians writing in a secular and materialistic culture not especially sympathetic to sexual abstinence. It is all too easy to adopt contemporary criticism at face value, making it sound like a modern tabloid critique of public figures.

On the other hand, it is easy to become romantically pietistic, not least when gazing at 'bare ruin'd choirs', and accept too readily what might not unfairly be seen as mediocre, uninspired and pedestrian.[121] More prevalent than sexual shortcomings appear to have been sloth and quarrelling. Many religious houses appear to have been long settled into an undemanding routine. For many, the liturgical round continued to inspire; but maybe sheer repetition caused some to become bored. The historian of the fifteenth-century English Cistercian houses concluded that[122]

the general level of monastic observance seems to have been pedestrian rather than bad or relaxed. Standards were undoubtedly lower [than earlier] and the inability to raise them seems to have stemmed from a general inertia, itself due to a departure from the vital and fundamental principles of the rule. There was too easy an acquiescence in the fallibility of human nature.

A scholar of the French church in a later period remarked that 'the greatest danger for monks is idleness'.[123] 'The general impression . . . of the state of the west-country monasteries on the eve of the dissolution', their historian noted, 'is that, with some notable exceptions, there were few houses guilty of gross depravity or serious abuse, but that there was little fervour in their religious life'; 'they were no longer regarded as power houses of the religious life nor as performing any longer a valuable, spiritual function to the glory of God or for the well-being of the whole of society'.[124] The later middle ages was 'neither a heroic nor a pioneering epoch in western monasticism'.[125] Though many religious houses lacked real spiritual fervour, few were obviously disgraceful: they may have needed reform but did not deserve outright abolition, concluded Christopher Haigh.[126] Were, Maurice Keen has asked, the 'fires of spiritual vigour and holiness of life' not burning rather low?[127] Susan Keeling found 'not gross corruption but . . . neglected opportunity',[128] while, according to Diarmaid MacCulloch, 'the general picture is one of conscientious, if uninspired and pedestrian observance of the rule, marred by occasional minor scandal and a good deal of run-of-the-mill ill-nature in the cloister'.[129] Were late medieval monasteries marked by spiritual and intellectual sloth, ennui and melancholia?[130] Qualifying such perceptions, Joan Greatrex stresses 'the constant need to take into account that most monks and nuns have always been frail human beings, neither intellectually talented nor spiritually remarkable'. As she further notes, 'Ordinary people lack the colour, the drama and the magnetic attraction that surround the rare breed recognised as heroes and saints; but with all their faults they are the backbone of their communities.'[131] Is that, however, more an argument for the critics than the defenders of late medieval monasticism? When George Gyfford defended Wolstrop, which had eight religious persons 'living very religiously', he wrote that 'There is not one religious person there but that he can and doth use either inbrotheryng [embroidering], writing books, with very faire hand, making their own garments, carving, painting, or graffyng [engraving]'. It will be noted that what Gyfford emphasised was not their devotion to religion.[132] And even so sympathetic a student of the monastic houses as Greatrex concludes that 'during the greater part of the two centuries preceding the dissolution monks . . . were afflicted by a form of accidie [*accidia*, that is sloth or torpor]'.[133]

Monasteries' relationships with landed families could increase such worldliness. Most had originally been founded by local noble or gentry families who offered land in return for prayers and intercession, and in some cases the links had remained, though more often families died out or descents had become complex, or the geographical centre of gravity of a family's estates changed. That has been presented as a fundamental weakness of monasteries: for Benjamin Thompson 'the seeds of the 1530s were sown in the very foundation of the monasteries, in the very attempt to devote perpetual resources to the welfare of the dead'. Inevitably such institutions would accumulate greater burdens over the years—obligations to remember a growing number of past generations—while they might find themselves with no resident and interested contemporary patron. 'To support suffrages with perpetual property was to encase religion in a framework of temporal exchange inappropriate to benefits which could be enjoyed out of time.' 'The result', Thompson insists, 'was monasteries doing nothing useful to living contemporaries.' 'The laity then had the perfect excuse to turn round and reform, or resume, the institutions which they had created to fulfil their own impossible expectations. They forced secularisation on the church, then reformed it for its lack of spirituality.'[134] But is this to judge monasteries solely by how far they satisfied the expectations of their first founders? Could they not, indeed did they not, develop wider social and religious functions, not confined to their benefactors (just as chantries were not purely and narrowly personal)? From the provision of lavish liturgies in monastic cathedrals to monasteries as centres of pilgrimage attracting large numbers of laymen and laywomen, from their charitable activities to the provision of education, monasteries could readily be seen as justifying their continuing existence, as the opposition to schemes of dissolution vividly showed. A marked later medieval development was the growth of confraternities within monasteries: the monks would make formal grants of confraternity in return for benefactions and then offer appropriate prayers and masses.[135] And, in the end, the argument that the dwindling links between monasteries and lay founder/patrons shows that monasteries were outdated merely clarifies why there was not more opposition to the dissolution from lay patrons: there were few such patrons. But it does not go very far to explain the motives behind the dissolution, and it is not clear that it says very much about the spiritual condition of the monasteries (as opposed to the political weakness of their position in the 1530s). Moreover, others would criticise monasteries precisely for allowing lay founders and their families to take *too great* an interest, notably in the choice of abbots. And monasteries continued to appoint noblemen as stewards—descendants of founders when possible, influential local landowners when not.

Noblemen continued to make use of monasteries. Henry, Lord Stafford, heir of the third duke of Buckingham executed for treason in 1521, complained that, because Wolsey compelled him to break up his household, he had been forced to board with his wife and seven children at an abbey for the past four years.[136] Corrodies—arrangements whereby laymen and women, often widows, paid monasteries a cash sum or lands and in return were given board and lodging in the monastery for the rest of their days— were a characteristic feature. Edward Walker, gentleman, occupied a suite of rooms on the south side of the cloister at Cleeve: for £27 he had been granted for life a chamber with an inner room for a servant together with meat and drink at the abbot's table and food and drink for his servant.[137] Obviously such arrangements could turn into an expensive liability for a monastic house; but if the actuarial calculations had been made correctly, corrodies could even be lucrative. Moreover, monasteries had little option but to agree to such requests, especially from kings, or local traders and officials.[138] Were late medieval monasteries consequently physically over- burdened by the presence of large numbers of staff, corrodians and guests, swamping the inmates? At Norwich, no fewer than 416 were fed in the early sixteenth century: there were just fifty-five monks.[139] Monasteries and nunneries also accommodated temporary boarders, including children, of whom there were twenty-six at the Benedictine nunnery of St Mary's Winchester in 1535.[140] Christopher Stapleton, very weak owing to continual sickness, went to the Greyfriars, Beverley, 'for change of air' in autumn 1536, as he had done at Hull the previous May till after midsummer, and the winter before.[141] None of that was new and, if it was an abuse, it was not a new abuse that could justify or explain the dissolution. But in so far as it lent the monasteries the worldly charm of a country house hotel or the liveliness of a prep school or the manifold bothers of a nursing home, it may have distracted monks from their religious duties and from their ascetic ideals.

Monasteries were becoming cosy, comfortable and inward-looking. Monks and nuns performed their duties, though perhaps not all of them, and lived, if not luxuriously, then at a higher level than most of their lay neighbours. The monks of Westminster Abbey largely observed the litur- gical round; they also ate and drank well, notably enjoying sizeable helpings of meat in contravention of the Benedictine rule.[142] The monks of Norwich Cathedral gradually relaxed the ban on the eating of meat in the thirteenth century.[143] There was indeed, as we have already noted, a Barchester flavour about monastic houses. Monks might be given monetary allowances to buy clothes and books; communal dormitories might yield to individual cells. According to a modern scholar, one who is generally sympathetic to the religious, 'there is no doubt that there had been a gradual breaking down of community life; individual monks were continuing to live under the same roof and share the same table—though even this observation requires some qualification—but they were no longer sharing daily in the kuinonia [communion] which is fundamental to the monastic life. The gradual accumulation over five centuries of customs and privileges had overlaid the living core of tradition concealing it from view; radical pruning was required for survival and fresh growth.' 'The attention of most monks appears to have been caught up in a pressing round of long-established duties, obligations, and related practices. As a result there was little time left for the cultivation of that bond of fellowship that is indispensable, for it lies at the heart of the common life.'[144]

And sometimes monks and nuns quarrelled. Often—how often?—the communal life was disrupted by clashes of personality. 'Envy, discord and anger . . . are the besetting sins of the common life wherever it is lived', a fellow of an Oxford college has declared knowingly.[145] 'It looks as if few medieval monasteries were without dissension.'[146] Ralph Tracy, prior of Sheen from 1496, was murdered in 1503 in an obscure episode by one Claudius Bryyandi at the instigation of one of his own monks named Goodwyn.[147] Backbiting is illustrated by the prioress of St James-outside-the-walls, Canterbury, who accused the sisters of the house of being public prostitutes: as John Thomson drily remarked, 'the historian may be pardoned some scepticism when the record notes that their ages were 84, 80, 50 and 36. Commonsense suggests that the prioress was defective in charity rather than the sisters in chastity.'[148] There were difficulties at Holme Cultram after a controversial election and the early subsequent death of the abbot: one of the monks was held on suspicion of having poisoned him. Subsequent interrogations revealed deep tensions between the monks.[149] The abbot of Leicester complained in 1534 that one of the monks, Hugh Whitwyke, who had been sent on the abbey's business to London, had stayed there for three months at a time, spending the money of the house and giving away sums of money (presumably to those he thought influential) in the hope of succeeding him. Some of the 'maliciously disposed brethren' had complained to the bishop against him and 'his brethren honest men'. How common was it for a monastery to be divided between 'maliciously disposed' and 'honest' monks?[150] A London Charterhouse monk claimed that if the monks spoke anything against the prior's mind they were threatened with imprisonment.[151] Hugh Cooper claimed that his fellow monks did not live virtuously, but rather enviously, unquietly, full of strife and dissension. He had known monks not speak to each other for half a year, yet boast of their goodness.[152] Richard Layton thought the abbot of Lichfield honest but that 'he hath here the most obstinate and factious canons that ever I knewe'.[153] The prior of Bodmin complained against his 'set of unthrifty canons'.[154] Yet all that does rather rest on hearsay: it is hard to verify such charges, though a degree of quarrelling, jealousy and misappropriation of funds rings true. Within monasteries, especially the larger monasteries, there was a hierarchy of administrative positions, with the head of the house at its summit; it is not hard to suppose that rivalries and lasting bitternesses were entirely possible.

Much depended on the quality of abbots. England was free from the Scottish practice of commendation, that is the appointment of a lay administrator, who might bring in his family and despoil the abbey, or (with the exception of Wolsey's election as abbot of St Albans) of a bishop as head. Nor were English abbeys the preserve of younger sons of noblemen. How exactly were abbots chosen? There was a variety of possibilities. Sometimes monks elected their own superiors, sometimes the key part was played by what we should call a sub-committee, sometimes by the pope, the crown, the archbishop, the bishop, noblemen or local gentlemen. Local laymen may have been most interested in monasteries as neighbours and landlords. Royal intervention was common in twelfth- and thirteenth-century England, declined thereafter until markedly escalating from the second half of Henry VII's reign.[155] Wolsey, ever reforming, took an increasing and close interest in monastic elections.[156] He exerted pressure on ageing and incompetent heads of houses to resign (in the absence of any formal system of retirement).[157] He evidently attempted to persuade Richard, abbot of Hyde, to give up on account of age and imbecility in 1526. The abbot flatly refused, saying that he was not so imbecile and impotent of body or wit: he was able to occupy his office to the pleasure of God, the increase of good religion and the wealth of his house. He was not minded to resign.[158] More effectively, Wolsey was involved in the resignations of at least eight (maybe ten) heads of houses, including Abbot Birkenshaw of St Werburgh's Chester in 1524 and Abbot Kirton of Peterborough in 1528.[159] As many as twenty houses referred elections to Wolsey.[160] The cardinal has been seen as sincerely reforming, for example personally examining all the inmates at Wilton, hard to explain other than because he wanted the best candidate.[161]

Abbots had very different styles. Marmaduke Huby (c.1439–1526), abbot of Fountains between 1494 and 1526, presided over the more than doubling of his house (twenty-two monks in 1495, fifty-two in c.1520), the rebuilding of the infirmary and the building of the tower. Richard Kidderminster (c.1462–1532), abbot of Winchcombe between 1488 and 1525/7, was involved in controversy with Henry Standish in 1512 and defended indulgences against Luther's attacks. His house became a centre for the study of theology, philosophy and literature. John Islip (1464–1532), abbot of Westminster between 1500 and 1532, oversaw the completion of the rebuilding of the new Lady Chapel. William More (1471/2–1552), prior of Worcester between 1518 and 1536, spent lavishly on entertainment, relatives and books. 'Leading what was essentially the life of a wealthy country squire', his biographer writes, 'he became a JP, was generous with hospitality, travelled with a retinue of up to twenty-five men, and maintained a fool. All the year round he laid out small sums on plays and other entertainments.'[162]

When visitors found neglect of buildings—the leaky roof in the dormitory so that rain fell on the brethren at night at Ramsey Abbey in 1518, or the ruinous dormitory, conventual church and infirmary at Peterborough in 1518—they blamed the abbots.[163] The visitors of the mid-1530s found considerable differences in the quality of heads of houses. Some, such as those of Brewerne and Chacombe, were learned in holy scripture; some, such as those of Canons Ashby and Wroxton, were unlearned. Some, such as those of Eynsham and Brewerne, kept their houses in good repair, while others, such as those of Clattercote, did not.[164] The prior of Boxgrove was 'a great husband'—he managed the priory's estates well—and kept great hospitality.[165] William Thirsk, abbot of Fountains, Huby's successor, had allegedly 'greatly delapidated' his house and wasted the woods.[166] The abbot of Shrewsbury could supply no inventory and kept no accounts; there was no infirmary, and when it rained they sat wet in the choir of the church.[167] Rowland Lee praised the prior of Leominster in November 1535 as being 'of as good reputation in these parts as the abbot of Reading in his parts'.[168] The crucial importance of the head of house emerges from such reports. In his translation of the Benedictine rule for women, Richard Fox, bishop of Winchester, set out the qualities necessary for a successful abbess—and they apply to abbots as well: not to be haughty, sour, obstinate, or self-willed; but rather to be diligent, attentive to detail and self-disciplined. These vices and virtues perhaps reveal what all too often was lacking.[169]

If the impression left by the royal visitors of the mid-1530s is rather mixed, there is no doubting the high standards of austerity and devotion met by the Carthusians, Observant Franciscans and Brigittines, new or reformed orders dating from the fourteenth century. They attracted substantial benefactions. There were seven new Charterhouses: Beauvale from 1343 (founded by Sir Nicholas Cantelupe), the London Charterhouse from 1361–71 (founded by Sir Walter Manny), Hull from 1377/78–9 (founded by Sir Michael de la Pole, later earl of Suffolk), Coventry from 1381/82 (founded by William, Lord Zouche), Axholme from 1395/97–8 (founded by Thomas Mowbray, earl of Nottingham), Mount Grace from 1397–8 (founded by Thomas Holland, duke of Surrey; though John de Ingleby was the prime mover), and then Sheen from 1414–15 (founded by Henry V), with never more than 200 monks in all.[170] The Charterhouses were an ascetic and contemplative order, strictly controlled by the Grande Chartreuse. 'Of all the monastic sites in England, this one', A.G. Dickens wrote of Mountgrace, 'reminds us the most forcibly that the desert of late medieval monasticism still had its fountains of living water.'[171] If Charterhouse monks lived in spacious sets of rooms, they also lived silent and solitary lives. 'Solitary life is the school of doctrine that leads unto heaven . . . The cell is the grave from this troubled life vexation/ And of heavenly life ye enter in consolation.'[172] It was the London Charterhouse that tempted Sir Thomas More. The Observant Franciscans were a reformed order of friars specially patronised by Henry VII. Henry VIII—admittedly in a letter to Pope Leo X, seeking his support for them—praised them lavishly. He could not sufficiently express his admiration for their strict adherence to poverty, their sincerity, their charity, their devotion. No order battled against vice more assiduously, none was more active in keeping Christ's fold.[173]

But to praise the Carthusians and Observants is implicitly to condemn the rest. To claim that prayers from the Charterhouses of Sheen and London, 'because of their merits . . . would be heard by God more favourably', to see the prayers of especially holy men and women as especially efficacious,[174] was to endorse a sort of spiritual elitism. Here Henry VII's letter of 10 February 1490 to Pope Innocent VIII is revealing. The king expressed himself 'convinced that the strictness of the Carthusian rule exceeds that of all other orders soever, in such wise that as the sacred canons permit the passage from a more lax mode of life to one more strict, it does not seem conformable to reason that any one professed of the Carthusian order should return in any manner to a rule less strict'. Referring to a monk who had transferred from the Cistercians to the Carthusians and back again, he was anxious that this should not set a precedent, 'lest they, vanquished by the importunities of their abbots, return from fish to flesh, from haircloth to broadcloth, from solitude to society: and lest, which is a still greater peril, this same evil embolden those who quite recently abandoned the world and entered the Carthusian order again to become worldlings instead of religious, at the instigation of the enemy of mankind'.[175] How far was to found a new monastery, and especially one in a new order, consciously to reject the rest?[176] Were the Carthusians too small a spiritual elite, too enclosed, to have exerted a wider influence?[177] Were they 'an exclusive and tightly knit spiritual aristocracy', supervising 'a seemingly slow and tight diffusion of texts'?[178] Were they too open to the demands of the powerful who endowed their houses?[179] Or were they still models?[180]

It is striking how many late medieval bishops felt that monasteries were in need of reform. Of course, monasteries were organic entities: all that grows decays, and, just as in a garden, weeding and pruning deadwood were perennial tasks. Reforming bishops are a recurring theme. Again, there were questions of jurisdiction involved here too. Many monasteries claimed exemption from episcopal visitation: many Augustinian and Benedictine houses, all Cistercian houses (an exceptional period in the 1480s apart), as well as the Dominican and Franciscan friars. The Benedictine houses of Bury St Edmunds, Evesham and St Albans enjoyed specially privileged exempt status. Erasmus was not alone in thinking it would be conducive to the concord of the church if monks were brought more completely under the authority of the bishops.[181]

Wolsey is remarkable for the vigour with which he sought to reform monasteries. On 12 June 1518 he wrote to the chapter of regular Augustinian canons meeting at Leicester. He insisted on learning as the greatest preservative of the catholic faith and as the great distinction between men and brutes. He could not observe without regretting that so few Augustinian canons applied themselves to study, and declared his determination to found a college for the order, the members of which would devote themselves exclusively to learning. In response, the chapter appointed him a brother of their order and submitted themselves entirely to his authority as a reformer. But they claimed, perhaps disingenuously, that they were nervous of taking measures against those who broke the rule for fear of being sued under the praemunire statutes; that nervousness made the discipline of the order ineffective.[182] Was Wolsey's assessment of the Augustinian canons' lack of learning altogether fair? A list of books which survives in part has been linked to the Augustinian priory of Thurgarton through an inscription readable under ultra-violet light which reads 'Liber Roberti . . . canonici de Thurgarton [This book belongs to Robert, canon of Thurgarton]'. The works 'listed closely correspond with the devotional reading of pious men and women in late-medieval England', including Catherine of Siena, Walter Hilton and Richard Rolle. A late fifteenth-century catalogue of books owned by the Augustinian abbey at Leicester—the abbey where the Augustinian canons were meeting in 1518—similarly offers evidence of 'substantial devotional interests'. Just how much weight can be placed on these lists is difficult to say, yet they do offer a warning against accepting too readily strictures on the ignorance of monks. Few of the books described can be identified with extant copies: but for these lists we should not know that Thurgarton and Leicester held any of them. It may well be that other Augustinian houses were similarly well stocked, and if so that would go a long way to qualifying Wolsey's complaints.[183] However that may be, in March 1520, following up his earlier intervention, Wolsey issued revised orders and statutes for the Augustinian canons, comprising eighteen articles. They were to hold a general meeting of the order every three years. Unsuitable persons and women were not to be admitted within the cloisters. The canons were not to leave the monastery. They were not to go hunting and hawking. They were not to wear furs and shoes such as worn by the laity. They were to keep the canonical hours.[184] Of course, what Wolsey was emphasising here was the traditional ideal. But the implication was that the rule had been honoured here more in the breach than in the observance. Wolsey 'looked to more rigorous application of the founder's rule, an enforced retreat from worldliness, reform through discipline'. He was a 'tough disciplinarian'.[185]

By the end of August 1518 Wolsey—who had first been appointed papal legate in May—was (jointly with Cardinal Campeggio) given powers to visit English religious houses, whether these were constitutionally exempt from episcopal jurisdiction or not. In December Wolsey summoned the bishops to meet at Westminster Abbey to discuss how the church should be reformed. Unfortunately the new constitutions, which were apparently drawn up then, have not survived. Wolsey and Campeggio were reappointed in June 1519 as legates for the reformation of monasteries—Wolsey's authority would be renewed in 1521, and amplified in 1524[186]—to which end Wolsey summoned abbots and priors to a conference at Westminster in November.[187] Polydore Vergil, the papal tax-collector in England turned historian, gave a jaundiced account of events. Wolsey berated the assembled monks for living a life very different from that which they had initially professed, for failing to devote themselves to letters and to good works, but instead concentrating on their own enrichment. He then held a visitation of Westminster Abbey itself, intending, according to Vergil, more to demonstrate his authority and to frighten the monks into making him gifts.[188] We may allow that Wolsey's motives were more sincere than Vergil (always quick to see the worst in him) credited. Wolsey was surely making a point as publicly as possible, namely that monasteries were not living fully up to their ideals and that none, not even Westminster Abbey, would be immune from episcopal oversight. And Vergil's chronology was awry since Wolsey's visitation took place in January 1519, several months before the general assembly of monks. Wolsey did go on to attempt a reformation of the Benedictines, to judge from their response (to which we shall return) to the instructions he sent them—seemingly restating the rules of their order.[189] Wolsey made some further visitations, to Much Wenlock, Shropshire, in 1523, and to Worcester Priory in 1525. And under his legatine powers Wolsey also appointed Edmund Audley (c.1439–1524), bishop of Salisbury, as his deputy—and presumably Wolsey acted similarly in other dioceses— to visit the nunneries in his diocese and take action against those guilty of

'misgovernance and slanderous living': in such cases nuns should be transferred to other houses.[190] That visitation in the diocese of Salisbury led to
the suppression of the nunnery at Broomhall, for unspecified 'enormities',
referred to by Henry VIII in his letter of thanks to the bishop for his care.[191]

What was Wolsey's intention behind all this activity? Convinced that all
was not well—a conviction he evidently shared with many other bishops,
and with scholars such as Erasmus—he clearly believed that visitations (or
inspections) would highlight shortcomings and then point the way to reformation, especially by the issuing of new 'constitutions' (present-day
managers would talk of 'action plans'). Of course, such inspections were
not always welcomed. Thomas, Lord Darcy, would attack Wolsey for 'the
orgueillous visitation and search that he rigorously and suddenly made' at
Syon.[192] And modern historians have been too quick to assert that Wolsey's
actions were driven, not by any spiritual concerns, but rather by a desire to
seize monastic wealth for his own ends. But if Wolsey was more vigorous
than other bishops, that reflected the extent of his powers and responsibilities, not least as papal legate. Many other bishops, it should be noted, were
similarly critical of the condition of monasteries and energetic in reforming
measures within their dioceses. Earlier, Richard Fox, bishop of Winchester,
had told Wolsey of his difficulties in doing within his diocese what Wolsey
had attempted in the whole country. To his surprise, he had found the monks
so depraved, so licentious and so corrupt that he despaired of any perfect
reformation.[193] In 1522 he told Wolsey that he had much business both of
correction and justice in hand: he was visting his cathedral and Hyde Abbey
every fifteen days.[194] Later he attempted to forbid nuns in his diocese from
leaving their monasteries, a measure which anticipated the policy of Henry
VIII and Thomas Cromwell in 1535 and aroused controversy.[195] Advised by
the abbess of Wherwell and the prioress of Witney that a basic weakness
was that the nuns insufficiently understood their rule, since it was in Latin,
Fox translated the rule of St Benedict into 'common, plain, round English,
easy and ready to be understood by . . . devout religious women', adding a
running commentary to the text. Fox's purpose was to strengthen the nuns'
commitment to their vocation, while gently reproaching them for being too
worldly. And if he was critical, and even at times despairing, of the state of
the monasteries, nevertheless he spent a good deal of his episcopal revenues
on rebuilding Netley Abbey, Southwark Priory and his own cathedral.[196]
John Longland, bishop of Lincoln, was concerned by the condition of
monasteries. Earlier—most likely at Wolsey's visitation—he had preached
to the monks of Westminster Abbey: 'woe unto them who do not devote
themselves to prayer and reading . . . but give themselves over to gourmand-
ising and self-indulgence'. 'What greater scandal or disgrace can there be

than men, consecrated and bound by solemn vows to God alone and divine worship, should buy in the open market meats, fish and all manner of other dainties for their table?' He asked them if they had struggled against the yoke of poverty and thrown it off and if they had borne the yoke of obedience and chastity patiently or not. And exhorted them 'let your frugal table, your hard bed, your mean clothing bear witness to your continual self-control . . . never let a book be out of your hand or out of your sight'. And in order for the monks to remain chaste, 'everywhere the company of women is to be avoided lest their beauty cleave to your heart'.[197] Once he had become bishop of Lincoln, Longland was much exercised by problems uncovered in several monasteries in his diocese. To Dorchester, Oxfordshire, where observance of services was lax, he sent injunctions which the abbot seemingly disregarded. To Great Missenden Longland made a special visitation and issued instructions in English 'for that ye be ignorant and have small understanding of Latin'. To Delapre, Northampton, he sent injunctions which he insisted be read 'lest in the course of time they be forgotten or any of you in future try to pretend to be ignorant of them'. The nuns of Elstow were told not to wear a low-cut dress or veil indistinguishable from those worn by women outside the nunnery. Longland also worked with Wolsey to secure the removal of the scandalous abbot of Thame.[198]

Wolsey shared the belief of many bishops that smaller monastic houses would be best suppressed and their revenues diverted to newer and more valuable pastoral purposes, namely grammar schools in towns and colleges at Oxford and Cambridge which would educate and train the clergy of the future. This was a practical realisation of the ideal implicit in contemporary critiques of the monasteries, most notably that of Erasmus. Wolsey dissolved some twenty-nine houses, a reform which has been given deserved recognition by Peter Gwyn. Since it has all too often been seen merely as Wolsey's self-glorification, it is important to emphasise that it was a shared policy. Archbishop Warham, for example, told a group of sixteen inhabitants of Tonbridge, Kent, that it was thought by Wolsey, 'and that I also thought the same', namely that it would 'stand better with the pleasure of God', and that it would be more for the 'advantage and commodity' of them and their children, perpetually to have forty children of that country brought up in learning, and afterwards sent to the university of Oxford, rather than to have six or seven canons resident in the priory in Tonbridge.[199] A notable earlier example was Bishop Alcock's suppression in 1496 of what he claimed was the dissolute and dilapidated nunnery of St Radegund and the creation on that site and from its revenues of a new college that we now know as Jesus College, Cambridge.[200] And far from being a corrupt prelate, Alcock, as we have seen, was admired even by John Bale for his sanctity.[201]

In November 1528 Wolsey secured a papal bull empowering him to inquire into the expediency of suppressing certain monasteries and to use their revenues and buildings for new cathedrals and dioceses. It permitted the mergers of monasteries with fewer than twelve inmates (a number symbolising the twelve apostles), especially affecting the many small houses of Augustinian canons with which Wolsey had earlier been much concerned.[202] In May 1529 Wolsey was granted executive powers allowing him to create new dioceses, to convert abbacies into bishoprics, to supress houses with low revenues, and to merge monasteries unable to support twelve monks or nuns.[203] The request for the bull spoke of the need for 'the conservation of religion', which could not be observed except in communities of a sufficient number: individuals scattered in small monasteries brought nothing but discredit on religion. By uniting monasteries which could not support twelve religious out of their fruits, they would 'make one perfect out of several imperfect'.[204] These bulls hint at the imminence of fundamental reform, thwarted by Wolsey's sudden fall.

But if closures and mergers were seen as essential and beneficial by most bishops, such a policy was far from popular. At Tonbridge all but three of the sixteen-strong delegation of townsmen who saw Archbishop Warham wanted the priory to remain.[205] At Bayham there was a small-scale rebellion.[206] Such local attachment to monasteries, however small and corrupt, is telling. When Wolsey fell in 1529 and it was open season for complaints against him, those drawn up by Thomas, Lord Darcy, included the hope that in future 'no abbeys nor houses of religion by untrue surmises pulled nor suffered to be pulled down, nor noble founders' wills broken . . . but royally maintained, and divine services upholden'. Darcy vigorously attacked 'the abomination, ruin, and seditious . . . violations used at the pulling down of abbeys by his commissioners and servants at his commandments, and the great robberies and spoilings', comparable to the worst acts of Luther.[207] And any reformer had perforce to walk over a minefield of privileges and financial rights which would lead to delays and make him unpopular.[208] In passing, it is worth noting that there is no contemporary evidence of opposition to dissolutions of nunneries on the grounds that their resources were being transferred to endow a wholly male college at Oxford.[209] Nor was the criticism by bishops of monasteries that they had ceased to be distinctive and that the services which they offered simply duplicated those available elsewhere.[210] The bishops' critique was rather that, on the one hand, monks and nuns were not living up to the continuingly valid ideals which they set themselves, and, on the other hand, that some part of their lavish resources could be more effectively used in other ways. They would have sympathised with the modern medievalist who noted that 'the unit cost of a monk was very high': the ratio of servants to monks, difficult though it is to calculate from surviving sources, was probably at least two to one, for example some forty monks in residence at Durham and 110 servants.[211]

Any modern British university historian who has lived through countless administrative reorganisations, and seen the consequences of, say, the restructuring of local government, will hesitate before pronouncing too confidently on the shortcomings of the monasteries of late medieval England. 'For forms of government let fools contest/ What'er is best administered is best.' But it is hard not to believe that some sort of overall rationalisation and reorganisation would have strengthened monasticism in general and left monasteries much less vulnerable to the charge that they squandered resources that could helpfully be redistributed and expended elsewhere, on colleges, on schools, and in the parish. The distinction made in the act dissolving the smaller monasteries in 1536 between smaller monasteries deserving dissolution and larger monasteries, 'the great solemn monasteries of this realm, wherein, thanks be to God, religion is right well kept and observed', which would remain, does seem to have empirical foundation. 'In general, the visitors discovered that the Benedictine monasteries, and especially the larger ones, were in a much better condition than the houses of the other orders.'[212] The royal visitors found little to criticise at Lacock ('as yet I can find no excesses', wrote John ap Rice, 'as for the house it is in good state and well ordered'), Glastonbury ('I doubt not that they will keep as good religion as any house in the kingdom') and Ramsey ('I pray God I may find other houses in no worse condition').[213]

But if late medieval monasteries, however conscientious in observance, were not all they might have been, if smaller houses were often inadequate, should the causes of repeated failures to be wholly and unceasingly committed to the monastic ideal be seen as rooted in man's fallen nature?[214] Were the rules which monks and nuns were supposed to follow simply asking too much? Was there an inescapable tension between the aspiration to renounce the world and the humdrum realities of human life? How committed were most monks and nuns to the religious vocation? Benedictines assembled in London by Wolsey's order (most likely in November 1519 or February 1520) responded lamentably to the instructions Wolsey had sent them, seemingly a restatement of the Benedictine rule. They agreed that many of the rules ought to be followed enthusiastically by all good monks, but 'in these stormy times . . . those who desire a life of austerity and of regular observance are few, and indeed most rare'. The number of monks and monasteries in England was too great to allow such rules to be enforced without provoking murmurs and mutiny. They begged Wolsey to modify the reform of their order in order not to drive the weak into flight, apostasy or rebellion, or to deter those who were intending to enter the order. There was no doubt that if Wolsey's reformation was conducted with too much austerity and rigour, there would be insufficient monks to fill the monasteries. In the present times, very few, they said, wished to live a life of austerity. Only the Carthusians, Brigittines and Observant Franciscans could do so. And if there were as many monasteries in England of those orders as there were of the Benedictine monks, 'certainly we do not see from where could be gathered such a multitude' so that their houses could be filled. All that was a remarkably damaging self-defence.[215] And there are individual examples of the same attitude. A would-be Charterhouse monk, evidently being denied admission, was unwilling to go to one of the northern houses, since he could not stand the cold.[216] The lawyer Christopher St German, a less impartial witness, reported how many said 'that religious men have the most pleasant and delicate life that any men have'. They spurned the ascetic life: they would neither hunger nor thirst. He questioned 'whether the rigour and straitness [strictness]' of their rules could be 'borne now in these days', and thought it 'better . . . to have an easy rule well kept than a strait [strict] rule broken without correction'.[217]

How far were monks and nuns unthinkingly absorbed in a more or less mechanical routine, with little time or stimulus to think about the larger issues? How far were religious vocations—like those of modern academics—stultified by the piling up of administrative tasks, by the burdens of the detailed administration of buildings and estates? Was there a loss, or a lack, of spiritual impetus and creative energy? Were new buildings a diversion of energy into worldly activities, for the benefit above all of heads of houses and senior office-holders, or rather evidence of high morale and prestige, of vitality and confidence? Were ruinous buildings evidence of negligence and slackness or a proper other-worldliness—or simply a reflection of an exaggerated definition of 'ruinous'? The abbot of Faversham offered two models of the role of an abbot to Cromwell, at a time when he was evidently being encouraged to consider retirement on account of his age. 'Admit the peculiar office of an abbot to consist . . . in journeying forth and surveying of the possessions of his house,' he said, and in that case a younger man might be more suitable. 'Again,' he continued, 'on that other side, if the chief office and profession of an abbot be (as I have ever taken it) to live chaste and solitarily, to be separate from the intromeadlyng [inter-meddling] of worldly things, to serve God quietly, to distribute his faculties in refreshing of poor indigent persons, to have a vigilant eye to the good order and rule of his house and the flock to him committed in God', then despite his age he could do that as well as ever.[218]

Of the monks at Westminster Abbey, 60 per cent held a time-consuming administrative post, forty out of fifty-seven at Canterbury in the 1530s; virtually all Durham monks after their noviciate could count on holding some office or other for the rest of their monastic careers.[219] How much did abbots and priors become administrators, as distant from their monks as university vice-chancellors are from academics today? When Cromwell's visitors banned monks from leaving their monasteries, many complained that this meant that they could not visit their lands and tenements: the abbot of Osney warned that this would prevent him from seeing that necessary repairs were made or from viewing 'such waste and spoil as many tenants will do if they may be sure their landlord will not nor may look upon their defaults'. Indeed, even one of the commissioners, John ap Rice, thought it 'over strait' since it prevented heads of houses from overseeing the husbandry on which their houses depended.[220] Certainly the running of their estates absorbed much of the energies of late medieval monks.

How far were monasteries victims rather than the beneficiaries of circumstances of their foundation? Had there, especially in the twelfth century, been perhaps over-enthusiastic foundations of monasteries by men of second rank who lacked the wealth needed to establish them on a sound footing?[221] There were no fewer than seventy-one new monastic foundations in the diocese of Norwich between 1066 and 1200.[222] A study of East Anglian nunneries noted their general under-endowment in the twelfth century.[223] Was there a gradual decline in the social status of founders and the wealth of their monasteries? In Norfolk St Benet at Holme and Norwich Cathedral Priory, the two richest houses in the county, together with a group of Benedictine and Cluniac houses founded between 1085 and 1113 (Thetford, Castle Acre, Bromholm, Binham, Wymondham), remained among the wealthier monasteries of Norfolk right up to the dissolution. They were mostly established near the castles or residences of their founders. But 'the later they were founded, the more likely were their founders to be of lesser status and they themselves to be poorly endowed': 'the ten houses founded after 1199 . . . were all at the bottom of the hierarchy of endowment'; 'the majority of the thirty-five endowed monasteries . . . were small, locally-based houses towards the bottom end of landowning society'. It was such houses that failed during the fifteenth century, leading to mergers with larger houses, or closures. Some twenty-five Yorkshire nunneries had been founded between 1125 and 1225, often poorly endowed. Only two had large incomes, Watton with £360, and forty-one nuns in the mid-1530s, and St Leonard's Hospital with £300. Five others had incomes over £50. But eleven had less than £22, one had just £8.[224] A modern parallel might be the under-endowment of the polytechnics, set up in the late 1960s,

and renamed as universities in 1992, though revealingly still often referred
to as the 'new universities'.

More telling, however, than the inadequacies of some, but by no means
all, heads of houses as a weakness of monasteries in the later middle ages
was the small size and poverty of so many of them, especially the small
Augustinian houses. Observance of the daily liturgical round must itself
have been difficult. At St Mary Magdalen priory, Bristol, a twelfth-century
foundation for canonesses, there were only two by the 1530s, together
with two servants.[225] At Stavordale near Wincanton, Somerset, 'there is
but two canons, which be of no good living': it had been so small that
Taunton had taken it over, though Richard Zouche, whose ancestors had
founded the house, would blame that on a lewd prior.[226] At Fordham priory,
Cambridgeshire, there was just the prior, and an aged monk 'at death's
door'.[227] It is not necessary to be a zealot for restructuring to believe that
such houses were hard to justify. And, setting aside such extreme examples,
there were many small houses that were clearly felt to be serving a purpose,
to judge from the evidence of bequests, and from the fuss that was made
when proposals for reorganisation and closure were put forward. How far
was it felt that abuses or shortcomings were worth putting up with because
the monks (or their deputies) nonetheless said masses for the souls of
countless benefactors languishing in purgatory?[228] Houses of Augustinian
canons had been founded with pastoral considerations in mind: unlike
Benedictine monks, Augustinian canons ('the unsung heroes of the
Gregorian reform movement . . . who brought the tenets of reform to the
populace'[229]) were explicitly expected to minister to lay needs, and, however
few the canons, they could obviously offer something. No doubt that
explains local attachment to such houses. And many if not most had been
founded when the population was much higher than after the Black Death.
Yet, all the same, making a strong case for them is not easy. Twelve monks
or nuns were reiterated as the canonical minimum number in the papal bull
secured by Wolsey in November 1528,[230] and surely Wolsey and reforming
bishops were right that an effective monastery required such a complement.

Was there, then, no general reform movement in the centuries before the
dissolution? Were there no charismatic monks offering outstanding spiritual leadership?[231] Certainly there seem to have been few if any monks who
were widely praised as exemplars of christian piety. 'Overall, one gets the
impression', Richard Hoyle has concluded, 'that monks no longer contributed much in the way of spiritual leadership to the world in which they
lived.'[232] Was Christopher St German right to suggest that a comparison
between monks past and monks present was 'as great diversity as between
heaven and hell'?[233] Or does that reflect the patchiness of fifteenth- and

early sixteenth-century sources? If there was a spiritual revival in the later middle ages, it was in the mystical writings of a Walter Hilton or a Julian of Norwich (1342–c.1416), an anchoress in Norwich who wrote *Revelations of Divine Love*. If a good deal of that emerged from within monasteries, in many respects such individualistic mysticism risked leaving monasteries as beached whales, overtaken or left to one side by changing ideals. There was no general monastic revival in late medieval England. The later fourteenth and fifteenth centuries did see some rejuvenation of the monastic ideal, as the foundation of the Charterhouses, Observant Franciscans and Brigittines shows. But those foundations were not followed by others. However pure and inspiring, they were few in number, and they had little influence on the conduct of other religious houses. Henry V's experiences are to the point here, showing how high ideals were not easily translated into practice. One of his projects, that for a Celestine abbey, failed to get off the ground for lack of funds. He had considerable difficulties in staffing the Brigittine house at Syon: in the end he secured just half the numbers required, taking short-cuts in quality. At Sheen Charterhouse he recruited some thirty instead of the forty he sought. If so determined and wealthy a founder as Henry V was forced to compromise, how much more true would that have been of lesser patrons?[234] Moreover, the standstill of work after his death confirms his personal involvement and vividly illustrates how plans could go awry.[235] Sheen's dependence on property formerly in the hands of alien priories entangled it in complex, long-running and time-consuming disputes with several foreign abbeys in the 1430s and 1440s and beyond, showing how ideals and practicalities were enmeshed.[236] These new foundations at Sheen and Syon damaged existing Charterhouses because monks left them for the new houses.[237] Moreover, consideration of Henry V's purposes shows how piety and politics intermingled. Was Henry in part fulfilling his father's vow of founding three houses in expiation of his part in the deaths of Richard II and Archbishop Scrope?[238] More generally, were these new foundations the best way to further the devotion of the Carthusians and Brigittines? Would it not have been preferable to have strengthened existing Charterhouses? Impressive too is how the fortunes of Sheen and Syon revived under Edward IV who (it has been claimed) saw them as enhancing his royal credentials, rather than from any conspicuous personal piety. His mother Cecily and his wife Elizabeth were granted special licences to attend masses at Sheen (breaching the absolute prohibition on the admission of women) as was Margaret Beaufort.[239] Monastic revival was subordinate to monarchical needs. And while Henry V's works of piety are indeed impressive, it is hard to see the Charterhouses and the Brigittines as the advance party of a monastic revival overall. Not only did descendants of founders

add little to the existing houses of their ancestors, but fifteenth-century
noblemen and gentlemen in general did not found monasteries. Henry V
did, as did his son Henry VI (if Eton and King's College Cambridge are
allowed as a kind of monastery); but 'in the fifteenth and early sixteenth
centuries, no one had the money with which to establish a monastery on the
classic high medieval lines'.[240]

It has been suggested that 'the greatest indictment of late medieval
monasticism is that in an age when the demand for intercessory prayer
for souls of the dead had expanded, those classes who had for centuries
been main benefactors of religious houses, which had been founded primarily to fulfil this function, now undramatically but en masse eschewed their
spiritual ministrations and sought salvation through the establishment
of chantries and obits in parish churches'.[241] Of course, it may simply be
that colleges and schools and almshouses were cheaper because they were
less lavish; in the fifteenth century the cost of founding a monastery on
traditional lines had become prohibitive. Colleges of secular priests associated with chantries were, indeed, founded by noblemen and gentlemen in
substantial numbers: over seventy between 1350 and 1530, of which
Fotheringhay, Northamptonshire in 1411, and Tattershall, Lincolnshire in
1439, are but two prominent examples.[242] Yet such college-chantries, with
their emphasis on liturgy and intercession, were surely inspired by monastic
ideals, and it is wrong to see them as opposed to monasteries.[243] Furthermore,
it may have been felt that there simply were sufficient large monasteries
throughout the country, with adequate endowments, and that there was no
pressing call for more. That allowed, chantries and fraternities may have
offered more laymen more direct involvement, indeed control. And parish
churches were an increasingly common focus of parishioners' piety: there is
a revealing contrast between the increasing and substantial commitment of
parishioners to St Margaret's Westminster and their lack of involvement in
Westminster Abbey.[244] Even so, it is notable that many did still leave
bequests to monasteries or request burial within them. Study of surviving
wills from the fifteenth and early sixteenth centuries suggests that some
15 to 20 per cent of testators, especially the more affluent and of higher
social rank, made bequests to monasteries.[245] When would-be reformers
such as Thomas Starkey asserted that 'we may not give all our possessions
to nourish idle men in continual prayer', he was admitting that many still
did support the monasteries.[246]

So how far, despite the paucity of wholly new foundations, did monastic
ideals permeate national life, even when not constantly followed: were they
still a point of reference? Did the Carthusians serve as a model after all?[247]
Was lay spirituality still heavily influenced by monastic ideals?[248] Was the

devotional mysticism, the 'mixed life', recommended by writers such as Walter Hilton, an attempt to bring the austerity and contemplation of the cloister and the cell into the homes of everyman and everywoman?[249] In the Low Countries such a *devotio moderna* as elaborated by Johannes Ruysbroeck (1293–1381) and his follower Gerard Groote (1340–85) led to the founding by Groote of the community of the Brethren of the Common Life in Deventer, which then spread throughout Flanders. There were no such houses in England, nor the *beguinages* (groups of semi-religious women living together in chaste and simple households, characteristic of the Low Countries and north-west Germany), maybe because such establishments might have seemed risky in the shadow of the heresies associated with Wyclif and because episcopal control was tighter. But the impulses underlying Hilton's 'mixed life' and the *devotio moderna* were similar— and both can readily be seen as a refashioning of the asceticism and devotion at the heart of the monastic ideal.[250] Was not the daily routine of devotion followed by Cecily (1415–95), duchess of York—matins on rising at seven o'clock, a low mass in her chamber, divine service and two low masses in the chapel, reading of works by Walter Hilton, St Bonaventure, the Golden Legend or the Revelations of St Brigitte over dinner, praying till the first peal of evensong, sung evensong in the chapel, reciting her dinner-time reading to those present at supper, followed by prayers in her private closet at the end of the day—and many other aristocratic ladies, a comparable domesticated version of the monastic model?[251] Were the books of hours so characteristic of late medieval devotion not replete with additions made to monastic services in the ninth to the eleventh centuries—'a striking indication of the power of the monastic innovators to express the spiritual impulses of their own age and to form those of the future'?[252] Were not the virtues reflected in the lives of saints to whom pilgrimage was made very much monastic virtues: humility, voluntary poverty, chastity, charity, obedience?[253] Were the hermits and anchoresses of medieval England in their individual ways also responding to the impulses underlying monasteries? And the ramifications of the heavy investment in chantries and masses, which we have already noted, are hard to square with any suggestion that belief in prayer and intercession, central to monasteries, was declining. The aspirations which reforming bishops had for parish clergy were very close to the monastic ideal.[254] Asceticism had not lost its resonance. Interestingly, in 1530, after his fall, Cardinal Wolsey spent five weeks at Sheen: it was remarkable testimony to the monks that he agreed to wear the hair-shirts they gave him, and that he was still wearing one of them when he died.[255]

But if the ebb and flow of monastic idealism was a recurrent phenomenon of the middle ages, if the history of monasticism was 'a history of alternating decline and revival', then that prompts the thought that reform and revitalisation were also possible.[256] How conceivable was a further burst of monastic reform, leading to a new wave of spiritual perfectionism? In a long view, the history of christian monasticism from its beginnings in the solitude of the Egyptian desert was a succession of attempts to institutionalise the living of an ascetic and holy life, usually reactions against what was perceived as the failure of earlier attempts. 'No order', Christopher Harper-Bill has noted, 'could hope to perpetuate the radical reforming zeal of its founding fathers.'[257] St Benedict's Rule (though the uncertainty of authorship makes any precise argument awkward), Fleury, the reforms of Dunstan (archbishop of Canterbury 959–88), Aethelwold (bishop of Winchester 963–84) and Oswald (archbishop of York from 971), the Cluniac reform, Lanfranc at Bec (even if he was not reforming anything specifically), the Grande Chartreuse, the Cistercians, the Augustinian canons, the Premonstratensians, and then the various orders of friars, can all be seen in such terms—even if the methods varied and the abuses or neglect against which each was reacting were not the same, and if the Augustinians, Premonstratensians and friars on the one hand saw their mission as very much in this world, while the monastic orders focused on the intercession provided by their own communities. There had been waves of revival: the ninth and tenth centuries had witnessed a great revival of Benedictine monastic life, culminating in the heyday of classic monasticism in the tenth and eleventh centuries. Characteristic of these waves of revival were monks seeking a purer, a more exclusive, a more intense, a more ascetic way of life, through the literal observance of the rule of St Benedict, most vividly illustrated by the Cistercians from the late eleventh century. They began with a secession from Molesme in 1075, and then rapid expansion came in the early twelfth century under Bernard of Clairvaux: one house in 1112, ten in 1119, 344 in 1153 (some, perhaps a majority, absorbing earlier foundations, especially Benedictine houses now 'rebranded as Cistercians but not direct offshoots of Citeaux').[258] This remains true even though much of what has often been presented as Cistercian growth was more the selective adoption of Cistercian customs by already existing houses, something that seems less the case in England and Wales, where houses such as Tintern, Rievaulx, Whitland were clearly colonial foundations from the beginning.[259] Other reformers wanted closer involvement in the world: the Augustinian canons, who took the whole world as their monastery, and the friars, with their emphasis on preaching in towns.[260] Meanwhile, the older Benedictine monasteries lived on, perhaps in 'crisis as some have said', certainly no longer at the cutting edge of monasticism, but simply continuing, in the century 1050–1150 that saw so much innovation, though with some rethinking of the rule, 'accepted as part of the order of things . . but not as tremendous facts in their society'.[261] In the twelfth century there was a newer vision of monastic life, a reaction against material prosperity.[262] Cluny's emphasis on poverty, its saintly men, illustrates that well. And in the late thirteenth and early fourteenth centuries fundamental changes were made by the English Benedictines to their religious life, imposing greater centralisation, and introducing new forms of devotion, but in many ways relaxing the demands of the rule of St Benedict—perhaps recognising realities, or, as in the eyes of some recent historians, a 'bold attempt at modernisation', yet more plausibly to be seen as a falling away from the austerity and rigour of the past, and no less real for being 'the result of deliberate policy' than of neglect.[263]

Was a renewed attempt at spiritual purification still possible from within the late medieval monastic order? Arguably, of course, that is just what Luther's call was, though he came to reject fundamental aspects of monasticism. The renewal of European monasticism, the emergence of new orders such as the Jesuits, in the age of the catholic counter-reformation, shows the continuing potential vitality of the monastic ideal. Could such a revival have been born in England? It is hard to say that it could not. It is often a characteristic of such movements that they arose from small and accidental beginnings, from the inspiration of some unusually pious and charismatic monk or nun. Were there 'hidden seeds of renewal and reform'?[264] Philippa Tudor has written of 'a sense of religious renewal' in the early sixteenth century, pointing to the emphasis on poverty, charity, obedience, prayer, personal examination of conscience, all tempered by moderation, that she found in contemporary religious books.[265] Could that have developed into a much larger religious revival in which monasteries would be central? One of the London Charterhouse monks had a revelation just after Prior Batemanson died in which he saw him and the previous prior both kneeling before the Trinity and making intercession for the Carthusians. In the revelation the monk was told that the cloth the monks wore was too fine, that they should not eat from pewter plates, that they should keep two rather than three habits in store. Interestingly, it was agreed to change the monks' cloth in the light of his revelation. There may have been something in the implicit charges of extravagance: the king's commissioners thought their fare dainty, noting that a meal that served twelve of the monks would, in their opinion, adequately serve twenty.[266] Nonetheless, the detail of the monk's revelation testifies to the continuing power of the ascetic ideal just a year or two before the dissolution.[267]

Maybe reform was impossible: Abbot Green of Leiston forsook his house in 1531 for the hermit's life in the marshes by the sea, presumably despairing of imposing asceticism on his monks.[268] But one must fairly note the limits of the ascetic ideal too. Another London Carthusian monk, Nicholas Rawlyns, claimed to have been tricked into making his profession. The 'religion'—rule—was 'so hard', what with fasting and watching, he moaned; there were hardly any monks who were not unwell; if he continued under the rule, it would shorten his life, which was an understandable, but worldly, concern.[269] A canon of St Osyth, Thomas Solmes, said that during the twelve years he had been there he had never willingly borne the yoke of religion: he would rather die than live such a miserable life any longer.[270] Much in this chapter has emphasised the achievements of the monasteries and the continuing appeal of the monastic ideal. But since the monasteries of late medieval England did not produce a revival, it is fitting that this chapter should end with examples that perhaps explain why they did not.

9

HERESY

Richard Hunne was convicted of heresy, as we have seen, though the evidence against him was, to say the least, ambiguous: the martyrologist John Foxe got himself tied in knots in trying to recruit Hunne to the pantheon of proto-protestant martyrs. And the Hunne affair acutely raises the wider significance of dissent. Was there a surge of organised heresy in the early sixteenth century? Did it weaken the late medieval church? Should it be seen as a stepping-stone on the way to a greater reformation? Or has the significance of dissent been exaggerated, at the time by orthodox bishops and polemicists, a little later by the first protestants who were looking for a medieval ancestry, and over the past century by modern scholars wholly dependent on the records created by just those churchmen and divines? Yet, if dissent has been given too much weight, counter-heresy—the measure the authorities took against what they saw as heresy—has been too little appreciated, not only as a potential weakness but also, in some ways, as a strength of the late medieval church.

Until the late fourteenth century there was little sign of any significant and substantial religious dissent in England: one estimate is that there were some forty-five cases in the previous two centuries.[1] That the late-fourteenth-century Oxford theologian John Wyclif (d. 1384) articulated heretical beliefs is indisputable, even though he was never pronounced an heretic while he was alive and even though his opinions were not formally condemned until the Council of Constance in 1415. He does not seem to have been influenced by continental heresies but rather to have elaborated his ideas through his own study of the scriptures. He attacked what he saw as superstitious popular practices: he denounced indulgences, prayers for the dead, chantries, prayers to the saints, the cult of the Virgin, pilgrimages to the images and bones of saints. He rejected the teaching of the church on the mass, not least the recent use of the host in processions such as those associated with the cult of Corpus Christi. He attacked the wealth of the church, its institutionalised system of patronage which, he confessed, had once ensnared him too in the sins of hypocrisy and ambition, and argued that prelates should not serve as rulers and judges. He denounced monasticism. He sought to reduce the difference between layman and priest: laymen should not make confession to priests. Only morally perfect clergy deserved respect. The Bible was the only sure basis of belief and it ought to be made freely available to the laity in a vernacular translation.

Wyclif's teachings were undoubtedly revolutionary in potential and if they had been adopted by Richard II and become government policy historians would not be referring to them as 'the premature reformation'. But neither Richard II nor Henry IV nor Henry V would have any truck with what they saw as heresy. For a brief period in the 1390s several of the knights at Richard II's court appeared to show sympathy, promoting and protecting clergy and scholars clearly influenced by Wyclif, and owning Wycliffite texts; yet such sympathy only went so far, and modern scholars may have given it too much weight. Indeed, they may have found it too readily. Wyclif would undoubtedly have felt contempt for funeral pomp but it is risky to deduce that knights who asked to be buried modestly were his followers. And most noblemen and knights were staunchly orthodox. Episcopal persecution, reinforced by the parliamentary statute *De haeretico comburendo* of 1401 that permitted the burning of heretics, inaugurated an effective repression, with William Sawtry, a priest, the first to be burnt; though for a generation or more a variety of manuscript writings clearly influenced by Wyclif continued to be produced. Further discredited politically by Sir John Oldcastle's rising in 1414 and by an abortive plot in 1431, Wyclif's ideas disappeared from the universities of Oxford and Cambridge, and continued to be largely rejected by the nobility and gentry. Henry V and Archbishop Arundel of Canterbury took an especially vigorous line against what they saw as a damnable heresy.[2]

How far did Wyclif's heresies—which were increasingly described as 'lollardy', in an attempt to discredit Wyclif's ideas by associating them with unsophisticated popular heresies,[3] deploying a middle-Dutch word that meant 'mumbler or babbler of prayers'[4]—nonetheless survive in the fifteenth century? Should we agree that 'native heresy, or "lollardy", unquestionably remained alive in early sixteenth-century England'?[5] Should we imagine 'groups of fervent readers, listeners and learners', skilled artisans, weavers, wheelwrights, smiths, carpenters, shoemakers and tailors, meeting together in taverns and in their own homes to read, listen and discuss the scriptures?[6] Did they share manuscript books of translated extracts from the Bible and commentaries? Was this a 'coherent, living movement' demonstrating that Englishmen and Englishwomen had an overwhelming desire to read the scriptures in English? Did it herald the demands of the laity for a more active role in the life of the church? Was it thus part of what has long been seen as the long struggle of the laity to gain supremacy within the English church between 1450 and 1660—in short, did it anticipate and contribute to the reformation?[7]

It is clear that there was a great deal of 'lollard' writing in the early fifteenth century. Such works referred admiringly to Wyclif or quoted his writings directly. They treated the nature of the eucharist, seen (contrary to the teaching of the church) as remaining bread and wine, they asserted the futility of oral confession, they made criticisms of pilgrimages and images and voiced anti-papal sentiments in general.[8] Thirty surviving manuscripts contain some 294 anonymous sermons on these lines (though, intriguingly, some of them were in the libraries of impeccably orthodox houses—Syon, the Franciscans of Shrewsbury and the nuns of Barking Abbey).[9] But after c.1420 little new material was produced, and, while dating such texts is not at all straightforward, it is certainly hard to find any writing of this type that *must* be later than 1440. Even the copying of manuscripts was very limited.[10] It is puzzling, given the very high volume of orthodox devotional works that was published in the first generation following the invention and diffusion of printing, that no lollard work was printed before c.1530. The most obvious explanation is that by the mid-fifteenth century lollardy had long ceased to be an intellectually creative force. No writers, no prophets, no great names of dissent are known from the mid-fifteenth century. If the church authorities remained vigilant, official denunciation of lollardy became more routine and less insistent in the decades after the 1430s, again confirming that sense of decline.[11] The curious case of Reginald Pecock (b. c.1392, d. in or after 1459), bishop of Chichester, summoned before the archbishop of Canterbury in 1457–8 over his allegedly heretical writings, does not much qualify that. Pecock may well have been a victim of political manoeuvres reflecting the larger conflicts of the late 1450s and the charges of heresy against him cannot be taken at face value. Nothing in his writings offered anything but a robust defence of orthodoxy. But the way he went about it—especially writing in English and engaging in a kind of dialogue with those whose views he was refuting— might have made him appear less than orthodox, indeed made him vulnerable to the charge that he was himself an heretic. He was certainly original and forceful in his writings. That he evidently thought it necessary to rebut heresy might be taken as evidence of its continuing strength in mid-fifteenth-century England, but his very confidence that an orthodoxy which incorporated his own questioning approach would triumph argues the other way.[12] Moreover, while investigations into heresy can be found in several dioceses, not many heretics were discovered and prosecuted in these years, a trend not convincingly to be explained away on the grounds of the indifference of the authorities or a loss of documentation.[13] 'Absolute silence in ecclesiastical records may simply mean that, as long as they were not too vociferous, they were left in peace';[14] or it might simply mean that there were very few who could reasonably be accused of heresy in these years. 'The history of lollardy from then [the 1420s] until the Reformation is,' Jeremy Catto has vividly written, 'at best, the history of a felony with no more coherence than a history of murder.'[15]

In the early sixteenth century there was unquestionably a revival of the episcopal persecution of heretics. How many were accused of heresy and where were they discovered?[16] In 1506 over sixty from Amersham and over twenty from Buckingham were accused. Two of them were burnt, William Tylesley or Tilseworth at Amersham, Father Robert Cosin at Buckingham. The rest, in what John Foxe called 'the great abjuration', did penance, bearing faggots, wearing badges and, in some cases, being branded in the cheeks.[17] One of them, Thomas Chase, was subjected to further interrogations and kept in prison: according to Foxe, he was strangled, but his death was declared by the authorities to have been suicide.[18] In the next two or three years two more were burnt, Thomas Barnard and James Mordon, and thirty-three did penance.[19] In 1521 the incoming bishop, John Longland, carried out a large-scale inquiry in the Chilterns, including Amersham and Chesham, and also Newbury, Berkshire, and Burford, Oxfordshire: four were burnt, around fifty abjured and did penance. According to John Foxe, some of those who had abjured earlier now gave evidence against others, notably Robert and Richard Bartlett. The Bartletts confessed, and named several more heretics, including their father, brother and sister, and in Robert's case his wife; all that led to a further series of detections.[20] Accusations of heresy were made on a comparable scale elsewhere. In Kent some five people were burnt and nearly fifty abjured between April 1511 and June 1512, mostly from Tenterden, Halden, Ashford, Maidstone, Benenden and Cranbrook.[21] In Coventry, somewhere between forty-nine and sixty-seven people were accused and one burnt in 1511–12: in 1520, seven of those who had earlier abjured were now burnt, and one more in 1520–1.[22] In London there were twenty-three accused in 1510–11, one in 1512, two in 1517, six or seven in 1518, and four in 1521.[23] In 1527–8 some fifty people were accused in and around Steeple Bumpstead, Essex.[24] The Chilterns,

Kent, Coventry, Essex and London were the places in which the greatest numbers were accused. In the diocese of Hereford there were eight between 1505 and 1511. There were four burnings between 1505 and 1511 followed by a further accusation in 1512 in the city of Norwich. Three men and their wives together with another woman in Bradford-on-Avon, Wiltshire, were dealt with in spring 1514, with further cases in December that year, two more abjurations in 1516, one burning in 1517 and another abjuration later that year, and four more in 1518–19.[25] There were two burnings in Devizes, Wiltshire, in 1516, one in 1517, and one in 1518.[26] In other parts of the country there were isolated cases. There was one in York in 1512;[27] one in 1511 and one in 1514 in the diocese of Worcester;[28] one in Plymouth in 1506;[29] one in Bristol in 1511–12;[30] one burning in 1508 in Chipping Sodbury, Gloucestershire;[31] one case in Walton-on-Thames, Surrey, in 1513–14.[32] There were no cases of heresy in the diocese of York between 1513 and 1527, in the diocese of Hereford between 1512 and 1528, or in the diocese of Norwich between 1513 and 1529.[33] In some parts of the country the diocesan registers yield no cases of heresy at all: this is true of the dioceses of Durham, Ely, Carlisle and Chichester. Nor is there any record of heresy in Wales.[34]

What should be made of these numbers? They are most commonly inter-preted as showing that 'the survival of lollardy into the sixteenth century is a fact'.[35] 'It seems clear,' Anne Hudson confidently claims, 'that there was a substantial number of lollards, or at least of men and women who at some stage had shown sympathy with lollard causes and teachings.'[36] And they can obviously be presented to suggest that there was a rising tide of heresy and, consequently, increasing concern on the part of the authorities. Yet that would be misleading. The numbers involved are tiny, totalling a few hundred at most from an adult population of over a million. These are rare and isolated cases, not a surge. There were some in the late 1500s, rather more immediately after 1511, and again a cluster in the early 1520s, but, after that, there were hardly any until 1527–8. In a few places a significant proportion of the population was involved, between 10 per cent and 25 per cent (historians differ) of the population of Amersham and surrounding villages in 1521; but, against that, it must be noted that the incidence of heresy as measured by these trials was highly geographically concentrated. Those accused in the diocese of Lincoln in 1521 came from Amersham, Beaconsfield, Chesham, Denham, Missenden and Uxbridge, familiar place names from the modern Metropolitan line, as well as from Wycombe, Marlow, Iver, Henley and Windsor, not far away. There were also cases in Burford and Witney. But most of the large diocese of Lincoln was not affected.[37]

It is all too easy for historians to slip into heightened language when glossing what is meagre evidence. Joan Boughton was burnt in 1495, her daughter Lady Young (widow of a lord mayor of London) was probably burnt later, and a London goldsmith, John Barrett, was convicted of heresy in the 1500s. Is it fair to deduce from those two certain and one probable cases that 'heterodoxy infiltrated the [London] livery companies at the highest levels'?[38] It might be objected that the surviving records are incomplete. But for Foxe we should know next to nothing of the heretics accused between 1518 and 1521.[39] There may have been more prosecutions the records of which have been lost. And so it is possible that those heretics whom we know the authorities detected were just the tip of the iceberg and that there were thousands more who were never detected or troubled. As two scholars have argued, 'there can be little doubt that heresy drives uncovered only a very few of the total number of heretics';[40] and 'those accused were surely only a few among a greater group: many no doubt managed to escape the questioning of the bishops' officers'.[41] There is no certain way of disproving such claims, but it is worth remarking that John Foxe offered a resoundingly different interpretation of the effectiveness of episcopal repression. 'Neither were there any assemblies, nor readings kept, but both the persons and also the books were known; neither was any word so closely spoken, nor article mentioned, but it was discovered. So subtilely and sleightly these catholic prelates did use their inquisitions and examinations, that nothing was done or said among these "known-men", so covertly, fifteen or twenty years before so covertly, but it was brought at length to their intelligence.'[42] If Foxe was right, then the submerged section of the iceberg may not have been very large, as Haigh, reworking the laws of physics, puts it.[43] What between them Foxe and the surviving episcopal registers tell us is, most likely, what there was. And that means that the number of heretics was low.

Our knowledge of what those accused of heresy had believed and done comes from the records created by the ecclesiastical courts that tried them. How far depositions in such trials accurately recorded what the accused had said is moot. And in many cases we lack the original records but depend on the edited transcriptions printed by John Foxe in his martyrology. Let us, nonetheless, begin by taking these records at face value. The richest vein of evidence on the activities of those accused of heresy in these years is offered by the visitation carried out in Essex by Geoffrey Wharton, vicar-general to Cuthbert Tunstall, bishop of London, in 1527–8, which led to interrogations and trials in which a number of people from Steeple Bumpstead, Essex, and the nearby county town of Colchester, confessed and renounced their heresies.[44] John Tyball, churchwarden of Steeple Bumpstead, confessed that seven or eight years earlier he had obtained the gospels in English, especially St John's Gospel and the epistles of Peter and Paul. He clearly recognised that he should not have possessed them as he burnt them on hearing of the interrogations. From his reading, and especially from Paul's Letter to the Corinthians, Tyball had been led to a range of errors and heresies, which he then discussed with and taught to others, including Richard Fox, parish priest of Steeple Bumpstead, with whom he read *Wyclif's Wicket*, a lollard text dating from the fifteenth century, and the scriptures. 'In process of time by reasoning of things contained in the said books, and disputing and instructing, he brought Sir Richard Fox to his learning and opinions,' the deposition noted.

Afterwards Fox, Tyball said, was 'infected with his errors and heresies'. Fox went on to convert others in his turn, exploiting the opportunity offered him as a priest to persuade people in the course of hearing their confession in Lent. When Robert Hempstead countered that Fox was going about 'to bring me in the taking that the men of Colchester be in' (that is to say facing interrogation by the episcopal courts), Fox had jibed, 'What man, art thou afraid? Be not afeared'. And so, through Fox's teaching and urging and encouragement, and because Fox was a priest, Hempstead allowed himself to be persuaded.[45] Thomas Hempstead—presumably Robert's brother— said that it was 'by the teaching and showing' of Fox that he had come to believe certain heresies.[46] Fox had also expressed heresy when hearing the confession of Edward Tyball, perhaps a relative of John Tyball.[47] He had argued with John Darkyn, mocking his orthodox opinions.[48] And two Austin Friars of Stoke-by-Clare said that Fox had converted them.

Fox was Tyball's great catch. Tyball also tried to persuade the other priests in the parish, William Stringer and one whom he called by his Christian name, Arthur, but despite all his reasoning he failed to convince them. Tyball also taught and instructed his mother and his wife, but evidently failed to persuade his wife to agree with what he said about the eucharist.[49] He taught heresy and read St Paul's epistles to Thomas Hills, a tailor's servant, and then Tyball and Hills went together to London to see the Austin friar Robert Barnes because of his reputation as a good man and because they wanted his advice about the New Testament. From him they bought a copy of William Tyndale's translation of the New Testament for 3s 2d (or 3s according to Hills), reading it in various houses, and eventually selling it to Richard Fox, the parish priest, or, according to another account, lending it to a Friar Gardiner who never returned it. Tyball named many more people with whom he had discussed these matters: John Smyth of Bumpstead, the Beckwiths at Colchester, William Pykas, John Girling, John Bradley, Thomas Parker and Friar Meadow of Colchester who abandoned his religion and married.[50]

Thomas Hills, Tyball's companion on the journey to London, was noted as a great reader among the servants of his master Christopher Raven, tailor of Witham.[51] Hills had been betrothed to a girl who had taught him the first chapter of James. A butcher of Coggeshall, now dead, had taught him the second chapter, and about the eucharist, pilgrimages and images. Hills had often come to Steeple Bumpstead with John Tyball who read him the epistles of St Paul and the evangelists and taught him heresy. He had gone with Tyball, Fox, one John Smith (who came often but kept his counsel and never offered his opinions) and two friars, Gardiner and Topley, to Bower Hall, to the house of a shipwright called Gilbert, and to the houses of two women whom he called 'mother Bocher' and 'mother Charte' where they read the New Testament in English and talked about heresies.[52]

Another detailed statement was made by John Pykas, a baker from Colchester. His mother had taught him heresy five years before, giving him St Paul's epistles in English. About two years ago he had bought a New Testament in English in Colchester from a Lombard merchant from London for 4s 'and read it thoroughly many times': he lent it to Robert Best, who could say the epistles of James by heart. But when Pykas heard it was forbidden, he gave it up, and returned St Paul's epistles to his mother. Later, he possessed several other allegedly heretical works: *The Prick of Conscience* (after the Wycliffite translation of the Bible, the medieval English text surviving in the largest number of copies, but a text going back to the mid-fourteenth century, before Wyclif, and so not clearly heretical); *Communicatio inter fratrem et clericum* (until he lost it) and another beginning 'O thou most glorious and excellent lord' (neither easily identified); and *The Seven Wise Masters of Rome* (though if this was a copy of the medieval romance *The Seven Sages of Rome* it was not obviously heretical).[53] He discussed his views with others, naming William Ryland, John Girling and Alice Gardiner.[54] He had listened to the sermon of Thomas Bilney, a Cambridge don who had preached in Ipswich, the 'most ghostly . . . that ever he heard in his life'.[55] But throughout Pykas had outwardly conformed, even confessing annually, 'but that people shold not wonder upon him'.[56]

Tyball, Fox, Hills and Pykas were evidently energetic in spreading their opinions. What precisely did they come to believe? Tyball declared that the eucharist was just bread and wine, basing this on his reading of a chapter of the Corinthians which he had since forgotten, and denying that a priest had the power to consecrate the body of Christ. He taught Hills that the eucharist was just a remembrance. He advocated priestly and episcopal marriage, drawing on St Paul's instruction that every bishop ought to be the husband of one wife and bring forth children. He denied the superior utility of confession to a priest, citing James's saying 'show your sins one to another'. He thought laymen might administer the sacraments as well as any priest, doubted the value of pilgrimages (refusing to join his godmother on pilgrimage to Ipswich) and of the practices of kneeling before images in church and setting candles and lights before images, 'for they be but stocks and stones'. He questioned the power of popes and bishops to pardon, though at some time he had been convinced that they had such power. Their mitres, rings, crosses and precious stones would be better given to the poor. Interestingly, and unusually for someone charged with heresy, he did believe in purgatory, from which the souls of sinners and evil-doers might be delivered by prayers. A year before, he had reasoned with Fox that there was no purgatory, and held that view for a time. He had also questioned the point of fasting. And he had said that sea water and running water were as efficacious as supposed holy water.[57]

Thomas Hills had learned from Tyball and from a now deceased butcher of Coggeshall that the eucharist was just a remembrance; the butcher told him that pilgrimages 'did not perfect a man', that men should not erect lights before images but rather have 'a burning love to God', that holy days not on Sundays should not be kept since they had been made not by God but by 'men of the church for their advantage'.[58]

The priest whom John Tyball had converted, Richard Fox, exploited the confession, as we have seen. On hearing Robert Hempstead tell him how he believed that 'in the sacrament of the altar is the very body of Christ', Fox contradicted him: 'For that is not the best way; but believe thou in the Father, the Son and the Holy Spirit, and not in the sacrament of the altar'.[59] Edward Tyball said that Fox had told him in confession in Lent that the eucharist was but a remembrance of Christ's passion.[60] Thomas Hempstead said that Fox had taught him the same view of the eucharist and also that pilgrimages were ineffective:[61] Fox had mocked John Darkyn's conviction that going on pilgrimage to Ipswich, Walsingham or Canterbury and lighting a candle of wax were good works.[62]

John Pykas, the Colchester baker, admitted that from his reading he fell into 'errors and heresies against the sacrament of the altar' which, he had said, was not the very body of Christ 'but only bread and wine'. He had spoken out against baptism which, he had said, should be only of the Holy Ghost, not by water. He criticised confession: it was enough for a man to show his sins privily to God without making confession to a priest. He repeated Thomas Bilney's dismissal of pilgrimages to saints as 'but stocks and stones' which 'cannot speak to a man nor do him any good'. He declared that the church had no authority to insist on fast days. Nor had popes and churchmen any authority to grant pardons.[63]

John Pykas's opinions and his teaching were confirmed by William Ryland of Colchester. Ryland testified how Pykas had discussed the eucharist with him. Pykas declared 'that in the host was but bread and the body of Christ was in the word and not in the bread and that God is in the word and the word is in God and the word can not be departed'; 'that bread was but in the remembrance of his passion'.[64] Ryland senior agreed that he and his son Henry had gladly heard Pykas teach such heresy which they believed to be true.[65] Pykas added that the Rylands father and son discussed the Lord's Prayer, the apostle's Creed, the epistles of James and John, and the beatitudes.[66] They often, Pykas said, talked against pilgrimages and worshipping images; Ryland senior spoke in favour of adult baptism; his son approved.[67] Ryland senior said that he had often heard Pykas and his son say that it was wrong to go on pilgrimage to the images at Walsingham or Ipswich or elsewhere: 'for they be but idols, and it is idolatry for to go there in pilgrimage, and they can not help themselves, therefore they can not help another man'. Ryland senior also said that he had heard Pykas and his son declare that 'we should pray only to God and to no saints'. On that point Ryland senior claimed that 'he hath often times rebuked his son for the said opinions, to whom his son would say yea father set your heart at rest and apply yourself to learn the true laws of God as I do'.[68] His son Henry was questioned by the bishop of London: Ryland junior agreed that the true body of Christ was in the sacrament of the altar and that pilgrimages were profitable, and denied having said that the Virgin of Ipswich was an idol.[69]

In all, Pykas admitted having declared that the eucharist was only bread and wine and just a remembrance, that it was unnecessary to confess sins to a priest, that pilgrimages and prayers to the dead were useless, that fasts should not be kept, that it was beyond the power of popes and bishops to issue pardons, that there was no baptism but of the Holy Ghost (which he had learned from the English New Testament).[70]

Such a set of opinions is comparable to those confessed in the earlier trials of heretics from Amersham, Coventry and Kent. The Amersham heretics had denied transubstantiation and purgatory, dismissed auricular confession and pilgrimages, made rude remarks about church bells and images ('lo yonder is a fair bell, an it were to hang about any cow's neck in this town'), and demanded English scriptures. These general beliefs were heightened by a little local colour. Richard Vulford and Thomas Geoffrey had justified their denial that the host was the consecrated body of Christ by citing an experiment carried out by two priests in Essex: they put a mouse together with the host in a pyx, and the mouse ate the host. Mistress Dolly claimed that when women went to offer to images of saints they did it to show off their 'new gay gear'.[71] The Kent heretics denied

transubstantiation, dismissed auricular confession, claimed that priests had
no greater powers than laymen, rejected the sacrament of extreme unction,
and saw pilgrimages and images as unnecessary since only God, not the
saints, heard prayers.[72] The Coventry heretics denied transubstantiation and
saw pilgrimages and the veneration of images as wrong.[73]

Such trial records are thus seemingly illuminating about beliefs; about the
ways in which family contacts could spread ideas and literature; about the
purchase, lending and giving of forbidden books; about the range of literature available; about the impact made by preachers; about the role of priests
in confession. Nonetheless, this still amounts to a very few people: in the
Steeple Bumpstead and Colchester trials, some nineteen men and fourteen
women. Even on their own account not all their relatives and friends were
brought in. John Tyball could not persuade his wife Alice that the sacrament of the altar was but a remembrance.[74] And all those accused from
Steeple Bumpstead and Colchester abjured their past views, and were ready
to detect others. It is all too tempting, yet very misleading to dramatise, to
claim, for example, that Steeple Bumpstead was 'a thriving centre of the
indigenous heresy' or that it 'represented a local tradition of Essex lollardy'.[75]
Most scholars have left the matter here, a handful noting how few heretics
there were,[76] but most have been content to present 'the lollards' as a significant dissenting minority, a real threat to the church, a harbinger of what
was to come. And, as such, 'the lollards' can clearly be taken to illustrate
the vulnerability of the church to criticism—and their criticisms as evidence
of the weaknesses, indeed the abuses, of the church. In this light Eamon
Duffy's vivid and positive portrayal of the church in *The Stripping of the
Altars* has, in some quarters, been fiercely criticised because it neglects the
lollards.[77]

It is worth pressing the analysis of these 'lollards' somewhat further. So
far we have taken the evidence from the trials of heretics essentially at face
value, as scholars generally have done. But that may be unwise. In doing so
we may, in consequence, simply be absorbing and reproducing the miscon-
ceptions and misperceptions of those who created our sources. Let us begin
by raising some doubts.

There is a striking similarity in the depositions made by those under
suspicion of heresy. In Coventry in 1511–12 the entries in Bishop Blyth's
register are extremely formulaic.[78] For example, what is recorded is often
standardised, with the name and address of the accused followed by two or
three clearly heretical views, expressed—and this is what is suspicious—in
identical, indeed, formulaic fashion. Yet is it likely that each suspect would
spontaneously have used the same words?[79] The authorities do not seem to
have been much interested in the complexities of the religious thought of

those whom they were prosecuting.[80] The depositions of John Pykas and William Ryland of Steeple Bumpstead in 1528 are improbably similar in places.[81] And on Ryland's testimony, several of those accused—Pykas, John Girling's wife, Dorothy Long, Thomas Parker and Robert Bate—said much the same about the sacrament of the altar being but a host, and the first three all referred to God being the word. According to William Ryland, John Pykas said 'that in the host was but bread and the body of Christ was in the word and not in the bread and that God is in the word and the word is in God and God and the word can not be departed. And that bread was but in the remembrance of his passion.' According to Ryland, John Girling's wife said that 'the sacrament of the altar was but an host and that the body of almighty God was joined in the word and the word and God was all one and might not be departed'. According to Ryland, Dorothy Long said 'that the sacrament of the altar is but bread and not the body of Christ and God is the word and the word is God and God and word cannot be sundered'. According to Ryland, Thomas Parker affirmed 'that the sacrament of the altar was but an host and bread and not the body of Christ'. According to Ryland, Robert Bate said that 'the sacrament of the altar was not the very body of Christ but only a host and all bread'.[82] It defies plausibility that each of these were independent and spontaneous opinions, carefully worked out and articulated.

If there was a single characteristic belief confessed by those accused of heresy, it was rejection of the orthodox teaching that in the eucharist the bread and the wine were miraculously transformed into the body and blood of Christ. Instead, the eucharist was seen as a remembrance of Christ. Yet despite apparently holding such convictions, those accused appear to have continued attending their parish church and in particular attending mass. Only one, Kathleen Bartlett of Amersham, was accused of not doing so.[83] Several served as churchwardens. Of course, that might have been tactical behaviour, designed to avoid suspicion. John Pykas, as we have seen, had conformed outwardly, even confessing annually, 'but that people shold not wonder upon him'.[84] More puzzling still is the evidence of bequests. What is to be made of those accused of heresy who, nonetheless, made orthodox wills and left bequests to confraternities, even to lights? The will of Richard Saunders of Amersham (d. 1524) has a conservative preamble: he left 3s 4d to the light before the rood at Amersham and £6 13s 4d for masses to be said for his soul. It is thus hard to treat him as a clear heretic.[85] Robert Durdant (d. 1524) of Iver Court, near Staines, left 8d to St Paul's, the mother church, 12d to the high altar at Staines, and 4d to every altar in his parish church.[86] John Collins of Betterton left his soul to 'almighty God and Our Lady saint Mary and all the holy company of heaven' and money to the curate of his parish church 'to pray for my soul'.[87] John Semand, fishmonger of Newbury, asked for his body to be buried in 'our lady's chancel' in Newbury parish church.[88] Such wills with their conservative formulae, their bequests for masses, to the light before the rood, and for the mother church, must cast grave doubt on the 'unorthodoxy', let alone the 'lollardy', of those accused. Can they really be explained away on the grounds that the testator was trying 'merely to smooth the passage of his will through probate'? Derek Plumb found fifty wills made between 1480 and 1550 by those accused of heresy as recorded in the pages of Foxe: of them no fewer than forty-three made conservative or non-committal wills. Does that not call into question their alleged heresy?[89]

And then there is the fact of overwhelming abjuration. Almost all those detected of heresy in the early sixteenth century formally renounced the heresies which they confessed and then performed the penance imposed upon them. Those who were convicted and burnt for heresy—a small number and a tiny proportion of those accused—were men and women who had previously abjured but were detected for heresy on a later occasion. Most abjured. John Tyball abjured.[90] Edmund Tyball abjured and was absolved: as a penance he had to carry a faggot before the procession at Steeple Bumpstead church the next Sunday, and hear high mass throughout.[91] Thomas Hills was to fast on bread and water for five days and go on pilgrimage to Ipswich.[92] Thomas Mathew was ordered to give 6s 8d in alms during five weeks in Lent, to prisoners in Colchester Castle and to the poor of the town, in bread and herrings, and to break the loaves before distributing them to the prisoners.[93] These were public penalties. Of course, defiance of persecution is a harsh test to apply to any religion, yet if lollardy had been a strong popular faith, it seems likely that there would have been more martyrs. The contrast between the 'great abjuration', to apply Foxe's term for what took place in Amersham in 1506, and the nearly three hundred burnt in Mary's reign is telling. These men and women lacked any concept of martyrdom as a validation of their beliefs.

And there is a further aspect of these confessions and abjurations that is pertinent here. Not only did most of those accused abjure, many of them went on to name, and so to incriminate, members of their families. Robert Bartlett of Amersham detected his brother, his wife and his sister; Richard Bartlett detected his sister and his father. John Collins of Burford detected his father.[94] John Pykas incriminated his mother and his brother.[95] It is thus hard to agree that households 'provided the context of strong affective bonds within which heresy could be broached, taught and discussed'.[96]

Did these men and women see themselves as heretics or deviants? Some of them may well have realised that others, especially those in authority,

might see them as heretics, but most may well have listened and dabbled
without quite grasping the dangerous significance of what they were doing.
After all, the overwhelming majority of those accused were artisans, not
men or women of education. It is revealing that one of the requests in the
Commons' Supplication against the Ordinaries in 1532 was that 'some
reasonable declaration may be known to your people how they may if they
will eschew the peril of heresy'.[97] How clearly did the church demarcate,
and laymen and laywomen recognise, the boundary between legitimate
criticism and unacceptable heresy? How far could, say, pilgrimages—especially if embarked upon lightly or for worldly motives—be criticised, indeed
satirised as Chaucer or Erasmus had done, without straying into heresy?
When John Pykas listened to Thomas Bilney's sermons against images at
Ipswich, did he realise that he was listening to what the church authorities
would regard as heresy? Would the church not have agreed that images of
saints were not to be worshipped like idols? How aware were those who met
to read sections of Bible in translation that what they were doing was
heretical? It is interesting that John Pykas (if he was telling the truth) did
not at first realise that the New Testament in English, which he bought for
4s, was a forbidden book. After all, he had bought it from Robert Barnes,
at the Austin Friars in London, not an obviously heretical institution: when
he heard that the Bible was prohibited, he gave it, also returning Paul's epistles in English, to his mother.[98] Richard Hunne, as we have seen, was post-
humously convicted of heresy on account of books found in his house.
Most damningly, he possessed a Wycliffite Bible. But did he realise its
heretical nature? Was possession of a Wycliffite Bible necessarily evidence
that its owners believed in heresies: were Henry VI and Richard III therefore
heretics? Was that Bible's previous owner, Thomas Downes, an heretic? Yet
in his will he left money for torches to burn in honour of the blessed sacrament and for 100 pounds of wax to burn before the crucifix, asking to be
buried before the image of the Virgin in his parish church.[99] What was
puzzling about Hunne's behaviour was that he displayed the Bible openly at
St Margaret's church, Bridge Street, and had it brought to his prison cell
after he was arrested—behaviour that would have been unlikely had he
thought that its possession would convict him of heresy.[100] Had those who
confessed to disbelieving that in the eucharist the bread and wine were
transformed into the body and blood of Christ consciously chosen to be
heretics, to set their faces against the church? Was the denial of transubstantiation necessarily a sign of defiant heresy? It could easily reflect some
untutored 'first principle' scepticism or misunderstanding. Nor was the
doctrine of transubstantiation so central or universally and unambiguously
agreed a part of the medieval church's thinking as might be supposed from

the pronouncements by the Lateran Council in 1215, and the term itself does not feature in the trials.[101]

At no point did any of those accused of heresy admit setting up alternative forms of worship, church services, let alone church organisation or rites of initiation. Even to see them as 'a special type of the late medieval fraternity' is to exaggerate.[102] They never called themselves 'lollards', nor were they accused of being 'lollards' or practising 'lollardy'. When they confessed, they might identify others as of that 'sect and learning', when they abjured, they renounced 'heresies' and 'damnable opinions'.[103] They lent and sold each other books, but in a somewhat haphazard way that makes talk of an organised distribution of books quite misleading. A comparison with the very effective distribution of Tyndale's translation of the New Testament and of books by Tyndale, Frith, Fish and other early protestants in the late 1520s and early 1530s makes that quite plain.[104] No lollard ever used the printing press to produce printed versions of Wycliffite texts. There were no lollard priests or ministers who administered the sacraments; at most, there were vaguely itinerant preachers or travelling teachers such as John Hacker—possibly the object of More's description of one who 'walked about as an apostle of the devil from shire to shire and town to town thorough the realm, and had in every diocese a diverse name',[105] or Thomas Man, burnt in 1518, who had been imprisoned in 1514, but later freed and had then 'associated and joined himself unto such godly professors of christ's gospel as he there could hear of', though he denied much of that.[106] But what they were scarcely merits the description 'wandering sectaries' or members of 'this fraternity'.[107] To claim that 'some of them attained enormous spiritual status among members of the sect' is to indulge in colourful writing.[108] None of them could be seen as a prophet, as a charismatic figure.[109] They seem on their own admission to have visited the few rather than the many. Hacker visited Christopher Raven, tailor of Witham, once or twice a year over four years; named three at St Margaret's Lothbury, a couple and a father-in-law; he named two who possessed forbidden books, a chandler whom he taught, three more 'disciples', a pointmaker, a bricklayer, several tailors, Mother Bristow, and another dozen listed. It is not a huge tally. Most were from London, with a few in Colchester, Braintree and Witham. Most of the communications were in private houses.[110] Yet this was a style of religion which, to have been effective, would have demanded charismatic preachers: it exaggerates to say, as Hudson does, that 'the communities themselves had effectively taken over from the individual preachers as teachers and maintainers of heresy'.[111] Talk of 'communities' enjoying 'contacts' with each other misleadingly reinforces the impression of coherence and continuity.[112]

Perhaps, however, there is another way of responding to all these puzzling features, and that is that our sources are highly misleading and that there was no such thing as 'lollardy' in the early sixteenth century. As we have seen, the number of 'lollards' was tiny, yet the suppression of heresy was declared to be the chief task of the convocation held in 1511. When founding Corpus Christi College, Oxford, in 1516, Bishop Richard Fox declared its purpose to be 'ad extirpationemque haeresium et errorum ac fidei ortho-doxe augmentationem [for the extermination of heretics and errors and to increase the orthodox faith]'.[113] John Longland evidently made the extirpa-tion of heresy his priority when he was promoted bishop of Lincoln in 1521.[114] In 1523 Cuthbert Tunstal, bishop of London, spoke of 'the great band of Wycliffite heresies'. It is interesting that when Elizabeth Barton, the nun of Kent, experienced her public vision at Court of Street in *c.*1525, the voice speaking in her belly 'spake also many things for the *confirmation* of pilgrimages and trentals, hearing of masses, and confession [my italics]' emphasising her felt need to reassert their value. Her later visions chiefly concerned the king's marriage, but also what were described as 'the great heresies and schisms within the realm', and 'the taking away the liberties of the church'.[115] Unquestionably the church authorities in the early sixteenth century were concerned, even obsessed, by what they saw as the challenge and the spread of heresy. It would be all too easy lazily to reproduce their conviction that heresy was indeed a persistent, even an increasing, threat to the teaching and authority of the church. But the seemingly dispropor-tionate character of the authorities' response to what, numerically, was a very small phenomenon should give us pause. How far, we should ask, did the church authorities 'construct' the heretics whom they accused?

Anyone suspected of heresy was dealt with by being asked a series of questions, a practice long established on the continent, and developed in England in the early fifteenth century as the appropriate way to deal with dissent. Yet there was a dangerous circularity in such methods. As anyone who has struggled to answer 'yes but' or 'in part' when confronted by a modern questionnaire will readily grasp, the questions posed can often determine the answers given. Bishop Longland's interrogatories in 1521 began by asking whether the suspect knew that people from Amersham had appeared before Bishop Smith on suspicion of heresy, whether the suspect knew that they had erred on the sacrament of the altar, whether the suspect knew that they had confessed their errors and done penance for them. The suspect was then asked whether he or she was 'of society' with those previ-ously dealt with, whether he or she had ever been detected of heresy, whether he or she had the reputation of being a 'known man', whether he or she had ever attended any readings, whether he or she had ever been in secret communication with them.[116] What made such questions tricky is that it would have been hard for any inhabitant of Amersham not to have been aware of the heresy proceedings of previous years, and a great many inhabitants would have known those who had abjured and would have had all manner of dealings with them. A casual social encounter with someone who had abjured years before could all too easily be read as taking part in a conventicle. A family relationship or a friendship could all too easily be seen as prima facie evidence of shared heretical beliefs. It was very hard in such a proceeding to establish one's innocence. It is impossible conclusively to prove a negative. And when those in authority suspect a conspiracy, any evidence, any response to questions, can be made to fit into that conspiracy. Some people caught up in such proceedings, perhaps especially those who were innocent, might come to think that the safest way out of their predicament would be to answer the questions put to them in the affirmative, reckoning that the penance that would then be inflicted on them would be less bad than what might follow if they denied, but could not disprove, what was insinuated against them. Anyone who had once abjured had all the greater reason to co-operate with the authorities in any future trials, for example as a witness, since the penalty inflicted on an abjured heretic who relapsed was death by burning. In such ways people, understandably, saved their own skins. But the consequence was that the authorities received answers and information that confirmed their suspicions and vindicated their inquiries into heretical beliefs and heretical behaviour. Investigations thus became self-reinforcing.

Foxe's account of the way in which John Longland, bishop of Lincoln, set about his task in 1521 is intriguing in these respects. His first aim, Foxe claimed, was to convict Robert and Richard Bartlett, two brothers who had abjured in the great abjuration of 1506. According to Foxe, he began by requiring several men (Foxe names five of them) to testify against the Bartletts. These witnesses had themselves earlier abjured and, Foxe, says, did not dare do anything but what was required of them, lest they were seen as having relapsed into heresy. And they all swore on the evangelists that the Bartletts were 'known men'. At that point the Bartletts' wives were asked to testify against their husbands. Then the two Bartletts were asked to name others, Robert beginning with his brother, his wife and his sister, Richard with his wife and his father. Then their sister Agnes was asked to give names; after refusing for a while, she detected others, including her brother Robert. Then Robert's wife Isabel at first denied and then confessed. There then followed around forty detections of others.[117] In his account Foxe makes Bishop Longland appear bent on blood, but we might allow either that Longland had received new information about the Bartletts or that, on taking up the duties of bishop, he had looked through the court records, uncovered the details of the trials of 1511–12, and resolved to see if those he saw as the most important and influential of the abjurors had lapsed in any way. Whatever his exact motivations, the way he set about it made it very likely that his fears and suspicions would be confirmed. And in other campaigns against large numbers of heretics, such as that in Coventry in 1511–12, it was evidence given by those first accused that led to formal accusation of others.

The consequent challenge for the modern historian is that such considerations make much of our evidence unsafe. When, for example, Agnes Wellys was interrogated about the sacrament of the altar, pilgrimages, images and the epistle of St James, she confessed, as did so many of the fifty-odd men and women under interrogation, that she had indeed held heretical opinions on each of these. Maybe she had; maybe she confessed that she had because that was what her interrogators believed that she believed.[118] When an historian concludes from 'an extraordinary identity between views abjured in the 1520 and those abjured in the 1420s' that 'all the essential theological and ecclesiastical teachings of early lollardy remain intact',[119] when another remarks that 'the general approach of the late lollards is not very different from earlier Wycliffite commentaries', might that precisely reflect the 'standardisation of the interrogatories' noted in the previous sentence rather than any true continuities?[120] When Thomas Hempstead listed those who were 'of the same sect and lernyng' and taken and reputed as 'known persons', when John Tyball identified those whom he believed were 'of the same learning and sect',[121] it would be mistaken to understand by the term 'sect' a group with a defined membership, and even more mistaken to suppose that Hempstead and Tyball saw themselves in this way. Although we do not have the questions which the authorities asked, it is very likely that what Hempstead and Tyball said was spoken in reply to the questions, 'Whom do you know who was of that sect and learning?' and 'Were they taken and reputed as "known persons"?' In other words, the labelling was that of the authorities.

When Tyball was asked if Thomas Mathew's wife was of his sect, he replied that he was not certain: for Tyball 'sect' meant 'beliefs', something of which he could not be sure, rather than the more easily verifiable membership of a distinct group of people.[122] When many of those under interrogation named members of their family and their friends and neighbours as sharing their views, that might be evidence that 'lollardy' was a 'gathered church', an 'underground' of 'close, secretive associations'; 'there can be no doubt that such meetings were going on all the time, behind closed doors'.[123] Or maybe again that was what the church authorities who interrogated the accused believed and expected them to confess. Given that churchmen began their inquiries with the conviction that heretics were an organised conspiracy, they had a strong interest that those accused of heresy not only confessed but also named others, since that would confirm that the authorities were correct in their conviction. Our evidence for an 'underground' church is no more than the replies given, under pressure, by a small number of men and women to the questions from inquisitors who pressed them to name their family and friends and to attribute to them the heretical beliefs that the authorities suspected all of them of holding. As John Foxe noted, 'they caused the wife to detect the husband, the husband the wife, the father the daughter, the daughter the father, the brother to disclose the brother, and neighbour the neighbour.'[124] It is thus indeed significant that so many of those prosecuted for heresy were prosecuted in 'groups of associated individuals',[125] but not in the way that the modern historian intended, more as an illustration of how the trials were conducted. When Hacker admitted going from place to place and named his contacts, as we have seen, was he both reflecting and confirming the authorities' fear that that was how heresy was spread?[126] And do the much trumpeted geographical continuities in the incidence of heresy over time reflect not so much the existence of regions of dissent, but simply the tendency of bishops, not least incoming bishops such as bishop Longland of Lincoln, to hold renewed investigations just where heretics had been found earlier, another self-validating process? Why was there a vigorous quest for heretics in the area around Amersham in 1521? Was it because Amersham had been investigated before? Did Longland deliberately set in motion a new inquiry in just those places that a quick scrutiny of the episcopal records would have shown him had been infested with heretics, as he would have seen it, in the past?

In short, were the 'lollards' then the witches of early Tudor England? Just as many women were to be accused of witchcraft in the late sixteenth and early seventeenth centuries, even though (a modern historian may be allowed to assert) there were no witches, so a small number of people were prosecuted for heresy in the early sixteenth century, but there were no heretics in any coherent or organised sense of the word. Were those men and women who were prosecuted for heresy no more than awkward or difficult people who had expressed some mild criticism of the church? Was it provoked by some misunderstanding or quarrel over financial matters? Did that criticism arise from a simple person's moralising in which the professed ideals of the church were set against the realities of the daily behaviour of priests? Or did it come from a commonsensical 'first principle' questioning of the plausibility of doctrines, such as that of transubstantiation, by an uneducated man or woman taking a literalistic approach because incapable of metaphorical thought? Did the church's lawyers and theologians then turn those who voiced such criticisms into more or less coherent heretics by their processes of examination, assisted perhaps by the prejudiced testimony of lay neighbours whom they had annoyed, not necessarily over religion, but possibly for what might have appeared as their self-righteousness? For were these supposed heretics more to be seen as moral elitists, as committed christians, who took the ideals of the church at face value only to fall foul of priest and bishop, and, sometimes, their neighbours? All that could be drawn upon to paint a dark picture of a persecuting and cruel church, in effect persuading those they accused of heresy to confess to heretical views that they had never held, at least not in so coherent a form.[127] Did the church authorities resort to intimidation, even torture, to secure confessions? Did the church authorities exploit the period between arrest and trial to subject a suspect to what amounted to a trial by inquisition, whose ostensible purpose was to investigate the ramifications of the alleged heresy and to secure information about accomplices, but which, at the same time, allowed the authorities to put pressure on the accused, possibly by physical torture, more likely by physical and psychological deprivation (cold, damp, dark isolation) or conversations intended to entrap?[128] Physical torture may not have been required: simply to spend several days imprisoned was bad enough.

We have seen how Richard Hunne was held under suspicion in the bishop of London's prison and clearly put under a good deal of pressure and maybe even subjected to rough interrogation. Foxe tells us that, in 1511, father Rogers in Amersham was held in the bishop's prison for fourteen weeks and 'cruelly handled with cold, hunger and irons'.[129] Thomas Chase was held in the bishop of Lincoln's prison called Little Ease, in the bishop's house at Woburn, where he lay 'bound most painfully with chains, gyves, manacles and irons, oft times sore pined with hunger'.[130] He died in prison and, according to Foxe, just as in the case of Hunne, his death was presented as suicide.[131] After William Pykas refused to swear on 27 March 1528, he was sent to the Lollard's Tower and put in the stocks: three days later he agreed to take the oath.[132] We lack reflections by those prosecuted in the early sixteenth century on how they had been treated. But a remark by a man later suspected of zwinglian sacramentarian heresy, Wolf Alarde of Calais, is intriguing in this context. He claimed that he had never spoken against the sacrament of the altar—but that, fearful of punishment, he had confessed that he had done so after the bishop's commissary, William Peterson, had encouraged him to do so, presumably in some sort of arrangement that we should recognise as a plea-bargain.[133] The reality of the pain and pressures of imprisonment must always be remembered.[134] More extravagantly, did the church authorities deploy the supposed need to deal with heretics as a justification for broader reform of the church, especially the moral reformation of the clergy that many bishops wanted in the early sixteenth century? Does that explain the waves of persecution between 1510 and 1512, persecution that came to an end once Archbishop Warham was confronted by secular responsibilities arising from war and because 'there were only so many heretics available'? One historian, citing no evidence, has offered this as an explanation for the vigorous but short-lived persecution of heretics in 1511–12: the burning of lollards was the quid pro quo for the moral reform of the clergy. That sounds too ingenious by far.[135] And if the procedures of any inquisition are necessarily tough, it must be urged that if the church authorities did turn men and women, whose mistake was to be too idealistic, into heretics, they may well have done so not from wanton cruelty or institutional self-interest but because they sincerely believed that heresy was an insidious and deadly threat to the souls of all christian men and women, a virus that could spread as fast and as widely as the plague.

The authorities throughout sought to save, rather than to destroy, souls. Heresy was the exercise of 'haeresis', that is to say a choice: it followed that those who had chosen false doctrine might be led to see the error of their ways and penitentially acknowledge their fault. That was the point of the procedures that led to abjurations. Bishops could be lenient. Even Foxe recognised this. Referring back to 'the great abjuration' in Amersham in 1506, he noted that William Smith, bishop of Lincoln, 'sent divers quietly home without punishment or penance, simply instructing them to go home and live as Christian men should. And he released many from the terms of their penance.'[136] Smith clearly saw them as faithful but misguided christians.

Nevertheless, did many churchmen too readily assume—sincerely and in good faith—that those who criticised them, or discussed the sacraments of the church, or voiced scepticism about practices such as pilgrimage, or dabbled in unorthodox literature, were manifestly fully paid-up members of an organised group, of an anti-church? Did churchmen in effect impose a stereotype, based on their institutional memory of late-fourteenth-century Wyclifism—an institutional memory which was itself a negative caricature of features of orthodox belief and practice—on what were much more diffuse and variegated notions and attitudes?[137] And if the church authorities may have placed those whom they accused of heresy in an ideological strait-jacket, attributing to them a stereotyped package of heretical beliefs and actions drawn from the late fourteenth century or earlier, did, paradoxically, John Foxe the martyrologist reinforce that view, though from an opposite standpoint, by suppressing or distorting any beliefs that he himself regarded as heretical, and so presenting those accused of heresies in the years before the break with Rome as holding more coherent, and crucially, more 'protestant', views than they actually did?

In many ways the importance of what has been discussed in this chapter has been exaggerated and its meaning distorted by those who have wished to link it to the development of protestantism in England. In his *Acts and Monuments*, John Foxe boldly presented the lollards as worthy and vital links in a great tradition, of which Wyclif was the morning star.[138] Most vigorously among modern historians J.F. Davis asserted that 'the English Reformation was really a process of religious change that gradually spread upwards from lollard artisans and merchants, to academic reformers of evangelism and erastianism, and then to the aristocracy'. He claimed that 'lollard congregations later coalesce[d] with the "hotter" sort of protestants' to produce further reformation.[139] Derek Plumb supposed that 'lollards remained a force in society during the years of the Reformation. They held on to their beliefs and they secured for themselves and for their descendants a nonconformist base from which later sects were to spring.'[140] Several historians have seen geographical continuities between those towns and villages in which lollards were found (parts of Kent, Colchester, the Chilterns, and quarters of London) and those places in which puritan nonconformity was to spread in the late sixteenth and early seventeenth centuries, and claimed that 'definite traditions of dissent . . . [can] be perceived in these areas, springing from lollardy itself'.[141] At a theological level, lollardy is held to have contributed to the English reformation 'a sacramentarian sectarianism that is purely native in character'.[142]

But there are great difficulties in any such claims. R.L. Williams, whose thorough examinations of the diocesan records have never been matched, determined that it is 'impossible to conclude from the available evidence that Lollardy was in any way a shaping force in the English reformation, either at the theological or the governmental level'.[143] As we have seen, whatever the vitality and ferment of religious writing, led and inspired by Wyclif, in the late fourteenth century, there is little to suggest that from the 1420s there was any developing or creative doctrine. Virtually no priests or university graduates in the early sixteenth century were accused of heresy along lollard lines; when Archbishop Warham voiced concerns in 1521, it was about the influence of Martin Luther, not Wyclif.[144] Yet it would be from within the church, especially from university-trained priests and friars, that the first protestant reformers tended to come.[145] Moreover, it is misleading to claim that 'lollardy professed the whole gamut of opinions that were later to be adopted by the reformation'.[146] That treats both 'lollardy' and 'the reformation' as theological monoliths. Above all, what it fails to recognise adequately is that the key lutheran doctrine of justification by faith alone is wholly missing from Wycliffite writings—and from the depositions and abjurations of early Tudor heretics in which the epistle of St James, with its stress on good works, was prominent. [147]

Less directly, had those English scholars who took an interest in Luther's reformation been influenced, perhaps as provincial children before they went up to Cambridge or Oxford, by Wycliffite writings or by popular lollards? There is only the most limited of tangential evidence, no more than tantalisingly vague hints, for any such youthful lollard influences on the early English reformers. Tyndale seems to have valued the epistle of St James, with its emphasis on good works, in a way Luther would not; certainly he vigorously criticised purgatory, pilgrimages, prayers to saints, and oral confession. Some scholars have seized on this to suggest that Tyndale's theology betrays some early, deep-seated, Wycliffite influences which make him a late lollard.[148] Did Tyndale pick up some native lollardy in his Gloucestershire childhood? That is purely speculative, and the paucity of heresy, as measured by the numbers accused in that area, tells against such claims. However ingeniously historians have argued, there is simply no documented evidence for Tyndale's lollardy or any lollard origins of his thought. Nowhere does he acknowledge any such influence.[149] It is wrong to see Simon Fish's *Supplication of the Beggars* (1529) as 'a polemic couched entirely in lollard terms':[150] lutheran influences were very strong.

Some of those accused of heresy in Steeple Bumpstead went to hear the preaching of Thomas Bilney, a Cambridge scholar much influenced by Luther. That does not prove that Bilney had earlier been influenced by rustic lollardy. Indeed, it is clear from Bilney's correspondence with Cuthbert Tunstal, bishop of London, that Bilney had fully espoused the central lutheran doctrine of justification-by-faith. So what made the preaching of Bilney attractive? If the evidence discussed above is taken as showing that there were a number of parishioners in Steeple Bumpstead—perhaps stimulated by their priest Richard Fox—who took a critical interest in religious matters, then it is not surprising that they should have gone to hear the preaching of university scholars. Bilney, though coming from a somewhat different direction, nonetheless confirmed their beliefs about images and pilgrimages. In so far as there really were comprehending 'lollards' (something this chapter has tended to question) they may have been a constituency ripe for conversion to protestantism. But that could not be presumed to be automatic, not least given differences over key doctrines, notably justification, and, above all, any such constituency, if it existed at all, was tiny.

And the attitudes of university scholars to Wyclif and lollardy in the 1520s and 1530s were decidedly mixed. Committed early lutherans would take up some Wycliffite texts and put them, for the first time, into print. Jerome Barlow and William Roye reprinted the tract *A proper dialogue between a gentleman and an husbandman* (dating from before 1413) in 1529–30 and (without acknowledgement) *The Lantern of Light* of c.1409–15. Also printed in these years were *A compendious olde treatise showing how that we ought to have the scripture in English*; *The examination of Master William Thorpe* (an autobiographical account of his investigation by Archbishop Arundel) and *The examination of the honourable knight Sir John Oldcastle*; *The praier and complaynte of the plowman unto Christe* (unmistakably lollard in sentiment, but no medieval manuscript survives) (1531).[151] But was not Wyclif here serving as a convenient 'father figure'? Did the reformers seek not doctrine but a pedigree?[152] As James Crompton has noted, 'Wyclif's influence was more consequence than cause' of the English reformation. 'The "myth" was important because it was a source of strength and inspiration to many after the emergence of the Reformers.' But there is little to suggest that any sixteenth-century writers had first-hand acquaintance with Wyclif's works: their sense of Wyclif was acquired indirectly from his clerical critics.[153]

Protestants sought to respond to catholic jibes against their novelty by emphasising their medieval ancestry. As John Foxe put it,

I find that as the light of the Gospel began more to appear, and the number of professors to grow, so the vehemency of persecution, and the stir of the bishops began also to increase . . . And this was before the name of Luther was heard of in these countries among the people. Wherefore they are much beguiled and misinformed, who condemn this kind of doctrine now received, of novelty, asking 'where was this church and religion forty years ago, before Luther's time?' To whom it may be answered, that this religion and form of doctrine was planted by the apostles, and taught by true bishops; afterward decayed, and now reformed again. Although it was not received nor admitted of the pope's clergy before Luther's time, neither yet is; yet it was received of others, in whose hearts it pleased the Lord secretly to work, and that of a great number, who both professed and suffered for the same, as in the former times of this history may appear. And if they think this doctrine be so new that it was not heard of before Luther's time, how then came such great persecution before Luther's time here in England? If these were of the same profession, which they were of, then was their cruelty unreasonable, so to persecute their own Catholic fraternity. And if they were otherwise, how then is this doctrine of the Gospel so new, or the professors therof so late starte up, as they pretend them to be?

'To see their travails, their earnest seekings, their love and concord, their faithful demeaning with the faithful,' Foxe concluded, 'may make us now, in these our days of free profession, blush for shame.'[154] Was Foxe, however, attributing to those accused of heresy a significance and a coherence which they did not in fact have? By editing out their eccentricities, and by eschewing any sustained analysis of beliefs, Foxe manages to present a more coherent picture of the heresies attributed by the authorities to those whom they accused of heresy in the decades before the break with Rome than is justified: by homogenising doctrine, and by treating those accused of heresy as heretics indeed, Foxe exaggerates the continuities.[155]

More tellingly, Robert Barnes, an Augustinian friar much influenced by Luther, made fun of the old Wycliffite texts of the four evangelists and certain epistles by Paul and Peter: 'which books the said friar did litle regard, and made a twit of it' when John Tyball and Thomas Hills from Steeple Bumpstead showed them to him. Instead he told them that Tyndale's translation of the New Testament was of 'more clearer English' and sold them a copy of it.[156] Indeed, 'the tools of critical scholarship and biblical exegesis developed by humanists such as Erasmus would have rendered obsolete the Bible translations of the Lollards.'[157] In short, the thrust behind early English protestantism came from university graduates, not from those artisans who were those most commonly accused of heresy. A lutheran reformation could not have been produced by them. As if in recognition of that difficulty, Diarmaid MacCulloch, writing of Elizabethan protestantism, ingeniously stresses its zwinglian, rather than lutheran, nature, and by so doing links it to lollardy, given some similarities between that and zwinglian teaching. Yet again the connection seems rather forced (setting aside what might seem a somewhat tendentious characterisation of the Elizabethan religious settlement that overlooks both lutheran and more traditional influences).

What emerges from this survey is that while some—but not very many— people expressed significant dissatisfaction with aspects of the teachings and of the practices of the late medieval church, the church authorities may well have misread, and labelled as heresy, what was rather resentment of its financial demands, idealistic criticism of the failings of priests, and first-principled literalistic questioning of intercessory devotional practices such as pilgrimages. No doubt marked by the experience of earlier periods and other countries that had been (or thought they were) affected by organised heresy, and, in the English case, by the years in the late fourteenth century in which Wyclif's unquestionably radical writings had been influential, late medieval bishops, supported by the secular powers, were active in its pursuit. Sermons were preached against heresy. Twice yearly in every parish, from 1434, anti-lollardy was proclaimed in the general sentence of excommunication.[158] Bishops founded colleges at Oxford and Cambridge to train priests to resist heresy. It was understandable that the church should have reacted so vigorously to what it sincerely saw as heresy. But that made the church vulnerable. In normal circumstances kings would ensure that resentment against any clerical injustices did not rise to unstable levels. Henry VIII intervened to protect the church in the turmoil produced by the death of Richard Hunne. But if one day a king were to wish to attack the church or to set in on a new course, the unease produced by heresy trials and the excessive harshness with which the church appeared to treat men and women who were, above all, moral idealists would offer fruitful opportunities for political manoeuvre that could quickly undermine the church. Yet it is worth unfashionably highlighting that, if heresy trials could in certain circumstances prove damaging, the broader campaign against heresy could be as much a source of strength. 'Historians on the whole have tended to invert the inquisitorial view of heresy as threat and anti-heresy as order, seeing the former as a sign of vitality in the church and the latter as an instrument of repression having a negative impact on society,' Ian Forrest has noted, going on to counter that 'heresy was the natural product of the church's aspiration to create a unified christian society' and that 'there was much vitality in the response to heresy'.[159] It is a mistake to suppose that persecution never succeeds, that efforts to maintain orthodoxy must always be sterile, and that persecuting bishops can quickly be dismissed. The vigour with which those heretics were dealt with shows clearly, however uncomfortably to us, the vitality of the late medieval church. And a brief glance at their persecutors shows very clearly that, far from desperately shoring up a crumbling edifice, they exemplified its continuing strengths.

Richard Fitzjames (d. 1522), bishop of London, Hunne's nemesis, had been warden of Merton College, Oxford, between 1483 and 1507. As a royal chaplain he preached at least ten times between 1491 and 1503; he preached six times at Paul's Cross between 1494 and 1498, and on various state occasions, including the death of Henry VII's queen, Elizabeth, in 1503. As we have already noted, he thought it central to the duties of a bishop—he became successively bishop of Rochester in 1497, Chichester in 1503 and London in 1506—to carry out ordinations of priests and visitations in person. Polydore Vergil would describe him as a father of great learning and the utmost goodness. We lack the detailed information to add flesh to the bare bones of his biography but there are sufficient hints here to call into question the uncomplicated characterisation of Fitzjames by Sir Geoffrey Elton as 'an old bigot'.[160]

Thomas Arundel (1353–1414), archbishop of Canterbury, exemplifies still more vividly how the same churchman could be both persecutor and pious reformer. Younger brother of Richard Fitzalan (1346–97), fourth earl of Arundel, Thomas was much caught up in the turbulent politics of Richard II's reign. Bishop of Ely at the age of twenty in 1373, archbishop of York from 1398, lord chancellor from 1376 to 1389, and again from 1391 to 1396, when he became archbishop of Canterbury, exiled in 1398 before returning with the successful usurper Henry IV, whom he crowned in 1399, lord chancellor again from 1406 to 1409 and 1412 to 1413, Arundel might seem the epitome of the aristocratic prelate heavily involved in politics and his part in the persecution of heretics no more than the defence of the unjustified privileges of the institutional church. Arundel was, undoubtedly, a vigorous persecutor of heretics, personally examining William Thorpe in 1407: Thorpe, as we have already noted in passing, wrote an account of his interrogation. In the same year Arundel enacted a series of constitutions for Oxford for the defence of the faith and the extirpation of heresy, extended in 1409 to cover every diocese. Preachers would need to secure a licence from their bishop; provosts and wardens in Oxford were to conduct monthly inquiries into the orthodoxy of what scholars were teaching; Wyclif's works were banned; no one was to translate the Bible into English without episcopal permission; priests were not to draw attention to the failings of the church before lay people, nor were they to argue over matters of faith outside the universities. It was Archbishop Arundel who secured the passage of the act *De haeretico comburendo* in 1401, which for the first time set down the penalty for heresy as death by burning, and, very likely, a statute of 1406 which explicitly gave justices of King's Bench, JPs, sheriffs and mayors authority to investigate heresy. In 1410 Arundel pronounced the artisan William Brady an heretic for denying the mass and attended his burning at Smithfield. Arundel's censorship has been seen as bringing to an end a golden age of religious writing—'original theological writing in English was, for a century, almost extinct'.[161]

So far, so wicked. Yet such a reading would fail to do justice to the seriousness, the depth and the sincerity of Arundel's religious convictions. Thorpe's account of his interrogation reveals Arundel 'as a surprisingly patient and humane interrogator, prepared to debate with Thorpe as an intellectual equal'. Receptive to the contemplative and mystical piety of the later fourteenth century, Arundel and the men whom he promoted did much to adapt it to the demands of ordinary life outside the monastic cloister. It was fitting that it was to Archbishop Arundel that Nicholas Love dedicated his *Mirror of the Blessed Life of Jesus Christ* in 1411. And Arundel gave Margery Kempe a sympathetic hearing as she told him about her weeping and her revelations.[162] Arundel thought it vitally important to promote christian truth and to repress error: 'original theological writing' was not his goal. It is most improbable that his *Constitutions* should have had such far-reaching effects as has been supposed. There was something inexplicably astonishing about the flowering of English writing in the second half of the fourteenth century: to expect to find Rolle, Hilton, Langland, Julian of Norwich, the Pearl Poet in every generation is to set the bar absurdly high. And if there was less metaphysical theology produced in the fifteenth century, that was a European, not simply an English, phenomenon, so not to be attributed single-handedly to Archbishop Arundel, though his emphasis on the need to set out true doctrine may have contributed. Yet the new Carthusian house at Sheen and the associated Brigittine house at Syon became centres of religious writing and copying—for example contributing to the dissemination of the *Imitation of Christ*. There was a remarkable flowering of musical composition, much of it liturgical: the music for the mass and motets on sacred subjects of John Dunstable (d. 1453) stand out. And Lancastrian bishops and noblemen were in various ways cultured men whose horizons were significantly and lastingly broadened during the decades of Lancastrian France as their patronage amply reveals. Prohibition of heresy did not entail theological or intellectual stultification.[163]

An even more striking example of persecuting churchman and pious reformer is that of Jean Gerson (1363–1429), scholar, theologian, preacher, chancellor of the University of Paris, cardinal, and indefatigable writer, who played a decisive part in the condemnation and burning of the Czech preacher and reformer Jan Hus at the Council of Constance in 1415 (and that despite the safe conduct which Hus had been given to attend the Council). On the face of it Gerson was an intolerant persecutor, despite his own strongly expressed desire for the institutional and moral reform of the church, his emphasis on the importance of the scriptures, his willingness to criticise wicked superiors, not least competing popes in the age of the papal schism, and his lack of sympathy for what he saw as superstition. Gerson and Hus should have worked together. There were many things 'introduced under the appearance of religion among simple Christians which it would have been more holy to have omitted'. Vividly, Gerson recounted the story of how Philip, king of France, had once been offered an image and told that he would live as long as he kept it intact. 'Full of faith', said Gerson, the king, repudiating superstition, 'threw the image into the fire to demonstrate his confidence in the power of God'. Gerson damned the *Romance of the Rose*, an early thirteenth-century poem about courtly love, as immoral and subversive. 'If I had in my hands the only copy of the *Romance of the Rose* and I knew it had a value of thousands of pounds, I would nevertheless ruthlessly cast it into the fire.' But Gerson insisted that 'the sense of scripture must be judged according to the decisions of the church, inspired and governed by the Holy Spirit, and not according to the free judgement and interpretation of the individual', and he never questioned the temporal power of the church or its hierarchical structure. And, chillingly, he believed that 'if a sinner does not wish to cure himself by amendment of his misdeeds, it is a mercy to force him to do so'. Yet Gerson was no complacent defender of the status quo: he did believe in reformation in the sense of making existing institutions work better. He attacked simony (the purchase of church offices), the misuse of ecclesiastical wealth, and the indifference of bishops, calling for regular visitations, 'the hinge on which the whole reformation must swing', defending the Brethren of the Common Life and their commitment to poverty, chastity and obedience. He wrestled long and hard with the challenges of the papal schism, gradually coming round to a conciliar position boldly held and consequent acquiescence in the deposition of three popes. And not only did Gerson think long and hard over the nature of the church and the authority of popes, in a series of more than five hundred sermons and studies he made remarkable contributions to the mystical theology of his day, advocating prayer over precise reasoning: 'it is preferable to have filial love directed towards God, than to have a keen intellect but cold, and illuminated only by study'. If anyone wants to be filled with the Holy Ghost, he once remarked, let him mount to the upper room of his soul, close the doors and windows of the senses, and then sit quietly, persevering in prayer. 'The perfection or happiness of the rational soul in this present life,' Gerson insisted, 'lies more in perfect prayer or mystical theology than in theoretical contemplation ... dry, restless, curious, ungrateful and proud.' 'Love often has access to places that are forbidden to learning,' he observed; 'contemplation does not reason, it beholds'. A close scholar has seen this as an attempt to bring the spirit of the monastery into the world of the University of Paris. Later in life, Gerson was more prepared to allow a place for the application of intelligence. And, taken as a whole, his thought seems inconsistent, indeed contradictory, as he perhaps recognised when writing that 'what is found harmful for one circumstance is fitting for another'; 'what is fruitful one day may prove arid the day following'. And no single work that he wrote has achieved the standing of a timeless classic comparable to the *Imitation of Christ* (which he has often been credited with writing). But whether Gerson is placed in the first rank of medieval philosopher-theologians or not, there is no doubting the creativity, richness and vigour of his writings or the extent of his influence 'as the most popular contemporary writer of the fifteenth century', successful because 'no fifteenth-century author knew the fifteenth-century public better than Gerson'. He urged, for example, those who sought his advice to read this or that author. What should a student do confronted by a huge number of books to read? 'Browse through some swiftly, just so you are not completely ignorant of them, and then bid them a final farewell. Consult others from time to time . . . but call upon a few as your constant companions.' In 1534 Thomas More, in the Tower of London, would frame his *Treatise upon the Passion* as a commentary on Gerson's *Monotessaron* (completed in 1420)—an attempt to write the four gospels as a single continuous narrative. Anti-heresy, as much in the case of Jean Gerson as of Thomas More, was manifestly not incompatible with vitality, however much we might regret it.[164]

EPILOGUE

A T the end of this exploration, it may seem that it has been the vulnerability of the church as much as its vitality which has been emphasised
throughout. That is no doubt a response, perhaps a salutary response, to
what has become the dominant positive interpretation of the late medieval
church. It also reflects the difficulty for historians of knowing just how
much inspiring spiritual leadership and pastoral guidance churchmen at all
levels gave. Disputes and delinquency leave a trail; the quietly effective does
not. Parallels with attempts to assess the quality of modern university
teaching spring to mind. And nothing in my presentation should be taken
to imply that there was anything inevitable about what was to happen in
England in the 1530s and beyond. Nor would the removal or the reduction
of the vulnerabilities discussed here have necessarily prevented the Henrician
reformation, though it might have been much more difficult for Henry VIII
to have accomplished what he did. The kind of devotion exemplified by
pilgrimage and intercession might well have perdured, as, arguably, it has in
many Mediterranean countries. Yet the vulnerabilities which have been
uncovered did leave the church open not just to criticism but, in some
circumstances, to contempt and violent opposition. Another scholar has
offered the metaphor of 'faultlines in the landscape' but, while that is
suggestive, it nonetheless rests upon the underlying inevitability of the
coming earthquake.[1]

It would only be fair to recognise that some of those vulnerabilities
reflect the human predicament more largely: hugely idealistic expectations,
realities that fell short. 'Nothing in the world is easier than to pick holes in
religious institutions. It is one inevitable result of human imperfection that

the higher the ideal aimed at by any endeavour, the more likely it is that practice will constantly fall short of profession,' Hamilton Thompson wrote with the monasteries especially in mind, though that formulation bears wider application.[2] And again it should be recognised that the circumstances of the 1530s, political, diplomatic and religious, were extraordinary. But for that concatenation, the church, which had long shown a remarkable capacity for self-renewal and revivification, would very likely have done so again. Many of the vulnerabilities we have been considering were closely connected with the very vitality for which there is also abundant evidence. It was an untidy profusion. A true understanding of the late medieval church needs to evaluate and to balance both vulnerability and vitality.

In case it has been the vulnerabilities that have seemed to dominate, it is fitting that this book should conclude instead by inviting the reader, once again, to stand at the west end of Cullompton church in Devon, and ponder what that tells us about those who created, maintained and used it. From that vantage point, taking care not to succumb to a sentimental romanticising that sees that period as an uncomplicated age of faith, it is hard nonetheless not to be impressed by the vitality, the commitment and the devotion of an institution and of a society that could offer so stunning a building to the glory, and for the worship, of a transcendent God.

NOTES

Unless otherwise stated, place of publication is London.

Preface

1. H. Trevor-Roper, *Princes and Artists: Patronage and Ideology at Four Habsburg Courts 1517–1633* (1976), p. 57 (which I heard as a lecture in February 1970); id., 'Spain and Europe 1598–1621', in J.P. Cooper, ed., *New Cambridge Modern History. IV: The Decline of Spain and the Thirty Years War 1609–48/59* (Cambridge, 1970).
2. J.L. Motley, *The Rise of the Dutch Republic. A History* (3 vols., 1906 edn.), iii. 456.
3. C. Wilson, *Queen Elizabeth and the Revolt of the Netherlands* (1970).
4. G.W. Bernard, review of E. Duffy, *The Stripping of the Altars: Traditional Religion in England c.1400–c.1580* (1992), in *Heythrop Journal*, xxxiv (1993), pp. 453–5.
5. J. Catto, review of C.M. Barron and J. Stratford, eds., *The Church and Learning in Later Medieval Society, Essays in honour of R.B. Dobson*, Harlaxton Medieval Studies, XI (Donington, 2002), www.history.ac.uk/reviews/paper.cattoJ.html

1   The Hunne Affair

1. *The Enquirie and Verdite of the Quest panneld of the death of Richard Hune wich was founde hanged in Lolars tower* (Antwerp, *c.* 1537?) (A.W. Pollard *et al.*, eds., *A Short Title Catalogue of Books Printed in England, Scotland and Ireland, 1475–1640* [rev. edn., 1986], no. 13970), fos. v–xiii, esp. fos. v–vii, xii–xiii*, printed in E. Hall, *Chronicle* (1809 edn.), pp. 573–4, 579–80 and in John Foxe, *Acts and Monuments* (1563 edn.), pp. 390–6. References to Foxe will throughout be given both to the edition cited from the website of the Humanities Research Institute, University of Sheffield (www.hrionline.ac.uk/johnfoxe/) and, for convenience, and given the evanescence of websites, to the widely accessible standard printed edition: John Foxe, *Acts and Monuments*, ed. S.R. Cattley and G. Townsend (8 vols., 1837–41), here iv. 183–204.
2. Thomas More, *A Dialogue concerning Heresies*, in *The Complete Works of St Thomas More*, VI pt. i., ed. T.M.C. Lawler, G. Marc'hadour and R.C. Marius (New Haven, CT, 1981), p. 318.
3. Hall, *Chronicle*, p. 573.
4. Foxe, *Acts and Monuments* (1570 edn.), p. 930 (Foxe, *Acts and Monuments*, iv. 183).

5. More, *Dialogue concerning Heresies*, in *Complete Works*, VI i, pp. 318, 326.

6. Ibid., 326; Thomas More, *The Apology*, in *The Complete Works of St Thomas More*, IX, ed. J.B. Trapp (New Haven, CT, 1979), p. 126.

7. C. Haigh, *English Reformations: Religion, Society and Politics under the Tudors* (Oxford, 1993), p. 78.

8. Foxe, *Acts and Monuments* (1570 edn.), p. 930 (Foxe, *Acts and Monuments*, iv. 183); S.F.C. Milsom, 'Richard Hunne's "Praemunire"', *English Historical Review*, lxxvi (1961), pp. 80–2.

9. R. Wunderli, 'Pre-reformation London summoners and the murder of Richard Hunne', *Journal of Ecclesiastical History*, xxxiii (1982), p. 218, suggests that this dispute may have provoked the church authorities 'to counter-attack against Hunne with a mortuary suit', but there is nothing to link these matters, and without Hunne's refusal to pay the mortuary the church authorities would not have been able to attack him; S. Brigden, *London and the Reformation* (Oxford, 1989), p. 99.

10. Milsom, 'Richard Hunne's "Praemunire"', p. 80.

11. This is my understanding of the implications of the cases discussed by R.M. Helmholz, *The Ius Commune in England* (Oxford, 2002), pp. 145–6, 179–80, which do not seem to me to support his conclusion that 'modern historians of the church have been faithful to the evidence when they have described the English mortuary payment as "particularly resented" or as "one payment to the clergy that rankled most"' (pp. 145–6, citing R.M. [recte N.] Swanson, *Church and Society in Late Medieval England* (2nd edn., Oxford, 1999 recte 1993)), p. 216, and P. Heath, *The English Parish Clergy on the Eve of the Reformation* (1969), p. 155. M. Harvey, 'Some comments on northern mortuary customs in the later middle ages', *Journal of Ecclesiastical History*, lix (2008), pp. 272–80, emphasises variation in local customs, and suggests that when the standard demand was an animal as well as a cloth, the payment of mortuaries could grate.

12. Milsom, 'Richard Hunne's "Praemunire"', pp. 80–2, drawing on T[he] N[ational] A[rchives], P[ublic] R[ecord] O[ffice], KB27/1006 mm. 36–7.

13. For an example, see Perys v. Grene (1517), TNA, PRO, KB 27/1024 m. 86, cited by Helmholz, *Ius Commune in England*, p. 147 n. 70.

14. Milsom, 'Richard Hunne's "Praemunire"', p. 81.

15. Thomas More, *Supplication of Souls*, in *The Complete Works of St Thomas More*, VII, ed. F. Manley, G. Marc'hadour, R. Marius and C.H. Miller (New Haven, CT, 1990), pp. 132–3.

16. Foxe, *Acts and Monuments* (1570 edn.), pp. 930–1 (Foxe, *Acts and Monuments*, iv. 183–4).

17. Foxe, *Acts and Monuments* (1570 edn.), pp. 932–3 (Foxe, *Acts and Monuments*, iv. 188); J. Fines, 'The post-mortem condemnation for heresy of Richard Hunne', *English Historical Review*, lxxviii (1963), pp. 528–31.

18. Simon Fish, *A Supplicacyon for the Beggers* (1528), ed. J.M. Cowper, Early English Text Society, extra series, xiii (1871), pp. 8–9; W.D. Hamilton, ed., *Wriothesley's Chronicle*, Camden Society, cxvi (2 vols., 1875), p. 9; Hall, *Chronicle*, p. 573; Foxe, *Acts and Monuments* (1570 edn.), p. 930 (Foxe, *Acts and Monuments*, iv. 183). cf. More's report, *Dialogue concerning Heresies*, in *Complete Works*, VI i. pp. 318–19.

19. P. Gwyn, *The King's Cardinal: The Rise and Fall of Thomas Wolsey* (1990), p. 35.

20. More, *Supplication of Souls*, in *Complete Works*, VII, p. 132; id., *Dialogue concerning Heresies*, in *Complete Works*, VI i, p. 324.

21. More, *Dialogue concerning Heresies*, in *Complete Works*, VI i, pp. 324, 328–30; R. Duerden, 'Authority and reformation Bible translation', in O. O'Sullivan, ed., *The Bible as Book: The Reformation* (2000), p. 22 n. 22.

22. Foxe, *Acts and Monuments* (1570 edn.), pp. 930, 938 (Foxe, *Acts and Monuments* iv. 183, 201). The tensions and ambiguities in Foxe's account are acutely explored by

S.J. Smart, 'John Foxe and "The story of Richard Hun, martyr"', *Journal of Ecclesiastical History*, xxxvii (1986), pp. 1–14.

23. Foxe, *Acts and Monuments* (1563 edn.), p. 394 (Foxe, *Acts and Monuments*, iv. 184).

24. Foxe, *Acts and Monuments* (1570 edn.), p. 938 (Foxe, *Acts and Monuments*, iv. 202).

25. Foxe, *Acts and Monuments* (1570 edn.), p. 931 (Foxe, *Acts and Monuments*, iv. 184).

26. Fish, *Supplicacyon for the Beggers*, ed. Cowper, p. 9.

27. *Enquirie and Verdite*, fos. v–vii, xii–xiii^v. The text was printed in Hall, *Chronicle*, pp. 573–4, 579–80. It was also printed by Foxe in the 1563 edition of *Acts and Monuments*, pp. 390–6 (Foxe, *Acts and Monuments*, iv. 183–204). But Foxe included only an abbreviated version in subsequent editions. In the 1570 edition Foxe explained that he was omitting many of the depositions relating to the Hunne affair because of their 'tediousness' and he simply gave a page reference (p. 395) to the 1563 edition: (1570 edn.), pp. 930–6 (esp. p. 935). See also the 1576 edn., pp. 773–5 (esp. p. 774), and the 1583 edn., pp. 810–11.

28. *Enquirie and Verdite*, fos. v–v^v; Hall, *Chronicle*, p. 574; Foxe, *Acts and Monuments* (1563 edn.), p. 391 (Foxe, *Acts and Monuments*, iv. 191).

29. *Enquirie and Verdite*, fos. vi–vi^v; Hall, *Chronicle*, pp. 574–5; Foxe, *Acts and Monuments* (1563 edn.), pp. 391–2 (Foxe, *Acts and Monuments*, iv. 191–2).

30. *Enquirie and Verdite*, fos. vi^v–vii; Hall, *Chronicle*, p. 575; Foxe, *Acts and Monuments* (1563 edn.), p. 391 (Foxe, *Acts and Monuments*, iv. 192).

31. cf. Gwyn, *King's Cardinal*, p. 38.

32. *Enquirie and Verdite*, fos. vii–viii; Hall, *Chronicle*, pp. 575–6; Foxe, *Acts and Monuments* (1563 edn.), p. 392 (Foxe, *Acts and Monuments*, iv. 192).

33. *Enquirie and Verdite*, fo. vii.

34. Hall stated that 'for a further truth to be declared in this abominable and detestable murder here shall follow the whole inquiry and verdict of the inquest word for word' (Hall, *Chronicle*, p. 573). Foxe insisted in his 1583 edition that he had reproduced 'word for word, the whole inquiry and verdict of the inquest' (*Acts and Monuments* (1583), p. 809 [Foxe, *Acts and Monuments*, iv. 202]). He may well have been convinced that that was what he was doing, but most probably, however, he took his text directly from Hall's *Chronicle* (Hall had omitted these same details). Both Hall and Foxe take the pamphlet at face value. What at once strikes the modern reader is that the account of Hunne's death and the subsequent investigations is prefaced by several pages (*Enquirie and Verdite*, fos. 1–4^v) of vitriolic denunciation of 'the hypocrisy and abominable living of whorehunters', in other words persecuting bishops seen as intent on keeping up 'the kingdom of fornicators and adulterers that they may live in all pleasure and idlenes, serving their bellies only and living more viciously than ever did the heathen'. If the pamphlet was manifestly not the product of objective study, that does not necessarily invalidate the evidence it presents, but it must raise some doubts about its reliability and comprehensiveness. It also includes a letter from Richard Fitzjames, bishop of London, to Thomas Wolsey: is this genuine?

35. This was partially noticed by J. Gairdner, *The English Church in the Sixteenth Century from the Accession of Henry VIII to the Death of Mary* (1912), pp. 29–30.

36. More, *Dialogue concerning Heresies*, in *Complete Works*, VI i. pp. 318–19.

37. *Enquirie and Verdite*, fos. x^v, viii^v–ix; Hall, *Chronicle*, pp. 576–8; Foxe, *Acts and Monuments* (1563 edn.), p. 393 (Foxe, *Acts and Monuments*, iv. 192–4).

38. *Enquirie and Verdite*, fo. x; cf. Hall, *Chronicle*, p. 578; Foxe, *Acts and Monuments* (1563 edn.), p. 394 (Foxe, *Acts and Monuments*, iv. 194).

39. *Enquirie and Verdite*, fos. vi^v–vii, viii; Hall, *Chronicle*, pp. 575–6. When did Joseph make his confession in the Tower of London? In the pamphlet it is presented as an integral part of the reasonings of the coroner's jury: yet Joseph was still at liberty on Wednesday, 6 December, when the jury reached its verdict (cf. Gairdner, *English Church*, pp. 575–6).

40. *Enquirie and Verdite*, fo. xi; Hall, *Chronicle*, p. 578.
41. cf. Gwyn, *King's Cardinal*, p. 36.
42. Smart, 'Foxe and "The story of Richard Hun, martyr"', pp. 1–14, esp. p. 13. On motives more generally see J.D.M. Derrett, 'The affairs of Richard Hunne and Friar Standish', in J.B. Trapp, ed., *The Complete Works of St Thomas More*, IX: *The Apology* (New Haven, CT, 1979), pp. 217–18.
43. *Enquirie and Verdite*, fo. vi; Hall, *Chronicle*, p. 574.
44. *The Customs of London otherwise called Arnold's Chronicle*, ed. F. Douce (1811), p. xlix.
45. Wunderli, 'Pre-Reformation London Summoners', pp. 222–4; *Enquirie and Verdite*, fo. vi; Hall, *Chronicle*, p. 574; cf. Gwyn, *King's Cardinal*, p. 38.
46. *Enquirie and Verdite*, fo. vii^v; Hall, *Chronicle*, p. 575.
47. cf. Gwyn, *King's Cardinal*, p. 39.
48. More, *Dialogue concerning Heresies*, in *Complete Works*, VI i, pp. 325–6; Hall, *Chronicle*, p. 573.
49. W.R. Cooper asked staff in the Public Record Office to explore the legal records in which this case might be found: they came across TNA, PRO, KB9/468 m. 14. Cooper drew on their discovery in his paper 'Richard Hunne', *Reformation*, i (1996), pp. 221–51. Unfortunately in crucial respects, as we shall see, Cooper misunderstood its meaning and significance. He also gives the call numbers of two further items relating to Hunne in the records of King's Bench but does not make any use of them: they are, however, crucial in explaining the course of events.
50. Unfortunately that date does not mark, as Cooper supposes, the completion of the inquest—'the inquest lasted 433 days' (Cooper, 'Richard Hunne', p. 236)—not least since the jurors reached their verdict on 6 December 1514, two days after Hunne's death, as is plainly stated in the document. It represents rather an important stage in the judicial proceedings.
51. It is a shame that W.R. Cooper, whose initiative led to the discovery or identification of these records, has failed to grasp their true meaning. Cooper misleadingly sees these sources as damning Horsey, when they do the opposite. Cooper cites Henry's instructions to Earnley, but misunderstands what was happening. He supposes that 'Horsey's indictment before the Court of King's Bench for the murder of Richard Hunne' was what prompted the king to act—whereas it is much more probable that what we have is a series of legal manoeuvres that followed the king's intervention earlier on. Cooper thinks that 'here we see him [Horsey] arraigned before King's Bench like any common layman on a charge of murder', but that is to take an anachronistic view of the operation of the legal process in Tudor England. Cooper insists that Horsey was not simply the beneficiary of 'a behind-the-scenes whisper from the king', and speculates that what happened was 'a string-pulling response by Wolsey' to Bishop Fitzjames's plea for his clerk. So determined, continues Cooper, were the judges of King's Bench to convict Horsey—'perhaps they had let it be known that they would ignore even the royal behind-the-scenes whispers'—that 'only the promise of a major royal embarrassment could have provoked such an extraordinary intervention on the part of the king'. But all this is to set things the wrong way about, to suppose that the legal proceedings to which these documents testify were the culmination of some state-administered investigation into a crime. If they were rather the consequence of the king's earlier decision to accept Horsey's plea of innocence, then Cooper's speculations become simply unnecessary (Cooper, 'Richard Hunne', pp. 232–3).
52. More, *Dialogue concerning Heresies*, in *Complete Works*, VI i, p. 326. More offered a similar account in *Supplication of Souls*, in *Complete Works*, VII, p. 133: 'after that the matter had been by long time and great diligence so far examined, that the king's highness, at length (as time always trieth out the truth) well perceived his innocence and theirs also that were accused and indicted with him: his noble grace when they were arraigned upon that enlightenment and therto pleaded that they

were not guilty, commanded his attorney general to confess their plea to be true, which is the thing that his highness as a most virtuous prince useth for to do, when the matter is not only just, but also known for just upon the part of the party defendant'.

53. Hall, *Chronicle*, p. 573; More, *Dialogue concerning Heresies*, in *Complete Works*, VI i, p. 326.

54. More, *Dialogue concerning Heresies*, in *Complete Works*, VI i, pp. 318, 326–7; id., *Supplication of Souls* in *Complete Works*, VII, p. 135.

55. *Enquirie and Verdite*, fos. xᵛ–xi; Hall, *Chronicle*, p. 578; Foxe, *Acts and Monuments* (1563 edn.), p. 395 (Foxe, *Acts and Monuments*, iv. 195). Creswell's testimony was among those omitted from the 1570 and 1576 editions before reappearing in 1583, p. 810.

56. More, *Dialogue concerning Heresies*, in *Complete Works*, VI i., pp. 127–8.

57. Foxe, *Acts and Monuments* (1570 edn.), p. 918 (Foxe, *Acts and Monuments*, iv. 126).

58. Foxe, *Acts and Monuments* (1576 edn.), p. 1165 (Foxe, *Acts and Monuments*, v. 419).

59. *Wriothesley's Chronicle*, p. 115; cf. S.E. Brigden, 'Popular disturbance and the fall of Thomas Cromwell and the reformers', *Historical Journal*, xxiv (1981), p. 264 and n. 55. Brigden says the pamphlet relating to Hunne might have been put together at this time.

60. Milsom, 'Richard Hunne's "Praemunire"', p. 82.

61. Foxe, *Acts and Monuments* (1570 edn.), p. 1911 (Foxe, *Acts and Monuments*, vii. 473–7).

62. It should be noted that Bishop Fitzjames's fears concerned 'my' clerk (*Enquirie and Verdite*, fo. xiᵛ), not 'any' clerk, as Hall (*Chronicle*, p. 579), followed by Foxe (*Acts and Monuments* [1563 edn.,] p. 395 (Foxe, *Acts and Monuments*, iv. 197)), influentially misrepresented it. This was first noticed by E. Jeffries Davis, 'The authorities for the case of Richard Hunne (1514–15)', *English Historical Review*, xxx (1915), pp. 477–88, at p. 477.

2 The Monarchical Church

1. J. Blair, *The Church in Anglo-Saxon Society* (Oxford, 2005), pp. 25, 33.

2. cf. R.W. Southern, 'Between heaven and hell', *TLS*, 18 June 1982, p. 652; J.L. Nelson, 'Society, theodicy and the origins of heresy: towards a reassessment of the medieval evidence', *Studies in Church History*, ix (1972), pp. 66–77.

3. E. Cameron, *The European Reformation* (Oxford, 1991), pp. 52–3, is perceptive here.

4. H. Mayr-Harting, 'Henry II and the Papacy, 1170–1189', *Journal of Ecclesiastical History*, xvi (1965), pp. 39–53 at pp. 39–40, 53; id., *Religion, Politics and Society in Britain 1066–1272* (Harlow, 2011), p. 94.

5. cf. J. Catto, *Journal of Ecclesiastical History*, lix (2008), p. 757.

6. L.G. Wickham Legg, *English Coronation Records* (1901), pp. xv–xix, xxi, xxiii, xxx–xxxi, 82/113, 251; J. Loach, 'The function of ceremonial in the reign of Henry VIII', *Past and Present*, cxlii (1994), pp. 51–3. A. Hunt, *The Drama of Coronation: Medieval Ceremony in Early Modern England* (Cambridge, 2008) is a good recent study.

7. D.M. Palliser, 'Royal mausolea in the long fourteenth century, 1271–1422', *Fourteenth Century England*, iii (2004), pp. 1–16; R.A. Griffiths, 'The royal dead in later medieval England', lecture delivered at Oxford, 12 Nov. 1993. I am most grateful to David Palliser for guidance.

8. Swanson, *Church and Society*, p. 89.

9. cf. P. Zutshi, in *Journal of Ecclesiastical History*, xxx (1982), pp. 461–3.

10. M. Prestwich, *Plantagenet England 1225–1360* (Oxford, 2005), pp. 275–7.

11. W.M. Ormrod, 'The West European Monarchies in the Later Middle Ages', in R. Bonney, ed., *Economic Systems and State Finance* (Oxford, 1995), p. 133.

12. Swanson, *Church and Society*, p. 116; G.L. Harriss, *Shaping the Nation: England 1360–1461* (Oxford, 2005), p. 60.

13. S.J. Gunn, 'Edmund Dudley and the church', *Journal of Ecclesiastical History*, li (2000), p. 515.

14. BL, Cotton MS, Vitellius B ii fo. 85.

15. TNA, PRO, SP1/31 fo. 10 (*LP*, IV i 299); N. Beckett, 'Sheen Charterhouse from its foundation to its dissolution', Univ. of Oxford D.Phil. thesis, 1992, p. 165; G.W. Bernard, *War, Taxation and Rebellion in Early Tudor England: Henry VIII, Wolsey and the Amicable Grant of 1525* (Brighton, 1985), pp. 128–9, 55–6.

16. M. McCormick, 'Liturgie et guerre des Carolingiens à la première croisade', in *'Militia Christi' e Crociata nei secoli XI–XIII. Atti dell'XIa settimana internazionale di studi medievali della Mendola* (Milan, 1992), pp. 209–40; id., 'The liturgy of war in the early middle ages: crisis, litanies and the Carolingian monarchy', *Viator*, xv (1984), pp. 1–23.

17. J.H. Denton, 'From the foundation of Vale Royal Abbey to the Statute of Carlisle: Edward I and ecclesiastical patronage', *Thirteenth Century England*, iv (1992), p. 127.

18. D.W. Burton, 'Requests for prayers and royal propaganda', *Thirteenth Century England*, iii (1989), pp. 25–9; id., 'Politics, propaganda and public opinion in the reigns of Henry III and Edward I', Univ. of Oxford D. Phil. thesis, 1985; A.K. McHardy, 'Liturgy and prayer in the diocese of Lincoln during the Hundred Years War', *Studies in Church History*, xviii (1982), pp. 215–27; ead., 'The English Clergy and the Hundred Years War', *Studies in Church History*, xx (1983), pp. 171–8.

19. J. Hughes, *Pastors and Visionaries: Religion and Secular Life in Late Medieval Yorkshire* (Woodbridge, 1988), pp. 26, 28–9.

20. McHardy, 'Liturgy and prayer'. W.R. Jones, 'The English Church and Royal Propaganda during the Hundred Years War', *Journal of British Studies*, xix (1979), pp. 18–30. cf. C. Tyerman, *England and the Crusades, 1095–1588* (Chicago, 1988), p. 327.

21. McHardy, 'Liturgy and prayer'; Jones, 'The English Church and Royal Propaganda', pp.18–30; J.A. Doig, 'Propaganda and public opinion and the siege of Calais in 1436', in R. Archer, ed., *Crown, Government and People in the Fifteenth Century* (Stroud, 1995), pp. 83–5. cf. Tyerman, *England and the Crusades, 1095–1588*, p. 327; A. Ruddick, 'National sentiment and religious vocabulary in fourteenth-century England', *Journal of Ecclesiastical Hisory*, lv (2009), pp. 1–18.

22. Beckett, 'Sheen Charterhouse', p. 41. cf. C.T. Allmand, 'Henry V, the Soldier, and War in France', in G.L. Harriss, ed., *Henry V: the Practice of Kingship* (Oxford, 1985), pp. 122–3.

23. A.K. McHardy, 'Religious ritual and political persuasion: the case of England in the Hundred Years' War', *International Journal of Moral & Social Studies*, iii (1988), pp. 41–58.

24. Beckett, 'Sheen Charterhouse', p. 72.

25. Doig, 'Siege of Calais'. p. 89.

26. *LP*, I i 627.

27. *Calendar of State Papers, Spanish*, iii (i) nos. 39, 43.

28. TNA, PRO, SP1/7 fo. 156 (*LP*, I ii 2636), *LP*, I ii 2641.

29. BL, Cotton MS, Vitellius B ii fos. 121–121a (*LP*, II i 108–9).

30. BL, Cotton MS, Vitellius B ii fo. 34 (*LP*, I i 1533).

31. cf. P. Contamine, ed., *L'état et les aristocracies: XIIe–XVIIe siècles. France, Angleterre, Écosse* (Paris, 1989), p. 673.

32. J.E. Cox, ed., *Writings and Letters of Thomas Cranmer* (Parker Society, 1846), pp. 281–3.

33. S. Raban, *Mortmain Legislation and the English Church 1279–1500* (Cambridge, 1982) for a complex survey.

34. C. Burgess, 'Strategies for Eternity: Perpetual Chantry Foundation in Late Medieval Bristol', in C. Harper-Bill, ed., *Religious Beliefs and Ecclesiastical Careers in Late Medieval England* (Woodbridge, 1991), pp. 9–14.

35. Harriss, *Shaping the Nation*, p. 313. Contrast the situation a little earlier: R.M. Haines, 'The episcopate during the reign of Edward II and the regency of Mortimer and Isabella', *Journal of Ecclesiastical History*, lvi (2005), pp. 661–3.

36. P. Heath, *Church and Realm 1272–1461* (1988), p. 267; Harriss, *Shaping the Nation*, p. 317.

37. Heath, *Church and Realm*, p. 307; R.G. Davies, 'Martin V and the English episcopate, with particular reference to his campaign for the repeal of the Statute of Provisors', *English Historical Review*, xcii (1977), pp. 309–44; M. Harvey, 'Unity and diversity: perceptions of the papacy in the later middle ages', *Studies in Church History*, xxxli (1996), pp. 145–69 at p. 152.

38. Heath, *Church and Realm*, p. 336.

39. Ibid., p. 344.

40. C. Harper-Bill, 'Who wanted the English Reformation?', *Medieval History*, ii (1992), pp. 66–77 at p. 66.

41. cf. Harriss, *Shaping the Nation*, pp. 323.

42. I owe this point to Tim Reuter.

43. cf. Heath, *Church and Realm*, p. 16.

44. *LP*, I ii 3140, TNA, PRO, SP1/9 fo. 95v (*LP*, I ii 3497).

45. *LP*, III i 600.

46. Denton, 'Edward I and ecclesiastical patronage', pp. 133–6.

47. cf. Heath, *Church and Realm*, p. 250.

48. cf. P. Zutshi, *Journal of Ecclesiastical History*, xxx (1982), pp. 462–3. I am grateful to Gerald Harriss for further suggestions on this point.

49. These paragraphs draw heavily on P.C. Saunders, 'Royal ecclesiastical patronage in England 1199–1351', Univ. of Oxford D.Phil. thesis, 1978, *passim*, a fine study which deserves publication.

50. J.A.F. Thomson, *The Early Tudor Church and Society 1485–1529* (1993), p. 90.

51. D. Lepine, *A Brotherhood of Canons Serving God: English Secular Cathedrals in the Later Middle Ages* (Woodbridge, 1995), pp. 22–3 citing T.W. Jex-Blake, 'Historical notices of Robert Stillington; Chancellor of England, Bishop of Bath and Wells', *Proceedings of the Somersetshire Natural History and Archaeological Society*, lx (1914), pp. 1–10; J.A. Robinson, 'Correspondence of Bishop Oliver King and Sir Reginald Bray', *Proceedings of the Somersetshire Natural History and Archaeological Society*, lx (1915), pp. 5–6.

52. For an interesting attempt at quantifying this, see C. Michon, *La Crosse et le Sceptre: les Prélats d'État sous François I et Henri VIII* (Paris, 2008), pp. 239–78, 311–13

53. I owe this formulation to Tim Reuter.

54. Heath, *Church and Realm*, p. 132.

55. Ibid., p. 133.

56. Swanson, *Church and Society*, p. 186.

57. P. Heath, 'Between reform and reformation: the English church in the fourteenth and fifteenth centuries', *Journal of Ecclesiastical History*, xli (1990), p. 659.

58. Prestwich, *Plantagenet England*, p. 286.

59. R.L. Storey, 'Episcopal king makers in the fifteenth century', in R.B. Dobson, ed., *The Church, Politics and Patronage in the Fifteenth Century* (Gloucester, 1984), pp. 90–3.

60. S.J. Gunn, *Early Tudor Government 1485–1558* (Basingstoke, 1995), p. 16; P. Cavill, ' "The enemy of God and his church": James Hobart, Praemunire and the Clergy of Norwich Diocese', *Journal of Legal History*, xxxii (2011), pp. 129–31, argues that Nix's letter should be dated to 1504 rather than the conventional date of 1507.

61. M.J. Kelly, 'Canterbury jurisdiction and influence during the episcopate of William Warham, 1503–1532', Univ. of Cambridge Ph.D. thesis, 1965, pp. 106–7, drawing on TNA, PRO, SC1/64/83, pp. 108–10.
62. John Skelton, *The Complete English Poems*, ed. J. Scattergood (Harmondsworth, 1983), Colin Clout, lines 108–11, p. 246.
63. Heath, *Church and Realm*, pp. 227, 329–30, 352.
64. Gwyn, *King's Cardinal*, p. 46; Kelly, 'Episcopate of Warham', pp. 119–20.
65. Swanson, *Church and Society*, p. 150.
66. The best discussion is Gwyn, *King's Cardinal*, pp. 46–50. Sir Geoffrey Elton (*Historical Journal*, xxi [1969], p. 161), saw this as simply a general conviction that 'the king ought to be free to do in England as he pleased', but not 'a practical philosophy based on a fundamental philosophy'. By contrast, John Guy has seen it as a 'denial of the pope's right to infringe his territorial sovereignty on the basis of the Petrine commission' (J.A. Guy, 'Henry VIII and the *praemunire* manoeuvres of 1530–1531', *English Historical Review*, xcvii (1982), pp. 497–8). F. Heal, *Reformation in Britain and Ireland* (Oxford, 2003), p. 33, notes that dispute arose from clerical assertiveness; cf. R.N. Swanson, 'Problems of the priesthood in pre-Reformation England', *English Historical Review*, cv (1989), pp. 863–4.
67. Kelly, 'Episcopate of Warham', p. 145. Curiously Standish was himself accused of offences under praemunire on 6 November 1518: he had allegedly been consecrated bishop by virtue of his bulls before the king's royal assent had been obtained to them, and he had allegedly used the bulls as authority for receiving the revenues due to him as bishop before doing homage for these revenues to the king. Standish acknowledged his guilt and was pardoned (J.J. Scarisbrick, 'The Conservative Episcopate in England, 1529–1535', Univ. of Cambridge Ph.D. thesis, 1955, pp. 45–6, from TNA, PRO, STAC 2/2 fo. 75).
68. 23 Henry VIII c.1 (*Statutes of the Realm*, iii. 362–3).
69. 25 Henry VIII c.3 (*Statutes of the Realm*, iii. 439); cf. 26 Henry VIII c. 12 (*Statutes of the Realm*, iii. 507–8).
70. 28 Henry VIII c. 15 (*Statutes of the Realm*, iii 671).
71. 25 Henry VIII c. 6 (*Statutes of the Realm*, iii. 441).
72. 27 Henry VIII c. 17 (*Statutes of the Realm*, iii. 549–50); 28 Henry VIII c. 2. (*Statutes of the Realm*, iii. 652).
73. 28 Henry VIII c.1 (*Statutes of the Realm*, iii. 651–2).
74. 28 Henry VIII c.3 (*Statutes of the Realm*, iii. 749).
75. TNA, PRO, SP1/112 fo. 120 (*LP*, XI 1246 (art.18)).
76. Gwyn, *King's Cardinal*, p. 53; J.G. Bellamy, *Criminal Law and Society in Late Medieval and Tudor England* (Gloucester, 1984), pp. 138–40; D. Wilkins, *Concilia Magnae Britanniae* (4 vols., 1737), iii 713; A.J. Slavin, 'Upstairs, downstairs: the roots of the Reformation', *Huntington Library Quarterly*, lxix (1986), p. 251.
77. J.H. Baker, *Oxford History of the Laws of England*, VI 1483–1558 (Oxford, 2003), pp. 531–8.
78. Hughes, *Pastors and Visionaries*, p. 328; *LP*, XIV ii 324; I.D. Thornley, 'The Sanctuary register of Beverley', *English Historical Review*, xxxiv (1919), pp. 393–7; J. Raine, ed., *Sanctuarium Dunelmense et Sanctuarium Berverlacense*, Surtees Society, v (1837).
79. R.H. Helmholz, *The Ius Commune in England: four studies* (Oxford, 2001), p. 67.
80. TNA, PRO, SP1/152 fo. 46 (*LP*, XIV i 1089).
81. TNA, PRO, SP1/131 fo. 9 (*LP*, XIII i 668), fo. 120 (*LP* XIII i 796); BL, Cotton MS, Titus B i fo. 468 (*LP*, XIII i 877).
82. Baker, *Oxford History of the Laws of England 1483–1558*, p. 546; Polydore Vergil, *The Anglica Historia of Polydore Vergil*, ed. and trans. D. Hay, Camden Society, lxxiv (1950), pp. 64–7; Thomas More, *Richard III*, in *The Complete Works of St Thomas More*, II, ed. R.S. Sylvester (New Haven, CT, 1963), pp. 27–33.

83. M.A. Hicks, 'The Yorkshire Rebellion of 1489 reconsidered', *Northern History*, xxii (1986), pp. 54–7; A.J. Pollard, *North-Eastern England during the Wars of the Roses: Lay Society, War, and Politics 1450–1500* (Oxford, 1990), pp. 380 n.56, 388; P.I. Kaufman, 'Henry VII and sanctuary', *Church History*, liii (1984), pp. 465–76.

84. J.H. Baker, ed., *The Reports of John Spelman*, Selden Society (2 vols., 1977), ii. 343; Baker, *Oxford History of the Laws of England 1483–1558*, pp. 547–50.

85. 22 Henry VIII c.14. (*Statutes of the Realm*, iii. 332–4).

86. 27 Henry VIII c. 19 (*Statutes of the Realm*, iii. 551).

87. This qualifies Helmholz's argument that what was happening was the alignment of the English law of sanctuary with the canon law proper of sanctuary—in other words, removing a series of anomalies and exemptions—rather than a straightforward assertion of royal authority over an unwilling church: *Ius Commune*, pp. 75–80.

88. TNA, PRO, SP1/112 fo. 120 (*LP*, XI 1246 (art.18)).

89. Helmholz, *Ius Commune*, pp. 68, 70–1.

90. e.g. G. Rosser, 'Sanctuary and social negotiation in medieval England', in J. Blair and B. Golding, eds., *The Cloister and the World* (Oxford, 1996), pp. 57–79.

91. Baker, *Oxford History of the Laws of England 1483–1558*, pp. 540–51; Helmholz, *Ius Commune*, pp. 16–81.

92. TNA, PRO, SP3/14 foliation illegible (*LP*, XIII i 696).

93. Helmholz, *Ius Commune*, p. 31; cf. p. 40 in general terms.

94. Rosser, 'Sanctuary and social negotiation', pp. 75, 79.

95. D. Fenlon, 'Thomas More and tyranny', *Journal of Ecclesiastical History*, xxxii (1981), p. 457 reflecting on Thomas More, *Richard III*, in *Complete Works*, II, pp. 37–9.

96. Kelly, 'Episcopate of Warham', pp. 60–1, 77–83, 91–2.

97. *LP*, I ii 2019.

98. *LP*, I ii 2098.

99. Henry's letter survives in two drafts, TNA, PRO, SP1/14 fos. 247–50 and BL, Cotton MS, Vitellius, B iii. fos. 122–125, summarised in *LP*, II ii 2871. T.F. Mayer, 'On the road to 1534: the occupation of Tournai and Henry VIII's theory of sovereignty', in D. Hoak, ed., *Tudor Political Culture* (Cambridge, 1995), pp. 11–30, esp. p. 26; id., 'Tournai and tyranny: imperial kingship and critical humanism', *Historical Journal*, xxxiv (1994), pp. 257–77; C.S.L. Davies, 'Tournai and the English Crown, 1513–1519', *Historical Journal*, xli (1998), pp. 1–26; M.R.J. Everett, '"Without recognisione of any superior": Henry VIII and Imperial Kinghtship, 1509–1533,' Univ. of Southampton M.A. dissertation, 2009.

100. Catto, 'Religious change under Henry V', pp. 108–10, 115; R.B. Dobson, 'The bishops of late medieval England as intermediaries between church and state', in J-P. Genet and B. Vincent, eds., *État et église dans la genese de l'État moderne* (Madrid, 1986), p. 236; Beckett, 'Syon Charterhouse', pp. 10–20, 74; Hughes, *Pastors and Visionaries, passim*.

101. J. Greatrex, 'After Knowles: recent perspectives in monastic history', in J.G. Clark, ed., *The Religious Orders in Pre-Reformation England* (Woodbridge, 2002), p. 42; Knowles, *Religious Orders*, ii. 182–4.

102. Beckett, 'Sheen Charterhouse', p. 148.

103. M.K. Jones and M.G. Underwood, *The King's Mother: Lady Margaret Beaufort Countess of Richmond and Derby* (Cambridge, 1992), pp. 173–201.

104. A.G. Little, 'Introduction of Observant Friars into England', *Proceedings of the British Academy*, x (1921–3), p. 464; Jones and Underwood, *The King's Mother*, p. 193.

105. *LP*, V 1649.

106. Foxe, *Acts and Monuments* (1570 edn.), p. 962 (Foxe, *Acts and Monuments*, iv. 241–2).

107. Henry VIII, *Assertio Septem Sacramentorum* (1521) (*RSTC* 13078); the best English translation is L. O'Donovan, ed., *Assertio Septem Sacramentorum* (New York, NY, 1908); *LP*, III, i 1220, BL, Cotton MS, Vitellius iv. fo. 96 (*LP*, III i 1233).

108. *LP*, III i 1297; cf. BL, Cotton MS, Vitellius B iv fo. 96 (*LP*, ii 1510), ii 1659.
109. *LP*, III ii 1574.
110. *LP*, XIV ii 400.
111. *LP*, III ii 1499.
112. *LP*, IV iii 5412.
113. *LP*, II ii 1592.
114. *LP*, IV i 40.
115. *LP*, IV ii 618.
116. *LP*, IV i 828.
117. *LP*, IV i 1760.
118. *LP*, IV i 40.
119. *LP*, IV ii 2446.
120. *LP*, IV ii 3438.
121. *LP*, IV i 40.
122. H. Gee and W.J. Hardy, eds., *Documents illustrative of English Church History* (1896), pp. 154–76.
123. *LP*, III ii 2652.
124. L.G. Duggan, 'The unresponsiveness of the late medieval church: a reconsideration', *Sixteenth-Century Journal*, ix (1978), p. 30.

3 Bishops

1. S. Thompson, 'The Pastoral Work of the English and Welsh Bishops, 1500–1558', Univ. of Oxford D.Phil. thesis, 1984, p. 225. When specific references about individual bishops are not given in this chapter, they may be found in the entries in the *Oxford Dictionary of National Biography* (*ODNB*).
2. C. Harper-Bill, 'Dean Colet's convocation sermon and the pre-reformation church of England', *History*, lxxiii (1988), pp. 199–200.
3. C. Harper-Bill, *The Pre-Reformation Church in England 1400–1530* (Harlow, 1989), p. 31.
4. 1 Timothy iii: 2–4; Titus i: 5–9.
5. C. Haigh, *English Reformations* (Oxford, 1993), p. 10, for a vignette; Thompson, 'English and Welsh Bishops', p. 220.
6. Compare D. MacCulloch, *Thomas Cranmer* (New Haven, CT, 1995), p. 108, with J.J. Scarisbrick, 'Warham, William (d. 1532)', *Oxford Dictionary of National Biography*.
7. C. Michon, *La Crosse et le Sceptre: les prélats d'état sous François I et Henri VIII* (Paris, 2008), pp. 117–19.
8. Skelton, *Complete English Poems*, ed. Scattergood, Collyn Clout, lines 130–1, 440, 694, pp. 250, 257, 264.
9. N. Orme, 'Two saint-bishops of Exeter: James Berkley (d. 1327) and Edmund Lacy (d. 1455)', *Analecta Bollandiana*, civ (1986), pp. 403, 412–18.
10. Tim Reuter suggested to me that the decline was evident from the late eleventh century.
11. K. Pennington, in *Speculum*, lxxviii (2003), p. 943; N. Tanner, *The Church in the Later Middle Ages* (2008), p. 8.
12. C. Richmond, 'The English gentry and religion *c.*1500', in C. Harper-Bill, ed., *Religious Belief and Ecclesiastical Careers in Late Medieval England* (Woodbridge, 1991), p. 142.
13. *LP*, IV i 623; I i 1052.
14. R. Rex, in *Journal of Ecclesiastical History*, lii (2001), p. 141; R.J. Schoeck, 'Alcock, John (1430–1500)', *ODNB*.
15. R.M. Haines, *Ecclesia Anglicana: Studies in the English Church of the Later Middle Ages* (Toronto, 1989), p. 228.
16. A.G. Dickens, *English Reformation* (2nd edn., 1989), p. 66.

17. R.G. Davies, 'The episcopate', in C.H. Clough, ed., *Profession, Vocation and Culture in Later Medieval England* (Liverpool, 1982), pp. 68–9.
18. TNA, PRO, SP1/47 fo. 170 (*LP*, IV ii 4152), fo. 155 (*LP*, IV ii 4136).
19. Cameron, *European Reformation*, p. 34.
20. Swanson, *Church and Society*, p. 80; Scarisbrick, 'The Conservative Episcopate', pp. 30–1.
21. cf. M. Keen, *English Society in the Later Middle Ages* (1990), p. 251.
22. W.A. Pantin, *The English Church in the Fourteenth Century* (Cambridge, 1955), p. 15.
23. Dobson, 'The bishops of late medieval England', p. 232.
24. MacCulloch, *Cranmer*, p. 130.
25. TNA, PRO, SP1/23 fo. 277 (*LP*, III ii 1972).
26. Thompson, 'English and Welsh bishops', p. 12.
27. Scarisbrick, 'Conservative Episcopate', p. 61.
28. Dobson, 'The bishops of late medieval England', p. 235.
29. William Tyndale, *The Practice of Prelates* (1530) (RSTC 24465), sig. B vi^v.
30. *LP*, XIV i 1220.
31. A point emphasised to me by Tim Reuter.
32. F. Woodman, 'The Gothic Campaigns', in I. Atherton, E. Fernie, C. Harper-Bill and H. Smith, eds., *Norwich Cathedral* (1996), pp. 179–93.
33. Thompson, 'English and Welsh Bishops', p. 212.
34. *The Itinerary of John Leland*, ed. L. Toulmin Smith (5 vols., 1907–10), ii. 98.
35. *LP*, IV ii 4507, 4509; TNA, PRO, SP1/49 fo. 107 (*LP*, IV ii 4513).
36. TNA, PRO, SP1/49 fo. 119 (*LP*, IV ii 4527).
37. Leland, *Itinerary*, iv. 62.
38. TNA, PRO, SP1/39 fo. 26 (*LP*, IV ii 2368).
39. *LP*, IV iii 6182.
40. TNA, PRO, SP1/57 fo. 270 (*LP*, IV iii 6571).
41. R.W. Dunning, 'Miles Salley, bishop of Llandaff', *Journal of Welsh Ecclesiastical History*, viii (1991), pp. 4, 6.
42. C. Richardson and J. Johnston, *Medieval Drama* (Basingstoke, 1991), p. 20.
43. cf. John XXII and the diocese of Toulon 1317–18, Rodez in 1317: N. Lemaitre, *Le Rouergue flamboyant: le clergé et les fidèles du diocèse de Rodez 1417–1563* (Paris, 1989), pp. 14–15.
44. Dobson, 'The bishops of late medieval England', p. 230, citing K. Eubel, *Hierarchia Catholica* (Munster, 1913–23), ii. 281–6. For Ireland see TNA, SP1/30 fo. 90 (*LP*, IV i 80).
45. C. Morris, *The Papal Monarchy* (Oxford, 1989), p. 388.
46. *LP*, XI 1427, BL, Cotton MS, Cleopatra E iv. fos. 316–316v (*LP*, XIII ii 111). Barlow's motives were, however, not simply administrative: he wanted to undermine the standing of St David, questioning whether that saint had ever been bishop there.
47. Thompson, 'English and Welsh Bishops', p. 223; Dobson, 'The bishops of late medieval England', p. 231.
48. Scarisbrick, 'Conservative Episcopate', pp. 1–21.
49. Thomson, *Early Tudor Church and Society*, p. 106; R.L. Storey, *Diocesan Administration in Fifteenth-Century England* (Borthwick Papers), xvi (2nd edn., 1972), p. 1.
50. K. Down, 'The administration of the diocese of Worcester under the Italian bishops, 1497–1535', *Midland History*, xx (1995), pp. 1–20 at p. 16.
51. Scarisbrick, 'Conservative Episcopate', pp. 32–3.
52. Ibid., p. 40.
53. Ibid., pp. 40–1.
54. Ibid., pp. 62–6.
55. *LP*, III ii 2207.
56. TNA, PRO, SP1/27 fo. 16 (*LP*, III ii 2795).

57. George Cavendish, *The Life and Death of Cardinal Wolsey*, ed. R.S. Sylvester, Early English Text Society, ccxliii (1959), pp. 178–9.

58. *LP*, IV ii 4649.

59. Cavendish, *Life and Death of Wolsey*, p. 144; Scarisbrick, 'Conservative Episcopate', p. 239.

60. F. van Otroy, ed., 'Vie du bienheureux martyr John Fisher, cardinal evesque de Rochester', *Analecta Bollandiana*, x (1891), p. 258; M. Dowling, *Fisher of Men: A Life of John Fisher 1469–1535* (1999), p. 54.

61. *LP*, IV ii 3904–6.

62. Storey, *Diocesan Administration*, p. 2.

63. TNA, PRO, SP1/53 fo. 252 (*LP*, IV iii 5533).

64. G. Williams, *The Welsh Church: from Conquest to Reformation* (2nd. edn., 1976), p. 518; id., 'Skevington [Skeffington, Pace], Thomas (d. 1533)', *ODNB*.

65. A.J. Louisa, 'Capon [Salcot], John (d. 1557), *ODNB*.

66. Thompson, 'English and Welsh Bishops', p. 11.

67. Ibid., pp. 14–15.

68. D.M. Smith, 'Suffragan bishops in the medieval diocese of Lincoln', *Lincolnshire History*, xvii (1982), pp. 21–2.

69. Down, 'Diocese of Worcester', pp. 11–12.

70. J.E. Cox, ed., *Writings and Letters of Thomas Cranmer* (Parker Society, 1846), pp. 290–1, from British Library, Harleian MS 6148 fos. 18–18v; p. 320.

71. Down, 'Diocese of Worcester', pp. 3–4.

72. Ibid., pp. 5–10.

73. 25 Henry VIII c. 26 (*Statutes of the Realm*, iii. 483); 26 Henry VIII c. 14 (*Statutes of the Realm*, iii. 509–10). According to the act, they were accustomed to be had 'for the more speedy administration of the sacraments and other good wholesome and devout things and laudable ceremonies, to the increase of God's honour and for the commodity of good and devout people'.

74. 26 Henry VIII c. 15 (*Statutes of the Realm*, iii. 509–10).

75. F. Oakley, *The Western Church in the Late Middle Ages* (Ithaca, NY, 1979), p. 291; Keen, *English Society*, p. 253.

76. *LP*, IV ii 3952 (*State Papers*, iii no. xliv pp. 126–7).

77. Thompson, 'English and Welsh Bishops', p. 10.

78. Down, 'Diocese of Worcester', p. 8.

79. M. Bowker, *The Secular Clergy in the Diocese of Lincoln 1495–1520* (Cambridge, 1968), pp. 19–23, esp. p. 22.

80. Oakley, *Western Church*, p. 292.

81. Down, 'Diocese of Worcester', p. 14.

82. Ibid., p. 13, citing P.S. and H.M. Allen, eds., *Letters of Richard Fox 1486–1527* (Oxford, 1929), p. 79.

83. cf. Storey, 'Diocesan administration', p. 18.

84. Thompson, 'English and Welsh Bishops', p. 77.

85. Ibid., pp. 35, 38, 178.

86. Ibid., pp. 223–4.

87. Ibid., pp. 115–16; K.L. Wood-Legh, ed., *Kentish Visitations of Archbishop Warham and his Deputies, 1511–12*, Kent Archaeological Society, *Kent Records*, xxiv (1984), p. x.

88. More, *Apology*, in *Complete Works*, IX, p. 203.

89. BL, Cotton MS, Cleopatra E vi fo. 243v (*LP*, VIII 963).

90. M. Harvey, *Journal of Ecclesiastical History*, xlv (1994), p. 344.

91. B. Usher, 'The deanery of Bocking and the demise of the Vestiarian controversy', *Journal of Ecclesiastical History*, lii (2001), pp. 434–55.

92. N. Orme, *Unity and Variety: a History of the Church in Devon and Cornwall* (Exeter, 1991), p. 54.

93. Thompson, 'English and Welsh Bishops', pp. 25–6.

94. Thompson, 'English and Welsh Bishops', pp. 25–6; R. Swanson, 'Universities, graduates, and benefices in late medieval England', *Past and Present*, cvi (1985), pp. 47–8.
95. TNA, PRO, SP1/153 fo. 101 (*LP*, XIV ii 177).
96. Thompson, 'English and Welsh Bishops', p. 34.
97. TNA, PRO, SP1/21 fo. 123 (*LP*, III i 1030); cf. Thompson, 'English and Welsh Bishops', p. 31.
98. Ibid., p. 35, from *Clifford Letters*, Surtees Society, clxxii (1952), pp. 84–5.
99. Ibid., pp. 25, 30–1, 43.
100. Ibid., pp. 31, 33.
101. Ibid., pp. 32–3 for examples.
102. Ibid., p. 46.
103. Ibid., p. 34.
104. Ibid., p. 30.
105. Ibid., pp. 39–42.
106. P. Tudor, 'Changing private belief and practice in English devotional literature, *c.* 1475–1550', Univ. of Oxford D.Phil. thesis, 1984, p. 42; B. Collett, 'The civil servant and monastic reform: Richard Fox's translation of the Benedictine rule for women 1517', in J. Loades, ed., *Monastic Studies: The Continuity of Tradition* (Bangor, 1990), pp. 211–28; id., ed., *Female Monastic Life in Early Tudor England. With an edition of Richard Fox's translation of the Benedictine rule for women, 1517* (Aldershot, 2002); id., 'Organizing time for secular and religious purposes: the *Contemplacion of Sinners* (1499) and the translation of the Benedictine rule for women (1519) of Richard Fox, bishop of Winchester', *Studies in Church History*, xxxvii (2002), pp. 145–60; id., 'Holy Expectations: the female monastic vocation in the diocese of Winchester on the eve of the Reformation', in J.G. Clark, ed., *The Culture of English Monasticism* (Woodbridge, 2007), pp. 147–65; J. Greatrex, 'On Ministering to "Certayne Devoute and Religiouse Women": Bishop Fox and the Benedictine nuns of Winchester diocese on the eve of the dissolution', *Studies in Church History*, xxvii (1990), pp. 223–35; M.C. Erler, 'Bishop Richard Foxe's manuscript gifts to his Winchester nuns: a second surviving example', *Journal of Ecclesiastical History*, lii (2001), pp. 334–7.
107. Hughes, *Pastors and Visionaries*, p. 156; Keen, *Social History*, pp. 255–6.
108. Skelton, *Complete English Poems*, ed. Scattergood, Collyn Clout, lines 132–41, p. 250.
109. TNA, PRO, SP1/29 (*LP*, VIII 839); *LP*, VIII 1019; cf. Richard Morison's comment that it was long since he had seen bishops in pulpits: *LP*, XI 1409; on Fisher, see M. Dowling, 'John Fisher and the preaching ministry', *Archiv für Reformationsgeschichte*, lxxxii (1991), pp. 292–3; cf. Thompson, 'English and Welsh Bishops', p. 168.
110. Foxe, *Acts and Monuments*, (1570 edn.), pp. 1251–2 (Foxe, *Acts and Monuments*, v. 174).
111. Tyndale, *Practice of Prelates*, sig. A vii.
112. C.S.L. Davies, in *English Historical Review*, cv (1990), p. 724.
113. C. Harper-Bill, 'Archbishop John Morton and the Province of Canterbury, 1486–1500', *Journal of Ecclesiastical History*, xxix (1978), p. 19.
114. Kelly, 'Episcopate of Warham', pp. 43–5.
115. Ibid., pp. 55–94.
116. Gwyn, *King's Cardinal*, pp. 278–81, 305–7.
117. BL, Cotton MS, Cleopatra F i. fo. 260v (Cranmer, *Writings and Letters*, pp. 304–6; *LP*, VIII 704).
118. A point emphasised to me by Tim Reuter.
119. Dowling, 'John Fisher and the preaching ministry', pp. 309, 297–8.
120. Tudor, 'English devotional literature', pp. 47, 56.
121. Harper-Bill, *Pre-Reformation Church*, pp. 31–2.
122. *LP*, III i 137, 1124.
123. *LP*, III i 77 (1, 3), from Wilkins, *Concilia*, iii. 662.

124. Haines, *Ecclesia Anglicana*, p. 228.

125. Thompson, 'English and Welsh Bishops', pp. 147–8.

126. *LP*, III i 1122; cf. Gwyn, *King's Cardinal*, p. 315; cf. Swanson, *Church and Society*, pp. 316–17, on Wolsey.

127. Cameron, *European Reformation*, pp. 43–5.

128. *LP*, III i 1122.

129. TNA, PRO, SP1/46 fo. 110 (*LP*, IV ii 3815).

130. Harper-Bill, *Pre-Reformation Church*, p. 33; Swanson, *Church and Society*, p. 317; Gwyn, *King's Cardinal*, pp. 464–9; G. Walker, *Plays of Persuasion* (Cambridge, 1991), pp. 105–32.

131. Harper-Bill, *Pre-Reformation Church*, p. 28.

132. Ibid., pp. 92–3.

133. Harper-Bill, 'Archbishop Morton', p. 2.

134. Davies, 'The episcopate', p. 51.

4 Clergy

1. N. Lemaitre, *Le Rouergue flamboyant* (Paris, 1988), p. 250.

2. R.N. Swanson, 'Problems of the priesthood in pre-Reformation England', *English Historical Review*, cv (1990), pp. 857, 848; J. Bossy, *Christianity in the West 1400–1700* (Oxford, 1985), pp. 65–6. On priests and the comforting of the sick see the sensitive discussion by P. Horden, 'Small beer? The parish and the poor and sick in later medieval England', in C. Burgess and E. Duffy, eds., *The Parish in Late Medieval England* (Donington, 2006), pp. 360–4.

3. Geoffrey Chaucer, *The Canterbury Tales*, general prologue, lines 479–82, in L.D. Benson, ed., *The Riverside Chaucer* (3rd edn., Boston, MA, 1987).

4. Harper-Bill, *Pre-Reformation Church*, pp. 50–1.

5. Swanson, 'Problems of the priesthood', p. 845.

6. *LP*, I ii 2862 (4).

7. P. Marshall, *The Catholic Priesthood and the English Reformation* (Oxford, 1994), p. 142.

8. TNA, PRO, SP2/m. fo. 199v (*LP*, V 1788).

9. TNA, PRO, SP1/97 fo. 37 (*LP*, IX 463 (2)).

10. Marshall, *Catholic Priesthood.*, p. 144.

11. Ibid., pp. 144–5.

12. TNA, PRO, SP1/91 fo. 170 (*LP*, VIII 496).

13. BL, Cotton MS, Cleopatra, E iv fo. 151 (T. Wright, ed., *Letters relating to the suppression of the monasteries*, Camden Society, xxvi (1843), no. lxxviii, p. 160; *LP*, XII ii 81).

14. TNA, PRO, SP1/142 fo. 223 (*LP*, XIV i 206).

15. D.G. Shaw, *The Creation of a Community: the City of Wells in the Middle Ages* (Oxford, 1993), p. 257.

16. P. Marshall, 'Attitudes of the English people to priests and priesthood, 1500–1553', Univ. of Oxford D.Phil. thesis, 1990, pp.199–200.

17. Marshall, *Catholic Priesthood*, pp. 51–3.

18. Ibid., p. 167.

19. cf. Cameron, *European Reformation*, p. 75; F. Oakley, *The Western Church in the Later Middle Ages* (Ithaca, NY, 1979), pp. 160–1.

20. Marshall, *Catholic Priesthood*, p. 125.

21. L. Wooding, in *Journal of Ecclesiastical History*, xlvii (1996), pp. 379–81.

22. Marshall, 'Attitudes of the English people to priests and priesthood', pp. 234–5.

23. Marshall, *Catholic Priesthood*, p. 163; id., 'Attitudes of the English people to priests and priesthood', p. 221; cf. Morris, *Papal Monarchy*, pp. 100, 172.

24. cf. Oakley, *Western Church*, pp. 160–1.

25. *LP*, IV, iii 5416.

26. Swanson, 'Problems of the priesthood', p. 845.
27. Thompson, 'English and Welsh Bishops', p. 107.
28. Ibid., p. 108.
29. cf. K.L. Wood-Legh, ed., *Kentish Visitations of Archbishop Warham and his Deputies, 1511–12*, Kent Archaeological Society, *Kent Records*, xxiv (1984), pp. xviii–xix.
30. N. Tanner, *The Church in the Later Middle Ages* (2008), p. 57.
31. A question posed of Flanders by J. Toussaert, *Le sentiment religieux en Flandre à la fin du moyen âge* (Paris, 1963), p. 51.
32. N. Orme, 'Popular religion and the Reformation in England: a view from Cornwall', in J.D. Tracy and M. Ragnow, eds., *Religion and the Early Modern State* (Cambridge, 2005), pp. 351–75 at 353–4 (these figures include household chapels); id., 'The other parish churches: chapels in late-medieval England', in C. Burgess and E. Duffy, eds., *The Parish in Late Medieval England* (Donington, 2006), pp. 78–94.
33. A. Watkin, ed., *Inventory of Church Goods temp. Edward III: Archdeaconry of Norwich*, xix (i–ii) (1947–8), ii.
34. C.H. Lawrence, 'The English parish and its clergy in the thirteenth century', in P. Linehan and J.L. Nelson, eds., *The Medieval World* (2000), p. 666.
35. J. Loach, 'Mary Tudor and the recatholicisation of England', *History Today* (Nov. 1994), p. 19; E. Duffy, *Fires of Faith* (New Haven, CT, 2009).
36. cf. Haigh, *English Reformations*, p. 42; J.R. Lander, *Government and Community: England 1450–1509* (1980), p. 133.
37. BL, Cotton MS, Cleopatra E, v fo. 304 (*LP*, XIII ii 147).
38. BL, Cotton MS, Cleopara E, vi fo. 329 (H. Ellis, *Original Letters illustrative of British History* (11 vols. in 3 series), III ii 337, *LP*, VIII 963).
39. N. Tanner, 'The reformation and regionalism: further reflections on the church in late medieval Norwich', in J.A.F. Thomson, ed., *Towns and Townspeople in the Fifteenth Century* (Gloucester, 1988), p. 137.
40. Swanson, *Church and Society*, p. 88; Lander, *Government and Community*, p. 131.
41. cf. also Marshall, *Catholic Priesthood*, p. 139.
42. Swanson, 'Problems of the priesthood', pp. 854–5.
43. Tim Reuter emphasised this point to me.
44. Marshall, *Catholic Priesthood*, p. 128. I am puzzled by Nicholas Orme's suggestion that the instructions given by Bishops Shaxton, Latimer, Lee and Veysey to priests to teach the Paternoster, the Ave Maria, the Creed and the Ten Commandments to children and young people were 'a new policy': N. Orme, 'Children and the church in medieval England', *Journal of Ecclesiastical History*, xlv (1994), pp. 565–6.
45. Marshall, *Catholic Priesthood*, pp. 90–1.
46. D. Lepine, *A Brotherhood of Canons Serving God: English Secular Cathedrals in the Later Middle Ages* (Woodbridge, 1995), pp. 137–9.
47. M. Dowling, 'John Fisher and the preaching ministry', *Archiv für Reformationsgeschichte*, lxxxii (1991), pp. 288–9.
48. For example, Phelip, late parson of St Mary Woolchurch (TNA, PRO, SP1/94 fo. 1 (*LP*, VIII 1000)); Thomas Corthorp, curate of Harwich (TNA, PRO, SP1/99 fo. 173 (*LP*, IX 1059)); Dr Lush, vicar of Aylesbury (TNA, PRO, SP1/144 fo. 112 (*LP*, XIV i 525)).
49. TNA, PRO, SP1/139 fo. 179 (*LP*, XIII ii 953).
50. BL, Cotton MS, Cleopatra E vi fo. 243v (*LP*, VIII 963). cf. *LP*, IX 1091, X 286, XIV i 334, ii app. 7.
51. Thomson, *Early Tudor Church and Society*, p. 316.
52. Cranmer, *Writings and Letters*, p. 283 (*LP*, VII 463).
53. TNA, PRO, SP1/97 fo. 37 (*LP*, IX 463 (2)).
54. 27 Henry c.25 (*Statutes of the Realm*, iii. 559–61).
55. Orme, 'Popular Religion and the Reformation', pp. 363–4. Great Walsingham, Norfolk, has a complete set of fifteenth-century benches (N. Pevsner and B. Wilson, *Norfolk 1: Norwich and North East Norfolk* (Harmondsworth, 1997), p. 486).
56. Thomson, *Early Tudor Church and Society*, p. 317.

57. Hughes, *Pastors and Visionaries*, pp. 146–8.
58. Tudor, 'Devotional Literature', p. 137; S. Powell, 'Mirk, John (*fl. c.*1382–1414)', *ODNB*; S. Powell, 'The Festial: the priest and his parish', in C. Burgess and E. Duffy, eds., *The Parish in Late Medieval England* (Donington, 2006), pp. 160–76.
59. N. Tanner, *The Church in Late Medieval Norwich 1370–1532* (Toronto, 1984), pp. 35–7.
60. Duffy, *Stripping of the Altars*, pp. 55–6.
61. Tudor, 'Devotional Literature', p. 40.
62. *LP*, XIII i 1106.
63. TNA, PRO, SP1/171 fo. 123 (*LP*, VIII 171).
64. R.L. Storey, 'Recruitment of English clergy in the period of the conciliar movement', *Annuarium Historiae Conciliorum*, vii (1975), pp. 290–313; J. Moran, 'Clerical recruitment in the diocese of York, 1340–1530: data and commentary', *Journal of Ecclesiastical History*, xxxiv (1983), pp. 20, 47.
65. Haigh, *English Reformations*, p. 44.
66. Moran, 'Clerical recruitment in the diocese of York', pp. 20, 47.
67. V. Davis, 'Rivals for ministry? Ordination of secular and regular clergy in southern England, *c.*1300–1500', *Studies in Church History*, xvi (1989), p. 104.
68. Harper-Bill, *Pre-Reformation Church*, p. 47.
69. Swanson, 'Problems of the priesthood', p. 862.
70. R. Whiting, 'Local responses to the Reformation', in D. MacCulloch, ed., *The Reign of Henry VIII* (Basingstoke, 1995), p. 206.
71. Ibid., p. 46.
72. R.N. Swanson, 'Learning and livings: university study and clerical careers in later medieval England', *History of Universities*, vi (1986–7), pp. 86, 97; id., *Church and Society*, p. 33.
73. Storey, 'Ordination of secular priests', esp. pp. 128–30 (Reg Ward has made a similar point based on a study of the diocese of Winchester in the eighteenth century); Harper-Bill, 'Dean Colet's convocation sermon', p. 207.
74. G. Williams, *The Welsh Church: from Conquest to Reformation* (Cardiff, 2nd edn., 1976), p. 519.
75. N. Orme, *Unity and Variety: A History of the Church in Devon and Cornwall* (Exeter, 1991), p. 53.
76. Swanson, 'Problems of the priesthood', p. 863.
77. Swanson, *Church and Society*, p. 38
78. Tanner, *The Church in the Later Middle Ages*, pp. 59–60.
79. Swanson, *Church and Society*, p. 54.
80. BL, Cotton MS, Cleopatra E vi fo. 243 (*LP*, VIII 963).
81. Swanson, *Church and Society*, p. 52; A.K. McHardy, 'Careers and disappointments in the late medieval church: some English evidence', *Studies in Church History*, xxvi (1989), p. 129.
82. Cranmer, *Writings and Letters*, pp. 364–5.
83. Swanson, 'Universities, graduates and benefices', p. 40.
84. Swanson, 'Learning and livings', p. 96.
85. M. Harvey, 'The benefice as property: an aspect of Anglo-papal relations during the pontificate of Martin V, 1417–31', *Studies in Church History*, xxiv (1987), p. 172.
86. Swanson, 'Problems of the priesthood', p. 845.
87. TNA, PRO, SP1/76 fo. 19 (Cranmer, *Letters and Writings*, pp. 240–1; *LP*, VI 447).
88. For an exploration, see Slavin, 'Roots of the Reformation'.
89. Bowker, *Secular Clergy*, p. 73.
90. Marshall, 'Attitudes of the English people to priests and priesthood', p. 263.
91. TNA, SP1/73 fo. 49 (*LP*, V 1703 (iii)).
92. 27 Henry VIII c. 63 (*Statutes of the Realm*, iii. 648).
93. 21 Henry VIII c. 13 (*Statutes of the Realm*, iii. 292–6).
94. 28 Henry VIII c. 13 (*Statutes of the Realm*, iii. 668–9).

95. TNA, PRO, SP1/100 fo. 89 (*LP*, IX 1147); cf. R. Whiting, *The Blind Devotion of the People* (Cambridge, 1988), p. 124.
96. McHardy, 'Careers and disappointments', p. 129.
97. C. Phythian-Adams, 'Rituals of personal confrontation in late medieval England', *Bulletin of the John Rylands Library*, lxxiii (1991), p. 83.
98. Swanson, *Church and Society*, pp. 46, 48; McHardy, 'Careers and disappointments', p. 119.
99. L.M. Stevens Benham, 'The Durham clergy, 1494–1540: a study of continuity and mediocrity among the unbeneficed', in D. Marcombe, ed., *The Last Principality: Politics, Religion and Society in the Bishopric of Durham 1494–1660* (Nottingham, 1987), p. 10.
100. McHardy, 'Careers and disappointments', p. 124.
101. C. Burgess, ' "For the increase of divine service": chantries in the parish in late medieval Bristol', *Journal of Ecclesiastical History*, xxxvi (1985), pp. 46–65.
102. Swanson, *Church and Society*, p. 62.
103. Lawrence, 'The English parish and its clergy', p. 656.
104. TNA, PRO, SP1/136 fo.166 (*LP*, XIII ii 403).
105. R.N. Swanson, 'Standards of livings: parochial revenues in pre-reformation England', in C. Harper-Bill, ed., *Religious Belief and Ecclesiastical Careers in Late Medieval England* (Woodbridge, 1991), p. 153.
106. Swanson, *Church and Society*, p. 62.
107. J. Pound, 'Clerical poverty in early sixteenth-century England: some East Anglian evidence', *Journal of Ecclesiastical History*, xxxvii (1986), pp. 389–96.
108. P. Mackie, 'Chaplains in the diocese of York, 1480–1530: the testamentary evidence', *Yorkshire Archaeological Journal*, lviii (1986), pp. 125–6; R.B. Dobson, 'Citizens and chantries in late medieval York', in D. Abulafia, M. Franklin and M. Rubin, eds, *Church and City 1000–1500* (Cambridge, 1992), p. 329.
109. Some interesting parallels may be found in F. Ciappara, 'The financial condition of parish priests in late eighteenth-century Malta', *Journal of Ecclesiastical History*, liii (2002), pp. 93–107.
110. These remarks are prompted by W.M. Jacob, *Journal of Ecclesiastical History*, lviii (2007), p. 586.
111. R.K. Turvey, 'Priest and patron: a study of a gentry family's patronage in south-west Wales in the later middle ages', *Journal of Welsh Ecclesiastical History*, viii (1991), p. 18.
112. Marshall, *Catholic Priesthood*, p. 170.
113. TNA, PRO, SP1/85 fos. 72–3 (*LP*, VII 991).
114. Christopher St German, *A Treatise concerning the division between the spiritualtie and temporaltie*, in *The Complete Works of St Thomas More*, IX, ed. J.B Trapp (1979), p. 187.
115. Phythian-Adams, 'Rituals of personal confrontation', p. 84; cf. Marshall, 'Attitudes of the English people to priests and priesthood', p. 175.
116. Marshall, *Catholic Priesthood*, p. 151.
117. Morris, *Papal Monarchy*, pp. 247, 288.
118. Lepine, *Brotherhood of Canons*, pp. 1–8.
119. Shaw, *Creation of a Community*, p. 257.
120. D. Lepine, 'The Courtenays and Exeter Cathedral in the later middle ages', *Transactions of the Devonshire Association*, cxxiv (1992), pp. 41–4.
121. R.B. Dobson, 'Cathedral chapters and cathedral cities: York, Durham and Carlisle in the fifteenth century', *Northern History*, xix (1983), p. 27.
122. Lepine, *Brotherhood of Canons*, pp. 89, 96–7, 104, 108–9, 145.
123. Cranmer, *Writings and Letters*, pp. 396–7; Lepine, *Brotherhood of Canons*, p. 17.
124. Lepine, *Brotherhood of Canons*, pp. 155, 160, 173.
125. TNA, PRO, SP1/113 fo. 30 (*LP*, XI 1371).
126. Keen, *English Society*, p. 258.

127. Marshall, *Catholic Priesthood*, p. 103.

128. Ibid., pp. 126, 236; Cameron, *European Reformation*, p. 34; cf. L. Wooding, *Journal of Ecclesiastical History*, xlvii (1996), pp. 379–81.

129. E. Duffy, *The Voices of Morebath: Reformation and Rebellion in an English Village* (New Haven, CT, 2001).

130. BL, Cotton MS, Cleopatra E vi fos. 350v–351 (*LP*, XI 210).

131. R.G. Davies, 'John Schorne (d. by 1315)', *ODNB*; R. Marks, 'A late medieval pilgrimage cult: Master John Schorn of North Marston and Windsor', in L. Keen and E. Scarff, eds., *Windsor: Medieval Archaeology, Art and Architecture of the Thames Valley*, British Archaeological Association Conference Transactions, xxv (2002), pp. 192–207, for the suggestion that Schorn miraculously conjured the devil *out* of the boot (p. 194). Schorn was never canonised but he was painted as a saint on the rood screens in three Norfolk churches, Cawston, *c*.1460, Suffield and Gateley (N. Pevsner and B. Wilson, *Norfolk 1: Norwich and North-East Norfolk* (Harmondsworth, 1997), pp. 430, 681; id., *Norfolk 2: North-West and South Norfolk* (Harmondsworth, 1999), p. 351).

132. N. Orme, 'Bishop Grandisson and Popular Religion', *Transactions of the Devonshire Association*, cxxiv (1992), pp. 113–14.

5 Lay Knowledge

1. R. Lane Fox, *Pagans and Christians in the Mediterranean World from the Second Century AD to the Conversion of Constantine* (1986), p. 330.

2. A. Cameron, 'The cult of the Virgin in late antiquity: religious development and myth-making', *Studies in Church History*, xxxix (2004), pp. 1–21; H. Mayr-Harting, 'The idea of the assumption of Mary in the west, 800–1200', *Studies in Church History*, xxxix (2004), pp. 86–111; M. Heimann, *Journal of Ecclesiastical History*, lx (2009), p. 866.

3. Blair, *The Church in Anglo-Saxon Society*, p. 3 for the definition, almost too capacious to be serviceable.

4. J. Blair and R. Sharpe, eds., *Pastoral Care before the Parish* (Leicester, 1992), most vividly A. Thacker, 'Monks, preaching and pastoral care in early Anglo-Saxon England', pp. 137–70.

5. cf. Henry Mayr-Harting's insistence that 'it is impossible to cite any Christian scholar or ascetic in early Anglo-Saxon history who thought it necessary or even right to wash his hands of his fellow men in order to devote himself to God'; H.Mayr-Harting, *The Coming of Christianity to Anglo-Saxon England* (Pennsylvania, PA, 3rd edn., 1991), p. 4; and pp. 242–3.

6. C.S. Drake, *The Romanesque Fonts of Northern Europe and Scandinavia* (Woodbridge, 2002).

7. Blair, *The Church in Anglo-Saxon Society*, p. 393.

8. Bede, *Historia Ecclesiastica*, ed. C. Plummer (Oxford, 1896), pp. 303–9, 163–8.

9. I draw on the stimulating sketch by R.W. Southern, 'Between heaven and hell', p. 652; cf. Nelson, 'Society, theodicy and the origins of heresy', pp. 66–77. S. Foot, 'Anglo-Saxon "purgatory"', *Studies in Church History*, xlv (2009), seems unnecessarily defensive about the coherence of what she shows.

10. Swanson, *Church and Society*, p. 276; Morris, *Papal Monarchy*, p. 494.

11. P. Tudor, 'Religious instruction for children and adolescents in the early Reformation', *Journal of Ecclesiastical History*, xxxv (1984), pp. 398–9, 392–3.

12. I. Green, *The Christian's ABC: Catechisms and Catechizing in England c.1530–1740* (Oxford, 1996), p. 16.

13. N. Orme, *From Childhood to Chivalry: The Education of the English Kings and Aristocracy 1066–1530* (1984), pp. 128–9.

14. N. Orme, *Education and Society in Medieval and Renaissance England* (1989), pp. 23–31 at p. 25.

15. cf. J. van Engen, 'The christian middle ages as an historiographical problem', *American Historical Review*, xci (1986), p. 543.
16. Duffy, *Stripping of the Altars*, p. 2.
17. C. Morris, 'Introduction', in C. Morris and P. Roberts, eds., *Pilgrimage: The English Experience from Becket to Bunyan* (Cambridge, 2002), p. 9. For comparable doubts see A. Murray, 'Piety and impiety in thirteenth-century Italy', *Studies in Church History*, viii (1972), p. 93; D. Wood, 'Discipline and diversity in the medieval English Sunday', *Studies in Church History*, xliii (2007), pp. 202–11 (on episcopal measures dealing with non-attendance).
18. Williams, *Welsh Church*, p. 511.
19. Orme, *Unity and Variety*, p. 58.
20. TNA, PRO, SP1/111 fo. 54 (*LP*, XI 1041).
21. BL, Cotton MS, Cleopatra E vi fo. 255v (*LP*, X 625).
22. A.A. King, *Liturgies of the Past* (1959), pp. 276–7.
23. P. Draper, 'Architecture and Liturgy', in J. Alexander and P. Binski, *Age of Chivalry: Art in Plantagenet England* (1987), p. 83.
24. King, *Liturgies of the Past*, p. 285; T. Webber, *Scribes and Scholars at Salisbury Cathedral c.1075–c.1125* (Oxford, 1992).
25. R.W. Pfaff, 'Prescription and reality in the rubrics of Sarum Rite service books', in L. Smith and B. Ward, eds., *Intellectual Life in the Middle Ages* (1992), pp. 204, 197–202. I am grateful to Tessa Webber for this reference.
26. Orme, *Unity and Variety*, p. 71; O.T. Edwards, 'How many Sarum antiphons were there in England and Wales in the middle of the sixteenth century?', *Revue Benedictine*, xcix (1989), pp. 156–8; W.H. Frere, ed., *The Use of Sarum* (2 vols., Cambridge, 1898–1901), i. xxxii; A.W. Pollard, G.R. Redgrave, W.A. Jackson, F.S. Ferguson and K.F. Pantzer, eds., *Revised Short Title Catalogue 1475–1640* (1976), pp. 70–2.
27. King, *Liturgies of the Past*, pp. 313–24. For detailed consideration of the differences between uses, see R.W. Pfaff, *The Liturgy in Medieval England: A History* (Cambridge, 2009).
28. R. Hutton, *The Stations of the Sun* (Oxford, 1996); id., 'The making of pre-reformation England', paper read at Institute of Historical Research, 11 February 1991; Duffy, *Stripping of the Altars*, esp. p. 11; D. Cressy, *Bonfires and Bells: National Memory and the Protestant Calendar in Elizabethan and Early Stuart England* (1990); V. Edden, 'The devotional life of the laity in the late middle ages', in D. Dyas, V. Edden and R. Ellis, eds., *Approaching the Medieval Anchoritic and Mystical Texts* (Woodbridge, 2005), pp. 39–40.
29. Lemaitre, *Rouergue Flamboyant*, p. 321.
30. Morris, *Papal Monarchy*, p. 298.
31. cf. C. Burgess, 'A service for the dead: the form and function of the anniversary in late medieval Bristol', *Transactions of the Bristol and Gloucestershire Archaeological Society* (1978), p. 189.
32. cf. Duffy, *Stripping of the Altars*, p. 91; B. Hamilton, *Religion in the Medieval West* (1986), pp. 44–5, 115–17. An especially vivid evocation of the mass is offered by V. Reinburg, 'Liturgy and the laity in late medieval and Reformation France', *Sixteenth-Century Journal*, xxiii (1992), 526–47.
33. 1 Corinthians:11:23–6
34. Bossy, *Christianity in the West*, pp. 67–8; J. Chiffoleau, 'La religion flamboyante (v.1320–v.1520)', in F. Lebrun, ed., *Histoire de la France religieuse*: tome 2: *Du christianisme flamboyant a l'aube des lumieres* (Paris, 1988), p. 130.
35. T. Wanegffelen, *Ni Rome ni Genève: des fidèles entre deux chaires en France au XVIe siècle* (Paris, 1997), p. 18; cf. Reinburg, 'Liturgy and the laity', pp. 533–8.
36. Oakley, *Western Church*, p. 88.
37. Duffy, *Stripping of the Altars*, p. 126.
38. *Victoria History of the County of Yorkshire*, iii. 42.

39. Oakley, *Western Church*, pp. 82–4; Morris, *Papal Monarchy*, p. 299; Chiffoleau, 'La religion flamboyante', pp. 78, 130–1, 181; id., *La Comptabilité de l'au-delà: Les hommes, la mort et la religion dans la region d'Avignon à la fin du moyen âge (vers 1320–vers 1480)* (Rome, 1980), p. 247; Toussaert, *Le sentiment religieux en Flandre*, pp. 123, 151, 157–8, 193.

40. Duffy, *Stripping of the Altars*, pp. 112, 116.

41. *State Papers of Henry VIII*, i. 163–5 no. xci (*LP*, IV i 2215); F. Kisby, ' "When the king goes a procession": chapel ceremonies and services, the ritual year, and religious reforms at the early Tudor court, 1485–1547', *Journal of British Studies*, xl (2001), pp. 44–75.

42. I owe this to Roger Bowers, from TNA, PRO, PROB 11/23 frame 99r.

43. C. Richmond, 'Religion and the fifteenth-century English gentleman', in R.B. Dobson, ed., *The Church, Politics and Patronage in the Fifteenth Century* (Gloucester, 1984), pp. 193–208; C. Carpenter, 'The religion of the gentry in fifteenth-century England', in D. Williams, ed., *England in the Fifteenth Century* (Woodbridge, 1987), pp. 53–74.

44. Swanson, *Church and Society*, p. 276.

45. Chiffoleau, 'La religion flamboyante', p. 108; Toussaert, *Le sentiment religieux en Flandre*, p. 68.

46. Tyndale, *Practice of Prelates*, sig. E viii–viiiv.

47. Duffy, *Stripping of the Altars*, p. 43.

48. S. Reynolds, 'Social mentalities and the case of medieval scepticism', *Transactions of the Royal Historical Society*, 6th. series, I (1991), pp. 21–42, esp. p. 24.

49. R.Knox and S. Leslie, eds., *The Miracles of Henry VI* (Cambridge, 1923), pp. 182, 212–13.

50. R.B. Merriman, ed., *Letters of Thomas Cromwell* (2 vols., Oxford, 1902), i. 104–9.

51. A.D. Brown, *Popular Piety in Late Medieval England: the Diocese of Salisbury 1250–1550* (Oxford, 1995), p. 13.

52. E. Danbury, *Historian*, xlvi (1995), pp. 8, 10.

53. A. Watkin, ed., *Inventory of Church Goods temp. Edward III: Archdeaconry of Norwich*, xix (ii) (1948), xix (i) (1949).

54. Ibid., pp. xxx–xxxi.

55. Ibid., p. xxxiii.

56. Ibid., p. lxxx.

57. Ibid., p. lxxxiii.

58. Ibid., p. lxxxvi.

59. Ibid., pp. xxxii–xxxiii.

60. Ibid., p. xxvi.

61. Ibid., pp. xxviii–xxix.

62. Ibid., p. xxxii.

63. Ibid., pp. xxvii–xxviii.

64. Ibid., pp. xxix–xxx.

65. Ibid., p. xxxii.

66. Ibid., p. lxxxix.

67. C. Sneyd, ed., *A Relation, or rather a True Account of the Island of England . . . about the year 1500*, Camden Society, old ser., xxxvii (1947), p. 29.

68. M. Williamson, 'Liturgical music in the late-medieval parish: organs and voices, ways and means', in C. Burgess and E. Duffy, eds., *The Parish in Late Medieval England* (Donington, 2006), pp. 197–209.

69. E. Duffy, 'The end of it all: the material culture of the medieval English parish and the 1552 inventories of church goods', in Burgess and Duffy, eds., *The Parish in Late Medieval England*, pp. 381–99, esp. pp. 384–91.

70. Nichols, *Pilgrimages by Erasmus*, pp. 44–5.

71. Chiffoleau, 'La religion flamboyante', p. 117.

72. Bede, *Historia Ecclesiastica*, ed. Plummer, p. 369.

73. E. Mâle, *The Gothic Image* (1910, tr. 1913), pp. 3–4, 7, 10, 15–17 and *passim*; cf. E.C. Rouse, *Medieval Wall Paintings* (4th edn., Oxford, 1991).
74. Mâle, *Gothic Image*, pp. 40, 45, 50–5, 60.
75. A. Weir and J. Jerman, *Images of Lust: Sexual Carvings on Medieval Churches* (1999).
76. Mâle, *Gothic Image*, p. 138.
77. Rouse, *Medieval Wall Paintings*, p. 38.
78. Mâle, *Gothic Image*, pp. 186–201; Rouse, *Medieval Wall Painting*, pp. 43–4.
79. Mâle, *Gothic Image*, pp. 208–21.
80. Ibid., pp. 233–61.
81. Ibid., p. 293.
82. Ibid., p. 294.
83. Ibid., pp. 183, 268–70.
84. C. Peters, 'Women and the Reformation: social relations and attitudes in rural England, *c*. 1470–1570', Univ. of Oxford D.Phil. thesis, 1993, pp. 270–8, 312–13.
85. Rouse, *Medieval Wall Paintings*, pp. 57–70.
86. A. Reiss, *The Sunday Christ: Sabbatarianism in English medieval wall painting* (Oxford, 2000), esp. pp. 1–3, 13–21, 52–3, 58, 60.
87. cf. A. Friedlander, 'On the provenance of the Holy Shroud of Turin: a minor suggestion', *Journal of Ecclesiastical History*, lvii (2006), pp. 457–77; D. Trembinski, '[Pro] Passio Doloris: early Dominican conceptions of Christ's physical pain', *Journal of Ecclesiastical History*, lix (2008), pp. 630–56.
88. Chiffoleau, 'La religion flamboyante', p. 118.
89. The case is vividly made in Toussaert, *Le sentiment religieux en Flandre*, esp. pp. 16, 66–8, 75, 79, 83, dismissing the liturgy as 'a lullaby for souls' (p. 83).
90. L. Salzman, *Building in England down to 1540: A Documentary History* (Oxford, 1952), p. 161.
91. M. Knight, 'Piety and devotion among the Warwickshire gentry, 1485–1547', *Dugdale Society Occasional Papers*, xxxii (1989), pp. 7–8.
92. A. Hamilton, 'Orthodoxy in late fifteenth-century glass at Leicester', *Transactions of the Leicestershire Archaeological and Historical Society*, lv (1979–80), pp. 22–37.
93. Morris, *Papal Monarchy*, p. 504.
94. Toussaert, *Le sentiment religieux en Flandre*, p. 81.
95. I owe this suggestion to Tim Reuter.
96. J. Chittock, 'The medieval wall paintings of St Mary and All Saints, Willingham', *Proceedings of the Cambridge Antiquarian Society*, lxxxi (1992), pp. 77–9.
97. P. Sheingorn, *The Easter Sepulchre in England* (Kalamazoo, MI, 1987), esp. pp. 34–44, 47–9, 57–60.
98. R. Marks, *Image and Devotion in Late Medieval England* (Stroud, 2004).
99. A.F. Johnston, 'What if no texts survived? External evidence for early English drama', in M. Briscoe and J.C. Coldewey, eds., *Contexts for Early English Drama* (Bloomington, 1989), p. 6; R.T. Davies, ed., *The Corpus Christi Play of the English Middle Ages* (1972), p. 23.
100. Johnston, 'External evidence', p. 6.
101. D. Mills, ed., *The Chester Mystery Cycle* (Kalamazoo, MI, 1992), pp. xii–xiii.
102. L.M. Clopper, 'Lay and clerical impact in civic religious drama and ceremony', in Briscoe and Coldewey, *Contexts for Early English Drama*, p. 127.
103. cf. M.E. James, 'Ritual, drama and social body in the late medieval English town', *Past and Present*, xcviii (1983), pp. 13, 17, reprinted in id., *Society, Politics and Culture* (Cambridge, 1986), pp. 16–47.
104. J. Goldberg, 'Craft guilds, the Corpus Christi play and civic government', in S. Rees-Jones, ed., *The Government of Medieval York*, Borthwick Studies in History, iii (1997), pp. 149–50; id., 'Performing the word of God: Corpus Christi drama in the northern province', *Studies in Church History*, Subsidia, xii (1999), pp. 145–70.
105. Duffy, *Stripping of the Altars*, p. 27.

106. L.M. Clopper, ed., *Chester*, Records of Early English Drama (Manchester, 1979), p. 27.

107. James, 'Ritual, drama and social body', p. 4.

108. Clopper, 'Lay and clerical impact', pp. 111, 112, 128.

109. M. Stevens, *Four Middle English Mystery Cycles* (Princeton, NJ, 1987), p. 13; James, 'Ritual, drama and social body', pp. 5–6.

110. Johnston, 'External evidence', p. 11.

111. H. Craig, *English Religious Drama of the Middle Ages* (Oxford, 1955), pp. 21–2, 29; C. Richardson and J. Johnston, *Medieval Drama* (1991), p. 3; Blair, *The Church in Anglo-Saxon Society*, pp. 486–9.

112. Chiffoleau, 'La religion flamboyante', p. 97.

113. cf. Southern, 'Between heaven and hell', *TLS*, 18 June 1982; Stevens, *Four Middle English Mystery Cycles*, pp. 64–5.

114. Stevens, *Four Middle English Mystery Cycles*, p. 65.

115. Clopper, 'Lay and clerical impact', p. 28.

116. Richardson and Johnston, *Medieval Drama*, pp. 24, 39.

117. Mills, *Chester Mystery Cycle*, pp. xi–xii, xx–xxi; Davies, *Corpus Christi Play*, p. 31; Stevens, *Four Middle English Mystery Cycles*, p. 14; Craig, *English Religious Drama*, pp. 133–4; James, 'Ritual, drama and social body', pp. 12, 21; Richardson and Johnston, *Medieval Drama*, pp. 13–15, 21–2, 24, 43–4; E. Prosser, *Drama and Religion in the English Mystery Plays* (Stanford, CA, 1961), pp. 21–2, 24–5; P. A. King, *The York Mystery Cycle and the Worship of the City* (Cambridge, 2006), p. 8, and for detailed elaboration, chs. 2–5.

118. Stevens, *Four Middle English Mystery Cycles*, pp. 12, 14.

119. A.F. Johnston, 'The plays of the religious guilds of York: the Creed play and the Pater Noster play', *Speculum*, l (1975), pp. 57–9, 71.

120. Stevens, *Four Middle English Mystery Cycles*, p. 275.

121. R. Woolf, *The English Mystery Plays* (Berkeley, CA, 1972), p. 303.

122. Richardson and Johnston, *Medieval Drama*, p. 65; Hughes, *Pastors and Visionaries*, pp. 286–8; Prosser, *Drama and Religion*, p. 25.

123. Stevens, *Four Middle English Mystery Cycles*, p. 231.

124. Ibid., p. 323.

125. Mills, *Chester Mystery Cycle*, pp. xxii.

126. The gilds were weak and subordinate to the magistracy in London and Exeter, argues Mervyn James, 'Ritual, drama and social body', pp. 23–5.

127. J.C. Coldewey, 'Some economic aspects of the late medieval drama', in Briscoe and Coldewey, *Contexts for Early English Drama*, p. 93.

128. A.F. Johnston, 'Parish playmaking before the reformation', in C. Burgess and E. Duffy, eds., *The Parish in Late Medieval England* (Donington, 2006), pp. 322–38.

129. Duffy, *Stripping of the Altars*, pp. 3–4; F. Lewis, ' "Garnished with gloryous tytles": indulgences in printed Books of Hours in England', *Transactions of the Cambridge Bibliographical Society*, x, part v (1995), pp. 577–90.

130. Duffy, *Stripping of the Altars*, pp. 62, 77–8; id., 'Elite and popular religion: the book of hours and lay piety in the later middle ages', *Studies in Church History*, xlii (2006), pp. 140–61; Tudor, 'Devotional literature', pp. 13–15, 130, 112, 91, 97.

131. M. Clanchy, 'Images of Ladies with Prayer Books', *Studies in Church History*, xxxviii (2004), pp. 106–22.

132. Clanchy, 'Images of Ladies with Prayer Books'; A. Walsham, 'Jewels for Gentlewomen: religious books as artefacts in late medieval and early modern England', *Studies in Church History*, xxxviii (2004), pp. 125–8; Duffy, *Stripping of the Altars*, pp. 214, 289–90.

133. M.K. Jones and M. Underwood, *The King's Mother* (Cambridge, 1992), pp. 171–201, 150–4; M., Clanchy, 'Images of Ladies with Prayer Books', pp. 109–11.

134. M.A. Hicks, 'Four studies in conventional piety', *Southern History* (1991), pp. 16–17.
135. Morris, *Papal Monarchy*, p. 309.
136. Duffy, *Stripping of the Altars*, p. 57; C. Cox, *Pulpits, Lecterns and Organs in English Churches* (1915).
137. *LP*, III ii 1527.
138. BL, Cotton MS, Cleopatra, E iv fo. 118 (*LP*, XIII i 634 (1)).
139. D. Daniell, *William Tyndale* (New Haven, CT, 1994), pp. 58, 100, 398.
140. Foxe, *Acts and Monuments* (1570 edn.), p. 1188 (*Foxe, Acts and Monuments*, v. 34).
141. Daniell, *Tyndale*, pp. 92–3.
142. Ibid., p. 100.
143. N.R. Ker, *Medieval Libraries of Great Britain* (2nd edn., 1964) lists manuscripts in the London Charterhouse (p. 122), Newcastle-upon-Tyne (p. 134), Syon (p. 186) and Thetford (p. 189). A.W. Reed, *Early Tudor Drama* (1926), pp. 3–4, notes a Bible bequeathed to Trinity Church, Coventry, by Richard Cooke, sometime mayor of Coventry, in 1507.
144. Daniell, *Tyndale*, pp. 99–100, disputing with Duffy, *Stripping of the Altars*, p. 79.
145. F. Higman, *Journal of Ecclesiastical History*, xlix (1998), p. 728.
146. J. van Engen, 'The christian middle ages as an historiographical problem', *American Historical Review*, xci (1986), pp. 519, 522, 529–30, 528, 550.
147. The treatment of popular religion in K.V. Thomas, *Religion and the Decline of Magic* (1971) is perhaps open to such a reading. Euan Cameron shows that late medieval theologians wrote vigorously against just such superstitious beliefs and practices: E. Cameron, *Enchanted Europe: Superstition, Reason, and Religion, 1250–1750* (Oxford, 2010), esp. pp. 70–1.
148. P. Morison, 'The miraculous and French society, *c.*950–1100', Univ. of Oxford D.Phil. thesis, 1983, pp. 111–12.
149. P. Griffith, in *Continuity and Change*, ix (1994), pp. 355–7.
150. cf. Bishop Saint Papoul, the mysterious spring, and the associated pilgrimage at La Plaigne (Chiffoleau, 'La religion flamboyante', p. 75).
151. S. Reynolds, 'Social mentalities and the case of medieval scepticism', *Transactions of the Royal Historical Society*, 6th series, i (1991), p. 38; cf. Morris, *Papal Monarchy*, p. 6. That is also the thrust of much writing by Ronald Hutton.
152. cf. Cameron, *Enchanted Europe*, p. 314.
153. Blair, *The Church in Anglo-Saxon Society*, pp. 167–9, 179.
154. Morison, 'The miraculous and French society', p. 113.
155. cf. V. Flint, *The Rise of Magic in Early Medieval Europe* (Oxford, 1991), p. 407.
156. Harper-Bill, *Pre-Reformation Church*, pp. 66, 88.
157. *LP*, III i 567.
158. Swanson, *Church and Society*, p. 276.
159. Chiffoleau, 'La religion flamboyante', p. 142.
160. J. Chiffoleau, *La Comptabilité de l'au-delà: Les hommes, la mort et la religion dans la région d'Avignon à la fin du Moyen Âge* (Rome, 1980, rev. edn., Paris, 2011), p. 219 (citations are from the 2011 edition).
161. R.N. Swanson, *Indulgences in Late Medieval England: Passports to Paradise?* (Cambridge, 2007).
162. Chiffoleau, 'La religion flamboyante', p. 145.
163. A. Vauchez, *Les laics au moyen âge: Pratiques et expériences religieuses* (Paris, 1987), p. 34.
164. Hughes, *Pastors and Visionaries*, p. 233.
165. Ibid., pp. 286, 288.
166. cf. C. Morris, in *English Historical Review*, xcvii (1982), p. 411; N. Tanner, in *Journal of Ecclesiastical History*, xlvii (1996), p. 727.

167. cf. Hamilton, *Religion in the Medieval West*, p. 73, though note remarks on the overlap between learned and popular religion, p. 199.
168. Cameron, *Enchanted Europe*, p. 138.
169. Keen, *English Society*, pp. 278–9.
170. B. Ward, *Miracles and the Medieval Mind* (Aldershot, 2nd. edn., 1987), p. 215.
171. Williams, *Welsh Church*, pp. 464, 477.
172. Morris, *Papal Monarchy*, p. 502.
173. Cameron, *Enchanted Europe*, p. 19.
174. cf. Morris, *Papal Monarchy*, p. 502: 'it is impossible to distinguish between christian and pagan magic'.
175. Duffy, *Stripping of the Altars*, pp. 15–18.
176. Ibid., p. 75.
177. Ibid. p. 72.
178. Ibid., pp. 214, 231.
179. Ibid., p. 269.
180. Ibid., p. 275.
181. Ibid., pp. 277–8.
182. Ibid., pp. 279–81.
183. Toussaert, *Le sentiment religieux*, p. 274.
184. Quotation chosen by Keith Thomas as the epigraph for *Religion and the Decline of Magic*, p. xxi; Keen, *English Society*, pp. 296–7. 'For the typical peasant farmer', Helen Rawlings has noted of sixteenth-century Spain, 'religion was intimately related to the natural world around him. It was a hostile, unpredictable world that engendered a mentality ruled by fears and insecurities. Popular religious culture offered a safe passage, a means of explanation, protection and deliverance in times of hardship': H. Rawlings, *Church, Religion and Society in Early Modern Spain* (Basingstoke, 2002), pp. 89–90.
185. B. Nilson, *Cathedral Shrines of Medieval England* (Woodbridge, 1998). Of course, it could be argued that greater spending on religious works reflected the simple economic reality that after the Black Death survivors were often better off.
186. Knox and Leslie, *Miracles of Henry VI*, my count.
187. *LP*, IV ii 4404 (mass), 4428 (communion), 4440 (made will); 4542 (daily confession, communion at every feast).
188. *LP*, IV ii 4542.
189. T.G. Ashplant and A. Wilson, 'Present-centred history and the problem of historical knowledge', *Historical Journal*, xxxi (1988), p. 259; Cameron, *Enchanted Europe*, pp. 14, 17, 24, 26–7.
190. Swanson, *Church and Society*, pp. 276–7.
191. cf. Huizinga, *Waning of the Middle Ages*, pp. 154–6, 168, 179.
192. Williams, *Welsh Church*, p. 416.
193. Cameron, *European Reformation*, p. 15.
194. Morris, *Papal Monarchy*, pp. 298–9, 309.
195. Reinburg, 'Liturgy and the laity', 526–47.
196. Chiffoleau, *La Comptabilité de l'au-delà*, p. 253.
197. Huizinga, *Waning of the Middle Ages*, p. 163.
198. F. Riddy, 'Kempe, Margery (c.1373–c.1438)', *ODNB*.
199. G. Dickson, 'Revivalism as a medieval religious genre', *Journal of Ecclesiastical History*, li (2000), pp. 473–96.
200. Reinburg, 'Liturgy and the laity', pp. 545–6; Toussaert, *Le sentiment religieux*, pp. 79, 83–4, 216.
201. Toussaert, *Le sentiment religieux*, p. 119; L.G. Duggan, 'Fear and confession on the eve of the Reformation', *Archiv für Reformationsgeschichte*, lxxv (1984), pp. 153–75.
202. G.R. Elton, in *Journal of Ecclesiastical History*, (1993), p. 719.
203. Chiffoleau, 'La religion flamboyante', p. 23.

204. Chiffoleau, 'La religion flamboyante', pp. 127, 130.
205. Ibid., pp. 129, 132, 139, 173, 152, 153–4, 155, 174, 162.
206. Duggan asks if historians' portrayals of late medieval anxiety are all based on Luther's experience ('Fear and confession on the eve of the Reformation', p. 155).
207. cf. remarks by C. Cross, *Journal of Ecclesiastical History*, li (2000), p. 164.
208. William Langland, *Piers Plowman*, Passus I, lines 7–9.
209. *The Kalendar of Shepherdes* (1506) (RSTC 22408) (STC Films 153 A-).
210. W. Roper, *Life of More*, pp. 48–9.
211. *LP*, IV i 995.
212. 25 Henry VIII c. 4 (*Statutes of the Realm*, iii. 440).
213. P. Marshall, 'Fear, purgatory and polemic in Reformation England', in W.G. Naphy and P. Roberts, eds., *Fear in Early Modern Society* (Manchester, 1997), pp. 150–66.
214. cf. remarks in a different context by B.S. Gregory, 'The "True and Zealouse Service of God": Robert Parsons, Edmund Bunney and "The First Booke of the Christian Exercise"', *Journal of Ecclesiastical History*, xlv (1994), pp. 254–8.
215. Van Engen, 'Christian middle ages', p. 547; id., 'Multiple options: the world of the fifteenth-century church', *Church History*, lxxii (2008), esp. pp. 266–84; cf. Duffy, *Stripping of the Altars*, p. 210.

6 Lay Activity

1. R. Hutton, *The Rise and Fall of Merry England: the Ritual Year 1400–1700* (Oxford, 1994), pp. 49–50.
2. For a pair of case-studies see J. Middleton-Stuart, 'Parochial Activity in Late Medieval Fenland: accounts and wills from Tilney All Saints and St Mary's Mildenhall, 1443–1520', in C. Burgess and E. Duffy, eds., *The Parish in Late Medieval England* (Donington, 2006), pp. 283–301.
3. K.L. French, 'Women churchwardens in late medieval England', in Burgess and Duffy, eds., *The Parish in Late Medieval England*, pp. 302–21, esp. pp. 303–4.
4. D. Dymond, 'God's disputed acre', *Journal of Ecclesiastical History*, l (1999), pp. 464–97; R. Hutton, 'Seasonal festivity in late medieval England: some further reflections', *English Historical Review*, cxx (2005), pp. 72–3; Blair, *The Church in Anglo-Saxon Society*, p. 508.
5. Chiffoleau, 'La religion flamboyante', pp. 27, 80, 81.
6. C. Vincent, *Les Confréries médiévales dans le royaume de France: XIIIe-XVe siècle* (Paris, 1994), pp.176–7, 41, 47, 99–101, 187, 103.
7. Ibid., pp. 9, 109, 114, 185.
8. C.M. Barron, 'The parish fraternities of medieval London', in C.M. Barron and C. Harper-Bill, eds., *The Church in Pre-Reformation Society* (Woodbridge, 1985), pp. 13–14, 23–5.
9. C. Cross, 'Communal piety in sixteenth-century Boston', *Lincolnshire History and Archaeology*, xxv (1990), p. 33; Swanson, *Indulgences in Late Medieval England*, pp. 54, 122, 130, 135–6, 375–6, 437, 449.
10. Brown, *Popular Piety*, p. 140.
11. Tanner, 'Reformation and regionalism', p. 132.
12. Pollard, *North-Eastern England during the Wars of the Roses*, pp. 189–90.
13. Duffy, *Stripping of the Altars*, p. 142.
14. C. Burgess, ' "By quick and by dead": wills and pious provision in late medieval Bristol', *English Historical Review*, cii (1987), p. 839 n.7.
15. Vincent, *Confréries médiévales*, pp. 69, 104.
16. G. Rosser, 'Solidarité et changement social. Les fraternités urbaines anglaises à la fin du moyen âge', *Annales*, xlviii (1993), p. 1129.
17. Vincent, *Confréries médiévales*, p. 94.
18. Chiffoleau, 'La religion flamboyante', p. 152.
19. Vincent, *Confréries médiévales*, p. 99.

20. Rosser, 'Les fraternités urbaines anglaises', pp. 1132–3.
21. Vincent, *Confréries médiévales*, p. 18.
22. Ibid., pp. 21–2.
23. Ibid., pp. 59–60, 124–5; cf. Barron, 'Parish fraternities', pp. 24–5; Chiffoleau, *La Comptabilité de l'au-delà*, pp. 286; Rosser, 'Les fraternités urbaines anglaises', p. 1129.
24. cf. Vincent, *Confréries médiévales*, p.98.
25. Ibid., p. 26.
26. Ibid., p. 23.
27. Ibid., p. 24.
28. Ibid., pp. 19, 34.
29. Ibid., pp. 35–6.
30. cf. ibid., pp. 36, 186.
31. Ibid., p. 45.
32. G. Rosser, *Medieval Westminster 1200–1540* (Oxford, 1989), p. 286.
33. Whiting, 'Local responses to the Henrician Reformation', p. 212.
34. cf. Richmond, 'English gentry and religion', pp. 137–8.
35. C. Burgess, ' "For the Increase of Divine Service": chantries in the parish in late medieval Bristol', *Journal of Ecclesiastical History*, xxxvi (1985), pp. 51–9; R. Bowers, 'Aristocratic and popular piety in the patronage of music in the fifteenth-century Netherlands', *Studies in Church History*, xxviii (1992), p. 224; M. Williamson, 'Liturgical music in the late-medieval parish: organs and voices, ways and means', in C. Burgess and E. Duffy, eds., *The Parish in Late Medieval England* (Donington, 2006), pp. 177–242; Orme, *Unity and Variety*, p. 67; D.M. Owen, *Church and Society in Medieval Lincolnshire: History of Lincolnshire*, V (Lincoln, 1971), p. 100; Leland, *Itinerary*, v. 33.
36. Brown, *Popular Piety*, p. 174.
37. Vincent, *Confréries médiévales*, p.111.
38. Harper-Bill, *Pre-Reformation Church*, p. 68.
39. Dobson, 'Citizens and chantries in late medieval York', pp. 328–9.
40. Burgess, 'Chantries in the parish', pp. 59–62; Owen, *Church and Society*, p. 100.
41. Harper-Bill, *Pre-Reformation Church*, p. 74.
42. cf. Shaw, *Creation of a Community*, p. 264; B. Thompson, 'Monasteries and their patrons at foundation and dissolution', *Transactions of the Royal Historical Society*, 6th series, iv (1994), p. 111.
43. Beckett, 'Sheen Charterhouse', p. 87.
44. D. Postles, 'Penance and the market place: a Reformation dialogue with the medieval church (*c*.1250–1600)', *Journal of Ecclesiastical History*, xlvii (1996), p. 121.
45. C. Richmond, 'Religion', in R. Horrox, ed., *Fifteenth-Century Attitudes: Perceptions of Society in Late Medieval England* (Cambridge, 1994), p. 186.
46. A. Gransden, 'The History of Wells Cathedral *c*.1090–1547', in L.S. Colchester, ed., *Wells Cathedral: a history* (1982), p. 45.
47. *LP*, I ii 2617 (21).
48. Tanner, 'Reformation and regionalism', pp. 129–47; Haigh, *English Reformations*, p. 37.
49. *LP*, XIII i 1309 (12).
50. Whiting, 'Local responses to the Henrician Reformation', pp. 214–15.
51. Tyndale, *Practice of prelates*, sig E vi.
52. Dobson, 'Citizens and chantries in late medieval York', p. 313.
53. C. Richmond, *The Paston Family in the Fifteenth Century: the first phase* (Cambridge, 1990), pp. 167–205; id., 'Religion and the fifteenth-century gentleman', in R.B. Dobson, ed., *The Church, Politics and Patronage in the Fifteenth Century* (Gloucester, 1984), p. 195.
54. TNA, PRO, SP1/101 fo. 105 (*LP*, X 138).

55. M.A, Hicks, 'Chantries, obits and almshouses: the Hungerford foundations 1325–1478', in C.M. Barron and C. Harper-Bill, eds., *The Church in Pre-Reformation Society: Essays in Honour of F.R.H. du Boulay* (Woodbridge, 1985), pp. 134–6; cf. Lemaitre, *Rouergue flamboyant*, p. 357.

56. M. Hicks, 'The rising price of piety', in J. Burton and K. Stober, *Monasteries and Society in the British Isles in the Later Middle Ages* (Woodbridge, 2008), pp. 95–109.

57. Bowers, 'Aristocratic and popular piety', 223–4.

58. Lepine, *Brotherhood of Canons*, p. 16.

59. John Frith, *Purgatory*, sig A5, E4.

60. Chiffoleau, *La Comptabilité de l'au-delà*, pp. 355–67, xxxii–xxxiv; id., 'La religion flamboyante', p. 145.

61. TNA, PRO, SP1/98 fo. 146v (*LP*, IX 740).

62. 'Of the relyfyng of saules in purgatory', BL, Additional MS 37049 fo. 24v.

63. J. Scarisbrick, *The Tablet*, 13 Feb. 1993, p. 212.

64. *LP*, VI, 585; C.Tyerman, *England and the Crusades 1095–1588* (Chicago, IL, 1988), pp. 309–11.

65. Thomson, *Early Tudor Church and Society*, p. 29.

66. Owen, *Church and Society*, p. 126; Duffy, *Stripping of the Altars*, p. 167; Lepine, *Brotherhood of Canons*, p. 143; BL, Cotton MS, Vespasian, C ii. fo. 117 (*LP*, III ii 2908), BL, Cotton MS, Vespasian, fo. 28 (*LP*, III ii 2617), BL, Cotton MS, Vespasian C ii fo. 25 (*LP*, III ii 2591); R.B. Tate, 'Robert Langton, Pilgrim (1470–1524)', *Nottingham Medieval Studies*, xxix (1995), pp. 182–90.

67. STC 15206.

68. J. C. Dickinson, *The Shrine of Our Lady of Walsingham* (1956), pp. 41–2.

69. *LP*, II, ii 3675; BL, Cotton MS, Caligula D vii fo. 28 (*LP*, II ii 3701); TNA, PRO, SP1/16 fo. 97 (*LP*, II ii app. 41); TNA, PRO, SP1/54 fo. 216 (*LP*, IV iii 5750 p. 2560).

70. BL, Cotton MS, Galba B v fo. 203 (*LP*, II ii 3199).

71. BL, Cotton MS, Caligula D vi fo. 239 (*LP*, III i 894), TNA, PRO, SP1/20 fo. 16v (*LP*, III i 905).

72. *LP*, III i 1285 p. 499.

73. *LP*, IV i 1792.

74. TNA, PRO, SP1/29 fo. 1 (*LP*, III ii 3476).

75. BL, Cotton MS, Otho C x fo. 216 (*LP*, X 40).

76. BL, Cotton MS, Caligula E i fo. 10 (*LP*, I i 1786); cf. B. Spencer, *Salisbury Museum Medieval Catalogue: part 2 Pilgrim Souvenirs and Secular Badges* (Salisbury, 1990), p. 31.

77. PRO, SP1/231 fo. 34 (*LP*, Addenda, i 29).

78. TNA, PRO, SP1/121 fo. 33 (*LP*, XII ii 21).

79. TNA, PRO SP1/112 fo. 142v (*LP*, XI 1260). I owe this to J.P.D. Cooper.

80. R. Finucane, *Miracles and Pilgrims: Popular Beliefs in Medieval England* (1977, 2nd. edn., Basingstoke, 1995), p. 205; Dickinson, *Walsingham*, p. 60; A. Savine, 'English monasteries on the eve of the dissolution', in P. Vinogradoff, ed., *Oxford Studies in Social and Legal History*, I (Oxford, 1909), p. 103.

81. *LP*, II i 395; TNA, PRO, SP1/136 fo. 50v (*LP*, XIII ii 257).

82. R.B. Dobson, 'The monks of Canterbury', in P. Collinson, N. Ramsay and M. Sparks, eds., *A History of Canterbury Cathedral* (Oxford, 1995), p. 149; *LP*, III i 695, 791.

83. Dobson, 'The monks of Canterbury', p. 140.

84. B. Spencer, *Medieval Finds from Excavations in London: 7. Pilgrim Souvenirs and Secular Badges* (2nd edn., 2010), pp. 37–133; W. Anderson, 'Blessing the Fields? A study of late-medieval ampullae from England and Wales', *Medieval Archaeology*, liv (2010), pp. 182–203 (for technical analysis of ampullae and speculation about how they were used).

85. cf. C. Brooke, 'Reflections on late medieval cults and devotions', in R.G. Benson and E.W. Naylor, eds., *Essays in Honor of Edward B. King* (Sewanee, TN, 1991), p. 42.

86. TNA, PRO, SP1/140 fo. 185 (*LP*, XIII ii 1142).

87. J.S. Craig, 'The "godly" and the "froward": protestant polemics in the town of Thetford', *Norfolk Archaeology*, xli (1990–2), p. 290 n.10.

88. BL, Cotton MS, Cleopatra E iv. fo. 72 (*LP*, XIII i 694); TNA, PRO, SP1/131 fo. 182 (*LP*, XIII i 863); W.D. Hamilton, ed., *Wriothesley's Chronicle*, Camden Society, 2nd. series, xi (1875), i. 80; Finucane, *Miracles and Pilgrims*, p. 205.

89. *LP*, VI, 247; Foxe, *Acts and Monuments* (1570 edn.), p. 1911 (Foxe, *Acts and Monuments*, vii. 475–6).

90. TNA, PRO, SP1/133 fo. 30 (*LP*, XIII i 1177): Hugh Latimer, *Sermons*, ed. G.E. Corrie, *Parker Society* (2 vols., Cambridge, 1844–5), ii. 395.

91. BL, Cotton MS, Cleopatra, E iv fo. 118 (T. Wright, ed., *Letters relating to the Suppression of the Monasteries*, Camden Society, 1st series, xxvi (1843), pp. 186–7; *LP*, XIII, i 634 [2]); Finucane, *Miracles and Pilgrims*, p. 205.

92. TNA, PRO, SP1/136 fo. 1 (*LP*, XIII ii 224).

93. TNA, PRO, SP1/136 fo. 119v (*LP*, XIII ii 346); BL, Cotton MS, Cleopatra E iv. fo. 267 (*LP*, XIII ii 367; Wright, *Suppression of the Monasteries*, p. 221); Finucane, *Miracles and Pilgrims*, pp. 205–6.

94. BL, Cotton MS, Cleopatra E iv. fo. 269 (*LP*, XIII ii 368; Wright, *Suppression of the Monasteries*, p. 224).

95. Foxe, *Acts and Monuments* (1570 edn.), pp. 1172–3 (Foxe, *Acts and Monuments*, iv. 706–7).

96. Leland, *Itinerary*: Howden, Yorkshire, i. 52; Sonning, Berkshire, i. 109; St Anne's chapel, Bristol, i. 134; Dunster, cliff chapel, i. 165; Bodmin, Devon, i. 180; Scilly Isles, i. 190; Our Lady in the Park, Liskeard, i. 208; Netley, Hampshire, i. 280; Southwick, Hampshire, i. 284; Penrhys, Glamorgan, iii. 16; St Baruch's chapel, Barry Island, iii. 24; Yale, Bromfield, iii. 70; Wirral, Hilbre point, iii. 92; Wakefield, Yorkshire, bridge chapel, v. 38; Appleby, Brougham, Westmorland, i. 47.

97. TNA, PRO, SP1/31 fo. 10 (*LP*, IV i 299).

98. TNA, PRO, SP1/129/fo. 12 (*LP*, XIII i 231); Finucane, *Miracles and Pilgrims*, p. 209, reads those words as evidence of decline and notes the absence of references to offerings in the commissioners' reports.

99. *Camden Miscellany*, v, Camden Society, lxxiii (1859), p. 11.

100. *LP*, VI 433 iii; VII 32.

101. TNA, PRO, SP1/136 fo. 118 (*LP*, XIII ii 345); Finucane, *Miracles and Pilgrims*, p. 206.

102. TNA, PRO, SP1/136 fo. 164 (*State Papers of Henry VIII*, i. 621–2 no. cxxii; *LP*, XIII ii 401).

103. TNA, PRO, SP1/137 fo. 80 (*LP*, XIII ii 516).

104. Thomas, *Religion and the Decline of Magic*, p. 85.

105. A.G. Dickens, 'The Last Medieval Englishman', in *Reformation Studies* (1982), p. 281; C. Richmond, 'Religion', in R. Horrox, ed., *Fifteenth-Century Attitudes: Perceptions of Society in Late Medieval England* (Cambridge, 1994), p. 195.

106. Thomas, *Religion and the Decline of Magic*, p. 31.

107. S. Walker, 'Political saints in later medieval England', in R.H. Britnell and A.J. Pollard, eds., *The McFarlane Legacy: Studies in Late Medieval Politics and Society* (Stroud, 1991), p. 85; D. Piroyansky, *Martyrs in the Making: Political Martyrdom in Late Medieval England* (Basingstoke, 2008), ch. 4, for a basic survey.

108. L. Lyell and F.D. Watney, eds., *Acts of the Court of the Mercers' Company 1453–1527* (Cambridge, 1936), p. 139.

109. B. Spencer, 'King Henry of Windsor and the London Pilgrim', in J. Bird, H. Clapman and J. Clark, eds., *Collectanea Londoniensia, Studies in London Archaeology and History presented to Ralph Merrifield, London and Middlesex Archaeological Society*, Special Papers, ii (1978), pp. 240–1.

110. cf. R.G. Davies, 'The Church and the Wars of the Roses', in A.J. Pollard, ed., *The Wars of the Roses* (Basingstoke, 1995), p. 145. The miracles are edited by P. Grosjean, ed., *Henrici VI Angliae Regis Miracula Posthuma, Société des*

Bollandistes, *Subsidia Hagiographica*, xxii (1935), and more accessibly by R. Knox and S. Leslie, eds., *The Miracles of Henry VI* (Cambridge, 1923), to which references will be given.

111. Nichols, *Pilgrimages by Erasmus*, pp. 1–2.

112. Spencer, 'Henry of Windsor', pp. 238–9; Spencer, *Salisbury Museum Medieval Catalogue: part 2 Pilgrim Souvenirs and Secular Badges*, pp. 52–3 ('an abundance of pilgrim badges found in Salisbury and elsewhere confirm that for perhaps two or three decades Windsor became perhaps the primary national pilgrim resort').

113. B. Spencer, *Medieval Finds from Excavations in London: 7. Pilgrim Souvenirs and Secular Badges* (1998), esp. pp. 189–92, and, slightly modified (2nd edn., 2010), pp. 189–92.

114. Foxe, *Acts and Monuments* (1570 edn.), p. 1387 (Foxe, *Acts and Monuments* v. 467); Spencer, 'Henry of Windsor', p. 244.

115. Knox and Leslie, eds., *Miracles of Henry VI*, pp. 166–7.

116. cf. J.W. McKenna, 'Piety and propaganda: the cult of Henry VI', in B. Rowland, ed., *Chaucer and Middle English Studies* (1974), pp. 72–88.

117. Spencer, 'Henry of Windsor', p. 240; cf. Lander, 'St George's Chapel', pp. 9–10. For a suggestion that Edward IV, suffering from gout, took the initiative, see Marks, 'Master John Schorn', pp. 199–200.

118. C. Ross, *Richard III* (1981), p. 226.

119. J. Hughes, ' "True ornaments to know a holy man": religious life and the piety of Richard III', in A.J. Pollard, ed., *The North of England in the Age of Richard III* (Stroud, 1996), p. 184.

120. Walker, 'Political saints', pp. 94–8.

121. Davies, 'The Church and the Wars of the Roses', p. 145; Spencer, 'Henry of Windsor', p. 241.

122. Walker, 'Poltical saints', pp. 86–7 for this 'admittedly speculative' hypothesis.

123. S. Anglo, *Images of Tudor Kingship* (1992), pp. 61–74.

124. J.M. Theilmann, 'Political canonisation and political symbolism', *Journal of British Studies*, xxix (1990), pp. 241–66, at 242, 265–6. cf. also J.R. Bray, 'Concepts of sainthood in fourteenth-century England', *Bulletin of the John Rylands Library*, lxvi (1984), pp. 40–77, esp. pp. 51–68; Walker, 'Political saints', pp. 77–106; J. Robinson, 'Pilgrimage and Protest: badges at the British Museum relating to Thomas of Lancaster and Isabella, queen of Edward II', in S. Blick, ed., *Beyond Pilgrim Souvenirs and Secular Badges: Essays in Honour of Brian Spencer* (Oxford, 2007), pp. 170–81

125. TNA, PRO, SP1/82 fos. 73–80v, bound in the wrong order (fos. 78–78v should precede fos. 77–77v), printed by L.E. Whatmore, 'The Sermon against the Holy Maid of Kent and her adherents, delivered at Paul's Cross, November the 23rd, 1533, and at Canterbury, December the 7th', *English Historical Review*, lviii (1943), pp. 463–75; W. Lambard, *Perambulation* (1596 edn. (RSTC 15176)), pp. 187–94.

126. Most probably 1526 (cf. Lambard, *Perambulation*, p. 189), but possibly a year or two earlier.

127. Lambard, *Perambulation*, pp. 189–92; J.E. Cox, ed., *The Writings and Letters of Thomas Cranmer* (Parker Society, 1846), pp. 273–4 (*LP*, VI 1546).

128. Cranmer, *Writings and Letters*, pp. 272–3 (*LP*, VI 1546).

129. *LP*, VII, 287.

130. Lambard, *Perambulation*, pp. 192–3.

131. Ibid., p. 193.

132. Whatmore, 'Sermon against the Holy Maid of Kent', pp. 464–6, 469, 471.

133. 25 Henry VIII, c. 12 (*Statutes of the Realm*, iii. 447).

134. Lambard, *Perambulation*, p. 192.

135. BL, Cotton MS, Titus B i. fo. 489v (*LP*, VI 1194); LP, VI 1589.

136. TNA, PRO, SP1/82 fo. 14 (*LP*, VII 17); *LP*, VII 72 (i).

137. J. Sumption, *Pilgrimage: An Image of Medieval Religion* (1975); Finucane, *Miracles and Pilgrims*; Morison, 'The miraculous and French society'.
138. *pace* Richmond, 'Religion', p. 195.
139. In October 1528 Archbishop Warham wrote to Wolsey that Elizabeth, a nun at St Sepulchre's, Canterbury, 'which had all the visions at Our Lady of Court Street' and was 'a virtuous woman', wished to speak to Wolsey, and had asked Warham to inform him (TNA, PRO, SP1/50 fo. 137 (*LP*, IV ii 4806)).
140. Foxe, *Acts and Monuments* (1583 edn.), p. 983 (Foxe, *Acts and Monuments*, iv. 580); Foxe, *Acts and Monuments* (1576 edn.), p. 792 (Foxe, *Acts and Monuments*, iv. 225); *Victoria County History, Buckinghamshire,* i. 303.
141. R. Whiting, *The Blind Devotion of the People* (Cambridge, 1988), pp. 54–5.
142. TNA, PRO, SP1/137 fo. 259 (*LP*, XIII ii 674).
143. Orme, *Unity and Variety*, p. 64.
144. Duffy, *Stripping of the Altars*, pp. 168–9.
145. Lemaitre, *Le Rouergue Flamboyant*, p. 384.
146. BL, Cotton MS, Cleopatra, E iv. fo. 316 (*LP*, XIII ii 11; Wright, *Suppression of the Monasteries*, p. 206).
147. TNA, PRO, SP1/152 fo. 1v (*LP*, XIV i 1053).
148. TNA, PRO, SP1/117 fo. 141v (*LP*, XII i 742).
149. TNA, PRO, SP1/124 fo. 140 (*LP*, XII ii 610).
150. R.M. Clay, *The Hermits and Anchorites of England* (1914), p. 187.
151. Southern, 'Between heaven and hell', pp. 651–2; Nelson, 'Society, theodicy and the origins of heresy', pp. 66–77.
152. Dickinson, *Walsingham*, pp. 41–2.
153. *LP*, I, i 1188.
154. British Library, Cotton MS, Vespasian F iii fo. 33 (*LP*, I ii 2268).
155. TNA, PRO, SP1/5 fos. 47–8 (*LP*, I ii 2283).
156. BL, Cotton MS, Caligula B vi fo. 249 (*LP*, III ii 2031).
157. BL, Cotton MS, Caligula B vi fo. 356 (*LP*, III ii 3481).
158. *LP*, III i 1285 (1).
159. TNA, PRO, SP1/22 fo. 63 (*LP*, III i 1284 (4)).
160. My counts from Leslie and Knox, *Miracles of Henry VI*.
161. Knox and Leslie, eds., *Miracles of Henry VI*, pp. 118–19.
162. Ibid., pp. 34–8.
163. Ibid., pp. 105–9.
164. *LP*, V, 607; Foxe, *Acts and Monuments* (1563 edn.), p. 1325 (Foxe, *Acts and Monuments*, vii. 489).
165. Dickinson, *Walsingham*, pp. 124–8.
166. *LP*, II, ii 3655, 3675; BL, Cotton MS, Caligula D vii fo. 28 (*LP*, II ii 3701).
167. cf. remarks by A. Martindale, 'The child in the picture: a medieval perspective', *Studies in Church History*, xxi (1994), pp. 208–9, on 'the totally miscellaneous sequence of problems' brought to thirteenth- and fourteenth-century saints.
168. TNA, PRO, SP1/102 fo. 85 (*LP*, X 364 (1)).
169. Leland, *Itinerary*, i. 109.
170. Craig, 'Thetford', p. 290 n.10.
171. TNA, PRO, SP1/102 fo. 95 (*LP*, X 364 (1)).
172. TNA, PRO, SP1/138 fo. 45 (*LP*, XIII ii 719).
173. BL, Cotton MS, Cleopatra E iv fo. 269 (*LP*, XIII ii 235).
174. TNA, PRO, SP1/136 f. 29 (*LP*, XIII ii 256).
175. TNA, PRO, SP1/102 fos. 85–100 (*LP*, X 364 (1)).
176. TNA, PRO, SP1/95 fo. 38 (*LP*, IX 42); J.H. Bettey, *Suppression of the Monasteries in the West Country* (Gloucester, 1989), pp. 170–1; Wright, *Suppression of the Monasteries*, pp. 58–9
177. Lambeth Palace, Talbot Papers, A 39 (*LP*, II i 1959).
178. Lambeth Palace, Talbot Papers, A 35 (*LP*, II i 1870).

179. TNA, PRO, SP1/48 fo. 206 (*LP*, IV ii 4418).
180. Haigh, *English Reformations*, p. 69; D. MacCulloch, *Suffolk and the Tudors* (Oxford, 1986), pp. 143–5, who dismisses it as 'a classic case of child hysteria and manipulation' (p. 145). cf. More, *Dialogue Concerning Heresies*, in *Complete Works*, VI i, pp. 93–4. Another contemporary miracle, of miraculous survival, was recorded at Doncaster. More than 300 people came to the image of Our Lady at the Whitefriars of Doncaster on the feast of St Mary Magdalen [22 July] when a miracle was rung and sung. William Nicholson and Robert Leche and his wife and children had been crossing the river Don at a ford, only to be overwhelmed by the current. They implored God and Our Lady of Doncaster, as, kneeling, did 'all the people being on the land seeing this piteous and heavy sight', praying to God and Our Lady, 'if ever she showed any miracle', to save Robert Leche's wife: safe, she then spoke to the people, saying that God and Our Blessed Lady in Doncaster had preserved her. Those who had escaped drowning declared the miracle on oath before the prior and convent, supported by witnesses (*Historical Manuscripts Commission*, Kenyon MSS, xxxv (1894), p. 1).
181. Keen, *English Society*, pp. 278–9.
182. cf. G. Williams, *The Welsh Church from Conquest to Reformation* (Cardiff, 2nd edn., 1978), p. 488; Morison, 'The miraculous and French society', p. 10.
183. W.H.C. Frend, 'The place of miracles in the conversion of the ancient world', *Studies in Church History*, xli (2005), pp. 11–21; cf. B. Bolton, *Studies in Church History*, xli (2005), pp. xv–xvii; A.M.L. Fedda, ' "Constat ergo inter nos verba signa esse": the understanding of the miraculous in Anglo-Saxon society', *Studies in Church History*, xli (2005), pp. 56–66.
184. Blair, *The Church in Anglo-Saxon Society*, pp. 142–3.
185. cf. B. Ward, *Miracles and the Medieval Mind* (Oxford, 1982), pp. 3–8, 10–11, 34; Williams, *Welsh Church*, pp. 488–9, 504; Sumption, *Pilgrimage*.
186. Wright, *Suppression of the Monasteries*, p. 16.
187. BL, Cotton MS, Cleopatra E iv. fo. 316v (*LP*, XIII ii 111).
188. cf. Williams, *Welsh Church*, pp. 488, 504.
189. N. Orme, 'Bishop Grandisson (1327–69) and popular religion', *Transactions of the Devonshire Association*, cxxiv (1992), pp. 107–18. Grandisson's letters are printed in M. Heale, *Monasticism in Later Medieval England 1300–1535* (Manchester, 2009), pp. 186–8.
190. Swanson, *Church and Society*, p. 289; Marks, *Image and Devotion*; Owen, *Church and Society*, pp. 126–7; Orme, *Unity and Variety*, p. 64; Duffy, *Stripping of the Altars*, p. 167; Aston, *Iconoclasts*, p. 21.
191. Foxe, *Acts and Monuments* (1570 edn.), p. 1387 (Foxe, *Acts and Monuments*, v. 467).
192. J.G. Nichols, ed., *Pilgrimages to Saint Mary of Walsingham and Saint Thomas of Canterbury by Desiderius Erasmus* (1849), p. 67.
193. G. Williams, 'Poets and pilgrims in fifteenth- and sixteenth-century Wales', *Transactions of the Honourable Society of Cymmrodorion* (1991), pp. 69–98 at pp. 77–8.
194. Williams, *Welsh Church*, p. 480.
195. Ibid., p. 486; Williams, 'Poets and pilgrims', pp. 78–9.
196. Duffy, *Stripping of the Altars*, p. 179; Morison, 'The miraculous and French society', p. 2.
197. TNA, PRO, SP1/102 fo. 103 (*LP*, X 364 (3)).
198. TNA, PRO, SP1/102 fos. 103–104v (*LP*, X 364 (3)).
199. TNA, PRO, SP1/95 fo. 38 (*LP*, IX 42); Bettey, *Suppression of the Monasteries*, pp. 170–1.
200. Wright, *Suppression of the Monasteries*, pp. 58–9, cited by Bettey, *Suppression of the Monasteries*, p. 172.
201. BL, Cotton MS, Cleopatra E iv. fo. 265 (*LP*, XIII ii 377 (ii)); Wright, *Suppression of the Monasteries*, p. 227.

202. *LP*, XIV, i 69 (2).
203. TNA, PRO, SP1/135 fo. 92 (*LP*, XIII, ii 101).
204. BL, Cotton MS, Cleopatra E iv fo. 267 (*LP*, XIII, ii 367), fo. 268 (*LP*, XIII ii 368), fo. 264 (*LP*, XIII ii 377); Wright, *Suppression of the Monasteries*, pp. 222, 224, 225.
205. BL, Cotton MS, Cleopatra E iv. fo. 319v (*LP*, XIII ii 200).
206. *LP*, XIV i 402.
207. W. Stubbs, ed., *Memorials of St Dunstan*, Rolls Series, lxiii (18), pp. 426–39 (I am grateful to Richard Sharpe for this reference).
208. *The Tablet*, 13 Feb. 1993, p. 212. 'What the reformation, and later scholars, came to call the prevalence of superstition is here treated as a true and attractive faith: for me much of it still looks like somewhat deperate superstition' wrote Geoffrey Elton, *Journal of Ecclesiastical History*, xliv (1993), pp. 719–21. 'Does he believe all these miracle cures?' Elton asked in his notes on Duffy's book (Elton room, Borthwick Institute, University of York).
209. Williams, *Welsh Church*, p. 520; N. Orme, 'Indulgences in the diocese of Exeter 1100–1536', *Transactions of the Devon Association*, cxx (1988), p.16.
210. Swanson, *Indulgences in Late Medieval England*, for an exhaustive survey; quotation at p. 31; Haines, *Ecclesia Anglicana*, pp. 183–91.
211. cf. P.A. Sigal, 'Les differents types de pèlerinage au moyen âge', in L. Kniss-Rettenbeck and G. Mohler, eds., *Wallfahrt kennt keine Grenzen* (Munich, 1984), pp. 79–80; Spencer, 'Henry of Windsor', p. 248.
212. Nichols, *Pilgrimages by Erasmus*, p. 2.
213. Williams, *Welsh Church*, p. 504; *VCH, Leicestershire*, ii. 6; *Historical Manuscripts Commission, Middleton*, lxix (1911), p. 384.
214. R.W. Dunning, 'Miles Salley, bishop of Llandaff', *Journal of Welsh Ecclesiastical History*, viii (1991), p. 5.
215. Nichols, *Pilgrimages by Erasmus*, pp. 5–8.
216. cf. Williams, *Welsh Church*, p. 488.
217. Foxe, *Acts and Monuments* (1570 edn.), p. 1185 (Foxe, *Acts and Monuments*, v. 29).
218. Foxe, *Acts and Monuments* (1570 edn.), p. 1188 (Foxe, *Acts and Monuments*, v. 34).
219. Foxe, *Acts and Monuments* (1583 edn.), p. 835 (Foxe, *Acts and Monuments*, iv. 239); A. Hudson, *The Premature Reformation* (Oxford, 1988), p. 469.
220. Spencer, *Salisbury Museum Medieval Catalogue*, pp. 7–12.
221. R. and C.N.L. Brooke, *Popular Religion in the Middle Ages: Western Europe 1000–1300* (1984), p. 23.
222. cf. H. Chadwick, *English Historical Review*, cv (2000), pp. 170–1.
223. Dobson, 'The monks of Canterbury', p. 137.
224. Aston, *Iconoclasts*, p. 21.
225. *Calendar of Close Rolls 1468–76*, pp. 298–9, cit. Spencer, 'Henry of Windsor', p. 240.
226. cf. for last point, C. Zika, 'Hosts, processions and pilgrimages: controlling the sacred in fifteenth-century Germany', *Past and Present*, cxviii (1988), pp. 25–64 at p. 64.
227. R.G. Davies, 'Religious sensibility', in C. Given-Wilson, ed., *An Illustrated History of Late Medieval England* (Manchester, 1996), p. 122.
228. More, *Dialogue concerning heresies*, in *Complete Works*, vi (i), pp. 231, 56; cf. Aston, *Iconoclasts*, p. 32.
229. Wriothesley, *Chronicle*, p. 80; BL, Cotton MS, Cleopatra, E iv fo. 72 (*LP*, XIII i 694); Williams, 'Poets and pilgrims', p. 76; 'time-honoured frauds' (Dickens, *English Reformation*, p. 158); Finucane, *Miracles and Pilgrims*, pp. 207–8.
230. TNA, PRO, SP1/138 fo. 40 (*LP*, XIII ii 709), *LP*, XIII ii 710.
231. TNA, PRO, SP1/129 fo. 94 (*LP*, XIII i 347).
232. TNA, PRO, SP1/136 fo. 171 (*LP*, XIII ii 409).

233. *LP*, XIII ii 710.
234. TNA, PRO, SP1/138 fo. 40 (*LP*, XIII ii 709), LP, XIII ii 710.
235. Wriothesley, *Chronicle*, p. 90.
236. Foxe, *Acts and Monuments* (1583 edn.), p. 1188 (Foxe, *Acts and Monuments*, v. 397).
237. Finucane, *Miracles and Pilgrims*, pp. 208–9.
238. TNA, PRO, SP1/129/fo. 12 (*LP*, XIII i 231); *LP*, XIII i 348; Wriothesley, *Chronicle*, p. 74; *LP*, XIV i 402; XIII i 644.
239. Finucane, *Miracles and Pilgrims*, p. 209.
240. TNA, PRO, SP1/129 fo. 210 (*LP*, XIII i 231).
241. Williams, *Welsh Church*, pp. 500–1; cf. P. Marshall's suggestion (from *LP*, XIII i 348) 'that the wires were only accessible after the rood had been prised away from the wall. The strenuous profession of ignorance and innocence by Abbot Dobbes and his brethren may thus have been quite genuine' ('The rood of Boxley', pp. 691–2).
242. TNA, PRO, SP1/129 fos. 94–4v (*LP*, XIII ii 347).
243. Nichols, *Pilgrimages by Erasmus*, p. 25.
244. Ibid., p. 52.
245. P. Sheingorn, *The Easter Sepulchre in England* (Kalamazoo, MI, 1987), pp. 58, 60; cf. Marshall 'The rood of Boxley', p. 692 and n. 13.
246. *LP*, XIII ii 200.
247. BL, Cotton MS, Cleopatra E iv. fo. 267 (*LP*, XIII ii 367); Wright, *Suppression of the Monasteries*, p. 222.
248. Dobson, 'The Monks of Canterbury', p. 136.
249. Whiting, *Blind Devotion*, p. 219. cf. C. Brooke's caution over the decline in pilgrim offerings at some, but not all, shrines (C. Brooke, 'Reflections on late medieval cults and devotions', in R.G. Benson and E.W. Naylor, eds., *Essays in Honor of Edward B. King* (Sewanee, TN, 1991), p. 42.
250. Savine, 'English monasteries on the eve of the dissolution', p. 104; C.E. Woodruff, 'The financial aspect of the cult of St Thomas of Canterbury', *Archaeologia Cantiana*, xliv (1932), pp. 22–5; M. Heale, 'Training in Superstition? Monasteries and Popular Religion in Late Medieval and Reformation England', *Journal of Ecclesiastical History*, lviii (2007), pp. 428–32, for salutary scepticism about *Valor Ecclesiasticus; pace* Duffy, *Stripping of the Altars*, p. 164.
251. cf. Hudson, *Premature Reformation*, p. 308.
252. TNA, PRO, SP1/129 fo. 120 (*LP*, XIII i 231).
253. BL, Cotton MS, Cleopatra E iv fo. 316 (*LP*, XIII ii 111).
254. TNA, PRO, SP1/157 fo. 67 (*LP*, XV 86).
255. *Daily Telegraph*, 8 Mar. 2003.
256. C. Morris, 'A critique of popular religion: Guibert of Nogent on "The relics of saints"', *Studies in Church History*, viii (1972), pp. 55–60; B. Bolton, 'Signs, wonders, miracles: supporting the faith in medieval Rome', *Studies in Church History*, xli (2005), p. 157.
257. J. Crampton, 'Leicestershire Lollards' in *Transactions of the Leicestershire Archaeological and Historical Society*, xliv (1968–9), pp. 11–44 at p. 38.
258. cf. Hudson, *Premature Reformation*, p. 403.
259. cf. ibid., p. 478.
260. BL, Cotton MS, Caligula D viii fo. 39 (*LP*, III i 1293).
261. D. Loades and C. Haigh, 'The fortunes of the shrine of St Mary of Caversham', *Oxoniensia*, xlvi (1981), pp. 62–72 at p. 67.
262. J. Strype, *Ecclesiastical Memorials* (3 vols. in 6, Oxford, 1822), I ii 388 (from BL, Cotton MS, Cleopatra E v fo. 139).
263. cf. M. Aston, 'Iconoclasm in England: rites of destruction by fire', in B. Scribner, ed., *Bilder und Bildersturm im Spätmittelalter und in der frühen Neuzeit* (Wiesbaden, 1990), pp. 175–202 at pp. 185–7.
264. A. Walsham, 'Reforming the waters: holy wells and healing springs in protestant England', in *Studies in Church History. Subsidia* xii (1999), pp. 227–55; ead.,

'Footprints and faith: religion and the landscape in early modern Britain and Ireland', *Studies in Church History*, xlvi (2010), pp. 169–83 (though whether it is fair to see this as reflecting an 'authentic protestant mindset' rather than an incomplete or ambiguous reformation is moot); ead., *The Reformation of the Landscape: Religion, Identity, and Memory in Early Modern Britain and Ireland* (Oxford, 2011), pp. 395–470, 555–67.

7   Criticism

1. A.G. Dickens, *The English Reformation* (2nd edn., 1989), pp. 317–18.
2. Skelton, *Complete English Poems*, ed. Scattergood, 'Collyn Clout', lines 913–15, p. 269, cf. 65, p. 248; 'Speke Parrot', line 500, p. 245.
3. *Calendar of State Papers, Spanish*, IV, i 367.
4. St German, *Divison between the spiritualtie and temporaltie*, in *Complete Works of St Thomas More*, IX, p. 177.
5. Gwyn, *King's Cardinal*, p. 43; D.J.A. Matthew, *Journal of Ecclesiastical History*, lix (2008), p. 114.
6. C. Haigh, in *English Historical Review*, c (1985), p. 843.
7. Cameron, *European Reformation*, p. 29.
8. TNA, PRO, SP1/69 fo. 121 (*State Papers of Henry VIII*, vii no. ccxvi pp. 349–50; *LP*, V 831).
9. R.W. Hoyle, 'The origins of the dissolution of the monasteries', *Historical Journal*, xxxviii (1995), pp. 275–305 (text of the 1529 petition on pp. 302–5).
10. F. van Otroy, ed., 'Vie du bienheureux martyr John Fisher, cardinal eveque de Rochester', *Analecta Bollandiana*, x (1891), pp. 338–44; Hall, *Chronicle*, p. 766.
11. St German, *Divison between the spiritualtie and temporaltie*, in *Complete Works of St Thomas More*, IX, pp. 194–5.
12. Leland, *Itinerary*, ii. 37.
13. Haigh, *English Reformations*, pp. 47–8.
14. Thomson, *Early Tudor Church and Society*, p. 289.
15. Whiting, 'Local Responses to the English Reformation', p. 25; C. Haigh, *Reformation and Resistance in Tudor Lancashire* (Cambridge, 1975), pp. 57–8.
16. 26 Henry VIII c. 15 (*Statutes of the Realm*, iii. 510–11); *LP*, IX 404.
17. *LP*, VII 523.
18. Haigh, *English Reformations*, pp. 40, 45–7; Marshall, *Catholic Priesthood*, pp. 216–18.
19. 27 Henry VIII c. 20 (*Statutes of the Realm*, iii. 551–2).
20. Tanner, *The Church in the Later Middle Ages*, p. 84.
21. Bowker, *Secular Clergy*, pp. 149–52.
22. St German, *Divison between the spiritualtie and temporaltie*, in *Complete Works of St Thomas More*, IX, p. 180.
23. *LP*, IV ii 1260.
24. TNA, PRO, SP3/5 fo. 22v (*LP*, VII 24).
25. cf. T. Scott, in *English Historical Review*, xcvii (1982), pp. 358–9.
26. Stevens, *Four Middle English Mystery Cycles*, p. 84.
27. Harper-Bill, *Pre-Reformation Church*, p. 62.
28. Thompson, *Early Tudor Church and Society*, p. 132; M. Ingram, 'Regulating sex in pre-Reformation London', in G.W. Bernard and S.J. Gunn, eds., *Authority and Consent in Tudor England* (Aldershot, 2002), pp. 79–96, esp. pp. 85–9.
29. Haigh, *English Reformations*, pp. 49–51.
30. Ibid., p. 73.
31. J. Baker, *The Oxford History of the Laws of England* VI *1483–1558* (Oxford, 2003), pp. 64–7. Baker has looked only at the period after 1495. He admits that by then such procedures were well established, and cites in passing a decision of 1465. It is thus unclear from his account just what was increasing, or changing.

32. Haigh, *English Reformations*, p. 76 citing TNA, PRO, SC1/44 fo. 83, a reference given him by Robin Storey; E.W. Ives, 'Hobart, Sir James (d. 1517)', *ODNB;* Cavill, '"The enemy of God"', pp. 127–50.

33. Gunn, 'Edmund Dudley and the church', p. 515; R.C. Palmer, *Selling the Church: The English Parish in Law, Commerce and Religion 1350–1550* (Chapel Hill, NC, 2002), pp. 25–6, 62, 68–9.

34. Gunn, 'Edmund Dudley and the church', pp. 515, 524, 526. Hobart and Fyneux are touched on in passing in a paper which offers a sensitive exploration of such contradictory attitudes to the church to be found both within the writings and the actions of Henry VII's notoriously rapacious minister.

35. *LP*, XV 453.

36. N. Tanner, *The Church in Late Medieval Norwich 1370–1532* (Toronto, 1984), pp. 141–54; id., 'The cathedral and the city', in I. Atherton, E. Fernie, C. Harper-Bill and H. Smith, eds., *Norwich Cathedral Church, City and Diocese, 1096–1996* (1996), pp. 259–61, 266–8; TNA, PRO, SP1/120 fo. 45 (*LP*, XII i 1177).

37. J.G. Clark, 'Religion and Politics in English Monastic Towns', *Cultural and Social History*, vi (2009), pp. 277–96.

38. Leland, *Itinerary*, i. 152, 295; J.H.P. Gibb, 'The fire of 1437 and the rebuilding of Sherborne Abbey', *Journal of the British Archaeological Society*, cxxxviii (1985), pp. 102, 104; G. Rosser, 'The cure of souls in English towns', in J. Blair and R. Sharpe, eds., *Pastoral Care before the Parish* (Leicester, 1992), pp. 273–4.

39. M.V.R. Heale, 'Monastic-Parochial Churches in late medieval England', in Burgess and Duffy, eds., *The Parish in Late Medieval England*, pp. 54–77, esp. pp. 75–6.

40. Brown, *Popular Piety*, pp. 171–3: but this does not face up to the problems raised by so awkward a relationship.

41. R. Dinn, '"Monuments Answerable to Mens Worth"': Burial Patterns, Social Status and Gender in Late Medieval Bury St Edmunds', *Journal of Ecclesiastical History*, xlvi (1995), pp. 243–4.

42. Dobson, 'Cathedral chapters and cathedral cities', p. 39.

43. Lepine, *Brotherhood of Canons*, pp. 114–15.

44. *LP*, VI 1601

45. Whiting, *Blind Devotion of the People*, p. 119.

46. Peters, 'Women and the Reformation', p. 197; Duffy, *Voices of Morebath*, p. 82.

47. TNA, PRO, SP1/2 fo. 50 (*LP*, VIII 584).

48. TNA, PRO, SP1/96 fos. 215–216v (*LP*, IX 429).

49. TNA, PRO, SP1/144 fo. 50 (*LP*, XIV i 423).

50. C. Tracy, 'The St Albans Abbey watching chamber: a reassessment', *Journal of the British Archaeological Association*, cxlv (1992), p. 104. cf. C. Oman, 'Security in English churches, AD 1000–1548', *Archaeological Journal*, cxxxvi (1970), pp. 90–8.

51. Marshall, 'Attitudes of the English people to priests and priesthood', p. 291.

52. Cameron, *European Reformation*, p. 49; Lander, *Government and Community*, p. 105; cf. Dickens, *English Reformation*, pp. 316, 323.

53. J.J. Scarisbrick, 'How the English Reformation happened', *Historical Review*, xiii (1992), 1; id., *Henry VIII* (1968), pp. 243–4. cf. M. Hicks, 'The English minoresses and their early benefactors, 1281–1367', in J. Loades, ed., *Monastic Studies* (1990), p. 167 n.9.

54. St German, 'Division between the spiritualitie and the temporalitie', in *Complete Works of St Thomas More*, IX, pp. 178, 181.

55. Skelton, *Complete English Poems*, ed. Scattergood, 'Collyn Clout', lines 133–41, 130–1, 440, 694, pp. 250, 257, 264.

56. Ibid., 'Collyn Clout', lines 276, 275–7; 75–80, 85–91, 324–5, pp. 253, 248–9, 254.

57. Ibid., 'Collyn Clout', lines 967–8, 204–19, 310–20, 585–8, pp. 270, 251–2, 254, 261.

58. Storey, *Diocesan Administration*, p. 20.

59. J. Huizinga, *Waning of the Middle Ages* (1955 edn.), pp. 179–80. cf. Colet's lament in 1511 that 'in this time also we perceive contradiction of the lay people', cited by Whiting, 'Local responses to the Henrician Reformation', p. 208.

60. Marshall, 'Attitudes of the English people', pp. 170, 238

61. TNA, PRO, SP1/122 fo. 59 (*LP*, XII ii 186 [38]).

62. S. Field, 'Devotion, discontent and the Henrician Reformation: the evidence of the Robin Hood stories', *Journal of British Studies*, xli (2002), pp. 6–22.

63. Ibid., esp. pp. 19–20.

64. cf. P. Marshall, 'Anticlericalism Revested [*sic*]? Expressions of Discontent in Early Tudor England', in C. Burgess and E. Duffy, eds., *The Parish in Late Medieval England* (Donington, 2006), pp. 373–80.

8   The Condition of the Monasteries

1. Still the best overall survey is M.D. Knowles, *The Religious Orders in England* III *The Tudor Age* (Cambridge, 1959). A good assessement of recent writing is offered by J.G. Clark, 'The religious orders in Pre-Reformation England', in id., ed., *The Religious Orders in Pre-Reformation England* (Woodbridge, 2002), pp. 3–33.

2. R.B. Dobson, 'English Monastic Cathedrals in the fifteenth century', *Transactions of the Royal Historical Society*, 6th series, i (1991), p. 158; B. Harvey, *Living and Dying in England 1100–1540: the Monastic Experience* (Oxford, 1993), pp. 154–9.

3. 27 Henry VIII c. 28 (*Statutes of the Realm*, iii. 575–7).

4. BL, Cotton MS, Cleopatra E iv fo. 135 (*LP*, XIII ii 744).

5. TNA, PRO, SP1/92 fo. 61 (foliation illegible) (*LP*, VIII 600).

6. BL, Cotton MS, Cleopatra E iv fo. 56v (*LP*, VIII 955).

7. BL, Cotton MS, Cleopatra E iv fo. 145 (*LP*, IX 772).

8. M.D. Knowles and R.N. Hadcock, *Medieval Religious Houses: England and Wales* (1971), p. 494, and for the most comprehensive gazetteer. cf. Harper-Bill, *Pre-Reformation Church*, p. 38; Swanson, *Church and Society*, pp. 83, 270; M. Oliva, *The Convent and the Community in Late Medieval England: Female Monasteries in the Diocese of Norwich, 1350–1540* (Woodbridge, 1998), pp. 67, 52.

9. R.B. Dobson, 'Cathedral chapters and cathedral cities: York, Durham and Carlisle in the fifteenth century', *Northern History*, xix (1983), pp. 23–5.

10. C. Harper-Bill, 'The English Church and English Religion after the Black Death', in W. M. Ormrod and P.G. Lindley, eds., *The Black Death in England* (Stamford, 1996), p. 98.

11. Oliva, *Convent and Community*, p. 70.

12. J. Greatrex, 'St Swithun's Priory in the later middle ages', in J. Crook, ed., *Winchester Cathedral Nine Hundred Years 1093–1993* (Chichester, 1993), pp. 144–5, 159.

13. Heale, *Monasticism in Later Medieval England*, p. 8.

14. J.H. Bettey, *Suppression of the Monasteries in the West Country* (Gloucester, 1989), pp. 11, 74; R.W. Dunning, 'Revival at Glastonbury, 1530–39', *Studies in Church History*, xiv (1977), pp. 213–22; A.J. Piper, 'Dr Thomas Swalwell, monk of Durham, archivist and bibliophile (d. 1539)', in J.P. Carley and C.G.C. Tite, eds., *Books and Collectors 1200–1700: Essays presented to Andrew Watson* (1997), p. 71.

15. Rosser, *Medieval Westminster*, pp. 259–60.

16. Dobson, 'English Monastic Cathedrals', p. 158; id., 'Recent prosopographical research in late medieval English history: university graduates, Durham monks and York canons', in N. Bulst and J.P. Genet, eds., *Medieval Lives and the Historian: studies in medieval prosopography* (Kalamazoo, MI 1986), pp. 188–9.

17. C. Cross, 'The origins and university connections of Yorkshire religious, *c.*1480–1540', *Studies in Church History*, Subsidia, xi (1999), p. 287.

18. R.B. Dobson, 'Life and death in Canterbury in the fifteenth century', paper read at the Institute of Historical Research, University of London, 1 Dec. 1989; Tanner, *Church in the Later Middle Ages*, p. 59.

19. R.W. Hoyle, 'The origins of the dissolution of the monasteries', *Historical Journal*, xxxviii (1995), p. 277.

20. Greatrex, 'St Swithun's Priory', p. 156.

21. Dobson, 'University graduates, Durham monks and York canons', p. 190.

22. Oliva, *Convent and Community*, pp. 18, 105–11.

23. B.J. Harris, 'A new look at the Reformation: aristocratic women and nunneries', *Journal of British Studies*, xxxii (1993), pp. 91–5, 111; Thomson, *Early Tudor Church and Society* (1993), p. 226.

24. TNA, PRO E36/119 fo. 96v (*LP*, XII i 901 (2)).

25. TNA, PRO, SP1/113 fo. 29 (*LP*, XI 1370).

26. Oliva, *Convent and Community*, p. 302.

27. Ibid., p. 108.

28. Brown, 'Lay piety in medieval Wiltshire', p. 257.

29. Oliva, *Convent and Community*, p. 301.

30. Harris, 'Aristocratic women and nunneries', p. 95.

31. Tanner, *Church in the Later Middle Ages*, p. 56.

32. R. and C. Brooke, *Popular Religion and the Middle Ages: Western Europe 1000–1300* (1984), p. 50.

33. Harvey, *Living and Dying*, pp. 118–22, 128.

34. Oliva, *Convent and Community*, pp. 75, 78, 81.

35. BL, Cotton MS, Cleopatra E iv fo. 284 (*LP*, XIV i 1321).

36. TNA, PRO, SP1/86 fo. 155v (*LP*, VII 1367).

37. Bowker, *Henrician Reformation*, p. 21.

38. cf. C. Barron, in *Journal of Ecclesiastical History*, xlviii (1997), p. 328.

39. I owe this formulation to Richard Davies.

40. Greatrex, 'St Swithun's Priory', p. 161.

41. For a most sensitive discussion of these themes see R.W. Southern, *Saint Anselm: A Portrait in Landscape* (Cambridge, 1990), pp. 148–52.

42. *LP*, V 607; Foxe, *Acts and Monuments* (1563 edn.), p. 1325 (Foxe, *Acts and Monuments*, vii. 489).

43. B. Harvey, 'A novice's life at Westminster Abbey in the century before the dissolution', in Clark, ed., *Religious Orders in Pre-Reformation England*, pp. 51–73; see now also J. Greatrex, *The English Benedictine Cathedral Priories: Rule and Practice, c.1270–c.1420* (Oxford, 2011), esp. pp. 50–88.

44. Oliva, *Convent and Community*, p. 98.

45. Y. Parrey, '"Devoted disciples of Christ": early sixteenth-century religious life in the nunnery at Amesbury', *Historical Research*, lxvii (1994), pp. 240–8, esp. 246–8.

46. C. Platt, *The Abbeys and Priories of Medieval England* (1984), p. 225.

47. TNA, PRO, SP1/95 fo, 148 (*LP* IX 160); TNA, SP1/98 fo. 40 (*LP*, IX 651); TNA, PRO, SP1/98 fo. 71 (*LP*, IX 694); TNA, PRO, SP1/98 fo. 94v (*LP*, IX 708); BL, Cotton MS, Cleopatra E iv fo. 272 (LP, IX 735); TNA, PRO SP1/100 fo. 94 (*LP*, IX 1150); BL, Cotton MS, Cleopatra E iv fo. 26 (*LP*, IX 1157); BL, Cotton MS, Cleopatra E iv fo. 234 (*LP*, X 103); *LP*, X 1449.

48. F.D. Logan, *Runaway Religious in Medieval England, c.1240–1540* (Cambridge, 1996), pp. 171–2; id., 'Departure from the religious life during the royal visitation of the monasteries, 1535–1536', in Clark, ed., *Religious Orders in Pre-Reformation England*, pp. 218–22.

49. J. Greatrex, 'On ministering to "certayne devoute and religiouse women": Bishop Fox and the Benedictine Nuns of Winchester diocese on the eve of the dissolution', *Studies in Church History*, xxvii (1990), p. 235.

50. C. Cross, 'The religious life of women in sixteenth-century Yorkshire', *Studies in Church History*, xxvii (1990), p. 316; ead., 'Community solidarity among Yorkshire religious after the dissolution', in J. Loades, ed., *Monastic Studies: The Continuity of Tradition* (1990), p. 247.

51. C. Cross, 'Monasteries and Society in sixteenth-century Yorkshire: the last years of Roche Abbey', in J. Burton and K. Stober, eds., *Monasteries and Society in the British Isles in the Late Middle Ages* (Woodbridge, 2008), p. 236; ead., 'The reconstitution of northern monastic communities in the reign of Mary Tudor', *Northern History*, xxix (1993), 200–4; C. Cross and N. Vickers, eds., *Monks, Friars and Nuns in Sixteenth-Century Yorkshire*, Yorkshire Archaeological Society Record Series, cl (1995), 4–5.

52. Bettey, *Suppression of the Monasteries*, p. 111.

53. Oliva, *Convent and Community*, pp. 123, 303–4.

54. Ibid., pp. 304, 374, citing *VCH Cambridgeshire*, ii. 301–2, *VCH Warwickshire*, iii. 78.

55. Cross, 'Religious life of women', p. 315; ead., 'Yorkshire nunneries in the early Tudor period', in Clark, ed., *Religious Orders in Pre-Reformation England*, p. 153; F.C. and P. Morgan, *Transactions of the Woolhope Field Club*, xxvii (1963), pp. 135–48 on ex-religious in Herefordshire.

56. J.G. Clark, 'Reformation and reaction at St Albans Abbey, 1530–58', *English Historical Review*, cxv (2000), pp. 314–17.

57. P. Cunich, 'The ex-religious in post-dissolution society: symptoms of post-traumatic stress disorder?', in Clark, ed., *Religious Orders in Pre-Reformation England*, pp. 227–38.

58. Dobson, 'English Monastic Cathedrals', p. 168; J. Greatrex, 'The English cathedral priories and the pursuit of learning in the later middle ages', *Journal of Ecclesiastical History*, xlv (1994), pp. 401–2.

59. Harvey, *Living and Dying*, p. 77.

60. Greatrex, 'English cathedral priories and the pursuit of learning', pp. 402, 409.

61. MacCulloch, *Suffolk and the Tudors*, p. 136.

62. R. Lovatt, *Journal of Ecclesiastical History*, lxii (2011), p. 606.

63. Clark, ed., *The Religious Orders in pre-Reformation England*, p. 12.

64. Heale, *Monasticism in Late Medieval England*, pp. 150–1; Greatrex, 'St Swithun's Priory', p. 159.

65. Greatrex, 'English cathedral priories and the pursuit of learning', pp. 398–411.

66. Greatrex, 'St Swithun's Priory', p. 153.

67. Henry of Kirkstede, *Catalogus de libris autenticis et apocritis*, ed. R.H. Rouse and M.A. Rouse (2004); R. Sharpe with J.P. Carley, R.M. Thomson and A.G. Watson, eds., *English Benedictine Libraries: the Shorter Catalogues* (1996).

68. Clark, 'Reformation and reaction at St Albans Abbey', pp. 304–8.

69. R. Bowers, 'The Lady Chapel and its musicians, c.1210–1559', in Crook, ed., *Winchester Cathedral*, pp. 247–53; id., 'The musicians of the Lady Chapel of Winchester Cathedral Priory', *Journal of Ecclesiastical History*, xlv (1994), pp. 210–37 (reprinted in id., *English Church Polyphony* (Aldershot, 1999), ch. V; id., 'An Early Tudor Monastic Enterprise: Choral Polyphony for the Liturgical Service', in J.G. Clark, ed., *The Culture of Medieval English Monasticism* (Woodbridge, 2007), pp. 21–54; D. Skinner, 'Marian anthems in late medieval England', *Studies in Church History*, xxxix (2004), esp. p. 169 n.4. For caution against exaggerating the role of monasteries, noting as well the part played by secular foundations and the indispensability of professional musicians, see R. Lovatt, *Journal of Ecclesiastical History*, lx (2009), pp. 155–6.

70. Stevens, *Four Middle English Mystery Cycles*, p. 309; G. MacMurray Gibson, *Theater of Devotion: East Anglia Drama and Society in the Late Middle Ages* (Chicago, 1997), pp. 107–35; J. Griffiths, 'Thomas Hyngham, monk of Bury, and the Macro Plays Manuscript', *English Manuscript Studies, 1100–1700*, v (1995), pp. 214–19.

71. J. Hughes, *Pastors and Visionaries: Religion and Secular Life in Late Medieval Yorkshire* (Woodbridge, 1988), for a magisterial treatment; K. Ghosh, *The Wycliffite Heresy: Authority and the Interpretation of Texts* (Cambridge, 2002), pp. 147–73

(for Nicholas Love); Nicholas Love, *The Mirror of the Blessed Life of Jesus Christ*, ed. M. Sargent (Exeter, 2005).

72. Duffy, *Stripping of the Altars*, pp. 81, 87.

73. V. Gillespie, 'Syon and the New Learning', in Clark, ed., *Religious Orders in Pre-Reformation England*, pp. 75–96.

74. J. Greatrex, 'The almonry school of Norwich Cathedral priory in the thirteenth and fourteenth centuries', *Studies in Church History*, xxxi (1994), p. 169, from *Valor Ecclesiasticus*.

75. Clark, ed., *The Religious Orders in Pre-Reformation England*, p. 25; Heale, *Monasticism in Late Medieval England*, pp. 54–5.

76. Heale, 'Monasteries and popular religion', pp. 433–6. Perhaps too much is made of this single example.

77. TNA, PRO, E36/119 fo. 96 (*LP*, XII i 901 (2)).

78. Hoyle, 'Origins of the dissolution', p. 277.

79. Harvey, *Living and Dying*, pp. 7–33, esp. p. 24.

80. Hoyle, 'Origins of the dissolution', p. 278 (from L. Stone, 'The political programme of Thomas Cromwell', *Bulletin of the Institute of Historical Research*, xxiv (1951), pp. 11–17).

81. BL, Cotton MS, Cleopatra E iv fo. 241 (*LP*, X 858).

82. TNA, PRO. SP1/104 fo. 30 (*LP*, X 916); fo. 32 (*LP*, X 917); BL, Cotton MS, Cleopatra E iv fo. 249 (*LP*, X 1166)

83. BL, Cotton MS, Cleopatra E iv fo. 249v (*LP*, X 1166).

84. TNA, PRO, SP1/104 fo. 246 (*LP*, X 1246).

85. BL, Cotton MS, Cleopatra E iv fo. 312 (*LP*, XII i 4).

86. TNA, PRO, SP1/132 fo.176 (*LP*, XIII i 1117).

87. TNA, PRO, SP1/136 fo. 86v (*LP*, XIII ii 306).

88. *LP*, XI 780 (2).

89. Michael Sherbrook, 'The fall of religious houses', in A.G. Dickens, ed., *Tudor Treatises*, Yorkshire Archaeological Society Record Series, cxxv (1959), pp. 89–142 at p. 94.

90. N.S. Rushton and W. Sigle-Rushton, 'Monastic poor relief in sixteenth-century England', *Journal of Interdisciplinary History*, xxxii (2001), pp. 193–216, esp. pp. 215–16; N. Rushton, 'Monastic charitable provision in Tudor England: quantifying and qualifying poor relief in the sixteenth century', *Continuity and Change*, xvi (2001), pp. 9–44.

91. J. Röhrkasten, 'Aspects of popular piety in late medieval London', paper read at the Institute of Historical Research, University of London, November 1991; id., 'Londoners and London mendicants in the late middle ages', *Journal of Ecclesiastical History*, xlvii (1996), pp. 450–1. J. Röhrkasten, *The Mendicant Houses of Medieval London 1221–1539* (Münster, 2004) is a fundamental study.

92. R. Whiting, 'Local responses to the Reformation', in MacCulloch, ed., *The Reign of Henry VIII*, p. 206.

93. Brown, 'Lay piety in medieval Wiltshire', p. 241.

94. Dinn, 'Burial Patterns, Social Status and Gender in Late Medieval Bury St Edmunds', p. 244.

95. M. Robson, 'The Grey Friars in York, c.1450–1530', in Clark, ed., *Religious Orders in Pre-Reformation England*, p. 119.

96. J. Catto, 'Franciscan learning in England, 1450–1540', in Clark, ed., *Religious Orders in Pre-Reformation England*, pp. 100–1.

97. For these sceptical observations see R.W. Swanson, 'The "mendicant problem" in the later middle ages', *Studies in Church History, Subsidia* xi (1999), pp. 217–38.

98. Hoyle, 'Origins of the dissolution', p. 276; *LP*, XIV ii 428; Oliva, *Convent and Community*, pp. 262–3.

99. *VCH, Cheshire*, iii. 143.

100. *VCH, Cumberland*, ii. 45.
101. Ibid., 156: from BL, Add. MS 24965 fo. 218.
102. Bettey, *Suppression of the Monasteries*, p. 15. Isabel Wygun, last prioress of Carrow Priory, Norwich, built herself a house to the west of the cloister which, in the opinion of Nikolaus Pevsner, 'in its sumptuousness and worldliness, almost seems to justify the Dissolution' (N. Pevsner, *North-East Norfolk and Norwich* (1962), p. 286).
103. 'The bright, showy garments of ecclesiastics shocked Boniface [St Boniface, 675–755], but his aristocratic contemporaries might have thought it odd if they had worn anything simpler': Blair, *The Church in Anglo-Saxon Society*, p. 136.
104. TNA, PRO, SP1/74 fo. 122 (*LP*, VI 107).
105. Bettey, *Suppression of the Monasteries*, pp. 30–4.
106. TNA, PRO, SP1/135 fo.35 (*LP*, XIII ii 32).
107. *LP*, XIII ii 340; BL, Cotton MS, Cleopatra E iv fo. 267 (*LP*, XIII ii 367; Wright, *Supression of the Monasteries*, p. 222).
108. TNA, PRO, SP1/137 fos. 129v, 131 (*LP*, XIII ii 554 (1) and (2)).
109. TNA, PRO, SP1/142 fo. 101 (*LP*, XIV i 101).
110. S. Jack, 'Of poverty and pigstyes: the household economy of the smaller religious houses on the eve of the dissolution', *Parergon*, i (1983), pp. 72, 74–5.
111. C. Cross, 'Yorkshire nunneries in the early Tudor period', in Clark, ed., *Religious Orders in Pre-Reformation England*, p. 146.
112. Bettey, *Suppression of the Monasteries*, p. 28.
113. TNA, PRO, SP1/79 fo. 58 (*LP*, VI 1142).
114. B.R. Kemp, 'Monastic possession of parish churches in England in the twelfth century', *Journal of Ecclesiastical History*, xxxi (1980), pp. 133–60; cf. M. Dilworth, *Scottish Monasteries in the Late Middle Ages* (Edinburgh, 1995), pp. 44–5: 'not only was pastoral care lacking, but the very concept of pastoral care did not seem to exist'.
115. Owen, *Church and Society*, p. 114; cf. K.L. Wood-Legh, ed., *Kentish Visitations of Archbishop Warham and his Deputies 1511–12*, Kent Archaeological Society, Kent Records, xxiv (1984), p. xv.
116. Haigh, *English Reformations*, pp. 43–4.
117. Harper-Bill, *Pre-Reformation Church*, pp. 38–9; id., 'Dean Colet's Convocation Sermon', pp. 195–6.
118. Platt, *Abbeys and Priories of Medieval England*, p. 137; B. Golding, 'Keeping nuns in order: enforcement of the rule in thirteenth-century Sempringham', *Journal of Ecclesiastical History*, lix (2008), pp. 657–79.
119. G.W. Bernard, *The King's Reformation: Henry VIII and the Remaking of the English Church* (2005), pp. 257–64.
120. Dilworth, *Scottish Monasteries in the Late Middle Ages*, p. 31.
121. The adjectives are those of Harper-Bill, *Pre-Reformation Church*, p. 39.
122. C.H. Talbot, ed., *Letters from the English Abbots to the Chapter at Citeaux 1442–1521*, Camden Society, 4th ser., iv (1967), p. 15.
123. J. McManners, in *Journal of Ecclesiastical History*, liv (2003), pp. 584–5.
124. Bettey, *Suppression of the Monasteries*, p. 20.
125. N. Tanner, *The Church in the Later Middle Ages* (2008), p. 47.
126. C. Haigh, 'Hammer of the monks', *English Heritage Magazine*, Mar. 1991, p. 13.
127. Keen, *English Society*, p. 263.
128. S. Keeling, 'The dissolution of the monasteries in the border country', in Marcombe, ed., *The Last Principality*, p. 43.
129. MacCulloch, *Suffolk under the Tudors*, p. 133.
130. Platt, *Abbeys and Priories of Medieval England*, p. 142.
131. J. Greatrex, 'After Knowles: recent perspectives in monastic history', in Clark, ed., *Religious Orders in Pre-Reformation England*, pp. 37, 40.
132. BL, Cotton MS, Cleopatra E iv fo. 249 (*LP*, X 1166).
133. Greatrex, *English Benedictine Cathedral Priories*, p. 330.

134. Thompson, 'Monasteries and their Patrons', pp. 123, 116, 122; id., 'Monasteries, society and reform in late medieval England', in Clark, ed., *Religious Orders in Pre-Reformation England*, pp. 173–80. A very similar line of reasoning is offered by John Blair as an explanation for the turning of the tide against the minsters of Anglo-Saxon England by *c*.800 after a great wave of foundation from the late seventh century (Blair, *The Church in Anglo-Saxon England*, pp. 132–4: 'Elite establishments made wealthy in a burst of concentrated enthusiasm must justify their inherited wealth as the generations pass, or see their prestige drain away. By 800 the novelty of minsters had worn off, and they no longer offered the only route to new and exciting things. Few of them still supported rigorous spiritual life, their intellectual achievements had tailed way, and moral reform was barely an issue. All too often, they could be identified with supplanted rivals or litigious kin, or perceived as greedy, self-satisfied consumers of scarce assets' (pp. 133–4)).

135. Heale, *Monasticism in Late Medieval England*, pp. 50–1.

136. *LP*, IV iii 6123.

137. Bettey, *Suppression of the Monasteries*, p. 17.

138. Harvey, *Living and Dying*, pp. 179–209.

139. Oliva, *Convent and Community*, pp. 230, 240.

140. Ibid., pp. 215–20.

141. TNA, PRO E36/118 fos. 71–1v (*LP*, XII i 392).

142. Harvey, *Living and Dying*, pp. 11, 38–41, 51–2.

143. B. Dodwell, 'The monastic community', in I. Atherton, E. Fernie, C. Harper-Bill and H. Smith, eds., *Norwich Cathedral: Church, City and Diocese, 1096–1996* (1996), pp. 237–8.

144. Greatrex, 'St Swithun's Priory', p. 161, ead., *English Benedictine Cathedral Priories*, pp. 329–32.

145. E. Christiansen, in *English Historical Review*, xcvi (1981), p. 854.

146. J. Nelson, 'Medieval monasticism', in J.L. Nelson and P. Linehan, eds., *The Medieval World* (2001), p. 588.

147. Beckett, 'Sheen Charterhouse', pp. 150, 156–7.

148. Thomson, *Early Tudor Church and Society*, p. 228; Wood-Legh, ed., *Kentish Visitations of Archbishop William Warham and his Deputies*, pp. 11–13.

149. TNA, PRO, SP1/78 fos. 115–115v (*LP*, VI 985), 117 (*LP*, VI 986), 118 (*LP*, VI, 987), 119–121v (*LP*, VI 988).

150. TNA, PRO, SP1/85 fos. 65v, 67v (*LP*, VII 1005).

151. TNA, PRO, SP1/85 fo. 101 (*LP*, VII 1047 (iii)).

152. TNA, PRO, SP1/86 fo. 155v (*LP*, VII 1367).

153. BL, Cotton MS, Cleopatra E iv fo. 162v–163 (*LP*, IX 1005).

154. BL, Cotton MS, Cleopatra E iv fo. 139 (*LP*, X 981).

155. M. Heale, ' "Not a thing for a stranger to enter upon": the selection of monastic superiors in late medieval and early Tudor England', in Burton and Stober, eds., *Monasteries and Society*, pp. 53–68. But the working assumption that the election from within a monastery is evidence of independence but the election of an outsider is evidence of external interference seems forced: Wolsey often favoured internal candidates.

156. Gwyn, *King's Cardinal*, pp. 317–28.

157. Thompson, *Early Tudor Church and Society*, p. 156.

158. TNA, PRO, SP1/39 fo. 54 (*LP*, IV ii 2394).

159. Gwyn, *King's Cardinal*, pp. 324–8.

160. Thompson, *Early Tudor Church and Society*, p. 157.

161. Gwyn, *King's Cardinal*, pp. 321–3; T. Stemmler, *Die Liebesbriefe Heinrichs VIII an Anna Boleyn* (Zurich, 1988), pp. 124–5 (*LP*, IV ii 4477).

162. A. Marett-Crosby, 'More, William (1471/2–1552)', *ODNB*.

163. C.H. Williams, ed., *English Historical Documents V 1485–1558* (1967), pp. 762–6; Wright, *Suppression of the Monasteries*.
164. TNA, SP1/97 fos. 28–28v (*LP*, IX 457).
165. TNA, PRO, SP1/97 fo. 74 (*LP*, IX 509).
166. BL, Cotton MS, Cleopatra E iv fo. 136 (*LP*, X 137).
167. TNA, PRO, SP1/101 fo. 135 (*LP*, X 165).
168. TNA, PRO, SP1/87 fo. 37 (*LP*, VII 1449).
169. Collett, 'Richard Fox's translation of the Benedictine rule for women', p. 217.
170. J. Catto, 'Religion and the English nobility in the later fourteenth century', in H. Lloyd-Jones, V. Pearl and B. Worden, eds., *History and Imagination: Essays in Honour of H.R. Trevor-Roper* (1981), pp. 52–3; Beckett, 'Sheen Charterhouse', *passim*.
171. Dickens, *English Reformation*, p. 40.
172. BL, Add. MS 37049 fo. 22v.
173. *LP*, I ii 2715.
174. Beckett, 'Sheen Charterhouse', pp. 69–71.
175. Ibid., p. 154.
176. Hicks, 'The English minoresses and their early benefactors', p. 160.
177. Keen, *English Society*, pp. 264–5.
178. Beckett, 'Sheen Charterhouse', p. 1.
179. cf. M. Heale, *Journal of Ecclesiastical History*, lxi (2010), p. 380.
180. Catto, 'Religious change under Henry V', p. 111.
181. *LP*, IV ii 4692.
182. *LP*, II ii app. 48; 4231.
183. T. Webber, 'Latin devotional texts and the books of the Augustinian canons of Thurgarton Priory and Leicester Abbey in the late middle ages', in Carley and Tite, eds., *Books and Collectors*, pp. 27–41.
184. *LP*, III i 693.
185. Hoyle, 'Origins of the dissolution', pp. 280–1.
186. *LP*, III i 1124, 1216; IV i 585.
187. *LP*, III i 475; 693.
188. Polydore Vergil, *The Anglica Historia of Polydore Vergil*, ed. and trans. D. Hay, Camden Society, lxxiv (1950), pp. 259–60.
189. *LP*, IV i 953 (mis-dated).
190. *LP*, III ii 1690.
191. *LP*, III ii 1863; TNA, PRO, SP1/24 fos. 34–7 (*LP*, III ii 2080).
192. TNA, PRO, SP1/54 fo. 206 (*LP*, IV iii 5749).
193. BL, Cotton MS, Faustina C vii fo. 221 (*LP*, III i 1122).
194. *LP*, III ii 2207.
195. TNA, PRO, SP1/110 fo. 46 (*LP*, IV iii 3815).
196. Greatrex, 'Bishop Fox and the Benedictine nuns of Winchester diocese', p. 224; Tudor, 'English devotional literature', p. 42; Collett, 'Fox's translation', p. 215; Thompson, 'English and Welsh bishops', pp. 154, 159.
197. M. Bowker, *The Henrician Reformation: The Diocese of Lincoln under John Longland 1521–1547* (Cambridge, 1981), pp. 7, 17–18, 109. Longland's strictures on the diet of the Benedictine monks of Westminster Abbey are readily supported by the details in Harvey, *Living and Dying*, pp. 34–71.
198. Harvey, *Living and Dying*, pp. 21–4, 27–8.
199. TNA, PRO, SP1/35 fo. 48 (*LP*, IV i 1470).
200. Heale, ed., *Monasticism in Late Medieval England*, pp. 166–8.
201. See above, p. 51.
202. *LP*, IV ii 4921 (2) (Rymer, *Foedera*, xiv. 273–4).
203. Rymer, *Foedera*, xiv 291–4; *LP*, IV ii 4900, iii 5638–9.
204. *LP*, IV iii 5607 (iii).
205. TNA, PRO, SP1/35 fo. 48; TNA, PRO, SP1/35 fo. 50 (*LP*, IV i 1470).

206. J.J. Goring, 'The riot at Bayham Abbey, June 1525', *Sussex Archaeological Collections*, cxvi (1978), p. 4.
207. TNA, PRO, SP1/54 fos. 204v, 206 (*LP*, IV iii 5749).
208. Gwyn, *King's Cardinal*, pp. 466–70.
209. I acknowledge discussions with Jackie Mountain on this point.
210. The thrust of B. Thompson, 'Monasteries, society and reform in late medieval England', in J. G. Clark., ed., *The Religious Orders in Late Medieval England* (Woodbridge, 2002), pp. 165–95.
211. Morris, *Papal Monarchy*, p. 542; Harvey, *Living and Dying*, pp. 146–78, esp. p. 153, for a remarkably acute analysis; M. Threlfall-Holmes, *Monks and Markets, Durham Cathedral Priory 1460–1520* (Oxford, 2005).
212. P. Cunich, 'The dissolution', in D. Rees, ed., *Monks of England: The Benedictines in England from Augustine to the Present Day* (1997), p. 154.
213. TNA, PRO, SP1/95 fo. 121 (*LP*, IX 139), fo. 148 (*LP*, IX 160), 253; X 103.
214. Greatrex, 'St Swithun's Priory', pp. 159–60.
215. W.A. Pantin, ed., *Documents illustrating the activities of the General and Provincial Chapters of the English Black Monks, 1215–1540*, III, Camden Society, 3rd ser., liv (1937), no. 283, pp. 123–4 (re-dated) (translation in *LP*, IV i 953 and in Heale, *Monasticism in Late Medieval England*, pp. 136–7); Gwyn, *King's Cardinal*, p. 273.
216. TNA, PRO, SP1/154 fo. 52 (*LP*, IV iii 5191).
217. St German, 'Division between the spiritualtie and temporaltie', in *Complete Works of St Thomas More*, IX, pp. 205–7.
218. BL, Cotton MS, Cleopatra E iv fo. 34 (Wright, *Suppression of the Monasteries*, p. 104, *LP*, X 484).
219. Dobson, 'English Monastic Cathedrals', pp. 170–1; id., 'University graduates, Durham monks and York canons', in Balst and Genet, eds., *Medieval Lives and the Historian*, p. 190.
220. TNA, PRO, SP1/95 fo. 121 (*LP*, IX 139), SP1/96 fo. 30 (*LP*, IX 215), fo. 163 (*LP*, IX 375).
221. J. Burton, *The Yorkshire Nunneries in the Twelfth and Thirteenth Centuries'*, Borthwick Papers, lvi (1979).
222. T. Pestell, *Landscapes of Monastic Foundations: The Establishment of Religious Houses in East Anglia c.650–1200* (Woodbridge, 2004).
223. Oliva, *Convent and Community*, ch. 1.
224. Thompson, *Early Tudor Church and Society*, pp. 105–6, 115.
225. Bettey, *Suppression of the Monasteries*, p. 12.
226. Wright, *Suppression of the Monasteries*, no. xix; Bettey, *Suppression of the Monasteries*, p. 14.
227. Wright, *Suppression of the Monasteries*, no. xxxvi.
228. cf. Harvey, *Living and Dying*, p. 210.
229. D.J. Power, in *Journal of Ecclesiastical History*, lx (2004), p. 580.
230. Gwyn, *King's Cardinal*, pp. 469–70.
231. cf. Greatrex, 'St Swithun's Priory', esp. pp. 159–61.
232. Hoyle, 'Origins of the dissolution', p. 276; Heale, *Monasticism in Late Medieval England*, p. 37.
233. St German, 'Division between the spiritualtie and the temporaltie', in *Complete Works of St Thomas More*, IX, p. 205.
234. Beckett, 'Sheen Charterhouse', pp. 30–6.
235. Ibid., pp. 105 ff.
236. Ibid., p. 139.
237. Ibid., p. 78.
238. Ibid., pp. 92–3, 97.
239. Ibid., pp. 133–4, 147–8.
240. Hoyle, 'Origins of the dissolution', pp. 276–7.

241. Harper-Bill, 'Dean Colet's Convocation sermon', p. 197.
242. Harper-Bill 'English Church and English Religion', in Ormrod and Lindley, eds., *Black Death*, p. 104.
243. cf. Keen, *English Society*, p. 262.
244. Rosser, *Medieval Westminster*, pp. 257–9, noting similar trends in Norwich and York.
245. Heale, *Monasticism in Late Medieval England*, p. 48.
246. cit. Thompson, *Early Tudor Church and Society*, p. 103
247. Catto, 'Religious change under Henry V', p. 111; Harper-Bill, 'Dean Colet's Convocation Sermon', p. 196.
248. cf. Beckett, 'Sheen Charterhouse', p. 75.
249. Hughes, *Pastors and Visionaries, passim.*
250. Ibid., esp. p. 351.
251. C.A.J. Armstrong, 'The piety of Cicely, duchess of York: a study in late medieval culture', reprinted in id., *England, France and Burgundy in the Fifteenth Century* (1983); Tanner, *The Church in the Later Middle Ages*, pp. 92–3.
252. R.W. Southern, *The Making of the Middle Ages* (1953), p. 153; E. Duffy, *Marking the Hours: English People and their Prayers 1240–1570* (New Haven, 2006), p. 5; id., 'Elite and popular religion: the book of hours and lay piety in the later middle ages', *Studies in Church History*, xlii (2006), p. 143; D. d'Avray, 'Continuities in medieval England', paper read to the Medieval Society, Institute of Historical Research, 21 January 1992.
253. Davies, 'Religious sensibility', in Given-Wilson, ed., *Illustrated History of Late Medieval England*, p. 122.
254. Lemaitre, *Rouergue flamboyant*, pp. 240–50.
255. George Cavendish, *The Life and Death of Cardinal Wolsey*, ed. R.S. Sylvester, Early English Text Society, ccxliii (1959), pp. 130, 182; Beckett, 'Sheen Charterhouse', p. 191.
256. Thomson, *Early Tudor Church and Society*, p. 360.
257. Harper-Bill, 'Dean Colet's Convocation Sermon', pp. 195–6.
258. Morris, *Papal Monarchy*, pp. 240–5; N. Vincent, *Journal of Ecclesiastical History*, lvii (2006), p. 577.
259. cf. C.H. Berman, *The Cistercian Revolution: The Invention of a Religious Order in Twelfth-Century Europe* (Philadelphia, 2000), and see review by J. Burton, *Journal of Ecclesiastical History*, lii (2001), pp. 720–2; J. Burton, 'Past models and contemporary concerns: the function and growth of the Cistercian order', *Studies in Church History*, xliv (2008), pp. 27–45.
260. Brooke and Brooke, *Popular Religion in the Middle Ages*, pp. 48–9.
261. cf. Greatrex, 'St Swithun's Priory', pp. 140; Morris, *Papal Monarchy*, pp. 260, 545; Southern, *Making of the Middle Ages*, p. 162.
262. J. van Engen, 'The "Crisis of Cenobitism" reconsidered: Benedictine monasticism in the years 1050–1150', *Speculum*, lxi (1986), pp. 279–304.
263. Clark, ed., *The Religious Orders in Pre-Reformation England*, pp. 11–12; Heale, *Monasticism in Later Medieval England*, p. 6.
264. Greatrex, *English Benedictine Cathedral Priories*, p. 332.
265. Tudor, 'English devotional writing', pp. 16–17.
266. BL, Cotton MS, Cleopatra E iv fo. 42 (*LP*, IX 283).
267. TNA, PRO, SP1/85 fo. 100 (partly illegible) (*LP*, VII 1047 (i)).
268. MacCulloch, *Suffolk under the Tudors*, p. 135.
269. TNA, PRO, SP1/100 fo. 94 (*LP*, IX 1150).
270. BL, Cotton MS, Cleopatra E iv fo. 26v (*LP*, IX 1157).

9 Heresy

1. A.E. Larsen, 'Are all Lollards Lollards?', in F. Somerset, J.C. Havens and D.G. Pitard, *Lollards and their Influence in Late Medieval England* (Woodbridge, 2003), pp. 59–72, at pp. 59–60. For earlier European heresy see the numinous survey by P. Biller, 'Through a glass darkly: seeing medieval history', in Linehan and Nelson, eds., *Medieval World*, pp. 308–26. For a more sceptical view of 'the Cathars', see M.G. Pegg, *The Corruption of Angels: The Great Inquisition of 1245–1246* (Princeton, NJ, 2001) and id., *A Most Holy War: The Albigensian Crusade and the Battle for Christendom* (Oxford, 2008), challenged, but not undermined, by P. Biller, 'Cathars and the natural world', *Studies in Church History*, xlvi (2010), pp. 89–110; id., *Speculum*, lxxviii (2003), pp. 1366–70, and B. Hamilton, *American Historical Review*, cvii (2002), pp. 925–6.

2. K.B. McFarlane, *John Wycliffe and the Origins of English Nonconformity* (1953) remains the most important survey and analysis. On Wyclif as theologian and philosopher see also A. Hudson and A. Kenny, 'Wyclif, John (d. 1384)', *ODNB*. Two rich papers by J. Crompton, 'John Wyclif: a study in mythology', and 'Leicestershire Lollards', in *Transactions of the Leicestershire Archaeological and Historical Society*, xlii (1966–7), pp. 6–34, and xliv (1968–9), pp. 11–44, hint at the substantial study he would have produced had he not died young. Many papers by Margaret Aston are significant too: they are collected together in *Lollards and Reformers: Images and Literacy in Late Medieval Religion* (1984) and *Faith and Fire: Popular and Unpopular Religion* (1993). D.G. Pitard, 'A selected bibliography for Lollard studies', in Somerset et al., *Lollards and their Influence*, pp. 251–319 is a fine tool of reference; see also Pitard's part-annotated and regularly up-dated bibliography of secondary sources on the Lollard Society website (http://lollardsociety.org.) Lollardy has increasingly been studied as a social, literary and gendered phenomenon.

3. G.H. Martin, 'Wyclif, Lollards and Historians, 1384–1984', in Somerset et al., *Lollards and their Influence*, pp. 237–50 at p. 239.

4. Crompton, 'Leicestershire Lollards', p. 11.

5. R. Whiting, *Local Responses to the English Reformation* (1998), p. 119.

6. M. Aston, 'Lollardy and Literacy', *History*, lxii (1977), pp. 347–71 at p. 353, reprinted in Aston, *Lollards and Reformers*, pp. 193–217.

7. C. Cross, *Church and People 1450–1660* (1976), p. 40; A.G. Dickens, 'Heresy and the origins of English Protestantism', in J.S. Bromley and E.H. Kossmann, eds., *Britain and the Netherlands*, ii (1964), pp. 47–66 at p. 59.

8. A. Hudson, *The Premature Reformation* (Oxford, 1988), pp. 20–2.

9. Ibid. p. 9.; J. Catto, 'Followers and helpers: the religious identity of the followers of Wyclif', *Studies in Church History, Subsidia* xi (1999), p. 160.

10. cf. R. Rex, *The Lollards* (Basingstoke, 2001), p. 88; A. Hope, 'Lollardy: the stone the builders rejected?', in P. Lake and M. Dowling, eds., *Protestantism and the National Church in Sixteenth-Century England* (1988) pp. 1–35 at p. 24. Possibly *Wycliffes Wycket* may be *c.*1470: that has been argued from its theological unsophistication and from the lack of reference to it in earlier trials: Thomson, *Early Tudor Church and Society*, p. 354 n.160; Hudson, *The Premature Reformation*, pp. 451–2, 11, 18.

11. Hudson, *The Premature Reformation*, pp. 18, 451–4: cf. Christopher Haigh's criticisms in 'The English Reformation: A premature birth, a difficult labour and a sickly child', *Historical Journal*, xxiii (1990), p. 451, and E. Duffy, *The Stripping of the Altars: Traditional Religion in England c.1400–c.1580* (2nd edn., 2005), pp. xxi–xxxii.

12. M. Bose, 'A reasonable faith? Bishop Pecock's religious projects', paper read at the University of Southampton, 2002; K. Ghosh, 'Bishop Reginald Pecock and Wycliffite Hermeneutics', paper read at Harris Manchester College, Oxford, June 2002; W. Scase, 'Pecock, Reginald, (b. *c.*1392 d. in or after 1459)', *ODNB*. cf. comments of Helen Rawlings on the comparable case of Friar Bartolome de Carranza y Miranda, archbishop of Toledo, arrested by the Spanish Inquisition soon after he took up office in 1559: 'while investigating heretical literature in Flanders at close quarters, he had

naturally absorbed the language of the reformers. In attacking their views, and using what the modern reader might judge to be a loose prose style, he exposed himself to the charge of sympathising with them': *Journal of Ecclesiastical History*, lvii (2006), p. 375.

13. Hudson, *The Premature Reformation*, p. 447; Rex, *The Lollards*, p. 88.
14. Crompton, 'Leicestershire Lollards', p. 14.
15. Catto, 'Religious change under Henry V', p. 114.
16. R.L. Williams, 'Aspects of heresy and reformation in England 1515–1540', Univ. of Cambridge Ph.D. thesis, 1976, remains the most thorough study of episcopal registers for the period.
17. Foxe, *Acts and Monuments* (1570 edn.), pp. 917, 943 (Foxe, *Acts and Monuments*, iv. 123–4, 214).
18. Foxe, *Acts and Monuments* (1570 edn.), p. 918 (Foxe, *Acts and Monuments*, iv. 125).
19. Foxe, *Acts and Monuments* (1570 edn.), p. 917 (Foxe, *Acts and Monuments*, iv. 124).
20. Foxe, *Acts and Monuments* (1583), pp. 774, 783–802 (Foxe, *Acts and Monuments*, iv. 123, 217–45); D. Plumb, 'The social and economic status of the later Lollards', in M. Spufford, ed., *The World of Rural Dissenters 1520–1725* (Cambridge, 1995), pp. 103–31, at 108, citing TNA, PRO, C85/115/13.
21. N. Tanner, ed., *Kent Heresy Procedures 1511–12*, Kent Records (1997), pp. x–xi.
22. S. McSheffrey and N. Tanner, eds., *Lollards of Coventry, 1486–1522*, Camden Society, 5th series, xxiii (2003), pp. 1–10.
23. Williams, 'Aspects of Heresy and Reformation', pp. 15–16, 19.
24. Ibid., p. 15.
25. Ibid., p. 19.
26. Ibid.
27. Ibid., p. 2.
28. Ibid., p. 8.
29. Ibid., p. 11.
30. Ibid., p. 12.
31. Ibid., p. 19.
32. Ibid., p. 17.
33. Ibid., pp. 2, 11, 17.
34. G. Williams, *The Welsh Church: from Conquest to Reformation* (Cardiff, 2nd edn., 1976), p. 532; Williams, 'Heresy and Reformation', pp. 11, 18.
35. Martin, 'Wyclif, Lollards and Historians', in Somerset et al., eds., *Lollards and their Influence*, p. 241.
36. Hudson, *The Premature Reformation*, p. 466.
37. D. Plumb, 'The social and economic spread of rural lollardy: a reappraisal', *Studies in Church History*, xxiii (1986); pp. 111–30; Hope, 'Lollardy', p. 4; Haigh, 'The English Reformation', p. 451.
38. Hope, 'Lollardy', p. 2, from A.H. Thomas and I.D. Thornley, eds., *The Great Chronicle of London* (1907), p. 252 and Foxe, *Acts and Monuments* (1570 edn.), p. 866 (Foxe, *Acts and Monuments*, iv. 228).
39. Hudson, *The Premature Reformation*, p. 35.
40. Thompson, 'English and Welsh bishops', p. 121.
41. Plumb, 'Social and economic status of the later Lollards', pp. 103–4.
42. Foxe, *Acts and Monuments* (1570 edn.), pp. 945–6 (Foxe, *Acts and Monuments* iv. 218).
43. Haigh, *English Reformations*, p. 55.
44. The sequence apparently begins with a Dutchman, Abraham Water, who confessed and abjured in July 1527, having preached in Colchester in April/May/or June (British Library, Harleian MS 421 fos. 9–10; [*LP*, IV ii 3267]), John Hacker who confessed on 20 and 27 January 1528 (BL, Harl. MS 421 fo. 11 [*LP*, IV ii 4029 (1)]), followed by John Pykas (before Dr Wharton in the consistory court on 2 March 1528 (BL, Harl. MS 421 fo. 15 [*LP*, IV ii 4029 (3)]), before Bishop Tunstall in the episcopal palace who administered articles on 3 March 1528 (BL, Harl. MS 421 fo. 15 [*LP*, IV ii 4029 (3)]),

and before Tunstall again on 7 March 1528 when he made a substantial confession (BL, Harl. MS 421 fo. 17 [*LP*, IV ii 4029 (2)]) after Henry Ryland had been questioned on 4 March and Thomas Mathew of Colchester had abjured before the bishop on 5 March (BL, Harl. MS 421 fo. 15 [*LP*, IV ii 4029 (3)]); there is also a different undated confession (BL, Harl. MS 421 fos. 21–2 [*LP*, IV 4175 (2)]), several more were examined on 19, 20 and 23 March (BL, Harl. MS 421 fo. 19 [IV ii 4175 (1)]); then on 28 April 1528 John Tyball confessed before Bishop Tunstall (J. Strype, *Ecclesiastical Memorials*, I ii 50 [*LP* IV ii 4218]); on 11 May 1528 William Bocher (Strype, *Ecclesiastical Memorials*, I ii 59 [*LP*, IV ii 4254 (1)], Robert Hempstead (BL, Harl. MS 421 fo. 27 [IV ii 4254 (1, 2, 3)]) and Thomas Hempstead (Strype, *Ecclesiastical Memorials*, I ii 61 [*LP*, IV ii 4254 (3)]); on 21 July 1528 Edmund Tyball (BL, Harl. MS, 421 fos. 28–29v [*LP*, IV ii 4545]) on 15 October 1528 Thomas Hills was examined (BL, Harl. MS 421 fo. 34 [*LP*, IV ii 4850)]. It is worth noting that our principal source, BL Harl. MS 421 fos. 7–35, is itself a fair copy of a much larger text which does not survive. The Harleian folios bear an original foliation which begins with xxxi–xxxii, continues with cxxix–cxxxii, clxx–clx, clxxxvi–clxxxx, clxxxxv–clxxxxvii, ccccxliii–lx. John Strype's early eighteenth-century transcripts supply some further depositions. And we also have Foxe's treatment in the *Acts and Monuments*.

45. Strype, *Ecclesiastical Memorials*, I ii pp. 60–1 (*LP*, IV ii 4254 (2)).
46. Strype, *Ecclesiastical Memorials*, I ii p. 62 (*LP*, IV ii 4254 (3)).
47. BL, Harl. MS 421 fos. 28–28v (*LP*, IV ii 4545 (i)).
48. BL, Harl. MS 421 fo. 28 (*LP*, IV ii 4545 (i)).
49. BL, Harl. MS 421 fos. 34–35v (*LP*, IV ii 4850); Strype, *Ecclesiastical Memorials*, IV ii. pp. 55–6 (*LP*, IV ii 4218).
50. Strype, *Ecclesiastical Memorials*, IV ii pp. 50–6 (*LP*, IV ii 4218).
51. BL, Harl. MS 421 fo. 11v (*LP*, IV ii 4029).
52. BL, Harl. MS 421, fos. 34–34v (*LP*, IV ii 4850).
53. BL, Harl. MS 421 fo. 17 (*LP*, IV ii 4029 (2)); Hudson, *Premature Reformation*, pp. 231, 485–7.
54. BL Harl. MS 421 fo. 25 (*LP*, IV ii 4175 (3)); BL, Harl. MS 421 fo. 22 (*LP*, IV ii 4030 (2)).
55. BL, Harl. MS 421 fo. 18 (*LP*, IV ii 4029 (2)).
56. BL, Harl. MS 421 fos. 17v–18 (*LP*, IV ii 4029 (2)).
57. Strype, *Ecclesiastical Memorials*, IV ii pp. 51–2, 54 (*LP*, IV ii 4218). cf. Foxe: one John Tibauld in trouble in 1533, four times in prison for Christ's cause: *Acts and Monuments* (1570 edn.), p. 1179 (Foxe, *Acts and Monuments*, v. 16).
58. BL, Harl. MS 421 fo. 34 (*LP*, IV ii 4850). Testimony identified as that of Hills from his account of visiting Robert Barnes with Tyball, see above, p. 212.
59. J. Strype, *Ecclesiastical Memorials*, I ii pp. 60–1 (*LP*, IV ii 4254 (2)).
60. BL, Harl. MS 421 fos. 28–28v (*LP*, IV ii 4545 (i)).
61. Strype, *Ecclesiastical Memorials*, I ii 62 (*LP*, IV ii 4254 (3)).
62. BL, Harl. MS 421 fo. 28v (*LP*, IV ii 4545).
63. BL, Harl. MS 421 fos. 17–18 (*LP*, IV ii 4029(2)).
64. BL, Harl. MS 421 fo. 24 (*LP*, IV ii 4175 (3)).
65. BL, Harl. MS 421 fo. 24 (*LP*, IV ii 4175 (3)).
66. BL, Harl. MS 421 fo. 22v (*LP*, IV ii 4175 (2)).
67. BL, Harl. MS 421 fo. 23 (*LP*, IV ii 4175 (2)).
68. BL, Harl. MS 421 fos. 24–24v (*LP*, IV 4175 (3)).
69. BL, Harl. MS 421 fo. 16 (*LP*, IV ii 4029 (3).
70. BL, Harl. MS 421 fos. 17v–18 (*LP*, IV ii 4029 (2).
71. Foxe, *Acts and Monuments* (1570 edn.), pp. 947, 953, 961.
72. Foxe, *Acts and Monuments* (1570 edn.), pp. 1453–5 (Foxe, *Acts and Monuments*, iv. 647–54); Tanner, ed., *Kent Heresy Proceedings*, pp. xii–xv, xxv; R. Lutton, *Lollardy and Orthodox Religion in Pre-Reformation England: reconstructing piety* (Woodbridge, 2006), pp. 157–8.

73. McSheffrey and Tanner, *Lollards of Coventry*.

74. Strype, *Ecclesiastical Memorials*, I ii 55–6 (*LP*, IV ii 4218).

75. J. Davis, 'Joan of Kent, Lollardy and the English Reformation', *Journal of Ecclesiastical History*, xxxiii (1982), p. 226.

76. Especially Haigh, *English Reformations*; Rex, *The Lollards*.

77. D. Aers, 'Altars of power', *Literature and History* iii (1994), pp. 90–105. See Duffy's defence in the preface to the second edition of *Stripping of the Altars*, pp. xxi–xxxiii.

78. McSheffery and Tanner, *Lollards of Coventry*, p. 15; J.P. Hornbeck II, *Journal of Ecclesiastical History*, lvi (2005), p. 156.

79. Hudson, *The Premature Reformation*, pp. 33, 37; Swanson, *Church and Society*, p. 335; Catto, 'Religious change under Henry V', p. 115; Cameron, *European Reformation*, pp. 70–1; Oakley, *Western Church in the Middle Ages*, pp. 177–8; Haigh, *English Reformations*, p. 54; Thomson, *Early Tudor Church and Society*, p. 353; cf. J.P. Hornbeck II, 'Theologies of sexuality in English "lollardy"', *Journal of Ecclesiastical History*, lv (2009), pp. 39–40: that 'nearly the same form of words' was used by twelve defendants accused of unorthodox views about marriage 'makes it all but certain that Archbishop Warham's officials painted their heresy suspects with the same brush'.

80. McSheffrey and Tanner, *Lollards of Coventry*, p. 15.

81. BL, Harl. MS 421 fos. 21–22, 24–25v (*LP*, IV ii 4175 (2, 3)).

82. BL, Harl. MS 421 fos. 24, 25, 25v, 26v (*LP*, IV ii 4175 (3)).

83. cf. Lutton, *Lollardy and Orthodoxy*, p. 169.

84. BL, Harl. MS 421 fos. 17v–18 (*LP*, IV ii 4029)).

85. *pace* Plumb, 'Economic and social status of later Lollards', p. 122.

86. Ibid., p. 121.

87. Ibid., p. 124.

88. Ibid., p. 127.

89. Ibid., pp. 121–2.

90. Strype, *Ecclesiastical Memorials*, I ii p. 50 (*LP*, IV ii 4218 (ii)).

91. BL, Harl. MS 421 fo. 29–29v (*LP*, IV ii 4545)).

92. BL, Harl. MS 421 fo. 35v (*LP*, IV ii 4850).

93. BL, Harl. MS 421 fo. 16v (*LP*, IV ii 4029 (3)).

94. Foxe, *Acts and Monuments* (1570 edn.), p. 946 (Foxe, *Acts and Monuments*, iv. 222); S.J. Smart, '"Favourers of God's word?": John Foxe's Henrician martyrs', Univ. of Southampton M.Litt. thesis, 1989, ch.1.

95. BL, Harl. MS 421 fos. 17–17v (*LP*, IV ii 4029 (2)).

96. Hope, 'Lollardy', p. 10.

97. R.B. Merriman, *Life and Letters of Thomas Cromwell* (2 vols., Oxford, 1902), i. 104–11.

98. BL, Harl. MS 421 fo. 17 (*LP*, IV ii 4029 (2)).

99. G. Walker, '"Known men", evangelicals and brethren: heretical sects in pre-Reformation England', in id., *Persuasive Fictions: Faction, Faith and Political Culture in the Reign of Henry VIII* (Aldershot, 1996), pp. 132–3; S. Brigden, *London and the Reformation* (Oxford, 1989), p. 107.

100. J. Fines, 'The Post-Mortem Condemnation for Heresy of Richard Hunne', *English Historical Review*, lxxviii (1963), pp. 530–1; J.A.F. Thomson, *The Later Lollards 1414–1520* (Oxford, 1965), p. 169.

101. cf. G. Macy, 'The Dogma of Transubstantiation in the Middle Ages', *Journal of Ecclesiastical History*, xlv (1994), pp. 11–41.

102. Hope, 'Lollardy', p. 30 n. 69.

103. For example, Strype, *Ecclesiastical Memorials*, I ii p. 59 (*LP*, IV ii 4254 (1)).

104. J. Davis, 'The Christian brethren and the dissemination of heretical books', *Studies in Church History*, xxxviii (2004), pp. 190–200.

105. For Hacker, BL, Harl. MS 428 fos. 11–14 (*LP*, IV ii 4029 (1)); Thomas More, *Dialogue concerning heresies*, in *Complete Works of St Thomas More*, VI i., pp. 268/35.

106. Foxe, *Acts and Monuments* (1570 edn.), pp. 941–3 (Foxe, *Acts and Monuments*, iv. 208–14).
107. Hudson, *The Premature Reformation*, p. 476.
108. Plumb, 'Social and economic status of the later Lollards', p. 134.
109. Hudson, *The Premature Reformation*, p. 459.
110. BL, Harl. MS 421 fos. 11–14v (*LP*, IV ii 4029).
111. Hudson, *The Premature Reformation*, p. 450.
112. *pace* Hudson, ibid., p. 456.
113. Thompson, 'English and Welsh bishops', p. 126.
114. Ibid.
115. Cranmer, *Writings and Letters*, p. 273 from BL, Harl. MS 6148 fos. 38–9.
116. Foxe, *Acts and Monuments* (1570 edn.), pp. 946, 948 (Foxe, *Acts and Monuments*, iv. 219–20).
117. Foxe, *Acts and Monuments* (1570 edn.), p. 946 (Foxe, *Acts and Monuments*, iv. 219).
118. Foxe, *Acts and Monuments* (1570 edn.), p. 946 (Foxe, *Acts and Monuments*, iv. 222–3).
119. Hudson, *The Premature Reformation*, pp. 456, 469.
120. Heal, *Reformation in Britain and Ireland*, p. 100; cf. similar remarks by Lutton, *Lollardy and Orthodox Religion*, pp. 157, 161.
121. Strype, *Ecclesiastical Memorials*, I ii p. 62 (*LP*, IV ii 4254 (3)); I ii p. 54 (*LP*, IV ii 4218).
122. Walker, ' "Known men", evangelicals and brethren', pp. 125–6. cf. M. Aston, 'Were the lollards a sect?', *Studies in Church History, Subsidia* xi (1999), pp. 165–72, 176–9 and J. Catto, 'Followers and helpers: the religious identity of the followers of Wyclif', *Studies in Church History, Subsidia* xi (1999), p. 143, for the meaning of 'sect' in this context.
123. Plumb, 'A gathered church', p. 146; G.R. Elton, *Reform and Reformation* (1997), p. 11; cf. discussion by Walker, ' "Known Men", pp. 124–5.
124. Foxe, *Acts and Monuments* (1570 edn.), p. 945 (Foxe, *Acts and Monuments*, iv. 218).
125. Hope, 'Lollardy', p. 12, or Lutton, *Lollardy and Orthodox Religion*, p. 162.
126. BL, Harl. MS 421 fos. 11–14v (*LP*, IV ii 4029).
127. *pace* Hudson, *The Premature Reformation*, p. 456.
128. cf. B. Bradshaw on the trials of the 1530s, review of J.G. Bellamy, *The Tudor Law of Treason* (1979), in *Journal of Ecclesiastical History*, xxxi (1980), pp. 361–5.
129. Foxe, *Acts and Monuments* (1570 edn.), pp. 917–18 (Foxe, *Acts and Monuments*, iv. 124).
130. Foxe, *Acts and Monuments* (1570 edn.), p. 918 (Foxe, *Acts and Monuments*, iv. 125).
131. Foxe, *Acts and Monuments* (1570 edn.), p. 918 (Foxe, *Acts and Monuments*, iv. 125).
132. BL, Harl. MS 421 fo. 19 (*LP*, IV ii 4175).
133. *LP*, VII 585.
134. S. McSheffrey, *Gender and Heresy: Women and Men in Lollard Communities 1420–1530* (Philadelphia, 1995), p. 13 citing Lich, Ct. Bk. fo. 24r; cf. J. Fines, 'Heresy trials in the diocese of Coventry and Lichfield', *Journal of Ecclesiastical History*, xiv (1963), pp. 169–70.
135. C. d'Alton, 'Heresy Hunting and Clerical Reform: William Warham, John Colet and the Lollards of Kent, 1511–12', in I. Hunter, J.C. Laursen and C.J. Nederman, eds., *Heresy in Transition: Transforming Ideas of Heresy in Medieval and Early Modern Europe* (Aldershot, 2005), pp. 103–14, esp. pp. 113–14.
136. Foxe, *Acts and Monuments* (1570 edn.), p. 946.
137. cf. comments by Marks, *Image and Devotion*, p. 256.

138. Martin, 'Wyclif, Lollards and Historians', in Somerset et al., eds., *Lollards and their Influence*, p. 240.

139. J.F. Davis, 'Lollardy and the Reformation in England', *Archiv für Reformationsgeschichte*, lxxiii (1982), pp. 82, 219, 224.

140. D. Plumb, 'A gathered church? Lollards and their society', in Spufford, ed., *World of Rural Dissenters*, p. 163.

141. Davis, 'Lollardy and the Reformation in England', pp. 221–2; D. MacCulloch, *Tudor Church Militant: Edward VI and the Protestant Reformation* (1999), p. 112. See Rex, *The Lollards*, pp. 119–31 for a comprehensive refutation. cf. comment that 'there were many descendants of lollards who were not dissenters', W.J. Sheils, *Journal of Ecclesiastical History*, xlvii (1997), p. 127. Those who would wish to argue for such long-run geographical continuities of belief may find it hard to account for the undoubted strength of puritan and non-conformist beliefs in seventeenth- and eighteenth-century East Anglia and Wales, regions in which what Eamon Duffy has called 'traditional religion' was seemingly strong in the later middle ages: why such a transformation?

142. Davis, 'Lollardy and the Reformation in England', p. 222.

143. Williams, 'Heresy and Reformation', p. 21.

144. *LP*, III i 1193.

145. Rex, *The Lollards*, p. 119.

146. Davis, 'Lollardy and the Reformation in England', pp. 220, 222–3.

147. Williams, 'Heresy and Reformation', pp. 25–6 (*pace* J. Guy, 'The Henrician Age', in J. G. A. Pocock, ed., *The Varieties of British Political Thought, 1500–1800* (Cambridge, 1993), p. 32: the lollards 'anticipated the reformers' solifidian platform'.

148. Williams, 'Heresy and Reformation', p. 27.

149. D.D. Smeeton, *Lollard Themes in the Reformation Theology of William Tyndale* (Kirksville, MO, 1986), esp. pp. 75–7, 251–5; C.R. Trueman, *Luther's Legacy: Salvation and English Reformers 1525–1556* (Oxford, 1994), pp. 41–2.

150. Hudson, *Premature Reformation*, p. 501.

151. Ibid., pp. 220–2, 11.

152. Williams, 'Heresy and Reformation', pp. 115–17, 25.

153. Crompton, 'John Wyclif', pp. 11–13.

154. Foxe, *Acts and Monuments* (1570 edn.), p. 945 (Foxe, *Acts and Monuments*, iv. 217, 218).

155. P. Collinson, 'Truth and Legend: the veracity of John Foxe's *Book of Martyrs*', in A.C. Duke and C.A. Tamse, eds., *Clio's Mirror: Historiography in Britain and the Netherlands* (Zutphen, 1985), pp. 31–54, reprinted in id., *Elizabethan Essays* (Zutphen, 1994), pp. 151–78; id. 'Truth, lies and fiction in sixteenth-century protestant historiography', in D.R. Kelly and D.H. Sacks, eds., *The Historical Imagination in Early Modern Britain: History, Rhetoric and Fiction 1500–1800* (Cambridge, 1997), pp. 37–68, and reprinted in id., *This England: essays on the English nation and commonwealth in the sixteenth century* (Manchester, 2011), pp. 216–44; T. Freeman, 'Fate, Faction, and Fiction in Foxe's *Book of Martyrs*', *Historical Journal*, xliii (2000), pp. 601–23; A. Walsham, 'Inventing the Lollard past: the afterlife of a medieval sermon in early modern England', *Journal of Ecclesiastical History*, lviii (2007), pp. 641–7.

156. Strype, *Ecclesiastical Memorials*, I ii. pp. 54–5 (*LP*, IV ii 4218 is very |compressed).

157. Trueman, *Luther's Legacy*, p. 44.

158. I. Forrest, review of R. Rex, *The Lollards, English Historical Review*, cxviii (2003), p. 484.

159. I. Forrest, *The Detection of Heresy in Late Medieval England* (Oxford, 2005), pp. 240–1.

160. Polydore Vergil, *Anglica Historia*, p. 130 n; Elton, *Reform and Reformation*, p. 57; S. Thompson, 'Fitzjames, Richard (d. 1522)', *ODNB*.

161. N. Watson, 'Censorship and cultural change in late-medieval England: vernacular theology, the Oxford translation debate and Arundel's Constitutions of 1409', *Speculum*, lxx (1995), p. 835.

162. J. Hughes, 'Arundel, Thomas (1353–1414)', *ODNB*; Catto, 'Religious change under Henry V', p. 112; Forrest, *Detection of Heresy*, pp. 29, 41, 49; N. Watson, 'Censorship and cultural change', pp. 822–64.

163. J. Catto, 'After Arundel? The closing or the opening of the English mind?' I am most grateful to Jeremy Catto for sight of this unpublished paper.

164. A. Combes, *La théologie mystique de Gerson* (2 vols., Paris, 1963–4) is a remarkable exposition; S.E. Ozment, *Homo Spiritualis* (1969); H.A. Oberman, *The Harvest of Medieval Theology* (1963); D. Hobbins, *Authorship and Publicity before Print: Jean Gerson and the Transformation of Late Medieval Learning* (Philadelphia, 2009), esp. pp. 32–3, pp. 80–2 (for Thomas More), p. 185 (public), though Hobbins exaggerates the novelty of Gerson as moralist and controversialist: see M. Clancy, *Journal of Ecclesiastical History*, lxi (2010), pp. 381–2; I.C. Levy, 'Holy scripture and the quest for authority among three late medieval masters', *Journal of Ecclesiastical History*, lxi (2010), pp. 40–68, for an attempt to show that Gerson was not so far from Wyclif on the authority of scripture; Cameron, *Enchanted Europe*, p. 131.

Epilogue

1. Field, 'Robin Hood stories', pp. 21–2.

2. A.H. Thompson, *The English Clergy and their Organization in the Later Middle Ages* (Oxford, 1947), p. 161.

INDEX

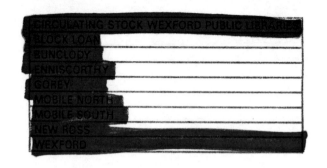
LAST IN CIRC:
27/03/18